Governance of Educational Trajectories in Europe

Also available from Bloomsbury

Agency and Participation in Childhood and Youth, edited by Caroline Sarojini Hart

Education and Disadvantaged Children and Young People, edited by Mitsuko Matsumoto

Education and International Development, edited by Tristan McCowan and Elaine Unterhalter

Global Education Policy and International Development, edited by Antoni Verger, Mario Novelli and Hülya Koşar Altinyelken

Governance of Educational Trajectories in Europe

Pathways, Policy and Practice

Edited by

Andreas Walther, Marcelo Parreira do Amaral, Morena Cuconato and Roger Dale

Bloomsbury Academic
An imprint of Bloomsbury Publishing Plc

B L O O M S B U R Y

LONDON • OXFORD • NEW YORK • NEW DELHI • SYDNEY

Bloomsbury Academic
An imprint of Bloomsbury Publishing Plc

50 Bedford Square
London
WC1B 3DP
UK

1385 Broadway
New York
NY 10018
USA

www.bloomsbury.com

BLOOMSBURY and the Diana logo are trademarks of Bloomsbury Publishing Plc

First published 2016
Paperback edition first published 2017

British Library Cataloguing-in-Publication Data
A catalogue record for this book is available from the British Library.

ISBN: HB: 978-1-4725-8952-1
PB: 978-1-3500-5338-0
ePDF: 978-1-4725-8954-5
ePub: 978-1-4725-8953-8

Library of Congress Cataloging-in-Publication Data
Walther, Andreas, editor. | Amaral, Marcelo Parreira do, editor. | Cuconato, Morena, editor. | Dale, Roger, editor. Governance of educational trajectories in Europe : pathways, policy and practice /edited by Andreas Walther, Marcelo Parreira do Amaral, Morena Cuconato, and Roger Dale.
New York, NY : Bloomsbury Academic, 2016.
Includes bibliographical references and index.
LCCN 2015045394 (print) | LCCN 2016005189(ebook) | ISBN 9781472589521(hardback) | ISBN 9781472589545 (ePDF) | ISBN 9781472589538 (ePub) | ISBN9781472589545 (epdf) | ISBN 9781472589538 (epub)
LCSH: Educational attainment–European Union countries. | Educational attainment–Social aspects–European Union countries. | Education and state–European Union countries. | Educational sociology–European Union countries. |
BISAC: EDUCATION / General. | EDUCATION /Educational Policy & Reform / General.
LCC LA621.83 .G68 2016 (print) | LCCLA621.83 (ebook) | DDC 370.94–dc23
LC record available at http://lccn.loc.gov/2015045394

Typeset by Fakenham Prepress Solutions, Fakenham, Norfolk NR21 8NN

Contents

List of Figures

List of Tables

Notes on Contributors

Karin Amos is Professor of Foundations of Education, International Comparative Education Research and Intercultural Education at the Institute of Education of Eberhard Karls University, Tübingen, Germany. Her current research interests focus primarily on international governance in education, the relationship between governance and governmentality and the relationship between political and pedagogical order formation.

Eduardo Barberis is Research Fellow at the Department of Economy, Society and Politics, University Carlo Bo of Urbino, Italy, where he lectures on Immigration Policy. His research interests include the socio-economic participation of migrants and minorities, anti-discrimination policies and the local dimension of social policies in comparative perspective.

Valérie Becquet is Professor of Educational Sciences at the University of Cergy-Pontoise, France. Her main research interests are youth participation and educational and youth policies. She analyses the ways in which young people get involved in associations and in public programmes (national and local youth councils, civic service) and their participation biographies.

Andy Biggart is Lecturer and Deputy Director of the Centre for Effective Education, Queen's University, Belfast, UK. His main research interests are concerned with the evaluation of educational interventions among disadvantaged groups, comparative educational policy and young people's transitions.

Felicitas Boron is a school social worker and interested in (youth) educational transitions, coping in the life course, educational trajectories and support of disadvantaged youth. She worked as a research assistant for the GOETE project.

Izabela Buchowicz is Assistant Professor of Economics at the Department of Education and Science Policy, Institute of Social Economy, Warsaw School of Economics, Poland. She has long-term research and teaching experience in the field of education policy, equal opportunities for young people and local policies, as well as in theory and practice of social policy.

Morena Cuconato is Associate Professor of Social Pedagogy at the Department of Educational studies of the University of Bologna, Italy. She teaches and carries out research in the areas of youth policies, transitions in the life course, youth welfare and European school systems in comparative perspective.

Roger Dale is Professor of Education at the University of Bristol, UK. His research interests include globalization, Europeanization and the governance of education, and sociology of education. Complementing and extending earlier works on the state and education policy, his current focus work is on the Education Policy in the European Union. He is co-editor of the journal *Globalisation, Societies and Education.*

Isabelle Danic is Lecturer and Researcher of Sociology at University of Rennes 2, France. She has contributed to European and national research projects on childhood and youth, on education and socialization in a life course perspective and on the spatial aspects of these phenomena.

Nicola De Luigi is Associate Professor of Sociology at the Department of Sociology and Business Law at the University of Bologna, Italy. The focus of his research is the analysis of the relationship between youth, education and the labour market as well as research methods and methodology.

Silvia Demozzi is Researcher at the Department of Education of the University of Bologna, Italy. Her teaching and research cover topics of oncological pedagogy; pedagogy of communication; relational skills in education; children, social and youth welfare services in Italy; childhood and adolescence illness; Gregory Bateson; Theatre of the Oppressed.

Manuela du Bois-Reymond is Emeritus Professor of Pedagogy and Youth Studies at the Leiden University, The Netherlands. Her fields of interest are transitions of young people, new learning theories and policies in and out of school contexts, young parenthood and intergenerational relationships.

Joanna Felczak is Assistant Professor of Economics at the Warsaw School of Economics, Poland. She teaches pedagogy and social rehabilitation. Her scientific and research interests include social rehabilitation, criminology and relations between the penal policy and the structure of the penitentiary system.

Ilse Julkunen is Professor of Practice Research in Social Work and Head of Discipline in the Department of Social Research at the University of Helsinki, Finland, and scientific leader of the Mathilda Wrede Institute, Finland. Her research concerns youth and marginalization, youth transitions and practice research in social work.

Yuri Kazepov is Professor of International Urban Sociology and Compared Welfare Systems at the University of Vienna, Austria. Previously he was based at the University of Urbino, Italy. His fields of interest are urban governance, citizenship and urban quality of life, and social policies in comparative perspective.

Hülya Koşar Altinyelken is Assistant Professor of Education and International Development in the Department of Child Development and Education at the University of Amsterdam, the Netherlands. Her research interests cover topics including migration and education, education policy transfer, education reforms, curriculum change, child-centred pedagogy, gender and mindfulness in education.

John Litau is Research Associate at the University of Frankfurt, Germany, and University of Tübingen, Germany. His research interests cover youth studies, especially regarding (educational) transitions, mobility, alcohol and qualitative methods.

Patricia Loncle is Senior Lecturer in Sociology and Political Science at the High School of Public Health in Rennes, France, where she is the Research Chair on Youth. She is a member of the Centre of Research on Political Action in Europe and leads the MA course Youth, Policies and Care. Her research focuses on youth policies and young people in the fields of social policy, health, education, leisure and youth participation.

Harry Lunabba is Lecturer at the Swedish School of Social Sciences, Sweden. His research interests are childhood, youth and gender studies as well as ethnographic and participatory research of welfare practices and social work.

Karolina Majdzińska is a doctoral researcher at the Warsaw School of Economics, Poland. Her research interests are: public policy; integration policy; refugees; social economy; social cooperatives; social exclusion and social integration.

Alessandro Martelli is Tenured Assistant Professor of Sociology in the Department of Sociology and Business Law at the University of Bologna, Italy. His research focuses on youth, youth policies at local and national level as well as on social protection policies.

Joanne McDowell is Senior Lecturer of English Language and Communication at the University of Hertfordshire, UK. Her research interests include educational linguistics, workplace discourse, identity construction in non-traditional occupations and gender in language. She is currently studying linguistic teaching strategies in the primary school classroom.

Marcelo Parreira do Amaral is Professor of International and Comparative Education at the University of Münster, Germany. His main research interests include international comparative education, education policy, international educational governance and its implications for educational trajectories, in particular issues of access to and equity in education.

Axel Pohl is Senior Researcher at the Institute for Regional Innovation and Social Research, IRIS e.V. in Tübingen, Germany, and at Goethe University, Frankfurt am Main, Germany. His interests focus on comparative research into transitions to adulthood, education and social policies for young people and on education in a migration society.

Risto Rinne is Professor of Comparative and International Education and Head of the Center for Research on Lifelong Learning and Education (CELE) at the Department of Education of the University of Turku, Finland, where he also leads the Doctoral Programme KEVEKO and the Finnish Doctoral Training Network FinEd. Main research areas include sociology of education, politics of education, comparative education and history of education.

Susan Robertson is Professor of Sociology of Education at the University of Bristol, UK. Her research focuses on the politics of education and the transformations of the state, the emergence of global and regional platforms, the changing role of teaching, social inequalities in learning and the outcomes of education. She is Director of the Centre for Globalization, Education and Societies and co-editor of the journal *Globalisation, Societies and Education.*

Veronica Salovaara is a doctoral student in sociology at the Department of Social Research at the University of Helsinki, Finland. Her main research interests are youth research and inequality in education.

Barbara Stauber is Professor of Educational Science at the Department of Social Pedagogy at the University of Tübingen, Germany. Her main interests are biographic transitions, gender and diversity studies, youth research with a specific focus on youth cultures, and reconstructive research methods.

Federica Taddia is a graduate researcher in lifelong education at the University of Bologna, Italy where she researches on topics connected to Intercultural Pedagogy, especially refugees and women's rights. At the moment her research and teaching focus on the question of migrants' integration.

Ulrich Theobald is a PhD student in Education Sciences at the University of Tübingen, Germany. His research focuses on the effects of global educational policies on actor constellations and steering mechanisms of schooling.

Jenni Tikkanen is a doctoral candidate in the Department of Education at the University of Turku, Finland. In her doctoral dissertation, she studies the effects that regional and social polarization of Finnish lower secondary schools have on students' planned life course trajectories. Her other research interests include European educational governance, multiculturalism and youth research.

Alessandro Tolomelli is Researcher and Assistant Professor of General and Social Pedagogy at the Department of Education of the University of Bologna, Italy. His main research focuses are epistemology of complexity, theory and methods of social and self-empowerment and Theatre of the Oppressed.

Mirjana Ule is Professor of Social Psychology and Sociology of Everyday Life at the Faculty of Social Sciences at the University of Ljubljana, Slovenia. She is Head of the Research Centre for Social Psychology. Her main research topics are life course studies, especially transition from youth to adulthood, intergenerational and parenthood research, gender studies, identity studies.

Andreas Walther is Professor of Social Pedagogy and Youth Welfare and Director of the Research Centre for Education and Coping in the Life Course at the Goethe University, Frankfurt am Main, Germany. His main research interests are youth research, transitions in the life course, child and youth welfare as well as international comparative analysis in social pedagogy and youth transitions.

Annegret Warth is Research and Teaching Fellow at the Institute for Social Pedagogy and Adult Education at the University of Frankfurt am Main, Germany. Her research interests are (international) youth and youth policy research, with focus on Turkey and peer group research.

Andreja Živoder is Researcher at the Research Centre for Social Psychology at the Faculty of Social Sciences of the University of Ljubljana, Slovenia. Her research topics include life course and identity studies, young people's educational and life choices and future planning.

Introduction: The Reshaping of Educational Trajectories in European Knowledge Societies

Morena Cuconato
University of Bologna

Roger Dale
University of Bristol

Marcelo Parreira do Amaral
University of Münster

Andreas Walther
Goethe University, Frankfurt

In the current educational discourses, a great emphasis is set on the notion of a *European educational space* (Nóvoa and Lawn, 2002; Dale and Robertson, 2009) with the concept of *lifelong learning* as one of its most powerful driving forces. In this direction, a trend has started in 2000 through the *Lisbon Declaration* of the European Council that envisaged Europe as 'the most competitive and dynamic knowledge economy in the world', with education – as the main tool to achieve global competitiveness and increased social inclusion – at the heart of this transformation (Jones et al., 2008: 32). This trend has been further developed in the ongoing *Europe 2020* strategy that gives a prominent place to education, with the aim of promoting lifelong learning, study mobility in the EU and taking-up of higher education in order to help young people's transition into work (EC, 2010; see also Daly, 2012).

This Europeanization of education has been operationalized through the work of supranational organizations – such as the *Organisation for Economic Cooperation and Development* and the *European Union* – and is implied in systems of comparative assessment like PISA (Programme for International Student Assessment) and mechanisms of governance like the Open Method of

Coordination, which calibrate the policies of member states around European-level objectives (Laval and Weber, 2002; Lange and Alexiadou, 2010; Lawn and Grek, 2012; Nordin and Sundberg, 2014). Targets agreed at European level, constant comparative analysis of progress towards them and a uniform measure of cross-national performance (in the form of PISA) should provide the framework in which the managers of increasingly autonomous educational institutions are encouraged and pressured to drive up national standards. Commenting on this trend, Nelly Stromquist argues that 'the diffusion of ideas concerning school "efficiency", "accountability", and "quality control" – essentially Anglo-American constructs – are turning schools all over the world into poor copies of romanticized view of private firms' (2000: 262).

At *institutional level*, private sector involvement and decentralization set the framework for the shaping of new educational governance in the name of competitiveness in a European knowledge economy. This trend has also brought the acceleration of educational marketization processes and, at the same time, as educational resources have been progressively cut down, led to an increase of social inequalities connected to individuals' educational chances.

According to Lawn (2013), this process seems to proceed through the deliberate exclusion of politics traditionally intended as the presentation of contestable programmes. He sketches a picture in which the:

> governance [of education] in Europe is developed through public–private partnerships, knowledge-based organizations, agencies, associations and markets … This activity is often out of sight and excludes politics. It thrives among new elite of technocrats, professionals and academics … They meet in associations or through projects or networks. They are solving problems, problems in the governing of Europe, through the collection, classification, and analysis of data, the parallel creation of standards or the accumulation of knowledge about problems and development. (Lawn, 2013: 20)

From this perspective, national systems of education are under pressure, as they do not succeed in enabling a larger number of students – in particular those among the most disadvantaged ones – to cope with the standards internationally required. National education systems and institutions, as we know them, are the result of long historical processes of institutionalization of cultural, social and political assumptions, values and norms of a particular society. Without doubt, institutional and organizational arrangements still have a pivotal effect on country-level differences in the efficacy and equality of education. In European countries, different education systems provide different levels of access to and accessibility of education, varying degrees of support to cope with its requirements and different ways of balancing societal and individual relevance of education. However, they are often taken for granted and become 'invisible' as frameworks, regulating the children and youth school careers and, in consequence, access to social positions and participation. In fact, in the globalized era of lifelong learning, early school leaving still represents one of the top concerns in the European and national educational agendas. In the knowledge society, education could be seen as a new and dangerous line of segmentation, determining either social inclusion or exclusion while persisting with the old elements of social inequalities connected to family background, gender and ethnicity (cf. Duru-Bellat, 2006).

At the *individual level*, young people nowadays – compared to their parents' generation – are confronted with societal *changes* that cause more and different disruptions and discontinuities in their life conditions (Walther, 2005; Bradley and Devadason, 2008). In the Fordist era, access to work was hierarchically pre-structured, but reliable in terms of equivalence between educational level and job position. In the knowledge society, the lack of the 'right' skills and knowledge becomes a predictor of future social exclusion, as individuals are socially excluded if they do not fit in with the dominant view of societies requiring the increase of human capital for their economic development. Moreover, the progressive Europeanization of education has taken place under the flag of the neo-liberal wave that invested EU policy as a whole according to the idea of a 'single market' set by the Maastricht Treaty of 1992. Accordingly, individuals – as market actors – are expected to become self-responsible agents in assessing, updating and promoting their own employability, while integrating the other life spheres. In schooling terms, students are now seen as enterprising individuals investing in their own human capital, neglecting the fact that their educational trajectories are the result of complex interactions between societal structures and individual–subjective action (Cuconato, 2014).

At *academic level*, this global climate of intense economic competition has brought a growing interest in European comparative studies, linked to the widespread belief in the key role of education as fuel for economic growth. Nowadays, mainstream comparative research is inspired by the need to create international tools and comparative indicators to measure the 'efficiency' and the 'quality' of education. This focus on the output of education risks disregarding the relation existing between education and individual life course in the knowledge society. Despite a still broad consensus in educational research that problems and dissatisfaction affect at most students with a poor (socio-cultural) family background, empirical studies on how reproduction of inequality through education occurs are not mainstream. Education tends to be regarded as a simple input factor into individual socialization processes determining outcomes in terms of later life chances, neglecting the effects of the life course on education, both in terms of education as an institution and as individual education processes.

Aiming at bridging this dichotomist view, the present book analyses how decisions in children's and young people's educational trajectories evolve by adopting an approach that combines a *life course* and a *governance* perspective on education. This means that *decision making* is not seen as an individual action but as the result of the interaction of multiple actors located on different scales between the local and the transnational. In processes of educational decision making a large number of stakeholders follow different interests and negotiate on the basis of different power and influence: state and local authorities, international organizations such as the OECD or the EU, research companies demanding qualified workforce, teachers and principals in schools, youth and social workers as well as other pedagogical experts and counsellors, parents and, last but not least, children and young people themselves.

To analyse the processes resulting from this complexity was the central objective of the project 'Governance of Education Trajectories in Europe. Access, coping and relevance of education for young people in European knowledge societies' (GOETE), funded by the European 7th Framework Programme for Research between 2010 and 2013. An underlying interest was to better understand how education systems and individual educational trajectories reflect the changing relation between education and social integration in the so-called 'knowledge society'. Complementary to mainstream educational research, which focuses on measuring educational outcomes, it aimed at analysing *how* educational trajectories of young people develop in different ways and patterns in different European education systems (for further information on the project see www.goete.eu).

The project involved eight European countries representing different contexts in terms of education systems, welfare states and labour markets, namely: Finland, France, Germany, Italy, the Netherlands, Poland, Slovenia and the UK. The research focused on the progression of young people from deprived social backgrounds throughout lower secondary education seen as embedded in *local school spaces* inasmuch as the relation between learning and education *in* and *out of school* was addressed. It thus covered the age group between 10 and 16 years, focusing on the transition from lower secondary education into upper secondary education or training (see Figure 0.1).

As the study concentrated on the interactive mechanisms of decision making in educational trajectories, it combined a *life course perspective* with *the governance perspective*. The governance perspective allows analysing *which* and *how* different actors are involved, and investigating *how* political decisions, public discourses on education, institutional programmes and individual preferences interact: inside and outside of school, between individuals and institutions, from the local to transnational level. The life course perspective, in contrast, combines this structural–institutional view with a perspective on the individual trajectory involving both the 'objective' movement through educational arrangements and subjective experience and meaning making. Combining these perspectives was operationalized with regard to three dimensions: the *access* to different stages of education, the individual *coping* with educational demands and the support available in this respect, and what makes education *relevant* for whom and how these different meanings are being negotiated.

In terms of educational trajectories – understood both as the institutionally expected progression in education and as the subjective experience that the individuals make of it – the category of *access* represents the very first segmentation line determining social inequalities. The phenomenon of early school leaving in particular shows how transitions into, within and out of education are affected by unequal starting positions, learning conditions and life perspectives according to class, gender, ethnicity, region and neighbourhood. The GOETE project analyses what schools do to prevent early school leaving and to what extent they provide young people from different social and ethnic backgrounds equal access to education, especially at *transition points* along their educational

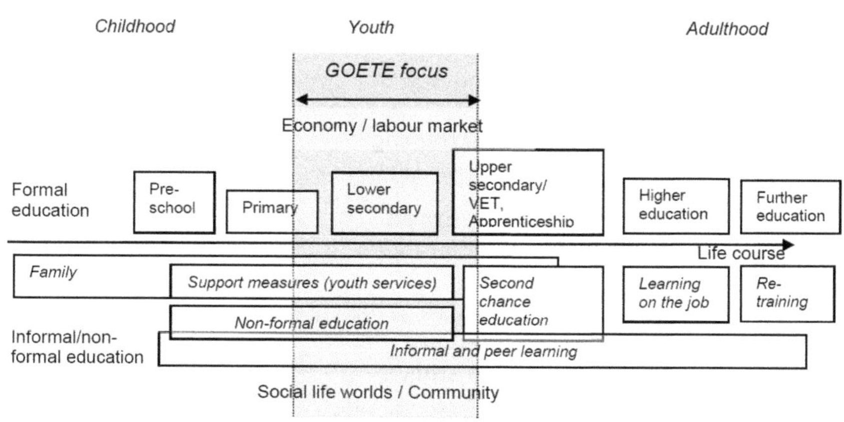

Figure 0.1 The focus of the GOETE project

trajectories. The focus set on transition is due to the liminal status that students experience in the moment of leaving one school level for progressing into another, having to bear the risk of making the wrong choice or to be hindered in their decision.

The project was structured in three phases: a preparatory *launching phase*, consisting of desk research intended to inform and prepare the *fieldwork phase*, which in turn was carried out through a combination of qualitative and quantitative research tools (mixed method approach) aiming at collecting the empirical findings to be used in the third, concluding, *analysis phases* (see Figure 0.2).

During the launching phase, the national research teams defined the sampling procedure for the ensuing empirical fieldwork, also preparing for contextualization of findings during the analyses. First, three regions per country were selected according to socio-economic indicators and – where applicable – different institutional structures, e.g. different school systems (e.g. Germany and the UK). Selection of regions took into account a country's levels of affluence and/or economic/industrial and socio-political contexts, particularly with regard to rates of economic development, employment and wealth. According to the same criteria, the teams selected three cities in the three regions and then, within the cities, different areas according to socio-economic indicator and population structure. The three schools selected were purposively to provide a broadly representative yet stratified sample so as to ensure inclusion of young people from deprived, average and affluent schools' catchment areas.

Based on this sample selection, national teams produced eight *country reports* used to contextualize the empirical work in the selected regions and

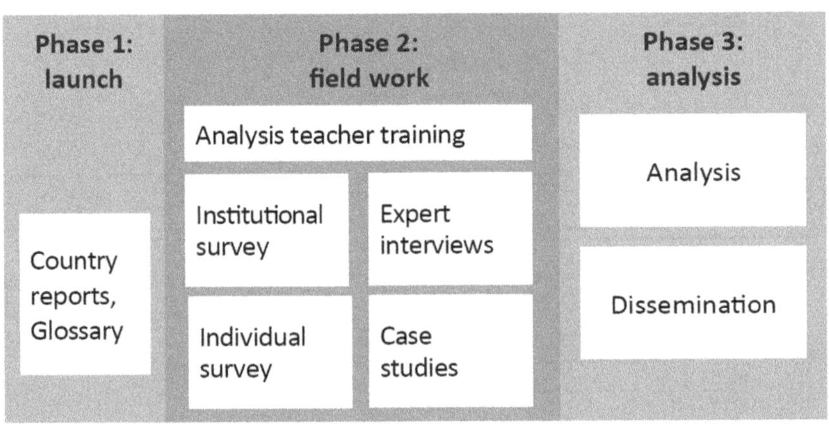

Figure 0.2 Structure of the GOETE project

cities. Furthermore, in order to enhance comparability, a glossary with key terms of the project was developed as a conceptual framework. The aim of such a glossary was not to 'homogenize' different understandings of these concepts, but rather to guarantee conceptual coherence during comparative analyses.

The *fieldwork phase* covered five empirical – qualitative and quantitative – sub-studies addressing different actors and actor constellations at different levels:

1 A *comparative analysis of contents of teacher training* aimed at understanding to what extent teachers are provided with knowledge on social aspects of educational trajectories and disadvantage as well as counselling skills related to assisting students in their educational and vocational orientation. The research was based on three major sources: questionnaires filled in by the GOETE partners, document analysis and expert interviews (N=65) in teacher training institutions (three per country). The data was analysed in a deductive way by means of content analysis, focusing on the following four dimensions: knowledge of theories and the current situation of educational disadvantage; diagnosis, support and counselling regarding individual learning processes; individualized teaching, handling of heterogeneity and differentiation in classroom; school career planning advice for decisions related to educational transitions and trajectories such as vocational guidance and occupational orientation of students in school.
2 Two *individual surveys* on school experiences and expectations with regard to *educational trajectories* from the perspective of students as well as parents. The student survey (N=6390) aimed to assess young people's subjective accounts and experiences regarding progression through their educational trajectories to date, as well as attitudes, expectations and aspirations towards their continued participation. The parental survey (N=3290) was used to assess parents' views in relation to school choice, progression, problems and support experienced to date as well as their expectations and their efforts for their child's future educational and employment career. The sample was stratified.
3 An *institutional survey* collecting the *views* of school principals on issues such as social inequalities in educational trajectories, transitions into and out of specific educational stages, early school leaving, the relation between formal, non-formal and informal learning as well as the present state and the future challenges of educational policy. The survey was conducted

through a web-based questionnaire with email invitations. The total number of respondents in the data is 984. The number of respondents per country varies between 38 (the UK) and 200 (Poland). On average, there were approximately 124 respondents per country. The response percentages varied between 34.5 per cent (Finland) and 3.4 per cent (the UK).

4 Eight *qualitative case studies on local school spaces* aimed at offering insight into the relationships between all the different actors involved (students, teachers, parents, employers, youth service, policymakers etc.) in shaping young people's educational trajectories at local level. The focus lay on understanding their different perspectives and on describing constellations of factors of access, coping and relevance in the educational trajectories and learning biographies of lower secondary education students. In each city, a school located in a disadvantaged area was selected – or better: a local school space (Maroy, 2004) – in order to get a grip on the relationships between school and out-of-school actors. Case studies included a sample of all actors involved in student trajectories: students, parents, teachers, principals, counsellors, youth and social workers, employers and local policymakers. Data was gathered from group discussions with students and teachers, individual in-depth interviews with parents (N=109) as well as with students during (N=195) and after they had left lower secondary education (N=109), reconstructing their trajectories up to entering the post-compulsory stage. Expert interviews were conducted with professional actors inside and outside school. These interviews were analysed in order to compare the different views of the actors and reconstruct interactive constellations. Interviews and focus groups were tape-recorded, fully transcribed and coded. Coding procedures were different in every country, although in order to get comparative results, every national team coded in a deductive way according to the five main thematic perspectives of the GOETE project (access, coping, relevance, life course and governance). A mix of *content analysis* (Mayring and Gahleitner, 2010), a grounded theory approach (Corbin and Strauss, 2008) and inductive procedures to spot new, unexpected issues, problems, constellations and so on was used. The majority of the countries used computer-aided software programs.

5 A *discourse analysis of educational governance* at national level with the objective to analyse processes and mechanisms of educational governance, current discourses and recent reforms at national level. This was operationalized through a critical discourse analysis of selected influential public documents as well as a series of expert interviews

with stakeholders at national level such as politicians, administration representatives, employers, researchers, trade union representatives, foundations etc. (N=208). While the previous studies focused on different groups of actors and placed their emphasis on different levels of analysis, this last investigated educational governance with a view to understanding governing discourses, policies and practices and how they shape and regulate educational trajectories, especially with regard to the first two transition points after primary school. Thus, it aimed at the 'higher' and 'wider' contexts of educational governance that frame, orient and set the challenges and shape the parameters and possibilities at local contexts and practices, hence influencing the outcomes of educational trajectories of individuals.

In the *analysis phase*, an attempt was made to integrate the different empirical findings from the previous sub-studies in a methodologically and theoretically meaningful way. This multilevel approach required, first, that the different sub-studies were analysed separately – nationally and cross-nationally – and, second, that overall thematic analyses were conducted that cross-cut different data sets from both quantitative and qualitative sources, thus bringing together the different levels into a *comparative multilevel analysis* along the themes of *life course, governance, access, coping* and *relevance*. This comparative process aimed at identifying and understanding different constellations of *governing educational trajectories* in the context of different *transition regimes*. The focus was on interactions between socio-economic, institutional and cultural factors inherent in current educational policy and practice, in relationships between education and welfare, in dominant discourses as well as in individual decisions and biographical orientations. By doing this, the project also explored how supranational, especially European, discourses were taken up at local and national level.

Overview of the Chapters

By combining a *life course* and a *governance* perspective on education, the present volume invokes a wide approach to students' educational trajectories in order to explain how they develop in the same structural context (i.e. selection versus comprehensive school system) according to the individual meaning attached to education and the strategies adopted to cope with it. The life course perspective focuses on how education is linked with previous, contemporary and subsequent (school) experiences and chances in individual lives. It integrates an institutional dimension inasmuch as, in modern societies, life ages and life stages are structured by (state) institutions, especially for what concerns education and the welfare state; and a subjective dimension because individuals construct their biographies on what they hold subjectively relevant. The governance perspective refers to how regulation of individual educational trajectories can no longer be seen as the product of educational institutions and state policies. In contrast, developments like the previously mentioned individualization, globalization or marketization have contributed to constellations of educational trajectories, which have to be conceptualized in terms of multilevel, multi-actor and multi-perspective processes. To this aim this book analyses on the one hand processes of decision making in individual student biographies, and on the other hand the contextualization of these decision-making processes in social contexts: families, schools – or better: 'local school spaces' (Maroy, 2004), municipalities, regions, national education systems and welfare states and – increasingly important – transnational policy contexts.

Two introductory chapters offer the conceptual and analytical framework of the whole book. In Chapter 1, 'Comparative Perspective on the Governance of Education in the Life Course', A. Walther, M. Parreira do Amaral, M. Cuconato and R. Dale introduce the theoretical and methodological interactionist approach of analysing young people's educational trajectories by combining the concepts of life course and governance, later operationalized into access to, coping with and relevance of education. Afterwards the authors present the model of qualitative multilevel analysis (Helsper et al., 2010) as the most adequate to take into account the methodological consequences of this interactionist approach, providing a heuristic modelling of educational processes across different levels of actors and meanings.

In Chapter 2, 'The Diversity of Education and Welfare Systems in Europe', J. Tikkanen, A. Biggart and A. Pohl present and discuss students' educational trajectories as the result of complex interactions between societal structures and individual–subjective action. This chapter provides contextual information for the subsequent analyses of educational trajectories in the European countries involved in the GOETE research. Two existing models and concepts of comparative education are discussed and applied to the countries: Allmendinger's model (1989) that distinguishes different levels of standardization and stratification of education systems; and Walther's transition regime model (2006). This permits us to highlight the main differences and common features of educational systems and to flesh out the contexts of education and of educational trajectories in the research countries.

Part 1 deals with the *governance of education* in terms of a conceptual tool for the interactions of different actors (state, market and civil society) at different levels (national, sub-national, transnational), with different mandates, competences and degrees of leverage power. In Chapter 3, 'Scales, Discourses and Institutions in the Governance of Educational Trajectories in Europe', R. Dale, Y. Kazepov, R. Rinne and S. Robertson focus on the high-level governance of educational trajectories, considering the different territorial levels at which it deploys. They present the wider contexts through which conceptions and practices of governance of educational trajectories (provision, distribution and likely consequences) are framed and different 'opportunity structures' produced, whose impact will be then discussed in term of access to, coping with and the relevance of education. In Chapter 4, 'Translation of Policy Instruments and Negotiation of Actors in Local School Spaces', K. Amos, P. Loncle, A. Martelli, E. Barberis, V. Becquet and U. Theobald illustrate how policy instruments related to the meaning of schooling as a key element in the lifelong learning regimes of late modern knowledge-based economies are shaped and translated, adapted and modified in the intersection between institution and actors (students, families, teachers, experts) at local levels. Attention is paid to similarities and differences across countries, and to the tools, practices, conditions, variables, perceptions, strategies, conflicts, challenges, opportunities and perspectives that explain the emerging patterns of (non-) participation and the interactions within local school spaces.

Part 2 deals with the *access to education*. In Chapter 5, 'Understanding the Interactive Emergence of Educational Inequalities through Access and Accessibility of Education', B. Stauber, M. Parreira do Amaral and I. Danic present this concept in relation to the overall approach combining the life course and the governance perspective, underlining the need for an analytical distinction between processes of social differentiation and differences or inequalities. The aim is to show which role both child–parent relations and educational staff members play during transition processes with regard to opening or narrowing access to education. In Chapter 6, 'Producing Accessibility through Discretionary Practices of Educational Professionals', E. Barberis, I. Buchowicz and N. De Luigi explore the points of view of parents and pupils in negotiating with school staff and the interactive processes in which practices unfold that can open up or close down access chances at a micro level and affect subjective perception of the accessibility of education. In doing this, the authors identify different constellations of interaction among pupils/parents and educational professionals (teachers, guidance counsellors, psychologists and youth workers, among others).

Part 3 deals with *coping with educational demands*. In Chapter 7, 'Educational and Vocational Guidance as Support Mechanisms in Schools', J. Felczak and I. Julkunen describe and analyse schools' support mechanisms for students at transition points occurring in the relationship between public education and welfare. The measures of educational and vocational guidance are analysed from the student perspective in order to reveal whether they are perceived as relevant, useful and effective and the different ways in which they are used by the young people. In Chapter 8, 'Cooperation and Problems of Recognition between Schools and Parents in Supporting Young People's Educational Trajectories', H. Koşar Altinyelken, S. Demozzi, F. Boron and F. Taddia discuss that while formal support and guidance focus on information and educational standards, young people look for recognition of their subjective needs, wishes and encouragement. This risks activating a continuing 'blame-game' and misunderstanding between families and school professionals undermining the efficacy of the existing support measures.

Part 4 deals with the *relevance of education*. In Chapter 9, 'Comparing the Views of Students, Parents and Teachers on the Emerging Notions of Relevance of Education', J. McDowell, A. Živoder and A. Tolomelli examine the notions of relevance of education as they emerge in the individual learner context, comparing the views of students with those of their parents and teachers involved in the transition processes. The analysis is conducted in terms of accessibility of education through the socio-economic position of families and characteristics of educational systems in respective countries. In Chapter 10, 'The Relevance of Informal Learning and Out-of-School Contexts for Formal Educational Transitions', V. Salovaara and J. Litau focus on how out-of-school learning is dealt with in schools and analyse to what extent different actors involved – directly and indirectly – in school education and educational trajectories are conscious and aware of young people's learning out of school, what relevance they ascribe to informal learning and how this is recognized and made visible or even supported in, through or in relation to school. The findings are first analysed according to the different actors, countries and theoretical perspectives and then according to the contribution of the knowledge society discourse to the meaning of informal learning for educational trajectories.

Part 5 deals with *educational transitions in the life course*. In Chapter 11, 'Students' Decision-making Strategies at Transitions in Education', M. Cuconato, K. Majdzińska, A. Walther and A. Warth provide an insight into how educational trajectories of so-called disadvantaged young people evolve differently. The authors theorize the concept of educational trajectories in terms of the interplay of life course and biography, the role of transitions and the meaning of decision making in this respect. This perspective is operationalized into three dimensions: ruptures, destinations and choice. The analysis develops the heuristic concept of 'doing transitions', highlighting that the relationship between education and the life course is to be viewed as a recurrent negotiation process among all actors involved in the process. In Chapter 12, 'Teachers and Parents as Actors in the Students' Educational Transitions', M. Ule, A. Živoder, H. Lunabba and M. du Bois-Reymond compare not only parents' and teachers' views but also teacher–parent relationships across different countries and (comprehensive or differentiated) education systems with the aim of reflecting on the implications of these perspectives for the decision making of students and on the discourses that these actors introduce into the decision making. The authors develop different constellations of teacher–parent relationships and discuss their potential effects on students' decision making in terms of institutional versus everyday life conditioning as well as societal discourses that are (re)produced in these relationships.

In a concluding chapter, 'Comparative Multilevel Analysis of Educational Trajectories', M. Parreira do Amaral and A. Walther introduce a meta-level discussion providing a more comprehensive picture of the different actors, perspectives and levels – and their interaction – involved in the emergence of young people's educational trajectories. Adopting an approach of multilevel analysis, the authors draw together the different data sources, actor perspectives and levels of meaning making presented and discussed in the previous chapters in an attempt to understand the interactive constellations of 'doing transitions' that become visible through the analytical–theoretical framework resulting from the combination of life course and governance. The model of the multilevel analysis builds on the idea of the integration of different perspectives, methods and data, but explores in more detail the relationships between the different levels under research. Therefore, it allows discussion of findings and insights from the previous chapters that are located at the different levels of analysis, and the interrelatedness of the levels and interactions involved in the emergence and evolution of individual educational trajectories.

1

Comparative Perspective on the Governance of Education in the Life Course

Andreas Walther
Goethe University, Frankfurt

Marcelo Parreira do Amaral
University of Münster

Morena Cuconato
University of Bologna

Roger Dale
University of Bristol

Introduction

This chapter introduces the reader to the theoretical and methodological approach adopted in analysing young people's educational trajectories. As discussed in the Introduction to this volume, researching the governance of education in the life course is based on the assumption that educational trajectories are the result of numerous interactions among multiple actors at different scales in decision-making processes throughout education. Further, we depart from the fact that educational trajectories can neither be sensibly seen as the sole product of educational institutions and state policies, on the one hand, nor be accounted for entirely in terms of rational individual choices and decisions on the other (Cuconato and Walther, 2015). Studying the governance of educational trajectories of young people meant, therefore, exploring how the actors involved at various scales actively or passively conceptualize, negotiate and organize individual educational trajectories. It involved revealing and understanding the wider contexts – for instance, discourses – by which these conceptions, interactions, institutions and regulatory practices are framed. It also required understanding the dynamic and interactive nature of governance processes since educational trajectories comprise countless individual and institutional choices/decisions that are greatly contingent and dependent on the actual interactions at local level that shape their outcomes without determining them.

Framing educational trajectories in such a dynamic and interactive way raised a number of conceptual and methodological issues that commanded attention and which will be discussed below. First, it has to think together the structural/institutional and individual/subjective dimensions of the topic at hand and overcome dichotomist views grounded in rational choice thinking that ascribes educational trajectories to: individual (rational) choices; determination by structural forces; or a universal (world) system of capitalist hegemony. Second, the very concept of educational trajectories requires not only taking into account different levels of analysis, different processes and activities but also accounting for the range of actors and institutions involved. Thus, studying educational trajectories requires a multi-actor and multi-level approach. Third, it entails looking into the intrinsically interactive and dynamic nature of the governance of educational trajectories and the decision-making processes they comprise. As such, a comparative perspective on educational trajectories entails both paying attention to location and context and identifying patterns or constellations of the governance of educational trajectories.

The chapter starts with the presentation of the concepts or better, the perspectives, adopted in framing our research: life course and governance. The *life course* perspective implies integrating a biographical perspective inasmuch as the institutionalized life course and the subjective biographies of individuals are interrelated in terms of structure and agency. This is especially relevant for the key question regarding the decision-making processes behind educational trajectories underlying the whole book. The *governance* perspective implies introducing the dimensions of educational discourses, scales and actors since state policies are no longer the sole or the main element involved in regulating educational trajectories. Drawing on existing concepts and research, the following section relates life course and governance to education and elaborates their conceptual interaction in producing educational trajectories. The second part of the chapter discusses the application of this conceptual approach to empirical research by focusing on access to, coping with and relevance of education throughout educational trajectories. All three dimensions are conceptualized in an interactionist way as social constructions that emerge from negotiations and power relations between different actors. The last section provides a discussion of the methodological approach consisting of a model for multilevel analysis that provides a heuristic tool for the analysis of educational processes across different levels of actors and meaning and a comparative approach to serve both as an interpretative framework and for contextualizing of findings.

Conceptualizing Educational Trajectories: A Life Course and Governance Perspective

In this section, we first present and discuss the two main conceptual perspectives adopted in conceptualizing educational trajectories in an interactive approach. First, we elaborate on the life course perspective towards education, then expound the governance perspective. By doing this, we aim to meet the conceptual requirements referred to above.

A life course perspective towards education

Referring to young people's learning and education in terms of educational trajectories implies a time perspective that evolves across stages and transitions; it also implies a space perspective connecting different contexts. Further, it involves a dynamic perspective inasmuch as transitions are crossroads at which further destinations are determined through choices and decisions. Finally, it implies conceptualizing education as an integral element of the interplay between the institutionalized life course and the subjective biographies of learners.

The *time* perspective of educational trajectories has been both underlined and undermined by the concept of lifelong learning: on the one hand, it explicitly refers to continuing learning and education across the life span on the other hand it decouples specific forms of learning and education from specific life phases (cf. Field, 2000; Jarvis, 2009). Further educational trajectories are related to *space* inasmuch as learning and education occur in specific contexts – not only lifelong but also life-*wide* – according to which learning is categorized as formal, non-formal or informal (Hodkinson, 2010). Thus educational trajectories are conceptualized as relating to learning inside and outside of schools. Educational trajectories are *dynamic* as they accumulate over the lifetime, in terms of formal certificates providing specific access to further education and to occupational careers, and also in terms of individual learning careers building on prior learning (cf. Bloomer and Hodkinson, 2000). In fact, educational trajectories emerge from a multitude of formal and informal educational situations, including explicit decisions such as continuing with a specific course after lower secondary school or implicit decisions such as following a lesson rather than joking with classmates.

Obviously, time, space and dynamics are interrelated inasmuch as certain decisions are scheduled at specific ages and bound to specific contexts. A theoretical framework appropriate to contextualize time, space and dynamics in educational trajectories is the relation between life course and biography. The *life course* is a 'social institution … in terms of a set of rules that orders a key area or a key dimension of life' (Kohli, 1985: 1) in terms of an 'age-based sequence of typical, socially defined conditions endowed with specific expectations (roles)' (Scherger, 2009: 532). This institutionalization is connected to the process of individualization in early modernity. Historical processes and events expressing the weakening of collective patterns of socialization such as reformation, enlightenment, industrialization and the French revolution contributed to the need for a secular order connecting individual lives with the societal division of labour. This order centred around the adult roles of paid employment and family work and was brought forward by the emerging institutions of the nation state: *public education* contributing to the emergence of a life phase – namely youth – meant to prepare children for adult roles, which includes allocation to (unequal) occupational and social positions, qualification in terms of providing them with skills to fulfil the respective roles, and integration (cf. Fend, 2006); welfare securing the life course by serving as incentive for a life centred around paid employment and as guarantee in case of job loss (cf. Mayer, 1997). This standardization of a 'normal' life course, however, depended also on a set of cultural norms, values and forms of knowledge. The disciplinary practices and the orders of knowledge and discourse, the evolution of which Foucault (1972) has reconstructed, contributed to the normality of a standard life course which became a shared model of 'good life' (cf. Kohli, 1985). This accounts at least for the period of Fordism which can be seen as the high time of life course standardization inasmuch as production, consumption and social policies were effective factors of the standardization of the life course with the specialized worker and the housewife as gendered prototypes (cf. Myles, 1993). Thus, the life course became a powerful orientation not only for educational and welfare institutions but also for individuals' life planning which is reflected by the concept of life course regime (Kohli, 1985: 1).

Obviously, standardization does not imply equality of life courses. In contrast, life courses are stratified according to occupational position, gender, ethnic origin or region. This is, for instance, reflected by the divide between vocational and academic strands in upper secondary education linked to a differentiation of both skills and status (cf. Lasonen and Young, 1998). In his study of 'cooling out' mechanisms, Goffman (1952) has analysed how education reconciles democratic promises of equal opportunity with capitalist competition. The meritocratic principle institutionalized in modern education systems encourages all to engage in the competition for social positions while also individualizing unequal outcomes of this competition; it both raises aspirations and helps to reduce them. Such cooling out is corroborated by professionals of the education system and other 'gatekeepers' in the life course such as medical doctors, psychologists, social workers or counsellors. 'In the best interest of the person' they undertake diagnostic practice: assess entitlements and capacities to identify which position fits best for whom (cf. Heinz, 1992). This shows that only in its relation to the labour market on the one hand and the welfare state on the other can the regulatory function of education be understood (cf. Allmendinger, 1989; Mayer, 1997).

Gatekeeping and cooling out are most articulate at *transitions* in the life course at which decisions are taken with regard to further destinations. Transitions in a most general sense are changes of social status in a lifetime perspective, mostly stimulated by institutional expectations related to age or the completion of scheduled pathways such as school. Transitions are situations of 'liminality' between positions with clear status and those with uncertain outcome – for society it is uncertain if individuals accept the offered roles according to the dominant normality; for the individuals it is uncertain if they will be the same after the transition. Transitions are, therefore, regulated and ritualized to reduce insecurity and uncertainty. Rites of passage (van Gennep, 1960) have first been analysed by anthropologists as social practices by which societies secure social reproduction across generational change (cf. van Gennep, 1960; Glaser and Strauss, 1971).

However, social and educational sciences have (re)discovered the issue of transitions only in the 1980s and 1990s. Due to the simultaneity of labour market flexibilization, increasing educational levels and sociocultural emancipation and related societal processes of individualization and pluralization, the life course underwent a process of de-standardization. The course and sequence of transitions was no longer self-evident but experienced – again – as insecure and uncertain. One way in which societies dealt with this renewed uncertainty was limiting the issue of transitions to the prolongation of youth transitions and to problems such as unemployment or early school leaving (cf. Kelly, 2000). This accounts as well for education as, for a long time, only transitions of school leavers who neither continued with education or training nor entered work (NEET) have been the main focus (Eurofound, 2012). However, with the discourse of lifelong learning, transitions into primary school, between primary and secondary school and into and out of higher education are also being addressed as transitions that might fail and therefore require support and control (Walther, 2006; Eurofound, 2014). In the meantime, transitions are analysed and addressed with regard to different life ages and areas of life from childhood to old age and from life styles to family (cf. Schröer et al., 2013). The heuristic value of the transition concept actually lies in its openness and its sensitivity for the individualization processes expressed and reinforced by the de-standardization of the life course.

Current discourses and regulations of transitions are expressions of how national education systems and welfare states contribute to specific normalities of the life course. At the same time, the renewed interest actually resulted from a situation in which existing concepts and standardized regulatory procedures were revealed to be no longer effective. The emergence of comparative transition research has therefore been concerned with analysing differences and commonalities between different nation states in addressing transitions – also stimulated by the interest in, and expectation of, discovering 'best practices' (see above). One of the outcomes of such research has been the model of *youth transition regimes*. Data from empirical research across a series of different studies was interpreted in the light of existing comparative models distinguishing different types of welfare states (cf. Esping-Andersen, 1990; Gallie and Paugam, 2000) or education systems (cf. Allmendinger, 1989). In correspondence with the theoretical framework developed above only a combination of education and welfare indicators was revealed as appropriate for the comparative analysis of youth transitions (cf. Walther, 2006; see also Tikannen et al., in this volume).

Understanding of educational trajectories and the transitions they involve, however, requires not only an institutional life course perspective but also a *biographical* perspective taking the subjective experiences and orientations of individuals into account. In contrast to the institutional life course which is structured by a linear sequence of social roles, biographical construction is structured by subjective meaning and continuity (Alheit and Dausien, 2000, 2002b). Biographies are identities over time involving resuming the past, imagining the future and linking past and future in present situations. Following Emirbayr and Mische (1998) and their iterative concept of agency, biography can also be seen as an aspect of individual agency which is structured by past experiences, evolves in imagined futures and articulates in coping with present situations (cf. Walther, 2012a).

Biography and the life course do not form a dichotomy but a duality inasmuch as biographies generate life course institutions and life course institutions provide key words for the construction of biographies; for instance, school entry represents for most children a stimulus to conceive of themselves and act like schoolchildren (cf. Helsper, 2004).

The duality of life course and biography that is articulated in transitions is also reflected with regard to education inasmuch as education can be understood in functional terms – attending formal education leading to certificates and justifying allocation to different occupational social positions – as well as in biographical terms. In a biographical sense, education means the reflection of learning processes leading to a transformation of the relationship between the self and the world and which can contribute to changed life orientations and agency (cf. Koller, 2011). In fact, biographical learning – or 'biographicity' (Alheit and Dausien, 2000, 2002b) – can and often does result from failure in formal education because the discrepancy between biographical aspirations and possibilities requires reflection. The often-missing link between functional education and biographical learning is *recognition*. In the formal education system, recognition is realized by standardized curricula and assessment. In biographical learning, recognition is dependent on direct interaction and implies both a general recognition as author of its own life history and recognition of specific learning and development. At transitions in educational trajectories, recognition occurs formally in terms of assessment and promotion, while individuals rarely experience recognition for biographical reflection involved in the decision making at transition (see Cuconato et al., in this volume). However, under conditions of educational governance shifting from a bureaucratic Fordist approach towards multi-actor and multi-centred coordination, the relationship between functional and biographical perspectives on education may need to be reconsidered. The following section introduces the governance perspective.

Governance as an analytical perspective in education

In this volume, the governance perspective implies analysing how educational trajectories are governed in the interaction of regulatory structures and actors. It is worth mentioning from the beginning that 'governance' is not a theory in the narrow sense of the term, but rather an analytic approach that calls attention to important shifts in perspective in the political field. These shifts in perspective refer to using the term 'governance' to conceptualize activities of regulation and governing for which traditionally terms such as 'steering', 'governing', 'control', 'interdependence' had been preferred. Governance addresses 'government', 'management', 'coordination', 'regulation' etc. among different agents within the state, the market, the economy and civil society structures in non-hierarchical and network-like structures (Benz et al., 2007; Ball and Junemann, 2012).[1]

Concisely, governance implies a shift from an actor-centred to an institutional-centred perspective of social coordination. It describes the movement away from exclusive state control over a range of aspects that constitute the substance of governing activities – funding, ownership, provision, policy, regulation – toward the involvement in these activities of a range of other actors – including the community, household, market (for-profit/not-for-profit). In that it emphasizes a plurality of actors, it shifts the focus to the *coordination of action* and implies a blurring of steering subjects and objects that are increasingly seen as mutually interdependent. Correspondingly, governance calls attention to a new mix of regulatory systems (hierarchy, market principle, majority rule or negotiation) but also to the effects of institutionalized regulatory structures. In our research context, particular attention was given not only to the effects of the different forms of organization of education and welfare systems, but also to the impact of discourses on the governance of educational trajectories. Here, the relation to the life course regimes referred to above becomes particularly visible. In addition, the governance perspective acknowledges that regulation may be the result of activities at different levels and scales – from the local through to the international. Thus, *multilevel systems* (Marks, 1992) provide a relevant reference point hinting at non-hierarchical forms of regulation, different game levels and network-like structures. In this multilevel perspective, it becomes clear that governance oftentimes takes shape as rescaling, i.e. shifting and increasing territorial levels of responsibility (Kazepov, 2010) and de-monopolization or devolution – that is, shifting and increasing actors involved in the policy process; moving governance tools to different scales is both the object and outcome of governing itself, which commands attention to the specific dynamics of governance. Further, the increased number and types of actors involved in regulatory processes call attention to tools and mechanisms of governance. In the governance literature, mechanisms beyond those employed in bureaucratic or legislative steering figure prominently. Not only do the types and potentials of the various actors differ, they also play out differently. Indeed, the outcomes of governance depend largely on the specific *actor constellations*, i.e. the different possible combinations of actors and modes of coordination that are termed 'governance regimes'.

The term *governance* has been used in many social science disciplines as an interdisciplinary 'bridging concept' (cf. van Kersbergen and van Waarden, 2004; Schuppert, 2005: 373). Instead of basing it on a consensual definition, the term governance is rather used in the description of new forms of steering/regulation and links various academic discussions on forms of collective decision making and implementation in political science, law and management (Schuppert, 2005), in sociology (Benz, 2004) and more recently also in education science (Altrichter et al., 2007),[2] inasmuch as it indicates a significant shift in emphasis relevant to all disciplines, 'namely from actor-centeredness to an emphasis on regulatory structures' (Schuppert, 2005: 374, own translation). Renate Mayntz refers to governance as comprising all forms in which public and private actors, separately or jointly, aim to produce common goods and services and solve collective problems. For her:

> Governance means the sum of all concurrent forms of collective regulation of social issues: from the institutionalized self-regulation of the civil society, through the diverse forms of cooperation among state and private actors, up to the action of sovereign state agents. (2004: 66, own translation)

One important aspect of the emergence of governance as a key political concept is that the term has emerged to signal shifts from an old to a new order (Jessop, 1999; see also Parreira do Amaral and Rinne, 2015). Related to this, governance has become an important term in educational policy and educational research as it points to profound changes in the area of education and its relationships to other societal sectors. These changes concern specifically the instruments and ways of steering, new forms of providing and organizing educational services, and the emergence of new actors in educational policy (Amos and Radtke, 2007; Amos, 2010).

As an analytical instrument, the term remains ideologically open and offers tools for the analysis of different types (regimes) of governance and of their transformations. A governance perspective can thus be integrated and combined with various social science theories, such as neoinstitutionalism, cybernetic and systems theory, network theory, theories of organizations, international regime theory or theory of regulation (cf. Benz et al., 2007; Amos, 2010).

According to Benz and colleagues (2007), governance appears as a political concept in a time of criticism and scepticism as to the possibilities of linear and hierarchical regulation of 'complex' social systems. Thus, its widespread usage points as much to a change of perspective on, as to profound transformations in, the forms of regulation and coordination of modern societies (Mayntz, 2006), and as a consequence especially of the spread of conceptions of New Public Management or 'New Governance'.

In the framework of this volume, the governance perspective implies analysing how different actors and constellations of actors – school, employers, administrations, policymakers, youth services, parents and students – on different levels and scales – local, regional, national, transnational/European – interact and communicate. In governance parlance, this would mean to coordinate their actions on issues of accessing and progressing within education, on students' legitimate needs of support and the responsibilities for providing support inside or outside school as well as on future skill and competence needs.

The chapters in this volume attend in particular to four aspects of the governance of educational trajectories: discourses, levels/scales, actors/constellations of actors and governance mechanisms. *Discourses* refer to the impact of overall discourses, for instance the discourse of the 'knowledge economy' or 'lifelong learning', but also of more localized ones such as professional discourses on the framing of both educational trajectories and of relevant issues, target groups and adequate interventions (see Parreira do Amaral and Rinne, 2015). The aspect of *levels and scales* refers to a 'scalar' division of labour between the various scales at which educational governance is carried out. There are two divisions of labour: a *vertical* division across the administrative levels of government at which the responsibility for particular activities rests – running from central government (and transnational bodies such as the EU) to local neighbourhoods; and a *horizontal* (or 'sectoral') division that refers to the degree to which the responsibilities for the activities of education systems are held by and within those systems themselves, and the degree to which they may be shared with other agencies, whether in the labour market or the area of guidance and counselling. For instance, it includes looking into the degree to which education is a single 'silo' and carries out all elements that fall under the heading of education in some level of isolation from other social and labour market sectors (see Dale et al., in this volume). One crucial advantage of the governance perspective is that it emphasizes a shift 'from actor-centeredness to an emphasis on regulatory structures' (translated from Schuppert, 2005: 374) without completely neglecting agency; rather it underscores the impact of constellations of actors involved in the governance of educational trajectories. Thus, the chapters in this volume pay special attention to the interaction of actors among themselves, e.g. teachers, parents and students, and also with structures and institutions: for instance, the opportunity structures embodied in different types of education systems (see Dale and Parreira do Amaral, 2015; Barberis et al., in this volume; Koşar Altinyelken, et al., in this volume). Finally, the chapters discuss – to different degrees – the impact of governance mechanisms on educational trajectories. Governance mechanisms include, for instance, the different ways educational pathways are structured and organized (see Tikkanen et al., in this volume), how access, guidance and support are provided (Felczak et al., in this volume), and also how each individual agency interacts with these governance mechanisms, producing outcomes that are neither purely an intra-individual process nor an automatic or deterministic translation of structural constraints into individual action, but rather the result of long processes of interaction, communication and negotiation (see Cuconato et al., in this volume).

Researching the Governance of Educational Trajectories: Access to, Coping with, Relevance of Education

In short, both governance and life course perspectives aim at conceptualizing the regulation of educational trajectories in interactionist terms. But how can a life course and a governance perspective be integrated and how can this be made fruitful for empirical analysis? What are relevant dimension and concrete issues in which a (changed) governance of educational trajectories can be made visible and accessible for analysis and understanding? Based on the theoretical perspectives developed above and the state of the art of educational research, three dimensions have been identified and subjected to empirical analysis in the further chapters of this volume: access, coping and relevance.

Access and accessibility

A first dimension which is obviously connected to the governance of educational trajectories is the question how access to education, as well as access between different types and levels of education, is regulated. Access is closely linked to the *structural and institutional* arrangements in the provision and delivery of education. Access to education is, thus, impacted by the different types of organization of education systems (e.g. selective, comprehensive, multi-tiered), by the specific organizational arrangements within schools and other educational institutions such as entrance and progression regulations, selection by ability, etc. and by sectoral policies (school choice, policies targeting particular groups, etc.). On the surface this is a primarily institutional question as age limits, school districts or performance in prior education are institutionally defined rules of access in most education systems at one level or the other (see Tikkanen et al., in this volume). However, institutional regulation of access is less universal and self-evident than it seems at first glance. Since the 1970s, research has repeatedly pointed out that social class correlates with access to different types and levels of schools reflected by different – or better, unequal – outcomes (cf. Bernstein, 1971/72; Bourdieu and Passeron, 1977; Willis, 1977). Much research has conceptualized social reproduction through education in a way that social origin appears as a determining mechanism. However, access regulation does not explicitly exclude children from certain schools based on their social origin, nor are all children from disadvantaged backgrounds underachievers. In fact, only in their interrelation do social origin and institutional regulation have a discriminating impact on children from certain milieus. This could, for instance, be due to a lack of institutional openness for heterogeneity of students with regard to language, ethnicity, gender or personal development; or school districts reflecting social milieus; or due to the unwritten expectation of schools that parents assist their children in doing homework or preparing for exams (Bernstein, 1971/72; Gomolla and Radtke, 2009).

But even the assumption and finding that socio-economic and institutional structures are effective only in their interrelation does not yet explain *how* they are related. The first factor that relates socio-economic factors with institutional regulation is societal *discourses*, i.e. dominant representations that contribute to the categorization of certain groups and individuals as different, deviant and/or deficient. Second, overarching discourses on underclass, migration and disadvantage are translated into pedagogical practices of 'othering' and 'cooling out' whereby individuals are ascribed individual deficits and are taught, counselled and supported in a way that contributes to reducing their educational and occupational aspirations. Third, the individual and collective practices of young people themselves are as significant as those of (and with) their parents. Although Willis's (1977) analysis expressed the expectation that 'working class kids' almost automatically 'get working class jobs', it revealed that reproduction does not occur by itself but depends on complex interactions between different actors and their cultural or subcultural, institutional or professional, formal or informal social practices. The question under what conditions young people from disadvantaged contexts become early school leavers, adapt to educational demands or even use education for social mobility, and the factors and actors involved in these constellations, is one of the central questions of the GOETE project. This implies however, that access is not something that does or does not exist, being broad or narrow, selective or universal, conditional or unconditional. Starting from a dialectic relationship of structure and agency, access as a structural property of education systems needs to be complemented by accessibility. *Accessibility* refers to the way in which individuals perceive and evaluate education as accessible or not. This includes their knowledge of formal regulations, their acceptance of conditions and anticipation of their ability to cope with the related demands. Both structural access to education *and* their subjective perception, interpretation and evaluation of education as accessible make young people *actually* access education (see Parreira do Amaral, Stauber and Barberis, 2015; Stauber et al., in this volume).

Coping and support

The dimension of coping refers to how individuals actively respond to the demands they encounter. Children and young people are subject to the expectation of taking the role of pupils and students and it is not up to them to accept or reject this role. Formally, this role is interpreted in terms of learning in a cognitive sense and coping is assessed by demonstrating curricular knowledge and competence in the classroom and exams. However, the role of pupils and students is much broader and deeper. First, it implies for the first time in the life course being reduced to certain aspects of the self and being sanctioned in case of non-fulfilment. Second, there are many facets of this role, which are formally not recognized. The concept of hidden curriculum has raised attention to the fact that succeeding in school requires adapting to hierarchical relationships and disciplinary rules (cf. Snyder, 1971). Then, there is plenty of evidence that the discourse of lifelong learning has also reached children and young people. They are aware of the relevance (see below) of formal education for later lives, which increases pressure and stress. Finally, school is also a place of peer and youth culture. While being a resource for individual identities and for coping with the alienating effects of school life, it also reflects social inequalities with its own dynamics of inclusion and exclusion; and it is in most cases either neglected or sanctioned by school (see Salovaara et al., in this volume).

The concept of coping has been developed in the context of developmental psychology to explain how individuals maintain capacity to act in critical life events (cf. Lazarus and Folkman, 1984). While identifying cognitive and emotional factors of human agency, it includes a normative perspective inasmuch as only strategies recognized as 'normal' are classified as coping – which is reflected by concepts such as 'productive coping' (Frydenberg and Lewis, 1993) or related perspectives such as 'positive youth development' (Catalano et al., 2004). This inbuilt normativity limits the potential for understanding individual action and agency. Böhnisch and Schefold (1985) have translated the concept of coping into a more sociological perspective by understanding any individual agency as a way of coping with uncertain and contradictory life conditions (*Lebenslage*). They follow psychological coping theory on the assumption that individuals in all situations aim at maintaining agency – in the very fundamental understanding of their capacity to act and to stay in control of their environment. However, they contextualize it with regard to the historical situation of the margins of modern welfare states and the de-standardization of the normal life course. Inasmuch as following the prescriptions of the 'normal' life course no longer guarantees the maintenance of agency, individuals are more and more compelled to develop their own strategies of coping with life on an everyday basis (*Lebensbewältigung*), especially in uncertain transitions which are identified as potential critical life events.

Following this understanding of coping, we refer to all actions of young people – in this case in the context of school – as attempts at maintaining their agency as individuals whether recognized by school in terms of learning and success or classified as failure, risk or deviance. We refer to coping, on the one hand, as a key to understanding what demands young people perceive, how they perceive them and how they respond to them. On the other hand, coping strategies reflect the social resources children and young people have at their disposal. This includes different sources of support – formal or informal, in and out of school – related to the learning or to the social aspects; and – similar to the relation between access and accessibility – the 'objective' availability of support needs to be complemented by young people's perspective. Do they find this support subjectively relevant and effective and do they evaluate the conditions as acceptable?; or, alternatively, what support do young people mobilize for what problems and what are the problems identified and addressed by school or youth services? (see Felczak et al., in this volume). The relation between coping and support needs to be analysed in terms of how involved actors aim at producing biographical fit between subjective and institutional definitions of needs and problems. At the same time, the perspective of coping and support in school relates to how education and welfare are coordinated both at the level of policymaking and the level of service delivery (cf. Allmendinger and Leibfried, 2003).

Relevance

The third dimension concerns the meanings of education. First, in what ways – and by what discourses – is the assumption established in society that education is relevant in general? Second, what makes education relevant for whom and how are different perspectives negotiated?

Relevance of education refers to an apparent societal consensus justifying compulsory education as a fundamental institution and element of the life course in modern societies, the importance of which is even increasing in knowledge societies in terms of lifelong learning. However, consensus does not necessarily imply a common and shared meaning of education. Here, it seems important not only to distinguish different actors with different interests, power and perspective but also to distinguish societal functions from declared aims.

Starting from the functional concept of education, a lesson from historical analysis of public education is that education serves to prepare individuals to fulfil a role in the labour force outside the family economy, to produce citizens identifying themselves with the nation state and to introduce the principle of meritocracy mitigating the contradiction between equal opportunities and inequality (see above). More recently, this function of education is being re-articulated in terms of 'employability' while the widespread use of the concept of 'competence' reflects that in the context of post-Fordism it is no longer possible to define employability in terms of concrete knowledge and skills. Instead, transversal abilities are required that can be adapted to and employed in diverse and changing contexts. Most education systems have modified curricula from an input orientation (issues to be taught) towards an outcome orientation (competences that students should acquire). This is also functional for the role of (secondary) education in legitimizing progression to further and higher education by providing students with the competences necessary to follow the respective studies. For example, German employers introduced the concept of 'trainability' (*Ausbildungsreife*) as a condition of access to apprenticeship training – even or perhaps because there is no consensus on what trainability implies (cf. Walther, 2015a). At the same time, the objectives of employability or trainability are too narrow to legitimize compulsory education as a public right and responsibility. Therefore, even modernized curricula include contents related to national culture and citizenship (cf. Young, 2007). This reveals that the changing relation between education and the life course reflects the contradictory processes of social change.

However, the relevance of education also has a biographical side. First of all, this impacts the children and young people who have to accept the role of pupil and student, to fill it with subjective meaning and to be motivated to go to school daily, follow the lessons and make an effort to do well. There is plenty of evidence that motivation is shifting in individual school careers students, from the pride of small children becoming schoolchildren to the boredom and alienation of older students who struggle to understand the purpose of what they are being taught (cf. Diepstraten et al., 2006). Student motivation has been studied extensively by cognitive psychology, concluding that both the subjective incentive of a certain goal and the subjective expectation to have control or the feeling of self-efficacy in achieving it are key factors of motivation (cf. Deci and Ryan, 1985; Heckhausen, 1991; Bandura, 1997). However, while didactics have focused on providing students with experiences of success and self-efficacy, little effort has been made in negotiating the meaning and relevance of school with students (as this would obviously contradict the function of school; see above). This means school relies mainly on extrinsic motivation, which includes also young people's apparent acceptance of the instrumental role of education for later opportunities (cf. Ule et al., 2014).

At the same time, the relevance of education from the perspective and experience of young people is not limited to the teaching and learning but includes also aspects of *being* in school. Obviously, this includes peers and youth culture for which school is a meeting point: laboratory, stage and market place (cf. Foljanty-Jost et al., 2008). Apart from this, young people often refer to everyday life experiences in school, including quality of lunch, state of toilets or lack of space for relaxation (cf. Ule et al., 2014; see also Salovaara et al., in this volume). Finally, parents also ascribe relevance to education which is reflected by their expectations of school success, their preferences for certain schools, by their ways of interacting with school and by their ways of advising and assisting their children in relation to school (see Ule et al., in this volume).

While it appears reasonable to study access, coping and relevance separately, the added value of analysing the governance of educational trajectories lies in exploring their links, relations and intersections. For example: access and accessibility reflect (self-)ascriptions related to age, gender or origin with regard to abilities of children in coping with education (understood in a normative way); coping strategies reflect how children and young people feel their subjective relevancies with regard to education are being recognized; existing access regulations and provision of support reproduce dominant relevancies like employability, etc. Access, coping (and support) and relevance are thus constructed by interactions at – and between – different levels of educational governance.

Multilevel Comparative Analysis: Methodological Discussion

The theoretical framing of the research object as discussed above aims at a complex conceptualization of 'educational trajectories' in terms of structures, institutions, individual and collective meanings (discourses) and their interactions at different levels of analysis. This multilevel approach entailed the inclusion of qualitative and quantitative methods and data in a mixed-method research strategy. Moreover, GOETE was designed as a comparative research study since the project departed from the assumption that educational trajectories evolve in, and result from, numerous interactions among multiple actors at different scales in decision-making processes throughout formal, non-formal and informal education. Thus, analysing the governance of educational trajectories implied looking into the specific spaces or contexts where they all conflate with the aim of identifying different constellations while at the same time recognizing common patterns and modes of governance. In sum, the research strategy required both a model for multilevel analysis accommodating qualitative and quantitative data deriving from the various levels/scales of analysis, and a comparative research design allowing for systematic case selection, providing an interpretative framework and serving the contextualization of findings. This multilevel comparative approach is discussed below (see Parreira do Amaral et al., in this volume).

In terms of *multilevel analysis*, the research strategy adopted in GOETE has been inspired by an approach to qualitative multilevel analysis proposed by Werner Helsper and colleagues. The original concept of qualitative multilevel analysis (Helsper et al., 2010) builds on the idea of the integration of different perspectives, methods and data (Denzin, 1970; Hantrais, 2009), but explores in more detail *the relationships* between the different levels under research. Qualitative multilevel analysis presupposes the systematic involvement of different levels of meaning and of aggregation of the *social* as well as the integration of the results obtained for each level in order to, first, conceptualize the research object in its complexity and establish a study that differentiates the various levels and aspects of a phenomenon and relate them to each other. It aims, second, at ensuring that data collection and protocols are as open as possible for each of the targeted levels. Third, it aims to collect data and protocols that are typical and meaningful for the respective level of meaning: for instance, for the level of individual social meaning, biographical or episodic narratives, interpretations, explanations or reasoning, etc., and for the level of institutional social meaning, legal/policy documents, statistical data, etc. Finally, fourth, it aims at reconstructing the meaning and analysing the material (for each independent level) with qualitative, interpretive methods for each of the included levels of an item. In this process, both the typical feature levels as well as the 'connection points' for other meaning levels need to be reconstructed; for this, the independently reconstructed patterns of level-specific meaning have to be related to each other and the 'bridges' or 'connection points' to the other meaning levels have to be connected.

The original approach, as suggested by Helsper et al. (2010), has been used for the integration of different *qualitative* data sets with an emphasis on interaction, respectively the interrelation of different levels. GOETE, however, includes both qualitative and quantitative data sets; one major necessity of the project was to extend the approach to integrate quantitative data, as well as to extend the original interactive perspective to different levels and to the interaction between different institutional actors. The multilevel analysis approach adopted in GOETE aims at providing 'bridges' and 'connection points' and at integrating the different perspectives of those involved (actors and stakeholders) rather than simply triangulating data sets and methods. It is important to note that it does not intend to provide a 'technique'[3] for the integration of the various data sets. The major contribution of this approach is that it rather offers a useful heuristic device for a much more differentiated and fine-grained theoretical understanding of issues related to access, coping and relevance of education throughout educational trajectories of young people. The following figure illustrates the adaptation of the original model in GOETE by distinguishing the different levels included in our research. The different levels discerned in the model, it should be noted, can be separated only analytically. In empirical research, for instance, elements of agency attributed to the individual level may as well be ascribed to 'the national' or 'the global' level. The dashed lines mark the permeability of the levels. The arrows point to the mutual interdependence of the levels, which are not thought of in hierarchical terms, but rather as systematic relationships.

In terms of *comparative analysis*, GOETE required a strategy allowing for systematic case selection and sampling criteria. Here we turned to typological

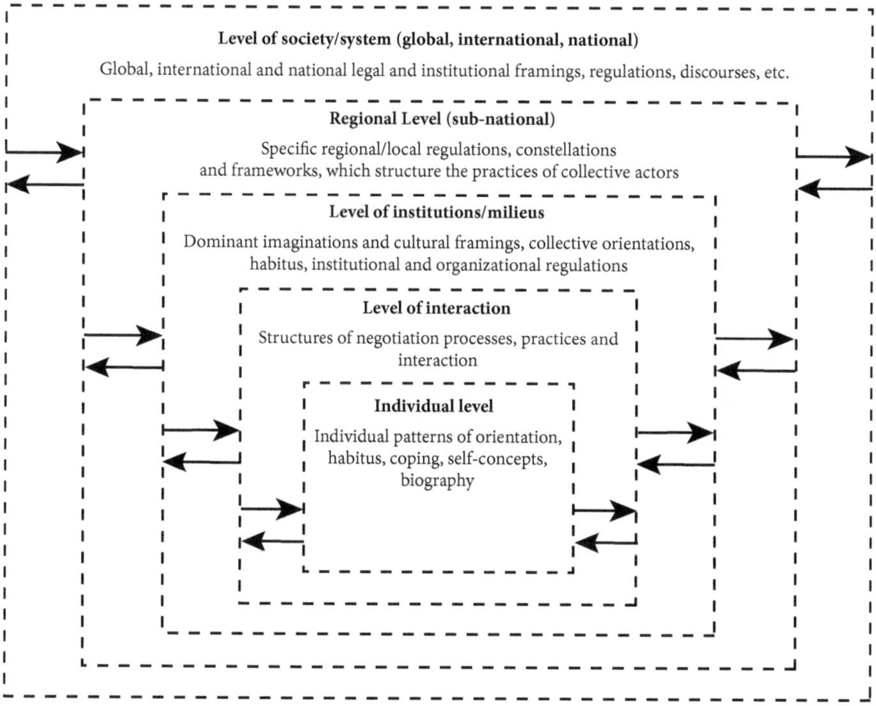

Figure 1.1 Model for multilevel comparative analysis

Source: Adapted from Helsper et al., 2010

and cross-national comparison (Allmendinger, 1989) in order to reach a balanced coverage and as many contextual variables as possible (cf. Tikkanen et al., in this volume). It also implied searching for an interpretative framework accounting for the interplay of individual agency and socio-economic, institutional and cultural elements. The model of 'Transition Regimes' proposed by Walther (2006) offered a broad set of categories useful in understanding the distinct realities and 'normalities' across the cases involved in the project by linking these differences and similarities to life course structures – which includes not only the education system but also welfare and the labour market, as well as cultural or discursive dominant understandings of young people (cf. Tikkanen et al., in this volume). The latter represents an important requirement for the adequate contextualization of findings. Finally, the different trajectories identified were analysed comparatively in terms of their framings and constellations. Instead of comparing the 'content' of these trajectories – which would remain at the surface, showing both similarities and differences – we opted to compare the institutional and the discursive 'opportunity structures' that frame them (cf. Dale and Parreira do Amaral, 2015; see also Dale et al., in this volume).

Conclusion

The purpose of this chapter has been to introduce the conceptual and methodological approach developed for the analysis of the governance of educational trajectories of young people in eight European countries. Educational trajectories were conceptually framed as dynamic and interactive processes which raised a number of conceptual and methodological issues. The combination of a life course and a governance perspective allowed for a complex conceptualization of the research object, attending to its multi-actor, multi-dimensional and multilevel nature. Three dimensions have been identified which lent themselves to empirical analysis – access, coping/support and relevance of education – as discussed in the various chapters of this volume. Finally, the chapter presented and discussed the methodological requirements of our research, which included developing a suitable model for multilevel comparison.

2

The Diversity of Education and Welfare Systems in Europe

Jenni Tikkanen
University of Turku

Andy Biggart
Queen's University, Belfast

Axel Pohl
Institute for Regional Innovation and Social Research, IRIS e.V. Tübingen

Introduction

Students' educational trajectories are the result of complex interactions between societal structures and individual subjective action. Thus, educational trajectories are crucially regulated by institutional and organizational frameworks, which diverge substantially across countries. National education systems and institutions, as we know them, are the result of long historical processes of institutionalization of cultural, social and political assumptions, values and norms of a particular society. They are, therefore, often taken for granted and become 'invisible' as frameworks regulating the trajectories of children and youth and, in consequence, they influence patterns of educational participation and subsequent social mobility.

According to current research, institutional and organizational arrangements have a pivotal effect on country-level differences in the efficacy and equality of education. In European countries, different education systems provide different levels of access to and accessibility of education, varying degrees of support to cope with its requirements and different ways of balancing societal and individual relevance of education throughout educational trajectories.

The aim of this chapter is twofold. First, it aims to highlight some of the key differences and commonalities across a range of European countries in terms of how educational systems regulate and provide access at different stages of young people's educational trajectories. Second, the chapter aims at making the institutional and organizational frames 'visible' by providing contextual information for the subsequent analyses of educational trajectories in different European countries included in the analyses later in this volume: Finland, France, Germany, Italy, the Netherlands, Poland, Slovenia and the UK. This chapter is based on the analysis of background country reports that were produced within the GOETE project in each of the eight countries. For these rather extensive reports, the country-specific partner teams reviewed national research data and analysed different policy documents around the five key thematic dimensions of GOETE: access, coping, relevance, governance and life course. Subsequently, a comparative analysis was conducted in the GOETE project so that the eight country reports were related to both European data and existing comparative models (see also Parreira do Amaral et al., 2011). Apart from this, information from Eurypedia (Eurydice, 2014), which is a European encyclopedia on national education systems, and descriptions of European guidance systems (Euroguidance, 2014) were also drawn upon in this chapter.

The first part of the chapter illustrates the legal–institutional frameworks regulating entry, progression and transition of pupils throughout their school careers. Here, the eight national education and training systems and their transition structures are presented. The second section focuses on the organization of educational and vocational guidance as one form of support highlighting various models based on the quality and uniformity of guidance services designed to assist young people making choices in relation to their educational and occupational trajectories. In section three, existing models and concepts that have been applied to comparative analyses of education systems are discussed and applied to the countries under analysis. Such models can serve as useful heuristic devices, both in terms of the initial sampling of countries and as a means of interpreting how differences and similarities in education systems and broader national policies relate to young people's educational trajectories. They can act as a conceptual lens for empirical analysis, reducing the complexities across individual systems through the creation of ideal types based on a number of key policy dimensions. Here we draw on Allmendinger's model (1989) that distinguishes different levels of standardization and stratification of education systems, as well as on Walther's transition regime model (2006) that classifies various regimes of regulation of educational transitions in order to cluster the participating countries in GOETE. Finally, in the concluding part, we highlight the main differences and common features of educational systems and flesh out the contexts of education and of educational trajectories in the research countries, thus providing a contextualization for the analyses pursued in the remaining chapters of the volume.

Education Systems as Legal–Institutional Frameworks

There is an ongoing process of homogenization of national education and educational policies in the European Union (Grek and Lawn, 2009; Lima and Guimarães, 2011). While education is outside formal EU legislation, the EU has nevertheless a strong interest in it. The initial and more prominent focus of the EU has been on cooperation in the field of vocational education and training but there is a growing interest in cooperation in, and steering of, both general education and the education systems as a whole (Naumanen, Leppänen and Rinne, 2008). This suggests an expanding influence of the processes of harmonization on national education systems in Europe. Of course, the EU is not the only supranational organization contributing to this type of educational unification, as other global actors such as the OECD and UNESCO have a significant influence on national educational policies and practices. Despite this trend, there are still notable national differences in the ways in which education systems are organized. This section illustrates the key features of the eight national education and training systems with an emphasis on their transition structures. The descriptions and juxtapositions have understandably required a certain amount of simplification of all the education systems but this is particularly the case in relation to Germany and the UK, due to their more heterogeneous systems. This is the result of the federal organization of education in Germany and the various differences across England, Scotland, Wales and Northern Ireland in the UK.

Pre-primary education

All GOETE countries have organized systems for pre-primary education with the exception of the Netherlands. In most of the countries included in this study, enrolment in pre-primary schools is voluntary; however, Poland has a compulsory year of pre-primary education.[1] Education is also compulsory for 4-year-old children either at pre-primary or primary level in Northern Ireland, but in other parts of the UK children normally start compulsory education between the ages of four and five depending on their month of birth. The national age of entry in pre-primary education varies between two (France) and six years old (Finland), and all countries have a high rate of participation in pre-primary education. This also applies in the case of the Netherlands. Although the Dutch system does not provide a separate, formal pre-primary school before compulsory education commences at the age of five, well over 90 per cent of Dutch pupils start primary education at the age of four.

Basic education

Basic education comprises primary and lower secondary education. While Finland and Slovenia have a single structure of primary and lower secondary education, a clear distinction between these two stages is more common in the organization of basic education in the GOETE countries. Primary education has the same key characteristics in all the eight countries; it focuses on basic learning and is free of charge. A school's catchment area is the basis of the allocation of primary school places used to varying extents in the majority of the countries, and the entry criterion is age. In the Netherlands and the UK, children enter primary schools at the age of four or five; in France, Germany, Italy and Slovenia, the entry age is six, and primary education starts in the year the child turns seven in Finland and Poland. At the end of primary education, regulation of pupils' transition to lower secondary education differs between the countries, particularly in terms of the role of school grades and teacher reports. There is no formal certification at the end of primary education in Finland, France, the Netherlands and the UK,[2] while in Germany, Slovenia, Italy and Poland pupils receive a formal certificate, although the organization of these certificates differs to some extent between the four countries.

Pupil performance levels, free school choice policies as well as schools' recruitment policies and the level of school autonomy are generally the central dimensions of access to lower secondary education. Because of the inclusive structure of primary and lower secondary education there is no real transition at this point in either Finland or Slovenia. In France, all children who have completed elementary school are automatically admitted into lower secondary school. In Italy and Poland, pupils who have obtained a final admission certificate at the end of primary school enrol in lower secondary education. In the UK, formal admission requirements are rare and admission is largely based on catchment area; however, in the case of oversubscription each school can set its own further criteria to allocate places. Germany and the Netherlands have stratified and selective lower secondary education systems where allocation into different school types depends primarily on pupils' grades. In the Netherlands, there are several options at the lower secondary level: pre-vocational secondary education (*VMBO*, four years), senior general secondary education (*HAVO*, five years) and pre-university education (*VWO*, six years). Pupils can also transfer to practical training (*PT*) if they are perceived as unlikely to obtain a qualification even with the provision of learning support. In Germany, the organization of the lower secondary system is also characterized by a hierarchical division with various tracks and different leaving certificates and qualifications according to the type of school. Depending on the federal state, there are up to five different types of schools at the secondary level. *Gymnasium* prepares students for university or for a combined academic and vocational qualification; *Realschule* leads to part-time vocational schools and higher vocational schools; and, after *Hauptschule*, pupils can enrol into part-time vocational education, which is combined with apprenticeship training. There can also be two types of *Gesamtschulen*, which are comprehensive schools either with different school types in the same building or with high, middle and lower streams in the same school.

Each of the GOETE countries has a formal process of assessment and certification at the end of lower secondary education. The end of compulsory full-time education occurs at the age of 16 in most of the GOETE countries, which often coincides with the end of compulsory schooling and the transition between lower and upper secondary education. This transition can also take place one or two years before the end of compulsory schooling (as is the case in France, Italy, the Netherlands and the UK) when one to two years of upper secondary education or part-time training is compulsory in certain situations.

Upper secondary education

For upper secondary education, each of the GOETE countries adopts different types of educational programmes. At a more abstract level, two common types can be distinguished: general education, which prepares students for tertiary education; and vocational education preparing students for both further studies and working life. General upper secondary education and vocational education and training can either be organized in separate programmes so that students must opt for one or the other, or they can be offered within the same structure. Vocational education and training is organized differently across the countries;

most often the provision is school-based, but the system is mixed in the UK (school-based, work-based or dual) and dual or mixed in Germany and the Netherlands. The dual systems combine vocational schools with apprenticeship training in a company.

The transition into upper secondary education is regulated by achievement, and it is common for students with higher academic achievement levels and grades to enter general upper secondary schools, while those with lower achievement records typically enter vocational education and training. While the regulation of the transition is formal in the majority of the countries, France and Italy regulate this transition informally so that upper secondary schools do not have official selection criteria but there is an invisible process of selection. In other words, all students who have completed their lower secondary education may enter the upper secondary level, but their orientation is at least partly determined by their performance level. There are no centralized entry requirements in the UK as schools and colleges set their own requirements. In Finland, Slovenia and Poland the grades obtained at the end of lower secondary education determine admission to an upper secondary school. In Germany, the precondition for entering a general upper secondary school is passing grade ten when not already enrolled in a *Gymnasium*. In the dual system of vocational education and training, admission depends on recruitment by training companies or organizations, while school-based training is regulated by age and grades. In the Netherlands, the upper secondary education system includes senior general secondary education (*HAVO*) and upper vocational education (*MBO*), which has various levels, and the length of study can vary between two and four years. The orientation made in the first years of pre-vocational secondary education (*VMBO*) determines which level students enrol into. It is also possible to access general secondary education at the end of the highest level of pre-vocational secondary education and from high levels of upper vocational education.

At the end of general upper secondary education, all the countries have national examinations providing certificates (e.g. the *Baccalauréat* in France and the *Abitur* in Germany). With regard to students' orientation at the end of the upper secondary level, the eight national systems are similarly organized: each caters towards entry to higher or further education, including universities and vocational education, or, alternatively, young people may leave education and enter the labour market.

Tertiary education

The minimum requirement for securing access to tertiary education is an upper secondary education certificate or its equivalent in all the GOETE countries. In most of the countries, there are other admission requirements, such as passing an entrance examination or submitting a personal record of achievement. When it comes to the regulation of access to tertiary education, three main levels can be distinguished: central or regional numerus clausus, institutional regulation and open access. There are differences in the cost of higher education for students; it is free of charge in Finland and Slovenia, mostly free of charge in Poland while the tuition fees vary in France, Germany, Italy, the Netherlands and the UK.

From the viewpoint of the education systems' transition structures, one of the central ways in which the eight national higher education systems differ from each other is the extent to which vocational education and training certificates provide access to the highest levels of education. In Finland, Italy, Poland and the UK it is possible to access tertiary education directly with a vocational education and training certificate. In France and the Netherlands, access is possible only through certain routes and, in Slovenia, access requires completed additional education. Germany is the only GOETE country where it is not possible to access the highest levels of education with a vocational education and training certificate.

Organization of Educational and Vocational Guidance

A number of interwoven societal developments and changes have taken place in the last few decades resulting in significant challenges for students planning their educational and occupational trajectories. Consequently, the future outlook and life experiences of young people have been transformed, for example, through labour market re-structuring with an increased demand for educated workers and more flexible employment practices (Furlong and Cartmel, 2007). In the field of education, alongside the emergence of the ethos of lifelong learning, there has been an expansion of educational opportunities and levels of participation (Müller and Wolbers, 2003). This has resulted in qualification inflation and a stronger link between educational qualifications and occupational positions (Gangl, 2003; Aro, 2014), combined with a greater range of alternative pathways within education systems. This increasing complexity and the associated risks in the labour market in making the wrong decisions has led to the need for additional support and information for students when deciding upon educational trajectories (e.g. OECD, 2003).

Educational and vocational guidance, as forms of general support, can address these needs only if they are widely available. The main goal of educational guidance is to provide help for students in choosing subjects and study programmes most suitable to their individual abilities and future aspirations as well as in overcoming learning and studying difficulties (e.g. Parreira do Amaral et al., 2011). Vocational guidance, on the other hand, is a service intended to assist individuals, both in terms of making choices about educational and occupational careers and in managing and succeeding within them (Watts and Kidd, 2000; Watts and Sultana, 2004). Hence, vocational guidance is not only available to students but it can also cover the progression in learning and work across the entire life course as choices relating to these two fields are closely connected.

While globalization has led to a substantial degree of inter-country convergence, especially in the practices of vocational guidance, there is also notable variance in the guidance systems reflecting national economic, political, social, cultural, educational and labour market characteristics (Watts and Sultana, 2004). Nevertheless, some similar features in the educational and vocational guidance systems of the GOETE countries can be distinguished (Stauber and Parreira do Amaral, 2013). In the majority of the GOETE countries, the Ministry of Education and Ministry of Labour administer the main guidance provision. Guidance about study choices and careers, which can be provided either within or in connection with educational institutions, falls typically under the Ministry of Education, while guidance about occupational careers is most often overseen by the Ministry of Labour. With the exception of Finland, private actors are also active in the guidance sector to greater or lesser extent in all the countries.

In order to discern the main similarities and differences between the provision of educational and vocational guidance in the GOETE countries, the eight guidance systems can be clustered by juxtaposing the central national features, such as the main guidance providers, the role of private actors, the strength of the connections with the labour market and the importance of families as a source of support and information (see also Tikkanen et al., 2015). Three main groups of guidance systems can be distinguished based on the uniformity of the availability and quality of the guidance services as well as the coverage of support for transitions both between educational levels and from education into the labour market. The threefold typology outlined below highlights the differences in the dominant logic of the organization of educational and vocational guidance, raises the question about the extent to which guidance provides individuals with the space and time needed for autonomous decision making and underlines the extent to which labour market demands are translated into adaptation and mechanisms of cooling out in the different guidance systems.

Educational and vocational guidance is available to students within schools, at least to some extent, in the majority of the eight countries. However, the guidance systems in Finland and Slovenia are predominantly *school-based*. Guidance is provided for students within schools by teachers and guidance counsellors or other internal experts. At the same time, vocational guidance provided typically by employment agencies is also at students' disposal. With regard to lifelong learning, the school-based guidance systems are characterized by a clear division of duties between the mutually complementary sources of guidance and by a relatively extensive support in transition phases.

In Italy, Poland and the UK, the provision of educational and vocational guidance is *particularistic*, and many significant guidance providers are located outside schools. These external bodies may include local or regional vocational training agencies, information and guidance offices, counselling centres as well as private agencies. A key characteristic of the particularistic systems is the significant variation in the availability and quality of guidance between regions and, in some cases, even between schools. Behind these differences are various factors, including a lack of regulation of the organization and provision of guidance at a national level, an insufficient coordination and unequal distribution of the guidance services, and regional and school autonomy in the delivery of guidance. Compared with the school-based systems, the role of family as a source of support and information is more significant in particularistic systems, due to the lower level of institutionalized transition support available for students.

In the *corporatist* systems of Germany and the Netherlands, guidance is provided by schools and labour market agents working in cooperation. Although these systems share many similarities with the particularistic group in terms of the significance of external sources of guidance and a lack of a uniform national guidance, the distinctive features of the corporatist systems are a strong market orientation and an involvement of certain labour market actors in vocational guidance on the basis of tradition, contract or consent. In these systems, cooperation between schools and labour market actors as well as direct contact between students and companies are both centrally important. This close connection has the potential to benefit students by promoting encounters with employers and facilitating employment opportunities after leaving education, but it also poses some specific drawbacks. It may impact greatly on students' decisions and career choices, and companies may use the cooperation with schools as a means to select the best or most suitable students.

In France, the system of educational and vocational guidance can be interpreted as a combination of both the particularistic and corporatist systems. It is particularistic in the sense that it is characterized by a great variety of services providing information and guidance, most of which are located outside schools. On the other hand, the corporatist nature of the French system is highlighted by the fact that certain actors in the labour market have strong stakes in vocational guidance. The most prominent feature of the system in France is a clear lack of coordination between the various providers and actors in the field of educational and vocational guidance.

Typologies as Heuristic Devices

The preceding section looked at some of the key aspects of the way the organization of education systems differs across the GOETE countries with a particular focus on access and accessibility to education. The following section takes a broader view and examines the education systems at the macro level drawing upon some of the conceptual models that have been used to compare European countries in terms of their educational structures. These are outlined and related to specific countries included in the current book. First, we draw on Allmendinger's model (1989) that distinguishes education systems along their levels of standardization and stratification (cf. Biggart et al., 2015), before examining Walther's transition regime model (2006) that classifies various regimes of regulation of educational transitions in order to cluster the participating countries in GOETE.

The function of models in comparative research

In comparative research, we can distinguish a variety of functions that models and typologies can take. If we simplify this variety to a small set of paradigmatic decisions and research strategies, these functions can be described along the axis of heuristic versus descriptive approaches and further distinguished in their function within the research process. In the following we focus on the latter, the decisions within a given research process, to demonstrate the benefits and limitations of models within comparative research.

In the GOETE research project, existing models were first of all used as sampling criteria in the selection of research countries. This served the purpose of reaching a balanced coverage of important categories highlighted by existing models. Comparative transnational analysis is based on contextual variation. It is vitally important, especially in small sample comparisons, to be able to cover as many contextual varieties known to be pertinent to the research subject, and to make their choices transparent and intersubjectively traceable to be able to draw valuable conclusions on the main unit of study.

As the main unit of study was the governance of transitions within the respective education systems, in order to grasp differences and similarities between countries, a first iteration was to look for a typology that would provide grounds for clustering the countries according to basic features and principles of education systems in general. A model that is widely used in comparative research on educational systems to achieve this is the one proposed by Jutta Allmendinger (1989). The model groups countries according to two main dimensions, the levels of stratification and the standardization of their education systems, and it has been applied to link these features to different labour market outcomes. *Stratification*, the first dimension, describes the degree of differentiation at given stages of the respective education system and the share of given cohorts reaching the maximum numbers of school years. Tracking of students into different tiers of the school system also plays an important part in this dimension. The stratification dimension combines these aspects into one measurement: the bigger the proportion of a cohort of students who reach the maximum of school years and the lower the differentiation into tiers, the lower the level of stratification is within a school system. In school systems with low stratification levels, tracking of students starts at comparatively later ages, the mobility between tracks is relatively high and curricula are fairly similar between the tracks. Taking up this measurement, Shavit and Müller (2000) found that in less stratified education systems the probabilities for students to reach tertiary education vary less between tracks than in highly stratified systems. In Allmendinger's study (1989), it could be shown that this dimension also impacts on students' labour market outcomes. Their occupational status is less determined by educational attainment in less stratified systems than in highly stratified ones.

Standardization, the second dimension, measures the degree of standardization of the content and the quality of education. The degree of standardization corresponds to the level of system-wide unification of aspects such as teacher training, curricula, exams and budgeting. The degree of uniformity in institutional arrangements determines the level of standardization in a given educational system. Allmendinger (1989) found that the degree of standardization has a significant impact on social mobility and how students' career trajectories are shaped. The concept has been taken up in research about equality and efficacy in education and proved to be a valuable factor in explaining differences between education systems (cf. OECD, 2005; Horn, 2009). It has also been applied to the field of vocational training, and it has been shown that the degree of standardization is clearly linked to the role of companies and schools as well as to school leavers' ways of entering the labour market (see Parreira do Amaral et al., 2011).

The countries covered in the GOETE study are classified according to Allmendinger's model in Table 2.1. This classification should by no means be understood as descriptive but as a first step of heuristics in the analysis of differences in how the organization of schooling might relate to the governance of educational trajectories. Considering the dynamic aspect of education policies, and therefore systems, this typology is to be used with particular caution. Nevertheless, a couple of distinctive features are apparent when looking at the classification. The GOETE countries fall into three different combinations of the two dimensions *stratification* and *standardization*. There are countries in our sample with high levels of standardization and low levels of stratification

Table 2.1 Categorization of the GOETE countries

		Stratification	
		Low	**High**
Standardization	**High**	**High-level comprehensive** Finland Slovenia	**High-level differentiated** France Germany Netherlands
	Low	**Low-level comprehensive** United Kingdom Italy Poland	**Low-level differentiated** –

Source: Based on Allmendinger's (1989) model

like Finland and Slovenia where all pupils and students follow the same track of education throughout their compulsory schooling. Therefore, there is less of a hierarchy and a smaller amount of segmentation during the stage up until the end of compulsory education and substantially lower levels of selection and grouping of students according to their abilities. At the same time, standardization is high and curricular development is regulated nationally. A second cluster of Italy, Poland and the UK belongs to the group of low standardization and low stratification. These education systems have a lower standardization of curricula and/or vocational training certificates. Additionally, their degree of differentiation between different tracks is similar to the first cluster and the level of selectivity is still quite low compared to the third cluster (high stratification/high standardization). The Netherlands, France and Germany can be grouped together in this respect with relatively high levels of selectivity and stratification. Compared to the second cluster, education systems in these countries certainly feature higher levels of standardization.

In the GOETE project, this model was used as a heuristic tool to analyse central mechanisms of governance by linking them to basic features of the eight education systems covered by the study. While Allmendinger's model refers to powerful dimensions of education systems at a macro level, it does not cover meso- and micro-level structures within education systems or the links between different levels in a governance perspective that was central for the GOETE project. Therefore, the project was based on a second, more comprehensive model, the concept of transition regime developed in the context of several previous international research projects on young people's transitions to work (McNeish and Loncle, 2003; Walther and Pohl, 2005; Walther, 2006; Walther, du Bois-Reymond and Biggart, 2006; Pohl and Walther, 2007). It refers to the 'regime' concept because it stresses the interplay between socio-economic, institutional and cultural factors with individual agency. The notion of 'regime' further emphasizes that the regulation of the life course needs to be coined in a more comprehensive fashion than purely institutional theory (cf. Parreira do Amaral et al., 2011). Therefore, the term 'normalities' is central to this approach, which looks into the link between different configurations of power and institutional arrangements under the angle of different resulting normalities.

The original model of transition regimes initially took up some of the work of Gøsta Esping-Andersen's *Three Worlds of Welfare Capitalism* (1990) and other concepts from comparative welfare research (cf. Walther, 2006). It has been further differentiated and refined during a series of empirical studies with a whole range of research rationales and methodologies. Because of its broad set of dimensions it seemed an ideal companion to Allmendinger's typology to inspire the research process not only in terms of sampling, but also as a source of focus to be considered at the stage of comparative analysis.

The model clusters countries into different regime types according to the following categories: young people's access to welfare, the responsibility for vocational education and training between school and companies, the structures of labour market entry, gender relationships in the labour market and structures of youth policy, as well as the cultural meanings of youth in general and disadvantaged youth in particular mediated by different 'climates of normality' (Walther and Pohl, 2005).

While Esping-Andersen divided the world of welfare into three, this typology distinguishes between four ideal-typical regimes. The liberal regime type found in English-speaking countries in Europe, in GOETE represented by the UK, is best characterized by the importance of the notion of individual 'rights and responsibilities'. According to this prioritization of market and individual, youth as a life stage is seen as a transition to early economic independence. This is underpinned by a highly flexible labour market as well as by a lowly standardized education system. Additionally, stratification starts rather late and standardization, especially in vocational education, is rather low. This contrasts with the employment-centred regime, represented in GOETE by Germany, France and in a less clear-cut case the Netherlands, where standardization is rather rigid in the field of vocational training. The dominant orientation of educational trajectories is the selection of young people into appropriate societal positions. In the universalistic regime, under which the Nordic countries can be subsumed, in the GOETE case Finland, education and youth are based on the idea of the development of citizenship. Education systems are therefore comprehensive and at the same time highly standardized. Italy, like other Southern European countries, belongs in the sub-protective regime where education and training provide rather unreliable pathways into the labour market, and where youth is regarded as a long waiting phase, due, among other factors, to the family-centred welfare system. The post-socialist countries covered in GOETE, Poland and Slovenia, cannot be subsumed under any of these regime types but rather form a very heterogeneous separate case. They have some of their socialist heritage in common, but the large differences and the high dynamics of post-socialist transformation make them extremely difficult to categorize.

In GOETE, this model served its purpose as a heuristic tool especially because it represented a way of linking contextual differences and similarities to life course structures that result from the interplay of cultural, institutional and

Table 2.2 Transition regimes across the GOETE sample

Dimension regime	Country	School	Training	Employment regime	Concept of youth	Concept of disadvantage	Focus of transition policies
Universalistic	Finland	Not selective	Flexible standards (mixed)	Open Low risks	Personal development Citizenship	Individualized and structure-related	Education Activation
Employment-centred	Germany France Netherlands	Selective	Standardized (dual)	Closed Risks at the margins	Adaptation to social positions	Individualized	(Pre-)vocational training
Liberal	UK	Principally not selective	Flexible, low standards (mixed)	Open High risks	Early economic independence	Individualized	Employability
Sub-protective	Italy	Not selective	Low standards and coverage (mainly school)	Closed High risks (Informal work)	Without distinct status	Structure-related	'Some' status (work, education, training)
Post-socialist countries	Poland Slovenia	Principally not selective	Standards in transformation (mixed)	Closed High risks	Mixed	Mixed	Mixed

Source: Parreira do Amaral et al., 2011: 44

socio-economic factors. The model also covers the dimension of governance that was central to the research question of GOETE in the way that it sharpens analytical lenses for the institutional processing of transitions and their links to individual biographical agency via the emphasis on motivational careers and their role for decision-making processes. The merit of the transition regime model for the GOETE project lays in the fact that it extends beyond the boundaries of education systems and includes labour market structures, welfare and youth services as well as dominant understandings of the individual. Thus, it was possible to distinguish dominant models of educational governance by putting a particular stress on different configurations of 'normality' and their embeddedness into different levels of analysis. The down side of the model was that it reduced the complexity of the comparison of education systems themselves. However, this disadvantage can be recompensed with more inductive research steps to avoid systematic blind spots potentially arising from its use.

Conclusion

This chapter has examined some of the specific features of the educational systems among the group of countries included in the GOETE project and located them within broader conceptual models of education systems and transition regimes within Europe. Educational credentials over the past few decades have become an increasingly important component at both the European and nation state levels in a bid to try to boost economic competiveness within an increasingly global economy, especially within the context of the current financial crises. The linkages between educational credentials and the labour market have become tighter in recent decades and as a result the pressures young people face in the contemporary European context have increased. Despite the fact that many young people, regardless of their educational credentials, will experience some form of disruption and disorientation in their education and early labour market trajectories, the highest levels of difficulties have tended to fall on those with the least resources and lowest educational credentials. Some commentators have even suggested that there is a real risk that this will open new structural divisions in Europe between the knowledge rich and the knowledge poor (Power, 2007).

Analysing the different educational systems and the broader policy context surrounding youth and welfare that are continually developing and adapting in response to social and economic change across each of the eight GOETE countries has highlighted a number of similarities and differences. Each of the national education and training systems included in the study remains quite distinctive, having developed independently over a long period of time and, while there may be aspects of convergence across different systems, the concept of path dependency remains strong in terms of development change (Pierson, 2000; Keep, 2006). Differences are less pronounced in the early stages of education, and while there are some differences in the age that compulsory education begins and in the provision of pre-school education, all countries provide a free accessible system of primary education. It is at the level of the lower secondary school that more radical departures begin to come apparent, in particular between selective and non-selective systems, the status of vocational training and flexibility within educational pathways. As strong educational credentials have become important for the majority of young people in the contemporary context, there has been a converging trend to delay specialization, and in this respect young people tend to remain more often in general forms of education rather than going down narrow vocational specialisms at an early stage. This process can be seen as a means adopted by young people to keep their options open (Wolf, 2011), in a context where the pathways through education to independent adulthood provide more opportunities, but at the same time have become more prolonged, uncertain and increasingly opaque. This serves to highlight the increasing salience of guidance and support in the planning of young people's educational trajectories. Although some education systems have well-established vocational guidance systems associated with the more stratified and selective systems within employment-centred regimes, the provision of more general support and guidance to help young people cope with the demands of the knowledge society remains variable. Higher levels of support are to be found in the school-based systems in Finland and Slovenia, while in Italy, Poland and the UK there is a lack of regulation and significant differences in the availability and quality of guidance.

Finally, the chapter introduced a number of conceptual models that aimed to serve as heuristic devices and to guide further analysis. While well-established distinctions are still relevant in terms of the stratification and standardization of education systems highlighted through Allmendinger's (1989) model, a much wider variety of factors are salient when considering young people's trajectories in a cross-national perspective. There is therefore a need to go beyond national educational institutional arrangements and to take account of the different contextual, cultural and socio-economic factors that also play a part in both differentiating access to the various pathways that young people follow and the different processes which govern and structure their journey. Here the model of transition regimes provided a useful starting point that moves beyond a sole focus on education systems taking account of labour market structures, welfare and youth services as well as dominant understandings of the individual. An initial distinction can be drawn between the liberal regime in the UK and the employment-centred regimes found in Germany, France and the Netherlands. The liberal regime gives emphasis to individual rights and responsibilities, where priority is placed on the market and individual as well as an expectation on youth to achieve early economic independence combined with a relatively flexible education system and labour market. In employment-centred regimes the dominant orientation of educational trajectories is the selection of young people into appropriate social positions, with a highly standardized and more rigid system of vocational training. Finland represents the universalistic regime characteristic of the Nordic countries where education and youth policy are based on the notion of development of citizenship, with a comprehensive and highly standardized education system. Italy is characterized as part of the sub-protective regime found in other Southern European countries, where education and training provide comparatively unreliable pathways into the labour market and, as a result, youth is characterized as a long waiting phase where continuing economic dependence is typically supported through the family-centred welfare regime. Finally the two post-socialist countries in GOETE (Poland and Slovenia) cannot be easily subsumed under any other regime types and while they do share some of their socialist heritage in common, they remain quite distinctive separate cases. These ideal typical models will be elaborated further and used to help guide the analysis in each of the subsequent chapters of this volume.

Part 1

Governance of Education

3

Scales, Discourses and Institutions in the Governance of Educational Trajectories in Europe

Roger Dale
University of Bristol

Yuri Kazepov
University of Vienna

Risto Rinne
University of Turku

Susan Robertson
University of Bristol

Introduction

The purpose of this chapter is to analyse the different ways that national education systems are governed and show how that shapes their focus, their preferences and their approaches, as these combine to form their 'education policy', and in particular how they shape the forms taken by educational transitions and trajectories through the *opportunity structures* that they offer. These issues are approached from two directions: the institutional forms and legacies of the different systems and how they shape what is *possible* for education systems; and the different ways that the purposes of education systems are framed and experienced at national level.

The first of these is addressed through an analysis of: (a) the combinations of scales – transnational to local – through which education is governed in the eight countries we analyse (Finland, France, Germany, Italy, the Netherlands, Poland, Slovenia and the UK); (b) the activities of governance involved; and

(c) the combinations of actors (state, market, voluntary organizations, etc.) involved in the work of educational governance.

The second is addressed methodologically, by comparing not the 'content' of the different countries' policies, but their perceptions of the problems they were facing and seeking to address through policy. The means we adopted for doing this was to try to identify the different opportunity structures which frame what seems desirable and feasible for education systems to achieve, and policymakers' responses to them. We examine in particular two highly significant opportunity structures. The first set of opportunity structures we consider is what we refer to as *institutional* opportunity structures. These are closely linked to forms of governance, for they are framed by the selectivities built into the existing forms and arrangements for determining and implementing education policy. The second set is what we refer to as the *discursive* opportunity structures which frame the set of policy choices seen as 'sensible, realistic and legitimate'. The main example we use here is the discourse of the knowledge-based economy in Europe, which confronts all eight countries, though, importantly for the argument of this chapter, each of them interprets and implements in rather different ways.

The chapter is organized in the following way. First, we focus on the concept of governance, its various meanings and how it is used within the chapter. Next, we elaborate on the concept of opportunity structure, and exemplify it through what we refer to as 'institutional' opportunity structures. The third part of the chapter develops the idea of discursive opportunity structures, and seeks to show how they operated in the eight countries, paying particular attention to the ways that their interpretations of the discourse of the European knowledge-based economy were shaped by their forms of governance of education. We conclude with a summary of how the eight countries' policies on educational transitions and trajectories were influenced by their different forms of educational governance.

The chapter draws on data collected in all eight countries. Two main types of data were collected. The first involved each country selecting and analysing three relevant policy documents, texts that shape – or attempt to shape – the ways that educational transitions take place. Three forms of such documents were analysed in each country: those relating to government policy, which we referred to as 'policymaker' documents; those generated by 'non-state policy shapers'; and what we referred to as 'commentator documents', especially from the media. These were all analysed through a common form of Critical Discourse Analysis. The second source of data was 100 expert interviews, following a common pattern of questions, carried out with representatives of each of the categories used in the document selection – policymakers, policy brokers and policy commentators. These were located at national, regional or local level depending on the regulatory and procedural systems present in different countries. This provided us with a rich and relevant source of data on the issues at hand, in forms that enabled cross-country analysis (for which, unfortunately, we have no space in this chapter).

Thus the chapter presents and discusses findings and insights from the empirical studies conducted in the participant countries, with a particular emphasis on the nature and forms of 'governance'.

The Governance of Educational Trajectories: Some Conceptual Clarifications

This section will show that the – increasingly varied and complex – forms, outputs and outcomes of governance result from and impact on the activities of many different people, working at many different levels, carrying out a multiplicity of activities and tasks related to governance. Governance 'works' through all scales, discourses and institutions without being reducible to any of them. All are essential; none are separately sufficiently decisive to determine outcomes. This is in part due to the remarkable resilience of the school as an institution, which is reflected in the continuing salience of the transition points themselves, across all the GOETE countries. This implies that dramatic or wide scale change is very difficult to achieve, or even to conceptualize. Governance works differently in the different countries (but still under the discursive umbrella of the *knowledge-based economy* and *lifelong learning*), according to the relative priorities attached to different purposes and forms of schooling, whether it be excellence in France, equality in Finland or alternative forms of secondary education in England. Those dominant discourses have the effect of concentrating governing activities predominantly around issues of access to the labour market, though our research recognizes that while the discourse appears homogeneous, it also showed that particular national and local 'labour markets' confronting individual schools and their students are unique and complex in their specificity, while still conforming broadly with the transnational discourse.

Our starting point is the assumption that, in European knowledge societies, understanding the nature and adequacy of education systems necessarily involves taking into account different combinations of individual, social and economic aspects. Studying this means exploring how educational institutions – actively or passively – conceptualize and organize individual educational trajectories, through the forms of governance on which they are based.

However, before we discuss the 'governance of educational trajectories', it will be helpful to elaborate on what we understand by 'governance'. The term has been criticized for its being 'notoriously slippery' (Pierre and Peters, 2000: 7). It is used in substantially different ways (as a practical, normative, melioristic, etc. concept) and amid diverging discussions in fields such as economics and foreign policy, among others, which makes it even more important to be clear about our usage (ibid.). Despite the polyvalences of the term, the essence of governance is that it does signal that the state – at national or sub-national level – is no longer the sole actor in charge of 'steering' society. Thus, governance not only points to new scales at which coordination takes place and to new actors involved in these processes, but also, as Rhodes points out, 'governance … signal[s] a change in the meaning of government, referring to a new process of governing' (1997: 15). Beyond this, governance refers to a range of mechanisms and functions – such as privatization, decentralization or recentralization – that are deployed to ensure the coordination of the education system (Dale, 1997: 274). In essence, governance describes the movement away from state control over a range of aspects which constitute the substance of governing activities (funding, ownership, provision, policy, regulation) toward a range of other actors – including the community, household, market (for profit/not-for-profit) and so on. Governance mechanisms can also be located in, and projected from, different scales, from transnational to local; and indeed, moving governance tools to different scales is both the object and outcome of governing itself.

As a political concept, governance emerged in a time of criticism and scepticism as to the possibilities of linear and hierarchical regulation of 'complex' social systems, which points as much to a change of perspective as to profound transformations in the forms of regulation and coordination of modern societies (Mayntz, 2006), and as a consequence especially of the spread of conceptions of New Public Management.

In this chapter, we give preference to an analytical use of the term, which sees it as a generic term for all the occurring patterns of steering, management and coordination of interdependence among states, as well as among state and economic or social actors, both individual and collective. Against this background, state hierarchy in the sense of 'government' appears then as just one of several possible patterns. For Renate Mayntz:

> Governance means the sum of all concurrent forms of collective regulation of social issues: from the institutionalized self-regulation of the civil society, through the diverse forms of cooperation among state and private actors, up to the action of sovereign state agents. (2004: 66, own translation)

Patrick Le Galès defined governance substantially as:

> a coordination process of actors, social groups and institutions that aims at reaching collectively defined and discussed objectives. Governance then concerns the whole range of institutions, networks, directives, regulations, norms, political and social uses as well as public and private actors which contribute to the stability of a society and a political regime, to its orientation, to its capacity to lead, to deliver services and to assume its legitimacy. (2004: 243)

Both these definitions inform our understanding of governance and our analysis. So, with respect to the changing nature of governance instruments and mechanisms, the main shift is the change from *government* to *governance*. While *government* earlier represented the nation state as having control over all key aspects of its national society, essentially through a process of tax and policy, now it gives way to *governance*, especially in the form of New Public Management (NPM) strategies.

Complexities and levels of educational governance

The links between national and local governance are rarely clear and are frequently perceived as ineffective, while a common finding of our research is that there is a range of forms of disjuncture between national and local levels. Rather than continuity between levels of governance, it may be that different discourses and practices at different levels of governance may carry different messages, aimed at different audiences. These complexities appear in many cases to be a consequence of different sets of policy priorities and forms of support at national and sub-national levels. They can lead to very different outcomes, from more participatory practices and local experimentation, thanks to school autonomy, to what can be referred to as forms of 'passive subsidiarity', where national policy proclamations and/or devolutions for more local autonomy are not accompanied by any form of support for either implementation or regulatory responsibility at the sub-national level (Kazepov, 2010; see also Chapter 4 in this volume by Amos et al.). These trends also reflect the changing nature and place of national policymaking in an era dominated by the transnational discourses of *knowledge-based economy* (KBE) and *lifelong learning* (LLL), which we will elaborate below. These take different forms in different countries, and at different levels of education systems, from national to regional and local, where, for instance, the responses (to the transnational discourses) at the level of national education systems have remained to a notable degree within the set of assumptions that surround the 'old' national economy discourse and the role of the State. The globalization and Europeanization of educational policy involve not only language, concepts, classifications and preferences per se but entangle in their webs a shared sequence of new cultural and political myths, sagas and beliefs, produced in a new space of meanings that swear allegiance to communality and progress. At the same time, reflecting those myths, our collective understandings of education as a whole and its relationship to concepts like equality, and social justice, or economy and culture are reshaped (Pereyra, 1993; Sultana, 1995, 2002; Lawn and Lingard, 2002: 299–303; Rinne et al., 2002; Simola et al., 2002).

In line with this understanding of governance, and against the background of the changes illustrated, we developed a framework in an attempt to capture the changes and their complexity in relation to the governance of education (see Figure 3.1). The questions addressed in the figure are: *who* does *what* at *what level*? The figure enables us to recognize key dimensions of the significant variations in the ways in which the division of labour in educational governance is achieved in the eight countries, in terms both of the activities and functions involved, and where they are carried out and by whom. Figure 3.1 distinguishes the *actors and institutions* (A axis) responsible for carrying out specific functions/activities (B axis). The former are – for the sake of parsimony – state, market, community and household, while the latter, *activities/functions* of governing, are funding, ownership, provision and regulation. The framework assumes that typically responsibility will be taken by hybrid groups of actors, such as state *and* community collaboration in provision, or public–private partnerships in funding, for instance. The *third* dimension to be taken into account is that of the *scales* at which all this takes place (C axis). Here, the governance of education may be discussed – both in analytical and empirical terms – at the supra- or international level, at the national level or at the relevant sub-national levels, namely regions or even municipalities (and neighbourhoods).

The *horizontal* level (A axis) refers to *who* the actors and institutions involved in educational governance are. It is clear that varying but increasing degrees of responsibility for the functions of education are carried out also by non-state

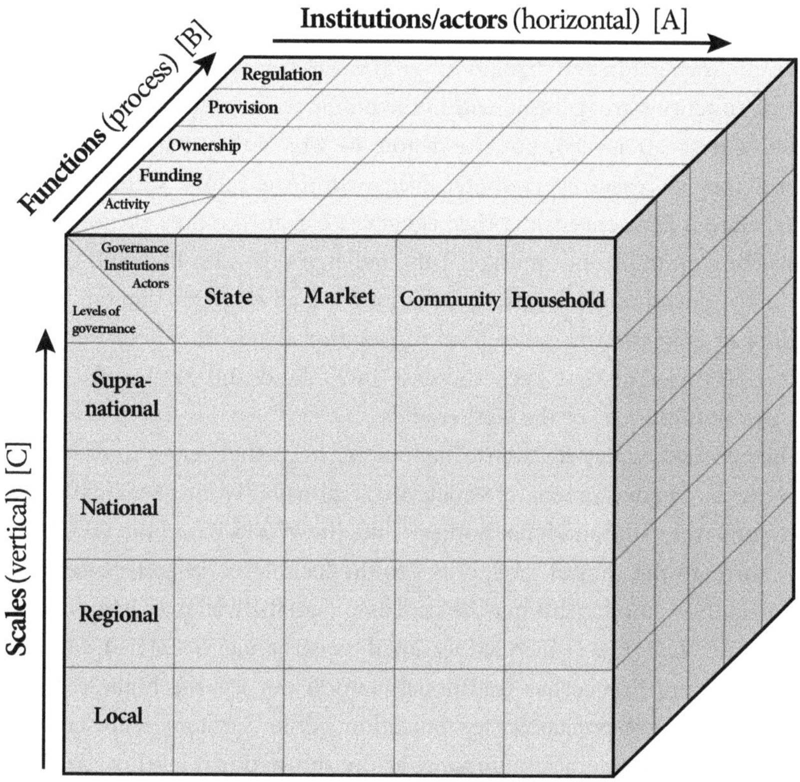

Figure 3.1 Activities, institutions and scales in the governance of education

Source: Adapted from Dale et al., 2012: 12, drawing on Dale, 1997

bodies in all the countries represented in GOETE. One clear example of this is the involvement of various religious organizations, usually in the provision of education (e.g. the Netherlands), but there are increasing numbers of other 'non-state' forms of educational provision, with apparent examples of 'privatization' of some educational activities such as the Academies in the UK. The extent to which this is the case varies across GOETE countries, with the very high levels of differentiation found in the Netherlands standing out at one end of the spectrum. No other of the countries under research deploys such a close relationship between the educational system and economic interests of (individual large) firms as Germany – which of course is not surprising, as the German dual apprenticeship system depends on companies. However, what is new is how directly new market tendencies are entering the system – with highly ambivalent effects.

The degree to which the different actors are involved in the process of educational governance relates to specific functions and activities (axis B) – funding, provision, ownership and regulation – and varies from country to country. Most of these functions are still held within the public realm of the state (even though at different scalar levels), but the degree to which they may be shared with other actors increases everywhere. Even within the public sector educational governance is influenced by other agencies, e.g. in the area of guidance and counselling on the labour market. This challenges the idea that, and the degree to which, education is a single 'silo', carrying out all elements that fall under the heading of education in some level of isolation from other social and labour market sectors. This has been the case in Finland and France, for instance, though not in the UK or the Netherlands.

The 'vertical' scalar division of labour (C axis) that refers to the administrative *levels* of government, at which the responsibility for particular activities rests, runs from supranational bodies – like the World Bank, the OECD or the EU – through the central level, down to the local level, in some cases even to local neighbourhoods. This may be seen as a 'spatial' division of labour, between the various scales at which educational governance is carried out. Along this dimension, France has traditionally stood out for the highest degree of centralization of responsibility for education, while Germany represents a clear contrast, with considerable autonomy at the sub-national level of the different *Länder*.

Changing scales might take similar directions (e.g. decentralization), but interacting with the existing institutional arrangements and path dependences might also produce much differentiated impacts and outcomes. They point to a tendency towards both 'spatial fragmentation' and temporal 'desynchronization' (Kazepov, 2010), i.e. changes which do not consider mutual effects on one another, and those consequences are producing an increasingly incoherent landscape[1] of multilevel educational systems. Changing scalar relations, therefore, might raise questions about the likely outcomes of rescaling projects for governing (with regard to access, coping and relevance of education in the life course) and for learners' trajectories: are some aspects deemed more or less important and at what scales, and what does this mean for social versus individual risk, protection or rights in education and educational spaces? What are the implications of such changes in the circumstances of equality of education and equity of education?

Discourses can be considered in addition to the three analytical dimensions discussed above, as a normative framing that cuts across all of them. In analysing educational governance it is crucial to consider them as potential drivers of change. For instance, in all participating countries an influential discourse on 'new governance' was identified that strongly informs discussions of educational policymaking and reform. The current debates on educational governance address different dimensions of the education system which are strongly consistent with the above-mentioned issues. Some recurring themes may be identified: (a) a shifting attention from 'bureaucratic-professional' (typically through planning, steering, organization and coordination, etc.) to 'post-bureaucratic' forms of regulation (Maroy, 2004), such as the 'evaluative state' and the 'quasi-market' models, in other words, from unilateral steering to coordination of action; (b) a view of education systems as complex systems which require a multi-level approach; (c) a decentralization of operative governance (school-based management); as well as (d) a turn to evidence-based policy and evaluation.

The different mixes of actors, institutions, functions and activities carried out in multiple level arrangements in the different contexts frame different *opportunity structures* within which young people's trajectories are embedded and transitions are governed. All of them are legitimized through narratives and discourses which shape current and future developments by channelling ideas, organizational and financial efforts, i.e. resources to make changes real.

Opportunity Structures as a Heuristic Tool

The basic conceptual tool we will employ in our analysis is that of 'opportunity structures'. In a sense, we can see the fundamental basis of the concept of opportunity structures as inhering in Marx's famous *dictum*: 'Men make their own history, but they do not make it as they please; they do not make it under circumstancees of their own choosing, but under already existing circumstances, given and transmitted from the past' (Marx, 1852: 7). Just so, in education systems we find already existing circumstances, in the form of what we refer to as opportunity structures, which include and frame the possibilities for present and future actions, with some of them more powerful and significant than others. What we are referring to as opportunity structures, then, can be seen as crucial forms of those 'existing circumstances', which might be expected to vary from country to country; that is to say that we need to investigate 'national' forms of discursive opportunity structures, though in this chapter we are able only to offer a methodology for establishing the basis of the focus and content of policy, and of the selection of apparatus for their implementation.

Opportunity structures shape conceptions of what is desirable (or undesirable), possible, feasible, etc. through existing assumptions about, or ways of talking and thinking about, or acting, what it might be possible, desirable, feasible to do in particular areas of activity. Some conceptions of opportunity structures see them as incentive structures, but that is not how they are seen here. Rather, they limit ideas of the possible, *proscriptively* rather than *prescriptively*. They frame conceptions of the desirable and the undesirable, the possible and the impossible, the attainable and the unattainable. More broadly, they can be seen as collections of norms, rules, institutions, conventions, practices and discourses which restrict or enable different sets of actors in determining and executing the actions they intend to pursue.

The nature and significance of opportunity structures has been well captured by Colin Hay (2002a). These structures are:

> selective of strategy in the sense that, given a specific context, only certain courses of action are likely to see actors realise their intentions. Social, political and economic contexts are densely structured and highly contoured. As such they present an unevenly distributed configuration of opportunity and constraint to actors. They are, in short, strategically selective, for whilst they may well facilitate the ability of resource- and knowledge-rich actors to further their strategic interests, they are equally likely to present significant obstacles to the realisation of the strategic intentions of those not similarly endowed. (2002a: 380–1)

That is, they have a shaping effect on the degree to which, and the forms in which, what count as 'policies', for instance, or acceptable and legitimate practices, are to be implemented through them.

Methodologically, we might see the idea of opportunity structures as providing a level of abstraction from which we may be able to understand and explain the *nature of* and *differences between* different national understandings of, and approaches to, educational trajectories and transitions more effectively. To put it another way, the opportunity structures approach leads us to focus on how the menu of choices, of policy and practice, is formed, as a preliminary to 'choosing' within it. It should also be clear that opportunity structures are analytic categories, not empirical ones. Policymakers and practitioners do not consult lists of possibilities, but necessarily, if unconsciously, act *within* opportunity structures which legitimate, favour and prioritize some forms of decision and action over others. Decisions and understandings about what counts as policy and practice in educational trajectories and transitions are not random, but – not necessarily consciously – follow particular framings of the possibilities over others. Our attempt is to introduce some distinctions among different types of opportunity structures, in order to fine-tune our analytical tools for further research.

The Knowledge-based Economy Discourse and the Governance of Educational Trajectories

One of the insights from our research is that the current educational reforms taking place in all of the GOETE countries are formulated by a specific set of broad *discursive* references, which, however, they interpret (discursively) and implement (organizationally) in very different ways. These references can be subsumed under three related 'discourses': *knowledge economy*, *lifelong learning* and *new governance*. From the governance perspective, it may be worth drawing attention to the fact that the activities as well as the actors of governance are changed in the 'knowledge-based economy'.

We need also to bear in mind that educational provision is still very much a national matter, and in the following section we will discuss the different national traditions of various kinds, which themselves represent powerful opportunity structures.

In what follows, however, we concentrate our attention on one of the most powerful narratives influencing the governance of educational trajectories, the discourse on the knowledge-based economy. This discourse may be viewed as containing and encompassing elements of the other two discourses named above inasmuch as the narrative of the knowledge economy implies a new vision for learning trajectories that are *lifelong*. These are entailing *new modes of governance* that will enable the successful management of the challenges involved in creating education and labour market systems as well as preparing individuals who rise to the challenge of the global knowledge economy. In seeking to specify as precisely as possible what seems to be the most useful representation of the changes, we argue that it would be more precise to speak of the *knowledge-based economy*, since the term 'economy' refers to specific modes of production in which knowledge is crucial, while 'knowledge society' remains rather vague while at the same time appealing as a neutral description of contemporary times. The term was forged in the late 1950s and 1960s to draw attention to a decisive change: the future economic and societal well-being of societies was said to not only depend on the classical foundations – resources, means of production and labour force – but on knowledge as a factor in its own right to drive economic and societal development through (primarily technological) innovation (see Schultz, 1961). Intricately related to this was the concept of 'human capital', which emphasized education as the key to economic growth, personal well-being and health, as well as to societal stability (see also Becker, 1975). Although the relationships have never been uncontroversial or scientifically proven (see Block, 1990), this rationale has become universally dominant. The strong link between education and societal progress is established and has become common sense for all nations. Bob Jessop powerfully frames the relevance of considering the discourse on the knowledge economy when he states that:

> whether or not the knowledge-based economy provides the most adequate description of current trends in contemporary economic development, the discourse of the 'KBE' has become a powerful economic imaginary in the last 20 years or so and, as such, has been influential in shaping policy paradigms, strategies, and policies in and across many different fields of social practice. (2008: 2)

In other words, the KBE became the key opportunity structure framing the expectations of national education systems.

From the 1980s onwards, the economic framework within which especially European nation states operate has changed in two highly significant ways. It has become a global rather than a national framework, and it has become knowledge- rather than production-based. In terms of the first, the ability of (European) nation states to control and steer their national economies has been transformed over the past four decades from a position rooted in *nationally*-based *productive industry*, to a position rooted in a *transnationally driven knowledge*- and *services*-based *sector* (Parreira do Amaral and Rinne, 2015).

Europe of the knowledge-based economy

The great harmonization project of Europe constitutes an important element by which the KBE discourse has been interpreted and become influential in Europe, with direct implications for education and educational governance. However, the nature of the European involvement in the issue of opportunity structures is quite important at a conceptual level, in ways that enable us to amplify somewhat the notion of discursive opportunity structure. Thus, while the discursive opportunity structures of member states are likely to be affected by pressures from the

European agenda, it is important to distinguish between agenda and opportunity structure. Essentially, the first contains and advances a 'project', while the second frames the possibilities through which a project might be realized. So, in a sense, the EU needs to locate opportunity structures through which its projects might be realized – and this is extremely difficult to achieve given its lack of authority over the education systems which themselves might act as opportunity structures for its projects. This is how we might explain, for instance, the lack of impact of the three major Communications of the decade of the 2000s;[2] they were seeking not so much to influence an opportunity structure, because they were not in a position to provide it, as to set a new agenda. In addition, as we will show below, an opportunity structure becomes more powerful in education when it is both nationally framed and includes an institutional opportunity structure.

This 'European KBE' project has gone through three rather distinct phases over the last decade (see Dale, 2007/2008). The first was the period following the Lisbon Agenda, which set 'Europe' the task of 'becoming by 2010, the most dynamic, competitive knowledge economy in the world, with sustainable growth, more and better jobs and greater social cohesion' (European Parliament, 2000: 5). Significantly, Lisbon also saw a key role for education in contributing to the European Social Model and European social policy, where the central features were 'investment in people' and 'building an active welfare state', i.e. effectively, 'productive social policy'. Investment in people meant that 'Europe's education and training systems need to adapt both to the demands of the knowledge society and to the need of an improved level and quality of employment' (European Parliament, 2000: 23). The second phase was characterized even more strongly by competitiveness, with a heavy emphasis on the need for Europe to move towards becoming a knowledge economy in a phase of increasing deregulation, as the new mantra of European political discourse (became) 'Growth and Employment' (Degryse and Pochet, 2012: 86). The third phase is essentially shaped by Europe's response to the global financial crisis, with the launch of Europe 2020 prioritizing 'budgetary reform and growth, without drawing any other lessons from the crisis' (Degryse and Pochet, 2012: 88). The later Europe 2020 initiative did, however, give a prominent place to education, with flagship programmes like 'Youth on the Move' which 'presents a framework of policy priorities for action at national and EU levels to reduce youth unemployment by facilitating the transition from school to work and reducing labour market segmentation' (European Commission, 2010a: 5).

In sum, at the European level education has been intrinsically connected to the goal of becoming a KBE. In all GOETE countries, the idea of being part of a global competitive knowledge-based economy represents an important element framing almost all education policy discussions. The knowledge-based economy represents the 'context of contexts', which functions in all countries as a 'macro spatial discursive framework and interspatial circulatory system' (Brenner et al., 2010: 202). It shapes and structures interaction patterns and institutional opportunity structures. In the knowledge-based economy discourse, key policy – and political – claims have emerged around issues such as increasing competitiveness and economic growth while maintaining social cohesion and welfare as well as preventing social risks. In this discourse these complex and not easily reconcilable social tasks have been conflated: more education is virtually automatically taken to mean more economic prosperity and welfare to the nations and people.

This form of representation of the problems and challenges brought about by the advent of the knowledge-based economy and its casting as a coordination problem – that is, the need to improve the fit between education and labour market policy, between the outputs of education institutions and the needs of the economy, as well as the need to better orchestrate the activities of the different professional actors responsible for the provision of education – has important implications for how education policymaking and the governance of education is framed, deliberated upon and implemented.

The wider changes in the political economy leading to the KBE discourse have at least two sets of implications for education: first, they imply changes in the conception of governance mechanisms and instruments used to 'steer' or 'govern' the education system, which also means changing the nature of the relationship between education and the economy sectors. Related to this, governance reforms appear as the most rational solutions. Second, the shift to what became known as the KBE involved important changes in the kinds of knowledge viewed as necessary and relevant, including a shift from canonical knowledge to 'key competencies' that are to be constantly 'refreshed' in the future – for which lifelong learning is a key term.

While the impact of the KBE discourse on issues and policies in the countries under investigation may be analysed at different levels and with reference to different aspects, we focus here on the governance reforms prompted to solve coordination problems between education and the labour market as well as between the different actors and stakeholders involved therein. However, as we noted above, the impact of the discourse has not been uniform, and it varies according to the different *national* political–institutional arrangements and levels of decision making. In effect, we might see it as representing a common context to which all countries have to respond, through the medium of their own discursive and institutional frameworks. Thus, although in all countries the need for a more efficient and transparent governance of education was articulated as an effective response to the challenges brought about by the knowledge-based economy, there are important differences in the emphases and aspects of educational governance (see Figure 3.2).

While in Finland, for instance, the policy options revolved around reforming the inter-sectoral coordination between education and social policy and, at the local level, a 'multi-professional cooperation' between social and educational professional staff was seen as a reasonable solution, the focus on the reforms in Germany was placed on the steering mechanisms in the field of education, with the aim of bringing about an improvement of the efficiency of the systems. Similarly, the reform debates in the Netherlands focused on 'quality' over 'equality'. In Italy, Poland and Slovenia, it rather concerned a rescaling of the relationships between the scales: in Italy between the local and regional level with the aim of countering the strong fragmentation of the field; in Poland and Slovenia between national and supranational level. Finally, the reforms in the UK centred on a recalibration of public and private tasks and setting standards, not structures (see also Dale et al., 2012). Figure 3.2 illustrates the different foci of governance reforms in the different GOETE countries.

'National' Opportunity Structures

The discussion put forward above raises significant issues around the nature and significance of national discursive opportunity structures and their profound importance in shaping education policies and practices. This raises important scalar issues despite the 'puzzling resilience' of *nations* in the context of Europeanized welfare states' (Barbier, 2008: 2).

There are two key issues here. The first is that the nation is the *space* in which any policy must be enacted – 'the bounded "sphere" within which solidaristic acts can be performed, shared and legitimized' – and the basis of those policies. Political culture is itself an historic amalgam of national discursive traditions as well as heir to institutional forms and frameworks (Barbier, 2008: 2). The second is the cultures through which education policy is framed: 'systems are anchored in territorial, material and linguistic determinations that cannot easily be circumvented, let alone dispensed with' (Barbier, 2008: 2), which clearly points to national 'cultural' assumptions, as a clear – and indispensable, because

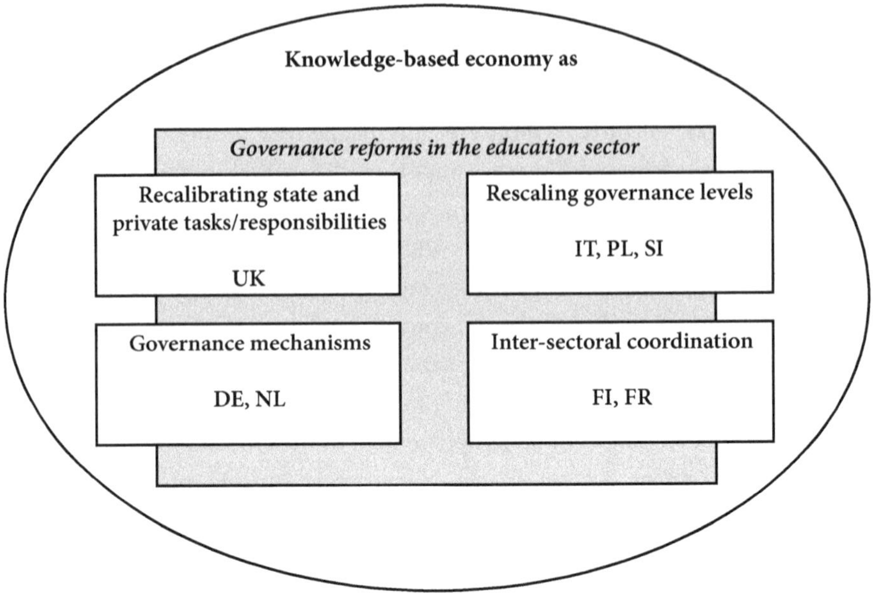

Figure 3.2 Knowledge-based economy as 'context of contexts'

Source: Parreira do Amaral and Rinne, 2015

education systems are taken as the key repository of that culture – basis of the determinations on which education policy rests.

One crucial point to be made here is that the various opportunity structures are to a degree nationally based and inflected, and differ from each other on that basis, though with considerable elements in common. As Ball puts it:

> National policymaking is inevitably a process of bricolage: a matter of borrowing and copying bits and pieces of ideas from elsewhere, drawing upon and amending locally tried and tested approaches, cannibalising theories, research, trends and fashions and not infrequently flailing around for anything at all that looks as though it might work. Most policies are ramshackle, compromise, hit and miss affairs, that are reworked, tinkered with, nuanced and inflected through complex processes of influence, text production, dissemination and, ultimately, re-creation in contexts of practice. (Ball, 1990; 1998: 26)

We should note that such bricolage is neither random nor uniform in its composition, and effects are themselves framed by national and local opportunity structures. Thus, a major rationale for adopting the opportunity structure strategy is that it does provide a means of *comparing* different national understandings of, and responses to, educational trajectories and transitions, and isolating and explaining those differences and their consequences.

Institutional Opportunity Structures

Framings of policy possibilities cannot be confined to the discursive level. They are equally relevant to our understanding of what we might call the 'institutional level' – essentially, the strategically selective set of institutional forms, political divisions of labour and so on that constitute the different organizational configurations that selectively frame and channel the local implementation of national policies. As Jessop puts it, 'a given state form, a given form of regime, will be more accessible to some forces than others according to the strategies they adopt to gain state power' (Jessop, 1990: 260).

Consequently, in this section of the chapter, we focus on the structures through which discourses and policies are transferred into practical rules, guidelines and frameworks that are intended to put 'policies' into 'practice'. In order to do this, we make quite extensive use of the concept of 'institutional opportunity structure' in analysing and comparing the means through which national policies of educational transitions are implemented. This is done both in order to 'problematize' them, i.e. not take them for granted as either natural or inevitable but to recognize them as particular political constructions, and thereby also to make them comparable at a higher level of abstraction than empirical description, which itself essentially denies the possibility of comparison.

By institutional opportunity structures, we mean the deeply ingrained conceptions about how education systems 'work', how they get things done, the set of rules, conventions, sedimented practices through which the system is administered. Such institutional and organizational frameworks powerfully channel and frame what is possible to achieve in and through education systems. The main institutional opportunity structure open to those wishing to intervene in areas of education practice is formed by the framework of the current system of educational administration and management in each of the countries we studied. This institutional opportunity structure sets limits to, and frames, but does not wholly control or shape, current or future policies and practices – and these in turn set key limits to states' capacity to shape policy and set limits to what could or should be done; institutional opportunity structures are sustained and instantiated in individual, organizational and inter-organizational activities and embedded in functionally differentiated institutional orders (e.g. what is the scope of the education system versus the health system?). These strongly sedimented practices shape the possibilities and likelihood of discourses to shape policy as instituted. They reflect deeply embedded assumptions about how national education systems are to be framed in order to deliver what governments, teachers, students and parents expect of them.

These structures are 'selective of strategy in the sense that, given a specific context, only certain courses of action are likely to see actors realize their intentions' (Hay, 2002b: 381). That is, they have a shaping effect on the degree to which, and the forms in which, 'policies' are to be implemented through them.

Our data show many examples of the ranges of different relationships, assumptions, tensions, etc. held by different bodies, at different levels of education policymaking and responsibility. But not only this: the institutional opportunity structures have a framing effect on the formulation of policy, since the likelihood of successful implementation is clearly influential on conceptions of the possibility of success.

So, recognizing the significance of institutional opportunity structures enables us to take into account the different national framings of what constitutes education policy, implementation and practice, as they are historically conditioned through distinct national path dependencies. For instance, in France the emphasis is on excellence, in the Netherlands on maintaining parental choice, Finland on equality, the UK on standards not structures – so that while their policies are all structurally selected by a common discourse, that organized around the KBE–LLL discourse, their opportunity structures are strategically selected by their historically conditioned discourses of what education is, how it should be administered and how it should be enacted. Though these policies may be contested, at national and other levels, the contestation takes place *within* the discursive opportunity structures provided by the KBE discourse on the one hand and national opportunity structures on the other. So, while opportunity structures do not determine education policies, they are implicated in the strategic selectivity of what will count as policies, their implementation and their enactment – for it is at each of these levels that we find key bases of significant and determining differences and patterns of relationships between national and sub-national education policies.

However, we should also note that *institutional* opportunity structures 'have both micro foundations and macro contexts. They are sustained and instantiated in individual, organizational, and inter-organizational activities but they are also embedded in functionally differentiated institutional orders' (Jessop,

2001: 1231). This means that we are able also to examine in some detail the 'enactment' of education policy. This takes place in schools as particular kinds of organizations, which are themselves intensely strategically selective of what can take place within them. This does not necessarily imply any deliberate obstruction by schools to policies determined elsewhere (though it may not rule it out); rather, it is that the everyday practices of schools are necessarily selective of what can and cannot easily be taken on; they operate through a logic of appropriateness rather than a logic of consequences. This is clearly evident in the large bodies of work on what is often referred to as the grammar of schooling (Tyack and Tobin, 1994), a set of more or less taken-for-granted features of what counts as schooling, like the length of the school day and year, the division of the student body into (equally sized) 'classes', staffed largely by specially trained cadres, and following particular prescriptions around appropriate content. These also vary quite considerably in terms of national traditions and styles.

Thus we can see how 'policies' directed towards improving educational transitions and trajectories are shaped and differentiated from each other – even as they are confronted by a more or less common EU agenda – at the levels of the national, the regional, the local and the practical.

Conclusion

The GOETE research programme had at its heart – as well as in its title – the recognition and demonstration of the nature and significance for educational transitions and trajectories of the ways in which they were governed. This enabled us both to take account of their broader implications for the understanding of education policies at individual country level, and to advance a means of enabling the identification of sources of differences between them. And that potential has been at the heart of this chapter, as we have attempted to show how the different ways that educational transitions and trajectories are defined, shaped and performed in different countries reflect and affect the processes and outcomes realized for the young people who pass through them.

The analysis we proposed in this chapter shows that discourses on KBE and LLL have ambiguous contents and meet a variety of ideological *Weltanschauungen* leading to different opportunity structures being construed and constructed through the medium of what remain essentially national structures.

Indeed, the complex mixes of scales, actors, type of processes and functions to be performed can have very different impacts. However, the effects of the

KBE and LLL on single countries' educational systems are always mediated through the contextual conditions that frame local opportunity structures. These conditions include (to different degrees and to different extents in the GOETE countries):

1 An institutional environment that effectively coordinates scales and actors across all possible combinations and through all processes;
2 A polity environment which supports and/or enhances the link between schools and firms and the knowledge transfer;
3 Strong investments in basic education and in (re)qualification through educational options at later stages in life.

Meeting these conditions eases pursuing the KBE and LLL goals of mainstream EU rhetoric, but lays out also the basis for potentially divergent opportunity structures. The ambiguities intrinsic in the processes involved – ranging from fostering participatory practices, capability enhancing solutions and local experimentation to cutting public expenditure in education and shifting responsibilities to families and local scales – both take different forms and deploy their effects unevenly on the changing forms, practices and outcomes of educational trajectories and transitions.

4

Translation of Policy Instruments and Negotiation of Actors in Local School Spaces

Karin Amos
Eberhard Karls University, Tübingen

Patricia Loncle
High School of Public Health, Rennes

Alessandro Martelli
University of Bologna

Eduardo Barberis
University Carlo Bo of Urbino

Valérie Becquet
University of Cergy-Pontoise

Ulrich Theobald
Eberhard Karls University of Tübingen

Introduction

Deep changes in educational governance become visible in places (schools, cities, regions) where different societal levels conflate into concrete practices, and where homogeneous supranational discourses are broken down and re-emerge at national and sub-national levels to demonstrate path dependencies and differences through the adaptation of these general trends to the contextual specificities (Dale and Robertson, 2009; Mons, 2009; Verger et al., 2012). As an example, the discourse on 'school autonomy' with its implications of improving democratic forms and completing the process of decentralization is adapted very specifically in the different countries and territories, due to their different resources, histories and path dependencies (Duru-Bellat and Meuret, 2001; Salamon, 2002; Loncle, 2011).

It is through the actors and activities of governance at the different scales (supranational, national, regional, local) that different 'opportunity structures' available for young people are framed at transition points (see Dale et al., in this volume). The increasingly varied and complex forms, outputs and outcomes of governance result from different actors, working at many different levels, carrying out a multiplicity of activities and tasks. Governance 'works' through all these levels, activities and people without being reducible to any of them: all are essential and none is itself sufficiently dominant to determine outcomes (Kooiman, 1993; Le Galès, 2004; Baer, 2009).

In this chapter, we try to analyse two mechanisms inherent to current structures and processes of educational governance in eight countries (Finland, France, Germany, Italy, the Netherlands, Poland, Slovenia and the UK): (1) the translation of apparently universal concepts and trends into local policies; and (2) the negotiation between different actors involved at the local level. While the mechanism of translation will be analysed with regard to the issue of school autonomy, the mechanism of negotiation is discussed with regard to the implementation of social support for students and the participation and influence of parents and students in school. Both issues represent a trend of involving new actors in educational governance, although it is unclear to what extent this involvement is realized in practice or is mainly a question of semantics. The following remarks serve as an initial framing of the issues we are concerned with in this chapter:

There is no doubt that discourses of 'responsibility' and 'partnership', 'autonomy' and 'self-regulation/self-organization', mask the coercion and the bureaucratic necessities that are still at work, although no longer easily recognizable as such (Rhodes, 1997; Geddes, 2000; Périer, 2012). And despite the fact that decentralization and school autonomy seem to offer greater opportunities for parental and student participation in the governing of schools and in supporting children, there is a very low level of involvement (Loncle et al., 2012). As a matter of fact, the new governance arrangements at the local level still fall within the realm of specialized professionals or voluntary organizations, rather than that of parents and students as individuals (Crozier, 2000).

Despite all the criticism of schooling, school is still of fundamental relevance for young people in contemporary societies, and has a concrete influence on students' life chances and trajectories. Among the factors and dynamics that intervene in the development of these trajectories, educational support and involvement of students and their families in everyday school activities and relations could improve (or weaken, if absent or problematic) the overall outcome. From this perspective, it is important to observe how support and involvement are implemented and conducted in local school spaces beyond formal discourses, recommendations, policy orientations and principles of governance. The question is, however, whether the power relations of schooling have really changed. Or is the proliferation of actors a semantic smoke screen masking the 'real' decision making?

The chapter is divided into three parts. First, it describes how policy orientations related to the meaning of schooling as a key element in the lifelong learning regimes of late modern knowledge-based economies are shaped and translated, adapted and modified, in the intersection between institution and actors (students, families, teachers, experts) at the local level, with a special focus on the translation, i.e. adaptation or appropriation, of the international discourse on school autonomy. Second, it also discusses the question of how roles, entitlements and power of taking action closely linked to educational transitions are negotiated, who the main actors involved are, what kinds of leverage they bring into the arena and how they interact in the negotiation process. The effects of the negotiation are crucial for the educational transitions and are important predictors for future status allocations. Third, focusing in particular on students' and parents' relation to school, it analyses to what extent structural possibilities exist for these actors to participate in the governance of education at the school level and in the regulation and delivery of services, and how far these actors are aware of their possibilities. Attention is paid to similarities and differences across countries, and to the mechanisms, practices, conditions, variables, perceptions, strategies, conflicts, challenges, opportunities and perspectives that explain the emerging patterns of (non-)participation and the interactions within local school spaces. We consider the socio-economic contexts that schools and educational relationships are embedded in (Nespor, 1997; Brint, 1998; Colombo, 2001; van Zanten, 2001; Maroy, 2006; Oberti, 2007; Mattioli and Volturo, 2014) to express our common concern with the way that modes of regulation emerge from and form complex patterns of interaction that impact schools and their immediate local environments.

Our study relies substantially on qualitative data coming from local case studies, where direct observation, interviews and focus groups were realized in order to reach an in-depth insight into the general structures of educational trajectories. We were also interested in the discourses and principles guiding them and the policy orientations that evolve from them. Therefore we also analysed documents and conducted interviews with high-level governance experts. Against this background, we wanted to see how these aspects interact with the individual agency of children and young people, their parents, teachers, principals and other educational professionals, and thus how all this comes to be translated into daily practices within local school spaces (see Walther et al., in this volume).

From International Policy Orientations to Practices at Local Level

In this section, we focus on regulations of school autonomy, devolution and the distribution of resources in relevant educational and welfare policies in our case countries, as institutional opportunity structures that affect decision making, policy debates and priorities in governing educational trajectories. These governance issues are targets of policy attention and reforms: for example, school autonomy has become a much-debated issue that usually has led to increased, but also varying, degrees of freedom (Eurydice, 2007; Fazekas and Burns, 2012), while more recently budget constraints (as an institutional response to the consequences of economic crisis) are a relevant intervening variable in this field that may affect the working of school autonomy itself.

Autonomy versus recentralization in European local governance systems

Schools and 'their' local spaces have to be studied with regard to the distribution of power and organizational dimensions. In our case studies, school autonomy has a long history, for example in the Netherlands (Eurydice, 2007). Elsewhere, it gained momentum mostly in the 1990s, when other rescaling processes, such as transferring authority and resources from higher to lower levels or vice versa (Robertson and Dale, 2006), were also taking place, including the more or less extensive devolution of powers in social, training and labour market policies that interact with educational policies in realizing students' transitions (Kazepov and Barberis, 2012). In Finland, for example, both education and social policy underwent a process of decentralization in the early 1990s, Italy did the same between 1997 and 2001, France enhanced its devolution process with laws in 2003–4, while Poland defined a brand new set of territorial bodies from 1990 onwards. Rescaling in education thus designates an adjustment process of policies or structures to what is politically deemed as adequate and/or necessary.

Rescaling in the form of devolving authority to lower levels of governance seems to belong to the past in many countries. While autonomization, decentralization and devolution processes are still taking place as a heritage of long-term implementation processes, voices critical of these reforms become more outspoken and influential. Whether reforms were based on concerns of efficiency or of effectiveness, often the outcome was far from meeting the high expectations and showed a worrying increase of fragmentation and inequality – to the point that a new recentralization process was initiated. Even in the most federalist educational system in our sample, Germany, where some 70 per cent of funds come from the regions (the *Länder*), the weight of initial central funding increased from 9 per cent to 14 per cent in ten years (Eurydice, 2013).

Current recentralization takes place through new governance tools aimed at coordinating local practice and wider policy goals: soft governance tools (e.g. the diffusion of good practices), arenas of negotiation (e.g. round tables involving local and national authorities) and selectivity and scarcity of resources (e.g. earmarking them according to priorities or evaluation procedures). The consequence is often an increased governance complexity.[1] Italy, for example, has lately become aware of the uneven outcome of its regionalization process. The symbolic policy of appointing a Minister for territorial cohesion in 2011 and the definition of national standards for curricula may represent a first step towards a new policy trend.

If we analyse discourses expressed in expert interviews and policy documents collected in the research project, most of the emerging problems seem to lie in the intersection between autonomization, devolution and endowments. Even though the devolution of tasks and the autonomy of school institutions have increased, funding is still mainly and firmly in the hands of the government, be it centrally or federally organized. Exceptions such as those in Poland or the UK do not tell us much about autonomy so far, since the latter depends not only on the sources of funding, and also on their structure (lump sum vs earmarked funds), and on the flexibility in the use of resources.[2]

There is a wide range of ways of regulating resources under the umbrella of 'autonomy'. Sometimes problems arise from a shortage of resources that does not result from retrenchment trends, but from structural governance problems: a better inter-institutional, inter-sectoral cooperation to ease transition can be restricted by earmarked funding in school budgets (a complaint reported, for example, in one German case). In other cases, autonomy is challenged due to inadequate resources, and there are also cases where school staff (especially management) plead for the de-bureaucratization of decision-making processes and more flexibility in the use of the available (scarce) resources, on the basis of school priorities.

It is not by chance that this request comes from those countries whose school autonomy on financial matters is more limited (OECD, 2012a) and where principals feel more disempowered (Aro et al., 2012), that is, Italy, France and Germany. At the same time, we could observe discontent in some Dutch cases, where most decisions are taken at school level and school autonomy is formally greatest: because school boards setting the agenda for several schools are increasingly reducing the autonomy of individual smaller institutions. These settings obviously have a crucial importance for the contents of relationships between actors and schools.

Local school spaces between actors and institutions: Constraints and opportunities

There is an extensive debate on the relationships between actors and institutions in the area of social and political sciences. One prominent example is the emphasis on 'actors' in what is known as actor-centred institutionalism (Scharpf, 1997). The concept of 'practice' and the associated 'community of practice' (Chaiklin and Lave, 1996; Wenger, 1998) have some heuristic potential in revealing the negotiated, changing and situated nature of the micro–macro link, suggesting a feasible way to link the collective (agency) and structural effects simultaneously. This provides an adequate framework for understanding the combined mechanisms of inequalities in the sense of structural determination, experience and contextual situations (meant as sets of both constraints and opportunities) in the study of educational trajectories in local school spaces. It is here that international discourses and semantics are translated and adapted by specific actors who bring specific leverage into the game. It is here that the specificity of policy instruments and the processes of negotiation may be studied in order to show their concrete effects.

The practices analysed in our case studies enable us to identify some key aspects of the ongoing educational processes. A first element pertains to the distinction between comprehensive and selective systems (see Tikkanen et al., in this volume): if the former generally offer smoother transitions from primary to lower secondary and then to the upper secondary school, other differences between the systems relating to how individuals are integrated are hard to discern. We would like to make a case for not attributing too much to system effects. On the one hand the power of general socio-economic and cultural dynamics overwrites, as it were, the logic and range of educational systems. On the other hand the local context (including in this case national, regional and local levels) presents a peculiar set of problems, patterns and resources that makes the 'scene' more complex. In other words, the effects of systems are 'toned down' from two directions: from the overall societal environment as well as from the specific relations schools are embedded in.

All the main actors' behaviours and dilemmas in local school spaces appear to be deeply affected by the dynamics of individualization which may be attributed – at least in part – to the power of dominant discourses and structures: in times of an increasing erosion of collective entities and devices (Castel, 2003), we find a reinforcement of the logics of categorization under an individualized perspective, that of an *individu par défaut*: an individual that is left alone with his/her vulnerabilities and difficulties (Castel and Haroche, 2001). This way of conceiving of an individual is also compatible with the currently promoted practices of life planning and self-construction through information and counselling. The conduct of life becomes a question of design, and this design is frequently inspired by science, or rather by scientization, as a dominant cognitive cultural mode. The computer supported self-tracking of behaviour and habits, and the role of experts guiding the life course. In short, what Han (2014) calls psycho power leads to the development of dispositions that facilitate individual attributions of decisions. In the end, it is the individual him- or herself who carries the 'risks' of these decisions (see also Cuconato et al., in this volume). Individualization can also mean that teachers and parents often emerge as conflicting actors (see also Ule et al., in this volume). Although they are affected by the same overall aims and programmes, they answer very differently to the challenges caused by frictions and contradictions generated at the macro level, which also shape local contexts and everyday school life. For example, 'inclusion' as a new task for schools may have very different implications depending on the respective focus on individualism (cf. UNESCO, 1994).

In their function as allocation agents, schools make use of and provide information that affects many relationships in the field, particularly in the interaction between school staff and students/parents. Information here relates first and foremost to meeting the challenges of schooling and getting help in coping with them, so that the role of schooling as the necessary, but not in itself sufficient, condition for societal participation can be completed successfully. The construction and delivery by school staff and experts (avoiding the risk of being self-referential, selective and/or hindering effective interaction) of the information that is most important for all the actors involved is a very important matter. Many complaints from students and parents suggest the need for significant improvement in this area, starting from the fact that parents prefer individual, face-to-face contact with teachers to web-based, digitalized cooperation. And although all educational actors share the idea that pedagogical work without active engagement of parents is incomplete and cannot fully accomplish its goals, in none of the countries of our sample could we discern an educational strategy on how to fully integrate them (du Bois-Reymond et al., 2012: 155).

A recurring issue both in the theoretical debate and in our empirical research is the tension between local school spaces and societal dynamics and politics that results from the introduction of school autonomy and an outcome orientation (seen as expression of liberalism and selectivity). Local contexts do not provide real opportunities to challenge or change macro-level decisions, and at the same time the claimed autonomy of local units within the education system appears not to be as extensive as it is alleged to be (Dale et al., 2012; du Bois-Reymond et al., 2012: 155). Many initiatives are nevertheless introduced by schools and local authorities to implement partnerships that enable links between education, social, cultural and health issues to be established. This tends to slightly soften education inequalities which are, of course, linked to social stratification. The main strength of local contexts lies in their proximity to the needs of the community and, most importantly in the case of education and (more generally) social solidarity. They show a high potential in terms of regional or infra-regional transition management, promoting partnership, networking and community development with schools and social work, the municipality, etc. as main actors in governance strategies to deal with financial cuts and dominant rhetoric. Somewhat paradoxically, it is again the supra-local level that puts these new frameworks and forms of collaboration on the agenda, such as those in the focus of our investigation, 'local school space' – or 'educational landscape' (*Bildungslandschaften*) – which are often used when policies directly link the national to the local level, circumventing, as is the case in Germany, the regional one. The possible advantages of such local collaboration are generally valued very highly:

> They have in common the chance to use existing resources in and out of school and, which is most important, create new resources by bringing together agencies and actors who operated up to then ignorant of each other's work. That is done by new combinations of actors, like assembling teachers, local employers, and municipality administrators, members of housing cooperation, youth workers, and representatives of minority/migrant and parent associations. They all may have in their different functions to do with multi-problem schools. Not always, and not in every country/city/school, do all these actors come together but, depending on educational and local resources, traditions, and financial means, there may be larger or smaller gatherings, more regularly or more irregularly conducted. (du Bois-Reymond et al., 2012: 162)

Nevertheless, if these initiatives and cooperation at the local level exist they are mostly optional, and the diversity of deliveries and the subsequent territorial inequalities (both within and between countries) is quite evident. The effectiveness of these actions depends on the local systems of actors and how far they are able to influence the (local) decision-making process (Martelli, 2007; Loncle, 2011). Our fieldwork revealed some critical aspects of the existing experience: a lack of evaluation of the effectiveness of the measures taken; tensions between projects and programmes due to the prevalence of many short-term as opposed to long-term projects; difficulties of internal commitment, common aims and internal governance; risks of weakening participation because of the excessive number of layers of decision and levels of actors. However, local cooperation appears to be one of the more promising and autonomous paths of local school spaces.

If this chapter's concern with the translation of policy instruments has created an expectation of great variation between countries, regions and local spaces, such an expectation needs to be toned down. In the final analysis, the rhetoric of individualism and partnership is countered by the persisting influence of social status on transition trajectories and decision making. The composition of the most successful and the most 'at risk' groups of students is quite similar in all countries of our sample; nowhere have we seen formerly underprivileged children and youth suddenly appearing at the top as a result of changes in the support measures made possible because of school autonomy.

Negotiation of Actors' Relationships at Local Level

This remark leads us to the analysis of negotiation contents between the actors involved. The given structural conditions – financial resources, laws and cultural norms – do not prevent them from being active and involved in influencing how educational trajectories are designed and managed in everyday life at the local level. According to the role they play (as parents, principals, teachers, experts) and their socio-economic status and their culture, they bring into the arena specific kinds of leverage, and interact in the negotiation process based on modes of information and participation that are school-specific. We first focus on the access and use of policy instruments set by local school spaces, and then consider the variety of actors involved in the framing of local governance issues, with a particular focus on the roles of students and parents.

Local policy instruments as 'cosmetic' answers to the structural problems of education systems

There is an ongoing process of homogenization of national education and educational policies in the European Union. One dominant issue concerns so called disadvantaged students. This issue is framed on all levels of educational governance by two main aspects: one is economic; the other relates to social justice. The first says that early school leavers or graduates who barely scraped by will not be successfully integrated into the labour market; the other says that in order to have social coherence and democratic stability, education is a necessary prerogative.

These aims are pursued against the background of very specific national traditions in dealing with disadvantage: Finland, with a long common education of all children in a comprehensive school system, arguably is the least selective; and Germany, with an early separation of educational trajectories after the fourth grade, can be taken as the most selective. However, despite these differences, we have found that there is no European country where the social origins of the children are irrelevant; the degree of the relation varies, not the relation as such (Dale et al., 2012).

In most of the countries of our sample, risks are seen as connected to weak social, educational and economic conditions of families. Of these, migrant children and youth are identified as a particularly significant educational at-risk group. Education policy focuses on the attributed deficits of individuals or the collective to which they belong. Hence, it consists in increasing and strengthening support measures, for example a strong focus on language acquisition in the case of migration as an indicator of disadvantage. For further illustration take the following snapshots as examples. In Finland the attainment rates, especially of young non-European females, are lower, their drop-out risk higher and their successful transition into upper secondary education more unlikely. In Germany, migration is a highly political issue and educational success is lowest for boys and young men from specific countries of origin (often not their own, but that of their parents). There is a strong correlation between social origin and educational attainment, although it is not so much the economic situation as parents' level of formal education that is important. These strong correlations lead to a questioning of the meritocratic claim that legitimizes schooling. The French situation is similar to the German, with the difference that in Germany migration is strongly emphasized and in France it is not. In France, as in other countries, there is a debate about which inequalities are due to the education system and which are not; whether and how educational responsibility is recognized and addressed. There is a general tendency to increase the resources and means of educational support, in the form of guidance, counselling, remedial education etc., rather than to question the basic structure of the education system.

Governance issues between general regulation and local dynamics

The complexities of schooling and the rising significance of education as an institution throughout the twentieth century have led to the situation where many actors are involved in shaping educational processes. In this section, we will take career counselling (see also Felczak at al., in this volume) and participation as two cases in point.

In terms of the first, our local studies have shown that what is intended as a major support for students can also be an obstacle depending on how the role is filled and interpreted. A case in point is Germany, where a highly differentiated support system has been established to aid students and their families, but may have very obverse effects. The possible obverse effects have two main sources: the lack of professional reflection of attributions and stereotyping, and the unclear or ineffective communication structures of the professional actors involved. For example, the comprehensive form of schooling called *Gesamtschule* that is slowly gaining importance as a response to the high reproduction of inequality revealed by the PISA studies (OECD, 2012a) is usually equipped with multi-professional teams to provide the necessary support structure. However, because teachers tend to be particularly stressed and overworked in these schools, not the least due to political pressure and high performance expectations, and the other professions (school psychologists and social workers) have their own professional procedures and organizational structures (i.e. they respond to organizational logics outside of schooling), feedback and communication loops may be a real problem. Similar observations have been made with regard to the Slovenian system, which is also characterized by a highly elaborate professional field of pedagogues and psychologists, including experts specializing in marginalized groups such as the children of Roma parents. The research report (du Bois-Reymond et al., 2012) discussing the findings in detail also took note of a remarkable tension: on the one hand, there is a proliferation of expertise and professionals to guide students and to facilitate difficult decision processes, but on the other hand, students are reported to feel left alone and to be burdened with the individual attribution of decisions. The explanation for this is that educational decisions are contingent, and dependent, on many factors, one of which is systemic. In other words, educational success depends on a number of variables and their constellations; there is no simple causality. Given the high legitimacy of causality in modern life, the presence of a 'scientized' and professional staff with multiple expertise by definition has legitimating power. Ever since so-called 'cooling out' processes were investigated more than fifty years ago (Clark, 1960), we know that support measures and career counselling in particular are highly relevant for making decisions which students quickly identify with (see also Walther et al., Cuconato et al. and Ule et al., in this volume). Today, all disadvantaged students have reason to be distrustful of advice given that is claimed to be in their best interest, because more often than not this advice will tell them that their expectations are too high and should be adjusted to reality (Walther et al., in this volume; see also Lipsky, 1980; Maynard-Moody and Musheno, 1990). As already stated in the section on 'autonomy', the system is not conducive to reversing the effects of social selectivity.

However, complementary to the proliferation of professional staff with academic training, we also find groups of lay people active in schools. The most important of these include volunteers in sport and music, as well as those belonging to the growing sector of public–private partnerships. They form collaborative networks which are often fragile and volatile, with unclear competencies and non-permanent funding.

Students' and Parents' Influence on the Negotiation Processes

Another set of actors may be identified in local school spaces that has more or less influence on negotiation processes. They do not belong to new professional groups, but are the most traditional key actors besides teachers: students and parents. Both benefit from various mechanisms for intervening in school governance. Nevertheless, we may ask what the 'real' extent of their power on educational trajectories is. Are they real partners in the construction of school spaces? Or are they simple users?

The question of students' influence on decision and participation processes not only varies greatly across the eight countries but is especially ambivalent as far as participation is concerned. With regard to this, the main questions are: who do students and parents represent and by whom are they represented? Are student and parent organizations to be seen as interest groups? Is there a homogenous group which we call students and another homogeneous group which we call parents? Clearly, this is not the case, although there may be issues of common concern. However, it needs to be emphasized that it is those students who are considered to be 'at risk' who belong to what becomes increasingly commonly termed as the precariat, whose parents may be chronically ill or unemployed, or both, who often have low educational degrees, who are most in need of having their interests defended. But it is this group that soon becomes disillusioned and frustrated and tired of fighting against overwhelming obstacles. And it is this group that has no 'voice' in their formal representations.

Parental participation is another area where diverse interests clash, even if formal bodies of collective participation exist. There are some issues of concern for all parents irrespective of their socio-economic or other backgrounds. All parents want good teachers who care about their students and who are dependably present to deliver their lessons. All parents want schools to be a safe and healthy environment. But there are also significant differences: some parents are very focused on the academic progress of their children and may even oppose their school complying with inclusion regulations and accepting students with special needs. We also know that immigrant parents are almost everywhere dissatisfied with the way they can, or rather cannot, become involved. There is evidence that injustice and inequity related to immigration are particularly frequently voiced in the UK, the Netherlands and Germany from our sample of European countries. The research report (du Bois-Reymond et al., 2012: 153) stated that parents with migrant backgrounds are aware that their children are at risk of receiving recommendations only for the lower tiers of secondary schooling, and these parents also complain about a lack of information of alternatives, especially about other ways to successfully master transitions. Conversely, as we know from parent associations, active and politically engaged parents complain that other parents are too unwilling, insufficiently interested or passive, and do not show signs of interest in the education of their own children, let alone of the next generation.

Against this general background, it is crucial to look at the local school system in order to understand the roles that parents and students play, and are empowered to play, in the school system. Specifically, the question of the available modes of participation at the local level is of particular importance. These roles are not mechanically ascribed, but the result of complex negotiation processes that largely depend on the structures and communication patterns established by local authorities who take an interest in balancing the power distribution between the various stakeholders.

How are parents addressed in the reform discourses? How is their collective belonging framed: as citizens? As users or customers? How do they realize the potential to participate in the decision process, in the regulation and in the delivery of services?

We cannot address in depth the underlying questions at stake here. But without doubt it is crucial to get to the underlying semantics. Are students and parents regarded as fully responsible actors in the system? What expert roles are ascribed to them? Are students considered as citizens in the making or are they addressed as equal partners? What role do they play in deciding on their own trajectories (Walther, 2012b; Martelli, 2013)? Finally, but not least importantly, what is the influence of the 'European education policy' (Dale and Robertson, 2009) on this issue?

A wide range of mechanisms

Formal spaces of students' participation have been created all over European countries. As reported by Eurydice: 'all European countries have introduced measures to promote the involvement of students in school governance', which can be considered as 'an encouraging signal of a widespread effort on the part of national authorities to foster democratic student participation' (Eurydice, 2012a: 39). Although these measures differ from one country to the next, this section will try to highlight overall tendencies.

The two countries where students' participation is institutionalized in secondary education are Germany and Poland. In those countries, three types of participation mechanisms (class representatives, student council, student representative in school governing bodies) (Eurydice, 2012a) are centrally defined and implemented in lower and upper secondary schools. In Finland, the UK and the Netherlands there are mixed situations between central regulations and local regulations, which means that students' participation can also be established across levels. Central regulations mainly concern student councils and student representatives in school governing bodies, while local regulations concern class representatives. This is the same in Slovenia where there is a mixed situation between central regulations in upper secondary schools and a tradition of local practices in lower secondary schools. In France and Italy, students' participation is more common in upper secondary schools than in lower secondary schools, but always based on central regulations.

There are also some differences between the mechanisms: student councils and student representatives in the school governing bodies are the most common institutionalized forms of participation. In student councils, students are the only members and they are not accorded formal decision-making powers within schools. For student representatives, students mix with other school actors and participate in the decision-making process.

The way of electing representatives varies according to the respective mechanisms and regulations. Class councils deal with class-level affairs and are generally comprised of teachers, parents and students. Class representatives are elected by the students in their class. The Eurydice report underlines that in the UK (England, Wales and Northern Ireland), 'class representatives are elected not to participate in class councils, but to sit directly on the student council at the school level', where they 'can raise class issues and report back to their classes'. There are different ways that members of a student council can be appointed. In France and Germany, they are directly elected by their peers; in Italy, the UK and Slovenia class representatives are appointed; in Finland, all students participate; in Poland and the Netherlands they take part in the definition of school procedures.

The Eurydice report concludes that the 'common role of students is consultative', mainly through class representatives and student councils, but also points out that when students participate in governing school bodies, they are part of the decision-making process. However, their real influence on the decision-making process depends on the influence that governing bodies have on school governance, their attributions and the number of student representatives.

Formal spaces of parents' participation

Several mechanisms of parental participation can be distinguished. The first refers to a rather conventional form in the context of hierarchical policymaking. Holding positions in a legally predetermined institution such as a school council is an example here. This way of participation implies a unidirectional form of parents' involvement since it does not foster cross-level communication within the education system. The different levels remain separate and interaction in circular form does not occur. While bottom-up decision making is possible, these processes can be better described by the term 'steering' than by the concept of governance.

The second and third possibilities comprise participation by direct or indirect communication with, or within, the organization.

One very progressive way is a form of direct communication in which parents are actively incorporated into the development process, for instance by being permanently integrated into decision-making groups to provide feedback.

Basically, this can happen on all levels from local to national. The difference from the conventional type of participation described above lies in the transgression of systemic borders. Making the parents part of processes which are genuinely subject to authorities such as school boards or other bodies, where cross-level decision making can become institutionalized (Altrichter and Helm, 2011: 19), does not automatically mean that they have a strong influence.

Ways of indirect communication with parents also imply mechanisms of participation outside schools. School choice is a good example here. Insofar as parents get their information about the characteristics and performance of different schools from third parties, they do not actively interact with the schools themselves. Again, this form of interaction is different from the conventional, unidirectional form of parents' involvement. In decision-making processes determined by classical steering, the different hierarchical levels can basically operate independently. Here, this is no longer the case. To stick to the school choice example, such governance processes rely on the role of parents. In contrast to the conventional, hierarchical decision-making model, both of these types of communication imply that parents become integrated into a form of closed-loop communication.

A fourth way in which parents can contribute to governance processes is by using channels which belong to other societal systems. In cooperation with actors from the economic system, such as companies or trade unions, they can for example put pressure on the education system with lobbying practices. Or they can constitute new actors by founding new independent organizations and consortia in order to pursue their interests. The difficulty here is the enormous heterogeneity within the whole group of parents. As mentioned before, the extent to which parents are actually willing to participate – and are capable of doing so – varies (Langer, 2011: 108).

The realities of students' and parents' participation

Beyond these mechanisms, we tried to understand in our surveys and case studies the extent and forms of student and parental participation. Of course, students and parents are not 'new' actors, but together with professional educators have existed since the beginning of modern schooling. Education in many countries is conceived of as parents' natural right and protected by the constitution (Eurydice, 2012a: 39). Compulsory schooling therefore severely limits the parental right to educate their child(ren). However, the forms and degree of these limitations vary greatly from one country to another. School systems expect families to adapt their way of life to school aims and expectations (Crozier, 2000).

Schools and families are traditionally seen as complementary: with teachers acting in place of parents, the understanding is that teachers assume the educative role during school time. With the rise of democratic participation as a standard within modern society, the necessity of including parents in the decision-making process has increased (Kränzl-Nagl and Zartler, 2010).

The semantics of governance, democratic participation and partnership should not obscure the asymmetry of the relationship between schools and parents/students. Two dimensions have to be considered: one is the various concrete possibilities to exert influence (with more possibilities in the Netherlands and Finland and fewer possibilities in France and Slovenia), while the other rests on the underlying legitimacy of the influence that various actors have within each system.

By definition, and according to relevant discourses, all actors should be equal in a partnership (Geddes, 2000). They have the same legitimacy and scope of influence. Politically and legally this is clearly not the case in the education field. The idea of students and teachers, or parents and teachers, as partners is essentially political, some may even say ideological. Educational partnership is a term often used internationally, but it obscures the fact that the relationship is not based on equal terms (Périer, 2012). Because of the way school and family are structurally related to each other, there is a general expectation by the school that parents take an interest in, and closely monitor, the progress of their child through the system. In France and in Germany, for example, it is an explicit expectation of the institution that parents are informed and follow their child's progress. This may lead to teachers and principals encouraging immigrant parents, for example, to attend language classes so that they are more able to understand information about career paths and options for their children. This expectation is met with an overall complaint that while some parents (mostly 'ethnic' Germans, middle class) comply with this expectation of collaboration between school and family, many do not. However, what is obscured in many of these discussions is the observation we made earlier: what it is exactly which unites parents, who on closer inspection appear as a very heterogeneous group.

In the eight countries, students and parents with an immigrant background are less included in the decision-making processes and less informed about the way the education system works. As a hypothesis, it seems likely that participation strongly correlates with the position of the student in the class and in the school. At-risk students are likely to be less informed and the system makes less effort to include them than high achieving well-adjusted students.

A somewhat surprising finding about the formal influence of parents and students in the different countries is that in the end, the specific structures of the welfare state or education system, and the mode of formal organization, centralized versus federal systems, do not make a difference for the most vulnerable students.

As with all mechanisms, it should not be forgotten that knowing how to use them is associated with power. As pointed out earlier in this chapter, parents and students are not a homogenous group. Social origin, socio-economic status and the disposable social and cultural capital are decisive factors. Thus, middle and upper class parents are not only the most active, but they also make most use of the possibilities they have. Conversely, a lack of active participation, especially on the part of parents, might easily be mistaken for not being interested in the progress of the child.

Beyond the formal role assigned, a key research object is given by reality and perceptions of participation and legitimacy. Our analyses allow us to say that, if 'partnership' is a frequently used word within the discourse of school governance, in everyday school life the different actors have not yet achieved an equal and collaborative pattern, specifically in the sense of the still insufficient and ineffective recognition of the role of parents and students. In this perspective we can partly explain the recurring complaint on the 'absent parent' (see also Koşar Altinyelken et al., in this volume) concerning in particular the more vulnerable, by contrast with the self-selection of 'collaborative' families among the middle-upper classes. In other words, the 'weaker' students and their families are perceived and classified, the stronger are the risks of their being excluded from participation mechanisms.

Conclusion

Local school spaces can be seen as arenas where general *discourses* and *norms* about education are translated into *practices*, and this requires researchers to confirm and/or discover the key issues and variables which characterize the interactions and negotiations among the actors in the field. The actors analysed here have been teachers and principals, experts, parents and students. The analysis has shown the relevance of three main aspects of the 'everyday life' of local school spaces.

First of all, under the perspective of governance processes affecting educational systems, the relationship between central and local levels still appears to be as fundamental as it is complex and ambivalent (that is, shifting from collaboration to conflict and vice versa), and to vary according to the different resources available in different local contexts.

Second, local school spaces, under the pressure of general discourses informing educational systems, appear to be deeply affected by dynamics of individualization, which is closely combined with the strong call for strengthening the support for students. The analysis has contributed to the idea that support and individualization may emerge as *liaisons dangereuses*, because the former are understood and planned within a framework where both needs and resources are connected to personal/familiar responsibilities, which are then mediated through practices driven by 'neutral' professionalization and scientization. The effect is that of leaving weak students and parents substantially alone, but also of challenging teachers in relation to the problems and contradictions produced by the macro/micro interaction.

Third, issues of participation remain at the very centre of the complex game of constraints and opportunities emerging within local school spaces in action. Information for students and families, particularly for the more disadvantaged ones, still appears to be insufficient both in terms of its quantity and in the ways it is delivered and made available. Parents' differential availability and ability to participate in school dynamics, which depends also on their social and cultural capital, is a major determinant and implication of this. The 'everyday' life of local school spaces thus proves to be a complex and contradictory process where a satisfying partnership among the different, heterogeneous actors still seems far from being reached, as a result of the difficult interactions between central and local levels, the persistence of the constraints suffered by families lacking social capital and of the force of the individualization process. Given these consequences of the persisting distance between school and families, local cooperation may possibly be one of the more promising ways to be followed and improved, so long as it is able to avoid individualizing ascriptions, and to include the point of view and the 'voice' of students and their families.

Part 2

Access to Education

5

Understanding the Interactive Emergence of Educational Inequalities through Access and Accessibility of Education

Barbara Stauber
University of Tübingen

Marcelo Parreira do Amaral
University of Münster

Isabelle Danic
University of Rennes 2

In current debates, the issue of access to education relates closely to a perspective that sees educational institutions as either reproducing or mitigating social inequalities. In discussing this issue, the chapter draws attention to the *interplay of societal structures and individual agency* in processes of reproduction of social inequality. It considers educational structures, policies and discourses but also the individual representations thereof when focusing the barriers and solutions to access issues that are perceived (or not) and/or created in the interaction of the different actors and levels involved.

The chapter first introduces the concepts of access and inequality. Drawing on findings from gender studies, postcolonial and critical studies on racism, it underlines the need for an analytical distinction between processes of social *differentiation* and their outcomes, i.e. *differences* or inequalities. Second, the interactive and intersectional character of access and inequality is differentiated with regard to four dimensions that are arguably crucial for a critical research on access to education. Here, the qualitative findings of the GOETE research on how young people and their parents perceive, experience and reproduce access to education show the interaction of children, parents and educational staff during transitions in terms of opening or narrowing access to education and elicit some findings on the quantitative approaches of GOETE. Here, transitions in educational trajectories are seen, thus, as heuristic moments, which allow us to analyse the multi-actor and multilevel nature of access to education and thus the interactional emergence of educational inequalities. A third section draws theoretical conclusions from the findings discussed and suggests the concept of *accessibility* of education. Compared to (equal) access, the notion of accessibility includes a more profound theoretical framing of the complex issue in the course of educational trajectories by thinking together societal structures and individual agency, and, importantly, it also includes a more pronounced critique of inequalities by pointing to the responsibility of all actors involved.

Introduction: Access to Education and Inequality

The concept of educational access is a central theme in the GOETE research project. In the framework of the knowledge society, it is most often associated with access to postsecondary and higher education or to lifelong learning. Debates around educational access focus on policies and measures aimed at widening and improving it, in particular in relation to gender, socio-economic status and ethnicity. In this way, the focus is set on the perspective that social inequalities and disadvantage are either reproduced/exacerbated or mitigated by educational institutions. This insight draws attention to structures and policies and to how they represent particular groups (e.g. girls or boys, children from ethnic minorities or from migrant backgrounds). Furthermore, educational access also touches upon issues of participation, which play an active – maybe decisive – role in achieving it.

One point of departure in the framework of the GOETE research has been the observed increasingly blurred link between 'increased access to education' and 'improved future professional prospects', as indicated by the growing number of highly qualified young people throughout Europe, and especially in southern Europe, without any professional prospects. Starting to reflect on the relationship between access and social inequality, an immediate difficulty is to distinguish between causes and consequences: what are processes and what are outcomes of processes of social differentiation? A closer look informed by insights from different fields of study, such as gender, migration, postcolonial and critical studies on racism, reveals that it is not only meaningful but essential to insist on an analytical distinction between the processes of social *differentiation* and their outcomes, which are *differences* or inequalities (see Gildemeister, 2004;

see accordingly the distinction made by Szalai, 2011, between minorities and minoritization). This has three main reasons and purposes: the first relates to a theoretical perspective which is critical of the reification of social phenomena as something given or 'natural' (Honneth, 2007; Przyborski and Slunecko, 2009); the second is guided by the analytical interest in exploring and making visible *how* social processes at different levels and their interplay (re)produce social inequalities. According to Foucault's idea that there are powerful social orders, which to a large extent work implicitly and throughout the agency of all actors involved, this chapter aims to put a spotlight on these social orders. In addition, the third purpose derives from a self-understanding of critical social science. We regard it as our job as social scientists to 'make visible' such mechanisms in order to clarify the (political) responsibilities of the actors involved with regard to the creation of access*ibility* to education for all young people.

The distinction between outcomes and processes of social differentiation is indeed crucial in order to avoid the trap of many current discourses, which equate the results of processes of social differentiation in the educational field to properties of the individual learners. The recent trend in psychological competence testing, e.g. in the context of large-scale school achievement research at the EU and the OECD level, provides important evidence of *how far* educational systems are able to help overcome or simply reproduce social inequalities. At the same time, however, it creates a crucial misunderstanding by turning social origin into an individual attribute of the learner. In the same direction, the relevance of 'competence' is mostly overstressed, while important issues of 'doing difference', i.e. the *ongoing interactional accomplishment* of social difference in the classroom as a powerful social space, of students' fluctuating experiences through educational institutions, are largely disregarded (see Helsper et al., 2008). Large-scale research on competence building often de-contextualizes data and in doing so neglects not only the extent but also the processes of reproduction of social inequalities within schools. We could even argue that referring to individual students as 'learners' de-contextualizes their situation: being a 'learner' represents *only one facet* of young people's lives, who even within the schoolyard have to perform many other roles, not only that of the learner. Instead, the complex range of roles, topics and transitions they concurrently find themselves in have to be considered, because it is exactly amid this multitude of transitions that educational trajectories are framed (see Walther et al., 2006; Stauber et al., 2007).

Conversely, social inequality cannot be regarded as a simple and automatic 'outcome' of 'unjust structures'; this could easily turn into an excuse for scientific as well as political or practical/professional disengagement. Instead, there is always a whole set of institutions and actors involved which either reinforce or mitigate the effects of structures. In theoretical terms, it is important not to limit the scope for individual agency in order to reveal *how* teachers, parents and students themselves struggle with educational systems, and *how* they try to co-shape this crucial social arena.

In order to come up against the current trend of de-contextualizing the success or failure of school transitions, and consequently of simplifying complex issues and obscuring the powerful social orders at play, this chapter *focuses on the processes* involved: How do educational processes construct social distinctions in the educational trajectories of students? How are demarcations such as ethnicity, class and background constituted? How is *social differentiation* being done? In the following sections, we highlight the issue of access(ibility) and social inequality as an interplay of four different dimensions or perspectives, and present the state-of-the-art research in this field, including the contribution of the GOETE research. By pulling together various strands of research, we hope to offer an innovative approach that emphasizes that *social differentiation* needs to be analysed in multi-dimensional and multi-disciplinary perspectives.

Interrelation of Structures, Institutions, Discourses, Representations and Individual Strategies: Multilevel Issues of Access and Disadvantage

With the aim of clarifying how we consider the interrelation of different levels of reproduction of social inequalities as a result of differential levels of access and accessibility to the educational system, in the following we discuss four dimensions or research perspectives: *a structural perspective, an institutional perspective, a perspective regarding discourses* and *a perspective of subjective positioning*. It is important to note that these four dimensions represent analytical distinctions that in reality can hardly be isolated from each other. While their content often overlaps, they call attention to different perspectives of the same phenomenon; for instance, while structural issues may be most closely associated with individual and/or collective features, we need to take into account that they themselves imply institutional, discursive and interactional aspects. These different dimensions thus possess a heuristic value and help us organize the various facets of the research field and object. After a short definition of each dimension, the current state of research relating to each of them will be presented in turn. This will help us to establish how and to what extent the GOETE research can contribute to this research field and to policy and practice.

The structural perspective

In a structural perspective, education is seen as one factor producing, reproducing or mitigating inequality among social groups defined by class, ethnicity, gender and other social categories. Inequality of access to education may be viewed as the result of differential access across social groups, but also geographic or spatial categories can be used to define unequal access to education. At a socio-structural level, these differences point to concrete relations of power that can be statistically and historically observed. The categories examined in research on educational disadvantage and inequalities have concentrated on different aspects since the 1960s: social class, gender, region, migration and ethnicity, and religion. While there has been a shift from a focus on girls (usually in rural areas) to boys (usually in urban settings and of migrant origin), most research places its focus on individual and/or collective socio-structural characteristics as well as on the life conditions of the concerned groups. Studies informed by theory of socialization and assuming deficit or dispositional properties of individuals or groups explain educational inequalities by referring to different language codes (Bernstein, 1971). In a similar vein, Bourdieu and Passeron (1970) elaborated their concept of cultural capital as an explanation for the reproduction of unequal life and educational chances based on socio-spatial differences.

The sociology of education has been especially concerned to demonstrate that education represents a key factor in reproducing structures of social inequality. While until the 1970s this meant that working class children 'inherited' the working class jobs of their parents (cf. Willis, 1977), more recently low educational attainment implies risks of social exclusion, especially for children and youth from disadvantaged backgrounds (cf. Castel, 2000; Vanttaja and Järvinen, 2006; Field et al., 2007). Moreover, some studies refer to social class-based decisions taken by parents concerning investment in the education of their children as a crucial 'social mechanism' in explaining educational inequality (see Boudon, 1974; Becker, 2000). This latter strand of research distinguishes between *primary* effects (e.g. the varying levels of financial and other resources parents have for supporting their children) and *secondary* effects (e.g. different educational aspirations of parents) (see Ditton, 1989; Breen and Goldthorpe, 1997; Stockè, 2007; Becker and Hecken, 2008; Grundmann et al., 2008; Hillmert, 2008). In agreement with results from Germany (Baumert and Schümer, 2001), GOETE findings indicate that the social milieu of the family influences both short-term transition decisions and medium-term trajectories in upper secondary schools (see Ule et al. in this volume; Biggart et al., 2015). However, as Gomolla and Rotter's (2012) evaluation of German data (Killus and Tillmann, 2012) has shown, the educational aspirations of parents with a Turkish or Russian background turned out to be much higher than of native German parents, which raises questions as to why this does not have a positive effect. The effect of class and gender on educational attainment has also been studied from a long-term perspective in seven European countries (for males, Breen et al., 2009; for females, Breen et al., 2010). The authors documented that 'class-based educational inequality declined in all of the countries' (Breen et al., 2010: 45). Currently, gender differences in educational attainment are changing and, according to several studies, girls now outperform boys in almost all OECD countries, both in secondary and tertiary education (OECD, 2009).

While taking account of the findings of these lines of research, GOETE emphasizes that the categories used to research educational inequality are not given, but rather socially constructed in complex processes of *social differentiation* (Gildemeister, 2004). Thus, the problem of access has to be first understood as a complex structural problem which has, however, to be dealt with actively. This theoretical consideration also has practical and normative implications, because it considers the organizing of access as a core task for all actors involved; analyses here must thus pay adequate attention to processes of social differentiation, which are mediated by structural aspects.

GOETE countries vary in the organization of their education systems. These differences relate to levels of differentiation or tracking, degrees of standardization and stratification, patterns of participation according to different socially constituted groups, transition points along the educational trajectories, their links between education and welfare systems and their foci on transition policies (for an overview see Tikkanen et al. and Amos et al. in this volume; cf. Parreira do Amaral et al., 2011: 187). All these features have a direct impact on how access is organized and negotiated. Through the GOETE parents' survey[1] it emerged very clearly that in comprehensive systems parental expectation with regard to their children's access to education is higher than in selective systems, and this could shape their support practices considerably. This insight has been deepened through the findings from our local case studies, which show that the limited students' access may be seen as an outcome of processes, structures, mechanisms and/or relationships within an unequal structural framework, a characteristic more prominent in selective systems than in comprehensive ones. One recurrent issue among the selective systems is the power structures that regulate access, up to the point where it comes to labour market entry. In this sense, Germany stood out in its very close relationship between educational system and economic interests (of individual or large firms), which of course is not surprising as the German dual apprenticeship system depends on companies. However, firms entering the school as part of the dual system is a new effect, with highly ambivalent outcomes, including the selection of those students who are fitting best to highly specified single firm needs (see du Bois-Reymond et al., 2012).

Access to the desired schools is strongly related to the characteristics of the respective educational system. The analysis of GOETE data according to Allmendinger's typology of educational systems (Allmendinger, 1989) has shown that parents in Finland (the only representative of the low stratification/high standardization group) are the most satisfied with the access to upper secondary schools (93 per cent), confirming that education is most accessible in countries where the educational system is less stratified and where there are fewer institutionally foreseen transitions in young people's educational trajectories. Correspondingly, parents are less satisfied (82 per cent) in countries where the educational system is highly stratified and complex (especially in the Netherlands, 78 per cent, and Germany, 80 per cent, while in France the proportion is considerably higher, 89 per cent) (see Ule et al. in this volume; cf. Ule and Živoder, 2013: 163).

Another important aspect is that *heterogeneity* is confined to students, with the teacher population still dominated by middle-class white teachers without any migration experience. In our comparison of teacher training in GOETE countries, gender-related issues also came to the fore:

> Regarding gender, it seems an overall phenomenon that the teaching profession, in particular the student teachers, is dominated by females. At the same time, the proportion of female teachers increases as the age of the target group of students decreases. In this case, (future) teachers are a very homogeneous group that obviously does not match the gender balance that students represent. In the case of ethnic or social background of (future) teachers, less data is provided. Most countries do not possess respective statistical data and experts are careful with comments, because they feel the political dimension of this aspect and its vagueness. However, teacher students are supposed to be a more homogeneous group than their future students. (see Cramer et al., 2012: 79)

This imbalance documents the structure and 'normality' of teaching as a profession, with the interplay of an ever lower social status of teachers and an increasing feminization of the profession, while still biased by middle-class origin, and difficult to enter for people from migrant backgrounds. Obviously, there is a need to recruit student teachers from *different* social backgrounds in order to achieve a heterogeneity of teachers which corresponds to the student population. Another structural issue identified refers to the inappropriateness of teacher training with regard to preparing teacher students for heterogeneity in schools and classrooms, in particular with teacher students not prepared to support the different needs of their students during transition processes (Cramer et al., 2012). Also, issues such as early school leaving, financial resources and the role of family deserve closer attention.

The institutional perspective

In an institutional dimension, two related aspects require attention. First, at the *macro level* of legislative and policy contexts especially, educational, social and immigration policies may produce disadvantaging and discriminating effects, which have to be carefully considered. This legal–institutional dimension provides the context and framework within which educational systems function, and is also partly reflected in them. One example from the GOETE Institutional Survey[2] may serve as illustration: free school choice policies, which are deemed to improve the responsiveness of schools to students' and parents' needs, and thus raise quality and performance standards, risk increasing students' socio-spatial segregation, as middle-class parents select the school for their children according to its reputation (and its location), producing inequitable effects such as 'white flight'.

The GOETE case study analysis confirmed these results. When looking carefully at the recruiting strategies of schools, such exclusion appears as something quite basic. As documented in the institutional survey of school principals, there is a tendency towards open enrolment giving way to higher student selection (England and Wales, and the Netherlands, top the table of institutional autonomy, while Finland seems to be heading in this direction). School principals across the GOETE countries intend to increase the possibility of their being able to select students according to achievement (see Aro et al., 2012: 50). The differentiating effect of how schools organize their recruitment has also become stronger: 'Education both qualifies and disqualifies individuals and thus functions as an instrument for both social inclusion and exclusion.

This dual nature of educational systems has strengthened' (Aro et al., 2012: 1). Wherever schools increase their scope for choosing students this can easily lead to more selection and social exclusion; even Finland's inclusive system starts to become undermined by such a selection process.

Referring to an overall idea of competitiveness, schools are also increasingly starting to develop their own regulations for selecting students and entering the competition for 'promising' students. The introduction of new forms of governance into the educational system not only enables, but in some instances pushes, state institutions to act like market-oriented firms, thus increasing selectivity in schools (Apple, 2006) and reducing the relevance of education to what is needed in the knowledge economy, which may in its turn have an impact on how access is perceived (Jessop et al., 2008; Lauder et al., 2012). Further examples could be presented, such as policies and programmes focusing on particular groups (e.g. children from migrant backgrounds) or on specific school levels and types (e.g. the depreciation of *Hauptschule* in Germany or vocational schools in the Netherlands) and the effects they produce for these groups in terms of access to further education and training. Thus, access to education is an issue which also concerns (welfare) policies broadly defined, raising questions of the equality of opportunities, coverage and flexibility (especially to cover multi-problematic cases, and cases not belonging to 'standard' mainstream welfare user categories). From this point of view, the issue of access is related to institutional *responsiveness* (capacity to read, meet and answer potential clients' needs) and *effectiveness* (capacity to achieve goals, taking up potential clients), and points to the principle of *universality* (limiting distortion due to implicit or explicit, intended or unintended, discriminatory profiling of potential clients).

A second important aspect in the institutional dimension may be seen at the *meso or organizational level*. Here the focus lies on the 'logics', 'structures' and 'operations' of educational institutions and how their decision-making processes affect different groups and regulate access to education. In this line of research, the concept of 'institutional racism' or 'institutional discrimination' has been recently borrowed from the debates over the Civil Rights movement in Northern America, according to which institutional discrimination does not derive from 'individual or group prejudice' (Gomolla, 2006: 47), but rather results from how 'organizational structures' and 'institutional logics' (procedures, routines, teaching practices, etc.) (Diefenbach, 2007) operate in schools and other basic institutions (see also Feagin and Feagin, 1986; Troyna and Williams, 1986). Institutional discrimination originates less from discriminatory single actions than from organizational features inherent to the system, which are mostly indirect and cumulative, deriving from the different institutions such as education, health, legislation, economy. This is why it is so pervasive in the professional culture of educational institutions and staff and why 'it is hardly recognized by individual professionals or even by the persons it disadvantages' (Gomolla, 2006: 48).

In this respect, it is also important to note that while direct or open discrimination exerts its effects in the differential treatment of formally equal individuals, institutional discrimination often emerges when all individuals are treated *equally* despite their uneven or unequal prerequisites, for instance when specific prerequisites such as supporting the children's homework by using 'basis knowledge' of the dominant society are taken for granted and other sources of knowledge are not taken into account. The usefulness of this analytical perspective emerged in research on the silent exclusion of children from migrant backgrounds in Germany. Gomolla and Radtke (2009) found mechanisms of 'institutional discrimination' that came about through the internal 'logics and pragmatics' of the *school as organization*. The school, according to the authors, reproduces educational inequality by utilizing pre-ascribed individual/collective attributes of the students and their families (the 'collective feature of national culture/language') (Gomolla and Radtke, 2009: 275). These serve as explanation and justification of institutional decisions regarding transitions/tracking from primary school to the different school types or tracks or to special needs schools. In addition, research on the transition from primary to secondary schools in Germany showed that the degree of continuity of a recommendation for a particular secondary school from a student's primary school teacher had a significant effect on the parents' decision about the actual transition of students (Gresch et al., 2010). Classroom composition can also influence a student's transition from primary to secondary school; both the composition according to achievement levels (reference group effect) and socio-economic differences can exert influence on the transition to one of the secondary school tracks available over another (Trautwein and Baeriswyl, 2007). Moreover, teaching arrangements may have different impacts on performance outcomes for boys and girls.

From interviews with parents, GOETE yielded some insights into their experiences with the institutions. In lower secondary schools, it is common for parents to find themselves in a double bind: on the one hand, parents are addressed as those responsible for the education of their children; on the other hand they are often regarded by teachers as incompetent concerning exactly this task. The missing recognition of their educational efforts has been reported by parents in all country cases (with the exception of Finland). This is experienced by them as institutional discrimination, where ascriptions to social origin, social status (living on benefits or not) and ethnicity intersect (see Kosar Altinyelken et al. and Ule et al. in this volume).

The discourses and representation perspective

In terms of the dimension of discourses and representation, we consider the issue of access to education as social phenomena influenced by dynamic power relations, which are expressed by practices of naming and representing. Against this background, we assume (inequality of) access to be shaped by different discourses – political, academic, 'scientific', professional, etc. – and therefore we included these discursive and representational aspects in our analysis. As there is not a unified concept of discourse,[3] we define it according to Fairclough (1992) as the set of meanings, rules and practices manifest in language use that orient the social construction of our political and social relations and institutions as well as cultural identities, which has practical consequences for the social world. Fairclough's notion of discourse, which does not disregard powerful social orders,[4] is of particular importance in the context of the GOETE research because it has inspired a wide range of theoretical and methodological considerations. Common to all of the varieties of what is known under the umbrellas of critical discourse studies and discourse analysis is a deliberate examination of the distinctions underlying specific discourses (see also Walther et al. and Dale et al. in this volume).

Thus, discourses on early school leaving, lifelong learning, key competences, accountability and excellence, among others, have an influence on the issues of access to education. All these powerful discourses are relevant for a better understanding of differently attributed relevance of education, for access problems as well as for support and coping with difficulties regarding specific groups. Through discourses, particular norms and values are 'normalized' and institutionalized, and consequently impact on the definition of a 'normal' life course and educational trajectory, on the relevance and usefulness of education, and on the criteria for identifying individuals who are considered as in need of support. Discourses affect the social representation of particular groups, thus influencing how individuals position themselves subjectively. They may be viewed as part and parcel of how educational trajectories are governed, and thus affect issues other than access. Furthermore, the positioning towards discourses may be examined to reflect certain interests and aims. In this regard, the representation and organization of different groups is also important, e.g. the question as to who has a voice in local school spaces, whether students and parents have an influence on school development, etc.

Research departing from this perspective provides fruitful insights into how particular groups are discursively constructed; for instance, the question of whether some students *have* special needs or *are in need* of special support to cope with school requirements has important implications for the issues of access. The question of 'how the meaning of students in need of special support is articulated' in Swedish schools has been discussed by Isaksson (2011: 115). According to this author, the expression '*having* special support needs' reveals educational attempts to 'correct' or 'normalize' students, while an understanding of students who '*are in need*' of special support would suggest instead that 'difficulties at school are interpreted as a result of the interplay between the individual and the environment' (Isaksson, 2011: 113), thus pointing to the need of a change in pedagogical or teaching arrangements, or to the elimination of barriers within the school or the classroom. Isaksson discusses a policy context in which the meaning of student's difficulties is mainly articulated as individual failures and not related to other aspects such as teaching arrangements or structural/organizational features. This discursive change concerning students' school difficulties is bound to shape the representation of particular students and impact on their access to further levels of education as well as their own subjective positioning.

In several countries, the GOETE research identified a widespread discourse on children and youth from migrant backgrounds (Germany, the Netherlands, Italy, Slovenia and the UK) which is 'ethnicizing' insofar as it very often and quickly points to issues of ethnicity and culture *as explanatory variables* for their failure and/or difficulties in the education and labour systems. Through this process ethnicity is turned into an *essence*. Here, it becomes clear that we need to pay attention to how professionals take over (causal or near causal) explanations from such discourses. In GOETE, we paid attention to such issues, and we will need to deepen our analysis regarding the 'explanatory' function of such discourses within the context of the overburdened working situations of teachers and other professionals within and around schools (see Dale et al., 2012).

In the framework of GOETE case study analysis, some other discourse patterns could be identified. Frequent references to a *discourse on competences* could be identified in the interviews with all groups of professionals (principals, teachers and even social workers) in and around schools. This idea of competence building is stuck in the logic of the individual achievement of relevant social competences and on their capitalization (see Riegel, 2012), and is far from understanding the reproduction of social inequalities in the context of asymmetric power distribution and how the cycle of this reproduction might be broken. This is another form of the 'invisibilization' of the mechanisms of 'doing difference', because this discourse refers to an *individualization*, *personalization* and also *psychologization* of – in our case – transition problems. In this respect a common example mentioned by teachers was 'if motivation is seen as a key element, then unmotivated students are regarded as being disadvantaged'. In this way, systemic risks and organizational inadequacies are transformed into individual risks and failures, which are in turn attributed to the students and their families. One trend which responds to this shift from social and educational responsibility to individual responsibility is the increasing number of private schools, private homework classes and the marketization of education, together with a vigorously developing *discourse of excellence*.

There is at the same time a *generalization* of problems, e.g. with regard to ethnicity. The fact that migrant students show more difficulties in their educational trajectories *quasi* automatically is interpreted in terms of cultural difference and often reduced to language problems. The fact that they are often performing much better in school is simply ignored, and there is only limited consciousness of the issues of institutional discrimination discussed above.

This is linked to practices of *othering*, by which, with Spivak (1985), we mean the hierarchical and generalizing ways of speaking about others, which can turn into a strategy of 'doing difference' (Fenstermaker and West, 1995). Again, ascriptions usually do not come alone: ascriptions regarding the local area frequently *intersect* with stigmatizing ascriptions regarding the low school level (of parents), gender and ethnicity. Such 'othering' legitimates the tracking and sorting out of students and tends to be stronger in the more strictly selective systems, such as Germany with its dual system. This is combined with the phenomenon that firms use the education system to pick out the best students ('creaming off'). The fact that so many social problems are not solved by social policy but have to be handled in schools is one reason why 'othering' could turn out as a (short-cut) problem analysis and coping strategy; an example of this is the tendency of experts, whenever they are asked to explain the effects and problems of selectivity, to stick to the same ideology on which selection is based: that some students are different from others, that some families are 'other' types of family, with completely different habits and value systems, etc. However, the reference to such discourses reproduces the main ideologies of handling societal problems (see du Bois-Reymond et al., 2012).

Complementary to 'othering' is a strong *discourse of normalcy*, i.e. assumptions about normal/average learning attainments and acceptable behaviour, mostly based on an unspoken white middle-class assumption of normalcy. Analytically it is interesting to ask how such discourses respond to current trends on the labour markets, and how individualizing discourses go along with discriminatory practices. Here, we can see the interplay of structural problems, institutional logics and individual agency with their reference to societal discourses. In this context, one could ask why discourses on self-responsibility and individualization seem to be especially strong in the ex-socialist country Slovenia, or if they are simply more noticeable here than in contexts such as the UK, where liberalism has a much stronger tradition (ibid.).

Looking at parents' interviews, especially interviews with migrant parents, one could reconstruct how critical voices are made silent by the powers of integration (Ploesser and Mecheril, 2012; see also Riegel, 2012). This points to the power dimension of social orders which are expressed and reinforced by discursive practices. At the same time, it is important to consider, with Wrana (2011), that people do not simply refer to discourses as a given, but that discourses only exist in the fact and the way of being referred to; and such references always represent a (perhaps minimal) modification of discourses.

The perspective of subjective positioning

On the dimension of individuals' subjective strategies, practices and positioning, access is not seen as a fixed attribute of educational systems but as constantly being processed, constructed and negotiated. This dimension focuses on agency and individual engagement, and also emphasizes 'how' these processes work. The different strategies, practices and positions of individuals involved in these processes are of interest because it is from here that the construction and negotiation processes of access can be studied. Furthermore, the interactions among the different actors involved need attention. Starting from the premise that educational trajectories unfold in institutional contexts and within structural frames, the individuals involved have some scope for agency. Therefore, professionals in the educational system such as teachers or school principals, and representatives of employment agencies and transitional firms, do have some degree of agency regarding the interpretation of their function as gatekeepers. However, the way they interpret this role differs according to different professional self-concepts and to different attitudes towards the educational system, both critical and affirmative, while prioritizing their tasks within the system.[5] There is always a certain scope for discretion – an aspect that is elaborated in more detail by Barberis et al., in this volume.

One important aspect related to this dimension may be termed 'positioning'. It refers to instances where students (or other actors) point to particular discourses to justify their decisions or to express their positions. Discourses become empirically relevant through the practices of positioning. It is important to ask about the functions of these strategies. Jürgen Budde et al. (2008) conducted research on the school playground, which provides interesting insights on how positioning refers to gender scripts and to how masculinities and femininities are reproduced, above all in the informal settings within school life. In addition, the research on students' biographies of Werner Helsper et al. (2008) refers to explanations for success and failure and how the positioning of students, parents and teachers co-constructs these student biographies. In our research, students both referred to an individualizing discourse by blaming their classmates for their lack of success, and showed a high level of sensitivity towards unjust treatment by teachers or institutional representatives (see du Bois-Reymond et al., 2012).

Regarding *Individual/Subjective Strategies and Positioning*, in the interviews with students, parents, teachers, social workers, regional transition experts and school principals, the GOETE case study analysis found many accounts in which people refer either to unjust structures, unjust treatment, pressures within school, uneven and insufficient access to resources, or discriminatory discourses. According to these findings, students seem to have a high sensitivity to the hierarchies that make some educational trajectories less accessible to them than others. They deal with that, and with how supportive the closer social context or professional experts in the field are experienced, in different ways, and this refers to the level of normality in which varying kinds of support could be anticipated in the respective systems.

> I found that amazing … that they went together with us to this place (the information centre of the career guidance) (and) instead of saying 'there you can get some information on your own', they took one day and went together with us to have this appointment, and this person working there explained to us, and students could also ask questions; that they (the teachers) reserved this time extra for us, this I found good. (Germany – Student: 327–9)

Parents, as soon as they address the issue of access problems, feel rejected rather than supported by the educational system and its representatives. There is a general complaint among experts from almost all countries that parents care too little – however, as soon as they engage in the educational trajectories of their own offspring, they may be seen to be 'disturbing' the system while they even experience *discrimination*, e.g. as migrated parents. Parental expectations with regard to the educational trajectory therefore could also be regarded as the result of a complex process of schools discouraging and disregarding parents that may have a negative impact on their expectations.

> I have to have this appointment with her (principal). Permanently she (principal) debases my children, calling them sexually deviant, ascribing something negative to them all the time. Some others – I don't tell the names – they really disrespect others, are sanctioned the very same way. But this is not the education he gets (at home). So I ask myself: why are all these children put into the same waste bag and beaten? This is unfair … My son is accused not being educated. And this I don't allow school to tell me. (Germany – Parent 5: 11)

From the point of view of experts, we found evidence of different professional conceptions among pedagogical professionals. Among these professionals were those who have the explicit task of improving access, either as head teachers in schools, school psychologists, school social workers or as external social workers. These experts partly understood their role as communicators and bridge-builders for young people and educational institutions with their own different area of expertise, for example firms, employment agencies, regional transitions systems, etc. Here we need to critically analyse *how* these professionals regard and fulfil their 'mission'. Taking into account the evidence of selectivity/exclusion effects of support regulations in selective systems this role is not innocent. Professionals often reported having to bring youth 'back to reality', which in most cases meant lowering students' aspirations and 'cooling them out'. Cooling out can take place either through restrictive, harsh and impermeable structures or by the intervention of experts from firms, employment agencies, social workers or career counsellors who give (discouraging) feedback on a student's achievement and advise lower educational tracks, thus making students develop 'realistic views' (see also Walther et al. in this volume).

> We make students reflect on the labour market perspective at national, regional and local level and we try to fight against the most common stereotypes, such as 'I'll do a job that makes me rich', 'I'll be a lawyer because my father is a lawyer'; these are very dangerous parental influences, we try to make them self-critical and well aware about the choice they have to make. (Italy – Teacher 10: 15)

These examples make visible 'that the extent to which cooling out mechanisms are inbuilt institutionally makes a difference from a biographical view, in as much as they imply aspects of alienation and disrespect while informal (family) influences in similar directions can (but need not …) be perceived as care and recognition' (Cuconato et al., 2013: 153; see also Cuconato et al. in this volume).

Accessibility: A Multi-dimensional and Multi-disciplinary Theoretical Approach toward Disadvantage

Against the above criticized perversion of processes and outcomes, of differences and differentiation, our purpose in this chapter has been to focus on the *accessibility of education* by pointing to different analytical levels – structural, institutional, discourse and representation and individual agency. Educational trajectories unfold and are shaped by accessibility as the result of an interplay of these different social levels: subjective experiences of structures within and outside the education system, 'soft' dimensions such as interpretations of institutional regulations by professionals (discretion power), macro-level structures of the education system and discourses on the normalities of a 'successful educational trajectory'. Accessibility is best understood as a dialectical relationship between these levels, while it is at the local level that these issues become effective: thus, it is at the local level that it might be best studied.

Against a perversion of outcomes and processes, of differences and differentiation, this chapter strongly underlines the point that access is not a given difference but results from a process of social differentiation in which structure is not regarded as determining, but as something which constantly challenges and is negotiated by individuals. Its basic consideration on the role of the interaction of structures and individuals (agency) is not only inherited from Giddens (1984), but also from interactionist theory (Fenstermaker and West, 1995), as well as a Foucauldian consideration on how discourse is acting through by individuals. It strongly contradicts an essentialist perspective: education is not accessible per se, but has to be made accessible. In this process, educational policies, educational institutions, but also the individual actors do play a role and have responsibility. Making education accessible is – in the broadest sense of the word – a political process.

Conclusion

This chapter has emphasized the theoretical perspective adopted in the GOETE project – life course and governance. This includes a *multi-dimensional approach towards social disadvantage*, which has been outlined above by distinguishing between the levels of structure, institution, discourse and individual practice, and also by focusing on the complex relationships between these levels. In this regard, we have tried to bring together on the one hand the considerations on *intersectionality* (Winker and Degele, 2011; Riegel, 2012) coming from critical race theory (Crenshaw, 1989), enriched on the other by the newer trends in gender theory, with multilevel analysis. Against this background, GOETE research points to the necessity of including macro-level institutional arrangements (e.g. policies and policy measures and programmes for particular groups) as well as intra-organizational aspects, such as institutional structures, decision-making mechanisms and logics, into the analysis of access and inequality issues in the education system, instead of solely focusing on students and their individual and socio-structural attributes. The qualitative parts of the research were of particular value in our attempt to describe and understand how policies aimed at increasing access impacted different groups differently, and how different ways to regulate access resulted in forms of institutional discrimination – or in terms of conscious strategies against it.

It is quite obvious that such multi-dimensional and multilevel approaches are not to be realized by one single scientific discipline; rather, it needs a *multi-disciplinary approach towards disadvantage, including sociology, social policy, psychology and educational sciences*. Here we suggest going beyond the level of interdisciplinary research, which still sticks to the borders of disciplines, and start to develop the transdisciplinary relevance of concepts and methodological approaches which are relevant to the same extent to educational research as to sociological research, to gender studies as to migration and diversity studies (see Stauber, 2010).

The main concern of GOETE in addressing this issue is to open up ways and means of understanding the fine-grained processes through which access is negotiated in systemically situated interaction. *Access needs to be experienced as a concrete option*. Therefore, the question is how, in which interactions and against the background of which discourses and which structures, accessibility – as the effective possibility of gaining access – is created or hindered.

The provision of access (and its research praxis) must be organized on different levels: it must pay adequate attention to structural and institutional barriers and solutions at the level of policy and programme (within educational organizations); it must consider that the subjectively experienced accessibility of educational pathways on the side of students and their parents is to be regarded as a result of such processes; it must conceive access and accessibility as communicating conduits, which interact through discursive practices and representations as well as individual strategies, practices and positioning. Through this normative implication of equity in terms of accessibility we are able to take up the considerations which Amartya Sen (2001) to has developed for his *capability approach*. While equal *access* does not necessarily consider the unequal prerequisites for getting access to education, and can indeed prolong inequality in and by the educational system, the notion of *accessibility* includes a much more profound critique by addressing mechanisms of doing difference within the ways educational trajectories are governed. This critique points to the responsibilities of the actors involved with regard to the creation of accessibility to education for all young people.

6

Producing Accessibility through Discretionary Practices of Educational Professionals

Eduardo Barberis
University Carlo Bo of Urbino

Izabela Buchowicz
Warsaw School of Economics

Nicola De Luigi
University of Bologna

Introduction

This chapter aims to provide evidence of micro-level relational processes of negotiation over individual educational trajectories, showing how they influence accessibility of education. The interaction of educational professionals and students in seeking help, and in advice support networks, will be studied and placed within structural constraints and opportunities given by national and local institutions.

In particular, we will focus on the balance between formal and informal support within local educational contexts. To disentangle how individual actions are framed within institutions, we will then focus on the role that educational professionals (teachers, counsellors, youth workers, school psychologists and the like) play as key actors coping with formal and informal expectations, following or breaking the rules according to their interests, needs and values in their interactions with colleagues, families and students. In this respect, with reference to the literature on street-level bureaucracy (Lipsky, 2010), our hypothesis is that the type and legitimacy of discretionary power used can influence the direction and success of professional practices – as we will show with some exemplary trajectories.

Results of the GOETE project will be used to disentangle such interplay of formal and informal support; discretionary and institutional constraints; results in terms of accessibility of education. This will first be achieved by analysing the institutional context as resulting in GOETE students' and principals' surveys, while exemplary trajectories will be derived from local case study interviews with parents, teachers, students and experts.

In particular, our quantitative analysis will focus on national, sub-national and individual-level variations in formal and informal support as a way of structuring spaces of discretion. Then, qualitative accounts of case stories will show potential effects of configurations of support and discretion on disadvantaged students: Who is supported and who is not? Which mandate do educational professionals think they have in supporting students? Which kind of discretionary power is used, and what is the goal of such an effort? How consistent is this with institutional mandates? What are the intended and unintended consequences of such discretionary support (or lack thereof)?

Students' Formal and Informal Resources in Context

Students encounter challenges and problems during their daily lives and educational experiences. These challenges and problems increase during early adolescence – the age group our research focuses on – a period characterized by profound changes involving mind, body, emotions and social relationships (Feldman and Elliott, 1990; Compas et al., 1995). Access to supportive relationships influences the way youths handle stressful situations depending on academic demands, environmental shifts (e.g. school transitions), learning and/or relational difficulties and changes in the nature and significance of familial relationships (Cauce et al., 1994).

Relevant literature abounds on children and adolescents seeking help and advice from individuals in their social support networks (Demaray and Malecki, 2002; Bokhorst et al., 2010). It has provided important information about the features and functions of help-seeking behaviours and orientations, yet several issues remain open. For example, there has been more attention to the quantity of available support (e.g. the number of individuals students can rely on) than on the interactions between different sources of support and the nature of the problems addressed (Cauce et al., 1994; Wills and Shinar, 2000).

Actually, individuals resort to different support systems according to the nature of their relationships with potential support providers, as it could be important to distinguish between them, especially during adolescence, when relationships are more frequently redefined and renegotiated. Moreover, research has not paid enough attention to analysing which individual characteristics and surrounding circumstances contribute to differentiating those seeking help from informal resources from those seeking help from both informal and formal resources, and if the two kinds of resources are mutually exclusive (Caplan, 1974; Cauce and Srebnik, 1991).

Thus, this section focuses on students in lower secondary education (or primary education in those educational systems where no lower secondary education is available), their help-seeking orientations and the resources they would turn to should they experience personal and academic problems.[1] The aim is to provide a description of the patterns of students' preferences for seeking help in order to frame contexts of interaction between relevant actors in the school system. Two major issues are addressed.

First, we focus on the type of resources students perceive as available, considering the rate reached by each type of potential resource. Second, we pay attention to the balance between various support providers and their combinations in students' perceived social support networks. In particular, we will analyse students' help-seeking patterns between informal support providers – such as family members (parents, siblings and other members of their household or family at large) and friends – and formal ones, such as teachers, counsellors, school social workers or psychologists, who provide support as part of their jobs as a structured activity based on professional and/or institutional mandates, utilizing professional resources. We also account for help-seeking variations in the balance between informal and formal resources according to some students' characteristics and territorial dimensions and how this may be related to institutional arrangements.

In the literature, some patterns of help-seeking preferences are generally acknowledged. A growing body of empirical studies has shown that children and adolescents tend not to seek help from professional sources, preferring to turn to their family members and friends (Boldero and Fallon, 1995). Indeed, despite the stereotype of conflicting relationships between adolescents and their parents, the latter remain a leading source of help, while friends become a fundamental emotional support that students start to engage more and more from early adolescence onwards.

In this perspective, teachers are fundamental in help relationships *within* institutional contexts; a resource labelled as informal in some research and formal in others, teachers often serve as secondary attachment figures, helping to satisfy children's needs in terms of encouragement, assistance and information. However, as some studies have pointed out, during adolescence, support from friends increases remarkably, whereas support from teachers decreases and support from parents remains stable, although parent–child relationships are seen by adolescents as less supportive and more conflicting (Cauce et al., 1990; Furman and Buhrmester, 1992; Arnett, 1999).

On the other hand, research on children's and adolescents' access to formal support services and professionals has underlined several barriers. The most common is the lack of knowledge about existing services within the school and the community and the concern about confidentiality, followed by fear about what services would do (Dubow et al., 1990; Sheffield et al., 2004). Furthermore, for those in disadvantaged situations, seeking help is often perceived as indicative of the inability to cope autonomously and considered proof of personal weakness. Therefore, it is more likely that working-class parents and families from migration backgrounds, for example, do not encourage their children to seek help from professionals, especially if they had previous negative help-seeking experiences, maintaining that they are able to manage problems on their own (Lareau, 2000; Deane and Todd, 1996). Thus, students from working-class or migration backgrounds struggle to achieve familiarity with school staff and professionals. They are unequally equipped to interact with institutions, and these interactions will contribute to inequalities in accessing formal support services.[2]

The service gap, that is, 'the gap created when those who need help do not receive it' (Raviv et al., 2000: 721), could be a result of the organization of children's help services, which is in turn related to the characteristics both of welfare and educational systems. However, we should not think of these systems just as macro, national frames of reference; they may affect more closely supportive interactions through the coordination, autonomy and institutionally tolerated (and promoted) degree of differentiation and discretion that opens up a wide scope for local administrations and schools to achieve an effective accessibility (especially for disadvantaged groups), also incorporating informal support resources in local networks (Kazepov, 2010; Sheard and Avis, 2011; Barberis and Loncle, 2015).

To investigate their support network, students were asked in the survey to whom they would most likely turn in case of problems with life in general and with their school experiences. They were provided a list of potential people and instruments and were asked to indicate which they perceived as a potential source of support. Figure 6.1 presents the share for single sources of support, rated separately by kind of problem. Expectedly, regarding problems with life in general, friends are the main source to whom students turn (87.5 per cent), followed at a short distance by mothers (80.3 per cent). Many respondents also indicated other family members, such as fathers (60.7 per cent) and siblings (51.0 per cent). Teacher is the most important figure among institutional help providers, indicated by one student out of five, while psychologists, school counsellors and social workers are located at the lower end of the scale.

The ranking of the sources students turn to in case of school problems is slightly different: at the top are mothers, while friends are second. The most important difference concerns teachers, positioned at the third place, even though other family members maintain a notable position. Similarly to problems with life in general, psychologists, school counsellors and social workers are positioned at the lower end of the scale.

Figure 6.1 shows also that mothers' and fathers' profiles of support are flat, while the profiles of friends, teachers, siblings and other family members appear quite irregular and varied according to the nature of their concerns. Most respondents perceive a relatively high degree of support from their teachers only for school problems, as shown also by previous investigations (Dubow et al., 1990; Cauce et al., 1994).

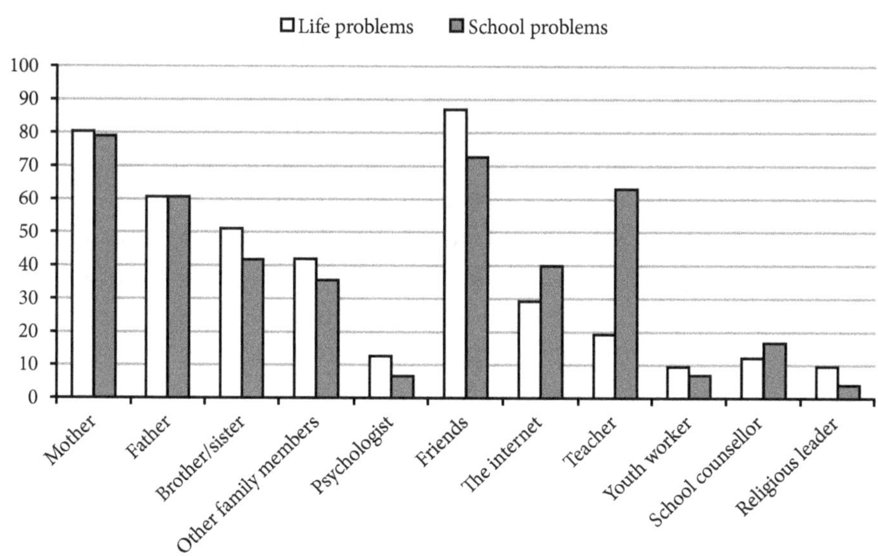

Figure 6.1 Seeking advice on life and school problems. Students who answered 'yes' for each source, in percentage points

If we focus on the structure and composition of students' perceived support network, only a few students did not indicate any source of support. One student out of three picked three sources, and three out of five did not exceed five. So, what are the most common arrangements in students' support networks, and which combinations of informal and formal support occur?

Among students picking just two sources in their support networks, the most usual choice combined mothers and friends for life problems, and mothers and fathers for school problems. This picture does not change much when three support persons are picked: mothers, fathers and friends is the prevalent arrangement.

Only when four sources of support are included does the most likely configuration to cope with school problems also include teachers. On the other hand, to find a sizeable presence of teachers in the support network for life problems, it is necessary to have a support network with five options.

Finally, access to other educational professionals (such as school counsellors or social workers) is widely indicated when the support network for school-related problems amounts to six units or more. To sum up, the probability to experience a balanced network of informal and formal potential support providers is higher when school problems are taken into account and increases along with the growth of the number of members.

For this reason, now the analysis will be focused only on students' help-seeking orientations for school problems. In particular, a specific question will be addressed: how do students seeking help from informal support only differ from those seeking help from both informal and formal support providers? In order to answer this question, a synthetic index has been made, grouping together possible combinations of different resources students turn to, according to the crucial distinction between formal and informal ones.

Overall, about one student out of four declares that social support is available from informal resources only, and about two out of three consider both informal and formal. About 5 per cent of the student interviewees do not fit into these two categories: 3 per cent do not indicate any kind of resources, and 2 per cent seek help from professionals and formal services only.[3]

As shown in Table 6.1, males are more likely than females to be seeking help from informal resources only. Generally, research explains this difference by referring to gendered behaviour and pointing out that women feel more comfortable in seeking help for their problems because help-seeking behaviour is considered to be consistent with traditionally feminine gender roles (Nadler, 1997; Johnson, 2001). So, we can suppose that also in our case male students may consider seeking help from informal resources as less threatening to their gender identity.

The association between students' help-seeking orientations and parents' educational levels is not linear but is quite telling nonetheless. Students living with parents with low educational levels are more oriented to informal resources only as opposed to students whose parents have upper secondary and tertiary educational levels. Probably, increases in parents' educational levels enhance students' levels of awareness, not only about the availability of formal resources in the school context, but also about the way to reach them and the kind of help provided. On the other hand, the (slight) difference between the two groups with more educated parents may be related to the strength of informal resources: students whose parents have a higher educational level can find proficient help in their informal network.

Now, to better frame our context, we have to consider also the territorial dimension: there is a significant difference in students' help-seeking orientations by country. Among the countries involved in the GOETE project, German cases have the highest share of interviewed students (44.4 per cent) who believe that social support is available from informal resources only, followed by Italian (37.1 per cent) and Polish cases (35.3 per cent). French and Finnish cases are positioned in an intermediate level (with 30.4 per cent and 26.1 per cent, respectively), whereas the UK, Dutch and Slovenian interviewees show the lowest percentage, around 15 per cent each.

Obviously, networks mixing informal and formal resources are the other way around: cases that amount to the highest levels are in Slovenia, the UK and the Netherlands (82.5 per cent, 79.9 per cent and 79.8 per cent, respectively), whereas German, Polish and Italian cases have lower rates: between 49.0 per cent (Germany) and 60.3 per cent (Italy).

Table 6.1 Students' help-seeking orientations by sex and parents' educational level (highest ISCED of either mother or father), in percentages

	Informal resources only	**Informal and formal resources**
Sex (N=6,309)		
Male	29.5	64.0
Female	25.3	72.0
Parents' educational level (N=4,460)		
No qualif. or lower secondary education	30.2	63.9
Upper secondary education	23.9	72.1
Tertiary education	26.6	70.2

These differences are not sufficiently explained by common modelling of welfare and educational systems, at least as measured by the well-known categorizations of Esping-Andersen (1990) and Allmendinger (1989), respectively. Other factors, e.g. parenting styles, family structures, relations and specific configurations of childhood services, may play a role that is not easy to disentangle here with available data.

However, there is another level of variation that is quite telling in our analytical frame: the variation between cases within national contexts. Figure 6.2 shows the variation (in percentage points) between the average national rate and the rate of the three cities analysed in each country, and shows that student help-seeking orientations can be very different within each country.

We are aware that we must not overstate the conclusions from these results: some differences are expected as part of the research design, aimed at choosing exactly cases portraying a plurality of intra-national differences. Nevertheless, this figure shows that the space for local networks, the configuration of place-specific coping strategies and the role played by specific support actors is highly variable even in the same regulation context, which allows formal (e.g. through local and/or school autonomy and decentralization processes) and informal (e.g. through different concentrations of socio-economic inequalities) degrees of variation. This also opens up different spaces for discretion, and we can have again an example from our students' survey and from the very same question on support sources. In this case, we will focus only on the role of formal sources of support.

Actually, network structures are influenced by nation- and place-specific factors in that they are tied to state regulations on available professionals, but also to regional and local regulations and practices. We can see this by analysing the intra-national coefficient of variation (CV), defined as the ratio of the standard deviation (σ) to the mean of the distribution (μ_x), for formal support providers.

In addition to the facts that available helping professionals work within institutional constraints that build up support paths for students (e.g. psychologists are mentioned mainly in Finnish, Polish, Slovenian and French cases; youth workers in Finnish and UK cases; social workers in cities in Slovenia, Poland, Germany and Finland), and that teachers (as mentioned above) are the most important institutional resource, the geography of support is quite variable.

On the one hand, we have a common level of CV at the individual level among countries and items, with a value around 0.25. This is true for psychologists, youth workers, counsellors and social workers. On the other hand, the

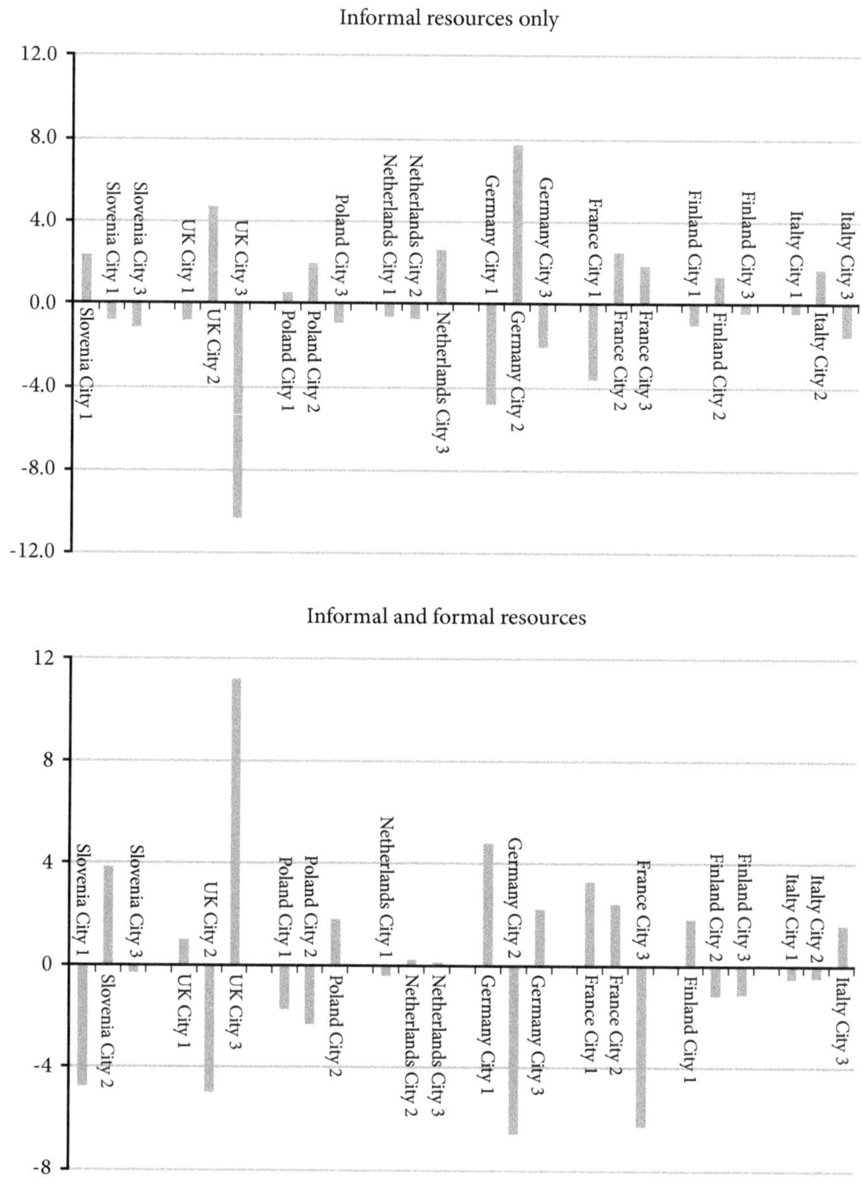

Figure 6.2 Differences in students' help-seeking orientations between average national rate and the rate of the three cities analysed in each country, in percentage points

CV that varies much more (around 0.37) is the role of teachers in coping with school problems: students perceive this resource very differently, and their confidence in seeking advice from teachers is highly segmented. So, we can suppose that their professional discretion (given also their key role: starting from the elementary fact that they spend much more time with students than any other professional mentioned above) is wider than that of other professionals involved.

This may also be in relation to the increased and redefined tasks 'assigned to teachers as a result of growing school autonomy and, more broadly speaking, decentralization' (Eurydice, 2008: 9): local partnerships and place-specific practices may have differentiated locally the experience of being a teacher and the responsibilities attached to the professional role as such.

In conclusion, some patterns emerged in students' help-seeking orientation, though this varies according to local circumstances, that may open up leeway for professional discretion. In the next paragraphs, we will contextualize the role that educational professionals can have at the micro level as makers of accessibility; then we will analyse what this means in interaction with some disadvantaged students, using information from qualitative case studies, i.e. interviews with students, parents, teachers and other relevant actors in school-centred professional networks.

The Steering Role of Educational Professionals

Teachers and other professionals can play quite a role in the lives of young people, as the role accorded to them in support networks mentioned above shows. In particular, they can have an influence in students' educational trajectories, thus playing a meaningful role in young people's future life courses through the opening up or the closing down of accessibility chances.

This role is influenced by institutional structures and regulations, defining the responsibilities teachers, counsellors and social workers have toward their students, according to the legislators and their institutional mandates. Regulations can frame the situation but cannot directly answer the variety of cases and potential solutions and consequences educational professionals have to take into account.

So, there is much room for their discretionary power: a constitutive part of educational jobs, which cannot be fully routinized (Maynard-Moody et al., 1990; Lipsky, 2010). Even if, and when, stricter rules are enforced to reduce their autonomy, this does not necessarily turn into a diminished discretion because the more a sphere is regulated, the more interpretation is needed: Lipsky himself maintains that 'street-level bureaucrats will also use existing regulations and administrative provision to circumvent reforms which limit their discretion'

(2010: 21). Also, discretion per se is neither positive nor negative: according to its use in context, it can have beneficial or detrimental effects (Goodin, 1986; Meier and Bothe, 2001; Evans and Harris, 2004). In our case (the interaction between students and educational professionals), we observed a varying impact of formal support on educational trajectories and accessibility: sometimes it was positive, with an effective motivational and supportive role; sometimes the impact was negative, discouraging and disempowering students in critical situations.

We suppose that actual outcomes are related to the intersection between top-down directives, their interpretation in local arenas, professional cultures and skills, individual standpoints, available resources, workplace conditions, practices and leadership (Spillane et al., 2009). So, when looking at educational practice at the micro level, it is important to frame it into meso and macro dimensions, too.

This also means that discretion is not necessarily illegitimate because there are different ways in which the interplay between bureaucrats and their institutions can be framed. Thus, we will observe the interaction between different individual practices, school cultures and educational principles in order to assess how they are related to specific uses of discretion. According to relevant literature (Galligan, 1990; Hill and Ham, 1993; Boote, 2006; Taylor and Kelly, 2006; Sosin, 2010) that takes into account the legitimacy and direction of discretionary decisions, we have identified: (a) discretion within the rule; (b) discretion among the rules; (c) discretion beyond the rule; and (d) discretion against the rule. Briefly, (a) is the case in which the rule foresees room for a street-level bureaucrat's autonomy and legitimates it; (b) is the case when (educational) professionals pick an option among various ones that are equally legitimate;[4] (c) is the case when cases are not targeted in any institutional norm and professionals have to piece together general principles and their own values, thus creating a rule and thus with a more blurred legitimacy; and finally (d) is the case when a professional actively violates a regulation that is considered to contrast with personal or professional values, interests and mandates. Clearly, this is the case where legitimacy is lower, even though a consensus can be created in a community of practice.

The role of educational professionals, and also their discretionary power, may have a specific impact on disadvantaged students: the analysis in the section on *students' formal and informal resources in context* showed their potential lack of linking social capital to interact with institutional players and a resort to informal support that is likely to be affected by similar lack of linking social capital. This means that some students, e.g. because of their social class and cultural background, may experience a limited accessibility to educational opportunities, notwithstanding that formal access is granted: the role of professional practices in limiting or expanding opportunities can be relevant in overturning a discouraging institutional frame or reinforcing it.

Besides professionals' individual skills and values, the chance to apply effectively spaces of discretion can be linked to constraining factors, e.g. the number of at-risk cases to be handled and the time and resources to do it. Professional motivation and commitment to 'invest' in cases that require non-routine answers cannot be considered independent variables tied to individual characteristics: they are constructed within the educational system, and involve selection, training and support of individual work as much as the creation of solid professional communities.

For example, the GOETE principals' survey shows different national (and sometimes local) leanings toward the support of specific disadvantages (e.g. the availability of remedial education and the attention toward special educational needs) and the prioritization of inequalities in education (Aro et al., 2012); in countries such as Slovenia and the Netherlands, for example, principals do maintain less than in other countries that students with difficulties should be supported, while more attention is given to 'gifted' students; also, from their point of view, factors negatively influencing school success vary. Ethnic background is mentioned more than the average by German and Italian principals, and social class by UK, Slovenian and French principals. At the micro level, these general approaches toward diversity become dilemmas for action: how is it possible and how much is it viable to support disadvantaged students in an efficient and effective way, avoiding stigmatization or discrimination?

To sum up, educational professionals can serve as gatekeepers for the access to further educational opportunities through their discretionary power, either grounded in rational decisions or in value-related (if not emotional) selection criteria, including personal theories of justice and fairness (Musheno, 1986; Kelly, 1994; Parding, 2007).

We suggest that this gatekeeping can produce both success and risks: on the one hand, rules may be made flexible and adaptable to individual cases; on the other hand, discrimination may arise as an unexpected outcome of individual understandings of fairness that possibly 'school teachers are not always able to orchestrate' (Kelly, 1994: 138).

Complex Interactions: Discretion and Accessibility between Structure and Agency

We will analyse here four case trajectories that have explicitly different links between individual agency, institutional constraints and professional discretion. These cases have been based on qualitative local case studies, with interviews with students, parents, educational professionals and experts that focus on the relational dimension of transition processes. Among twenty-four case studies and 195 interviews that we administered in eight countries, we chose four exemplary stories (resulting from nine interviews) that better exemplify the link between discretion and accessibility. For this reason, they should not be regarded as typical or representative of national contexts, even though they concern focal points in the operations of educational systems: these cases can be considered as 'outliers' at the margins of mainstream procedures, but they constitute challenges to the daily operations of the school systems, thus allowing for a reflection on educational professionals' discretionary agency.

Case studies

Case 1. Including by excluding: School 'godsons' and Marco

Marco is a sixteen-year-old boy living in Italy.[5] As a member of the school staff put it, he is one of the school 'godsons': semi-literate ex-students who have failed repeatedly and have dropped out to work, often in tiring jobs (e.g. night working hours). They are officially dropouts and are not expected to be found on school premises, but the school allowed them to get their lower secondary leaving qualification, as *privatista*.[6] Marco cannot attend regular classes, and he is not yet entitled to adult education.

Considered deserving, the school provides him with dedicated support and flexible lessons using free hours in teachers' schedules. This arrangement adopted informal strategies to achieve the desired goal: Marco is formally dropped out, so he is allowed to pass two school years in one, completing the proper final exams. Thus, paradoxically the school excludes him from regular education in order to better include him with an individualized path. Such an informal arrangement is given some sort of recognition by means of a written agreement between Marco and the school: it has no official status, but it is considered helpful to commit him.

In this case, we see that rules on school careers and dropouts, perceived as too rigid by the school staff, have been worked around via discretionary practices. A 'recovery' strategy is agreed upon and considered consistent with a 'true' mandate – i.e. helping the disadvantaged through an individualized path. The final outcome is an opening of access opportunities for some disadvantaged students like Marco.

With regard to the principles of the Italian educational system, this practice makes use of discretion beyond the rule because the school cannot find and use legitimate policy instruments to cope with Marco's case and 'invents' a solution. It also amounts to a discretion against the law because it bypasses rules on school attendance and dropouts.

Such use of discretion has limited legitimacy. Low institutionalization is paired with a high, active involvement of all the staff, with some sort of formalization of the agreement with the student, but also with a high emotional investment (as the definition of 'godson' somehow shows), with the risk that a bad school performance can be read as a 'betrayal' of a personal commitment.

Doubts can be raised on access criteria to discretionary support: the number of deserving dropout students is limited and their selection implicit as part of the opacity that such discretionary power can imply.

Case 2. Lost in the (computerized) machinery: Lila's difficult path

Lila lives in France and is a sixteen-year-old, mid-to-low achieving student from a large family, with an unemployed, young mother. Her post-*troisième* transition[7] has been problematic: she had no idea of her future school track, and the time to decide came without any effective guidance.

She could not talk with the guidance counsellor because she was available for an inadequate time in her school. This added to her apathy in making an appointment, bolstered by the difficulty in dealing with the institutions involved (for example, she hardly understood the different mandates of teachers and counsellors) and in coping with their mixed feelings about her future.

So, Lila made her decision with her mother only, choosing two distant options: photographer as her first choice and dental technician as her second. However, both of her choices were refused by the competent administration via the computerized system for vocational recommendations that allocates students matching requests, school results and available places.

However, she received this information very late (in mid-August) because the competent administration was not able to contact her. Only at this point did Lila discover that her choices had a poor chance of being accepted from the beginning because the tracks she requested were very popular and her school results were not good enough. At such a late stage and in a very short time, she had to choose a new future: to go to one of the few, unattractive places left or to repeat a year. In the end, she opted for a secretary course quite close to home.

In this case, we can see a lack of discretion that hinders accessibility or (more likely) a defensive use of discretion. First, there is a failure in the counselling process that did not point out the risks associated with her choices. While the counsellor was not involved and the school supervisor just shook her head, Lila's choice was approved and registered without any word from the class council. Lila has the impression that everyone but her and her mother knew she was going to crash into a wall, which also affects her trust in the system. She was deemed responsible and somehow blamed for her choice because the school professionals assumed that she should have known what to expect.

On the other hand, the depersonalization of controls through information technologies allows a further defensive strategy: blaming the software. However, it is just a step of a process that should involve students and families for two trimesters with the further possibility to appeal in case of persisting disagreement with the school staff.

Staff members have room for discretion that is used selectively. In the case of Lila, we can suppose that the diversion strategy she underwent was a defence against overworking. At the local level, the number of counselling professionals seemed inadequate for actual guidance needs, which may have resulted in the overburdening of counsellors. The shifting of responsibility in order to limit blame could be seen as a protection in an uncomfortable position.

However, this can be a hard hit on students and families with poor resources. Lila and her mother seemed quite unaware of the workings of the system; in fact, they did not even know that a scoring system was in place.

So, Lila bumped into every single bar of the bureaucratic cage, but this cannot be seen as a matter of luck. Rather, it is a risk affecting disadvantaged families who have a poorer understanding of the educational system. It is no surprise that Lila-like situations happen every year. In Aro et al. (2012), French principals are keener to consider 'the lack of places in the next educational level in the neighbourhood' as a factor negatively affecting transitions,[8] and a supervisor in Lila's school points out:

> Every year there are students coming out of the system with no destination . . . There are the students applying for vocational schools, where there's a case selection. They can have the place or not. In early July, we have the results of this assignment. There are maybe some fifteen students left in unclear positions,

> whether in a waiting list or not selected at all. Then, there's a readjustment board. In early July, we have vacancies in vocational schools, so we place two or three students, and the same happens in September. Later, for those left, we suggest repeating the last class, or – if they already did – we have vocational training tools. At the end, maybe there are the last two or three left. For them there's the employment agency.

We can consider this discretion in closing the door as a peculiar discretion within the rule that turns into an outcome beyond or against the rule. In a sort of 'work-to-rule' approach, relevant educational professionals apply the minimum standard regulations in a ritually bureaucratic way, limiting their personal involvement. Every actor involved seems able to justify his/her behaviour as legitimate, though this undermines the institutional mandate.

Case 3. A contested guidance: Henna's case

Henna's experience in the Finnish school system concerns the same issue but different procedures in a different national context, which our research in general proved to be quite rich in institutional support. However, 'discretion at the margins' of the system can happen everywhere. Henna is a low achiever who in primary school obtained additional lessons that were no longer offered at a later stage. This added up to problems in subjects where, according to her, some teachers used ineffective methods. Henna was granted additional classes but on a very small scale and with students from lower classes (which made it less useful for her).

When the transition to upper secondary school came closer, Henna turned to the vocational counsellor to ask for his help in gathering information about schools with a musical profile that she was interested in. However, the counsellor pointed out that her grades were not good enough. Henna was disappointed and felt that she could not count on his support, so she looked for information with her mother and found a couple of schools that seemed suitable that she opted for.

While Henna's lower secondary school did not organize visits to those particular schools, the counsellor helped her to join a visit with students from another school. However, at a later stage he did not tell her that entry exams to both schools that she was interested in were on the same day. As a consequence, Henna took only one, but she was not accepted. She regrets that the other school had lower thresholds, and she could have had a chance if only she was able to take that exam as well.

So, Henna had to return to the counsellor, and she was again disappointed as he suggested a vocational school while Henna preferred a general one. She followed the counsellor's advice reluctantly and applied to a school with a low admittance threshold in a town nearby; she was accepted. However, she did not feel comfortable, and, after only a week, she decided to move to another school (a general one) where she managed to find a place. Currently, Henna is satisfied with her school, although she is weak in some subjects.

Henna's case shows in another way how the same problem as Lila (the gap between individual expectations, guidance support and selectivity procedures) can be shaped. The scope of support provided is insufficient, and apparently small organizational decisions cumulate to make her transition harder.

The counsellor cools out Henna's expectations again and again and limits support to her only once she 'deviates' from the expected path. We see here a defensive use of discretion that can affect those with special guidance needs: a counsellor under pressure, responsible for many students, sees students like Henna as introducing 'dangerous' entropy into the system, so he/she answers by 'working-to-rule'. In the Finnish case, the problem seems magnified by the isolated work of different professionals, with teachers not contributing much to transition processes and by a systematic difficulty in placing students. Also, in this case, the GOETE institutional survey shows that Finnish principals are more worried by negative effects for transitions due to 'difficulties in obtaining a place of study'.[9]

Case 4. A long-term effect of supporting measures: Joanna's path toward educational professions

The fourth case moves the focus from actual student–professional relations to in-work motivation, practices and role modelling effects. Joanna is an educator working in a community day-care service in Poland and at the same time a former student of one of the case study schools. She comes from a troubled family with a deprived socio-economic background.

When she was a lower secondary student, her principal maintained that she was an eager student, despite a disadvantaged environment. So, she received special remedial education and, at the end of school, she was sent to a community day-care service.

She was able to complete general secondary school, and the educators from the community day-care service recommended that that she should study at a university far from home to increase her assertiveness in an environment distant from her troubled context.

She managed to earn a degree in education and decided to go back to her hometown to help children the same way she was helped: she started to work with the educators in the same service that had been so helpful to her. Currently, she coordinates the work of two offices, works as an educator in a day-care centre and manages a 'youth club' for children aged twelve to seventeen on a voluntary basis.

She is very committed and tries to show children that they are important, reproducing the role modelling practices she enjoyed years before with actions not strictly included in her institutional mandate (showing new options of behaviours and choices, establishing positive experiences in relationships with adults and endowing them with skills such as using computers or writing application letters).

This case shows that discretionary practices do not necessarily come via rational interests – as most of the literature on discretion as power maintains (including Lipsky) – but also from strong motivation and personal involvement. Her personal experience helps her to endure professional difficulties (and to possibly limit burnout that can strongly affect involved professionals).

In the past, teachers helped Joanna in a way for which she is still grateful. Now Joanna helps other children, and her personal experience helps her in her profession, in the understanding of students and their environments. Undertaking individualized actions may lead to long-term effects and investments in human capital that will have multiple profits in the future.

Conclusion

In this chapter, we have placed the role of educational professionals' discretionary power in relation to the need for support expressed by students in lower secondary education, analysing potential consequences that it can have in terms of accessibility. Sometimes new chances become open, making students' educational trajectories smoother; in others cases, students' opportunities were reduced (see Table 6.2). The use of discretionary power was similarly evident in different educational contexts. Even though our case study approach does not allow for 'grand' modelling, our findings show how different systems can be a frame for different needs for and types of discretionary power.

Professional, individual agency counts in implementing daily work, even when control mechanisms based on a 'rational' choice – like the French allocation software in the case of Lila – are set in place. In the educational institutions we analysed, we can identify some macro-institutional frames

Table 6.2 Case trajectories and professional discretion

Case	Country	Transition	Transition problem	Solution	Use of discretion	Type of discretion
Marco	Italy	Completion of ISCED 2	Early school-leaving	Individualized recovery path	Formal dropout, informal care, prioritizing 'deserving' students; proactive; opening up chances	Beyond the rule Against the rule
Lila	France	From ISCED 2 to ISCED 3	School choice and guidance	Late second-best school choice	Limitation of guidance; defensive; closing down chances	Within the rule Beyond the rule
Henna	Finland	From ISCED 2 to ISCED 3	School choice and guidance	Late second-best school choice and school transfer	Limitation of guidance; defensive; closing down chances	Within the rule
Joanna	Poland	From ISCED 2 to ISCED 3, from ISCED 3 to ISCED 5A	Disadvantaged family background and lack of family support	Institutional support	Prioritizing 'deserving' students; proactive; closing down chances	Within the rule

influencing how discretion is deployed. Actually, we can find all the types of discretion in different educational systems, to a different degree: those with an effective rule of the law, clear legitimacy and division of labour among sectors and professions, but also clear coordination tools and higher standardization (Allmendinger, 1989), are more likely to have an effective discretion within the rule; systems with an excess of rigidity in bureaucratization and juridification open spaces to less accountable forms of discretion (e.g. among the rules). Systems with poor institutionalization and low standardization are more likely to see a discretion beyond or against the rule.

However, as we mentioned in the section *the steering role of educational professionals*, because discretion is neither positive nor negative per se, this is still not enough to characterize cases, inasmuch as the same type of discretion can be used either to ease transitions or to bar some paths.

First, the level of professional proactivity: an opening of chances through discretion was available when societal goals were shared but available means were considered inadequate. This elicited the proactivity and personal involvement of school staff. In other cases, the discretion was used in reactive, defensive ways – especially when goals were less clear and the tools available became the only reference of professional work. In this case, the motivation to invest in discretion is less emotional and more strategic.

Second, we see that outcomes of discretion practices can open or close doors beyond the intention of the involved actors: the control over the process is important. When the discretionary practice is embedded in a structure of legitimacy, it is more likely to produce control over unintended consequences. This is clearer for discretion among the rules, but is also evident in an action against the rule that is strongly embedded in a professional community.

Third, discretion is rooted in power positions: even though it is an attribute of social professions at large, not every professional community has the same room for discretion or applies the same mix of types of discretion (Hupe and Hill, 2007). Actors placed in critical junctions of policy actions can more easily define strict professional boundaries and use a defensive discretion: the section on the steering role of educational professionals shows that teachers, who are obviously a key element in education, are the most used formal help but are also the most variable; the section concerning *complex interactions: discretion and accessibility between structure and agency* shows that guidance counsellors that can to a certain degree control access to their office (e.g. through appointments) and gatekeep access to information and educational opportunities, play a key role in two of the four exemplary trajectories we analysed.

Also, elaborations from the section on *students' formal and informal resources in context* show that there is a different use of formal resources according to territorial, gender and social class variables: this is related to the interaction between students' agency (e.g. gender and youth culture, linking social capital) and professional agency in the given social and institutional context. Professional agency is also shaped by a specific form of selectivity, even in the access to opportunities opened through discretionary practices. We should ask who is considered 'deserving' and hence advantaged by such practices. Our case studies show that there are barriers associated with accessing discretionary practices. Discretion by itself implies a definition of targets not based on explicit criteria. Even when we talk about the most legitimate and regulated types of discretion, the use of different solutions for different groups can turn into discriminatory practices (Keiser et al., 2004).

Because professionals enacting a discretionary practice are supposed to have an advantage – instrumental (e.g. reducing workload) or emotional (e.g. being acknowledged as good teachers) – they profile 'deserving' targets that allow an acceptable investment for either instrumental or affective reasons. However, the definition of deserving targets also implies the existence of undeserving ones. This can boost or undermine the equity of the system according to how discretionary practices reinforce or contrast with institutional advantages as far as gender, ethnicity and social class are concerned.

Policymaking in education should take into account discretion: juridification and control mechanisms – as the long record of studies mentioned in the section on *students' formal and informal resources in context* and our fieldwork proved – neither limit it nor are able to use it toward positive outcomes. More effectively, the construction of routine work should make a place for more reflection that is horizontal, peer and networked interaction within communities of practice (Wenger, 1998).

Part 3

Coping with Educational Demands

7

Educational and Vocational Guidance as Support Mechanisms in Schools

Joanna Felczak
Warsaw School of Economics

Ilse Julkunen
University of Helsinki

Introduction

The increasing importance of education in knowledge societies has led to growing pressure on students to achieve and succeed in school. At the same time, the composition of students has become more and more diverse with not only students from different social milieus but increasingly also with migration and ethnic minority backgrounds. Educational inequality does not only result from different access but is also related to different abilities and resources for coping with educational demands. The study Governance of Educational Trajectories in Europe (GOETE) investigated how students, especially those from deprived social backgrounds, actually do cope with educational demands and what support they receive in this regard (see Cuconato et al., in the Introduction to this volume). Evidence of a powerful discourse of individualism was found, putting students under pressure. Students often believe they alone are responsible for success or failure in their educational trajectories. They feel particularly burdened with decision making at transition points, which implies that more and better guidance and counselling are needed (Parreira do Amaral et al., 2013). These are the challenges that produce a situation of heterogeneity and diversity of needs among students in school. The multiple types of support, both learning and subject related, but also psychosocial and above all counselling, are particularly critical with regard to decision making at transition points. A variety of formal and informal support mechanisms have been implemented in schools to enable, assist and encourage young people through the challenges they encounter in school to facilitate a smooth transition. However, little is known on how efficient these support measures and mechanisms are and how they vary in different educational settings.

Rather than analysing efficiency of support, the chapter aims at describing and analysing support mechanisms for students in schools: what measures exist in the different countries and what role can these measures play in coping with school demands, in ensuring an adequate knowledge and skills base? How is career guidance perceived in the different countries and how do they differ when it comes to organization and integration in the curricula? In many cases support includes providing information, not only with regard to the labour market but also with respect to post-compulsory education, but clearly this is not sufficient with regard to the diversity and needs of students. The vast majority of students in contemporary secondary education aim at higher education rather than at direct labour market entry when they formulate their plans for post-compulsory education or training. US research has shown that the college-for-all ideal has weakened the link between students' educational expectations and their educational attainment, setting up a large number of underprepared students to fall out of higher education (Domina et al., 2011a).

The chapter relies on descriptions of the institutional structure of education systems in the eight countries involved, on the analysis of survey data with students, parents and school principals, as well as on a secondary analysis of the case studies involving interviews with students, parents, teachers and counsellors. The collected materials are the result of mixed-method studies conducted simultaneously in all eight countries involved: Finland, France, Germany, Italy, the Netherlands, Poland, Slovenia and the UK. The materials collected have been used for multilevel analyses and enabled comparison of both educational systems and actual realities of work with students (see Cuconato et al. and Walther et al., in this volume).

The chapter starts with discussing the meaning of school-related social support and locating the issue in the relationship between public education and welfare. This includes a discussion on whether and how education systems and welfare states play a role in what support mechanisms prevail. A focus is laid on measures and their role in educational and vocational guidance aimed at supporting students in decision making at transition points and their relevance from a student perspective. The final section discusses whether different constellations of support can be identified, whether these relate to different education systems and/or welfare regimes and what discourses and ideologies of education and support they reflect.

Support Mechanisms in Different Education Systems

'Support' describes different forms of strengthening people to cope with social and mental challenges in a more successful way. This can be done by informal communication among peers, members of families or neighbours, but also by formal support that is offered by professionals within different sectors. Findings show that various sources of support act independently and that young people can benefit from any sources of support (Wang and Eccles, 2012). Social support implies a broad range of methods, including mediation, empowerment and community work and may include material resources. A variety of support mechanisms have been implemented in schools and these vary within, as well as between, different countries. Welfare support in school has hardly been described and systematized in a comparative perspective. The relevance and width of support as perceived from different angles may differ, as may the mechanisms of support, but their role is in one way or another connected to young people's coping with school demands, in ensuring them an adequate knowledge and skills base, in preparing them for the demands in work life, and in preventing social exclusion, early school leaving and youth unemployment. Support relates to the changing societal conditions.

Recent studies (cf. Anthias, 2005; Tolonen, 2013) have opened new avenues for conceptualizing social class in ways that explicate the unequal positions of individuals in the labour market, and differing experiences and understandings of education. Young people aspire to reach at least the social status position of their parents, and therefore the perceived benefits of further educational attainment will vary with family background as well (Heinrich, 2014). It is low-income parents who are most likely to work in stressful, low-quality jobs that feature low pay, little autonomy, inflexible hours and few or no benefits, perhaps resulting in unsatisfactory child care or remaining without supervision. The risk of status demotion motivates investment in prolonged education. On the other hand, an opposite tendency is equally strong – children of lower-educated parents have lower incentives to complete a college degree than children of college educated parents, all else being equal. Socio-economic differences may take effect in choices at obvious transition points such as choosing the vocational high school track or enrolling in higher education (Reisel, 2011).

Another aspect contributing to educational inequalities is rising educational demands. Especially low-income children and their parents are classified as being unprepared for the demands of the twenty-first century. What seems to be crucial is high-quality early childhood education (Rusche and Jason, 2011; Chase-Lansdale and Brooks-Gunn, 2014). By identifying *students*' academic strengths and weaknesses, students are able to see not only how they have grown but also *what their potentials* are. Acknowledging these will be helpful to them in other academic endeavours (Domina et al., 2011b).

Support in school

Support mechanisms can be described as societal and institutional level responses to students' individual difficulties in school. Schools use a variety of strategies, interventions and programmes to increase social support. Many of the formal support services are geared towards educational challenges, but there are also other forms of support, such as school-wide programmes reducing bullying at school, classroom interventions or special support for learning difficulties. There is, however, little evidence of their efficiency; some of these efforts aim at improving school climates or well-being among students, and others are simply promising ideas that are tried out. Teachers and welfare workers in school systems can promote social support by making efforts to connect personally with students and through these interventions help students overcome the challenges in their lives. Often, the lack of economic/cultural resources in the family can make it more difficult for students to cope on their own. Different forms of support may provide important socio-cultural components with regard to mental, cognitive and emotional development of students in their environment in order to strengthen their competencies in coping with the challenges of everyday life (Caplan, 1974; Oerter and Montada, 2008).

From a comparative point of view it is interesting to see what forms of support are offered, which issues are covered and how the formal support is organized in schools in the countries involved. These can be analysed on the basis of how services are organized within or outside school and also with regard to whether they are directly or indirectly related to learning.

Support taking place inside schools and carried out by teachers, nurses, school social workers, school psychologists and other members of staff can be described as formal, as it is structured or planned, is often based on legislation and is carried out by trained professionals. Aro and colleagues (2013) found in their analyses of the GOETE project that generally indirect means of support, such as a school social worker or a school psychologist, were considered almost as important as those that are directly related to learning. The indirect support measures are focused, among other things, on mental and physical health and

Table 7.1 Formal support and services in relation to school

		Location in relation to school	
		Internal	**External**
Relationship to learning	**Direct**	1) Remedial instruction Special education classes Part-time special education Preparatory education for immigrants Homework classes	3) Private tutoring
	Indirect	2) Student welfare team School social worker School nurse School psychologist Use of support pupils	4) Municipal social work Youth work Youth psychiatry Employment service Work experience periods

Source: Aro et al., 2013

general well-being of students. This form of categorization raises issues of how support is organized but also how it connected to learning, even though one might conclude that all support in school is in one way or other related to learning. It remains unclear, however, what the forms of mechanisms are and how coherent and inclusive the support in school is.

Offering educational guidance has long been seen as important when it comes to students at all ages. It was over 100 years ago that definitions were formulated and a distinction was drawn between educational guidance and vocational guidance. Educational guidance relates to all the objectives of education, of which vocation is only one. Educational guidance is therefore more inclusive than vocational guidance (Educational Guidance, 1921). Still, the forms vary and have developed over time and it is of specific interest to study how vocational guidance is organized in the different countries involved and whether it plays a role in how inclusive vocational guidance is. From a comparative perspective, the chapter analyses different types of internal, external or mixed support, their relationships to teaching and the conception of guidance (e.g. labour market oriented, lifelong learning perspective, focus on disadvantaged students), and how it is provided in countries, so as to underline similar and different strategies conducted in the European countries involved in the study.

Support in Form of Career Guidance

There does not seem to be a clear cut definition of career guidance in school. It is more of an emerging concept that is dependent on the changing social conditions surrounding school. The OECD Career Guidance Policy Review defines it as 'services and activities intended to assist individuals, of any age and at any point throughout their lives, to make educational, training and occupational choices and to manage their careers' (OECD, 2004a: 11). Two elements are highlighted. First, it is about organizing, systematizing and providing access to *information* about the labour market and about educational and employment opportunities, when and where people need it. Second, it includes *counselling* in terms of assisting people in reflecting on their aspirations, interests, competencies, personal attributes, qualifications and abilities, and in matching these with available training and employment opportunities. Sultana and Watts (2004) show that the term 'career guidance' is slowly replacing the term 'vocational guidance'. Vocational guidance has focused upon the choice of occupation and has been distinguished from educational guidance focusing upon choices of courses of study. Career guidance brings the two together and stresses the interaction between learning and work. In reality, however, education guidance and employment guidance still coexist, overlap with, complement or even ignore each other.

In the perspective of building a strong European knowledge society as advocated in the Lisbon strategy, career guidance has been placed at the very top of the political agenda in most of the countries. As a main tool for achieving this ambitious goal, career guidance is largely seen as contributing to public policy objectives (OECD, 2004b). International research reveals that there are four fundamental trends in the sphere of guidance (Sultana and Watts, 2004: 36).

1 Fostering self-help: space is arranged equipped with computers and job-related data bases, and providing web based forms that can be filled in, as well as a call service where one can receive simple advice or talk to a person on duty that can analyse the client's situation. Such actions enable devoting more time to those who are in a difficult situation. Such form of counselling involves commitment from the aspect of searching for a job.
2 Differentiation: gradation of access to the service evolving in three stages, from self-service to service for groups (job clubs) and to intensive work with individual cases.

3 Decentralization: provision of guidance at local level which can adjust the actions to the specificity of the region, including local interests. Such actions, however, can deepen the differences and inequalities between the regions.
4 Outsourcing: guidance is delegated to specialized agencies and other entities, often private. Assistance provided by specialized agencies to the socially excluded must be of holistic form and consider various aspects of their lives.

New ways of offering career guidance outside of school are sought, especially those directed at students with special educational needs. Internships and other forms of experiential learning are a valuable learning opportunity and resource for many students, and perhaps even more so for those with special needs. Internships may help bridge the gap for students transitioning from the classroom to career by providing opportunities to gain marketable skills and helping them better understand how their disability may affect their career option. Outside the classroom, however, assisting students with special needs may present new questions and transitional challenges. The category of students with a disability is a complex one and encompasses a wide range of impairments, not necessarily visible but also 'hidden'. Each of those means a particular set of challenges with respect to disclosure, special needs and accommodation (Severance and Starr, 2011). The advantage of these programmes is better preparation for work than in the case of school-held classes.

Support Mechanisms in Career Guidance in Europe

Education and welfare systems as contexts of career guidance

A crucial prerequisite for comparative studies is taking account of the social contexts in which studied phenomena are embedded. In respect of career guidance, key aspects of these contexts are the structures of education systems as well as the way in which welfare services address children and young people while being in school.

In social sciences, comparative studies are frequently conducted on the basis of a comparison of welfare regimes referring to different modalities of access to and levels of social security (cf. Esping-Andersen, 1990). For Europe, Gallie and Paugam (2000) distinguish a universalistic welfare regime in Nordic countries, a liberal regime type in the English-speaking countries, an employment-centred regime in continental Europe and a sub-protective one in Southern Europe. Frequently, such studies leave out education. In the GOETE project, the welfare typology has been combined with Allmendinger's educational typology comparing the standardization and stratification of education systems. Stratification refers to both the differentiation between educational programmes of unequal status and the chances of reaching high levels of academic attainment. Standardization refers to the degree to which the quality and contents of education, such as teacher training, school budgets, curricula and school-leaving examinations, meet the same standards nationwide (Allmendinger, 1989). The resulting model may serve as an analytical framework and a step towards theorizing and generating hypotheses. The eight European countries can be clustered according to the extent to which educational trajectories are structured by hierarchically segmented or comprehensive tracks from primary to the end of lower secondary levels and the degree to which students have access to measures of support (see Table 7.2).

In *high-level standardized and differentiated systems* (France, Germany, the Netherlands) there is a substantial organizational differentiation, a medium to high degree of selectivity and transitions exist which represent a medium to high threshold from one education level to the next. The systems have inherent highly selective 'bottlenecks' and early decision-making points that have the potential to reinforce social and educational inequalities and disadvantage, thus offering less potential for providing effective access and mitigating inequalities. Support mechanisms are available not as a universal offer but addressing students classified as disadvantaged in a compensatory way.

In *high-level standardized and comprehensive* systems (Finland, Slovenia) organizational differentiation and degree of selectivity is low and no transitions in compulsory education exist. Thus the degree to which students are selected and grouped according to individual or group characteristics (e.g. level of achievement, language proficiency, etc.) is substantially lower. This type of system has the most potential for effectively providing access to education and

Table 7.2 Categorization of countries based on Allmendinger's typology

Standardization differentiation	**Low**	**High**
Low	Italy, Poland, UK	Finland, Slovenia
High	–	France, Germany, the Netherlands

Source: Allmendinger, 1989; Parreira do Amaral et al., 2013

mitigating inequalities, also because a diversity of support mechanisms are widely accessible.

In *low-level standardized and differentiated systems* (the UK, Italy and Poland) there is a medium degree of organizational differentiation, a low degree of selectivity and the existing transitions are 'smoother'. This, however, has to be seen in the context of the level of support pupils receive to cope with transitions: all three countries provide only little institutionalized (state) support. Pupils consequently have to count predominantly on the support of the family (often reproducing social inequalities), and they also experience less 'cooling out' processes.

However, the complex and multi-layered issue of educational (and support) systems calls for a methodology that takes into account three different levels: the (micro) level of individuals, the meso level of institutions and professional interactions as well as the macro level of society with regard to both education and welfare (see also Parreira do Amaral et al., 2013: 18).

The data material

One of the central objectives of comparative analyses is to relate findings to larger societal contexts (Dogan and Pelassy, 1990), the main purpose being to discover divergences or commonalities with regard to a phenomenon. Rode (2009) has emphasized that the issue of comparative research is to establish a relation between the phenomena, conditions and processes represented by the country cases. The chapter builds on research undertaken in the framework of the GOETE project that covers the period from transition from lower secondary education to transition into upper secondary education/ vocational education and training (see Cuconato et al., in the Introduction of this volume). Our comparative analysis with regard to career guidance relies on national background documents and expert interviews contributing to a comparison of how teachers are trained with regard to guidance issues (Cramer et al., 2012), a standardized survey with school principals on support mechanisms in their schools (Aro et al., 2012) and on local case studies, including expert interviews with teachers and out-of-school experts on how career guidance is set into practice in concrete local school spaces. The multi-sited ethnographic study in twenty-four different schools in eight countries provides the basis for the contextual actor perspective on career guidance (cf. Bledowski and Felczak, 2013; Koşar Altinyelken and Julkunen, 2013; Mellottée and Julkunen, 2013).

Degree of Integration

In recent years there has been a trend for career guidance based upon personal interviews to be supplemented with a curriculum-based approach. An emphasis upon lifelong learning and sustained employability greatly enhances the case for such an approach. As underlined in Table 7.3, the degree of integration of career guidance into curriculum can show how the countries are proceeding in this direction (cf. Mellottée and Julkunen, 2013).

As Table 7.3 illustrates, most countries include programmes of career education within the curriculum. Nevertheless, these vary in content and intensity and also within different school systems within a country. Some (in Germany, for example) focus mainly on understanding the world of work and its demands. Most, however, also include attention to self-awareness and the development of skills for making decisions (especially in Finland, and to a lesser degree in France) and managing transitions. In other countries, extents and contents have not been nationally specified and there is a broad variety between schools or territories.

Within the curriculum-based model three different types can be found in GOETE countries: on the one hand career guidance is included within the curriculum and, on the other hand, it is organized to help work on the development of skills for making decisions and managing transitions. Some countries include programmes of career guidance within the curriculum but keep them as separate programmes. These programmes are increasingly becoming mandatory in most of the GOETE project countries (mostly in Germany, Finland, the Netherlands and the UK).

In Germany, curricula are the responsibility of the *Länder* (regions) and their respective ministries. Around the year 2004, as a reaction to the PISA-shock, much of the curriculum was reformed, shifting from an input-based data system (describing teaching contents) to an output-based system of educational standards (what students should be able to know and to do: skills). For instance, the traditional subject *Arbeitslehre* focuses on understanding the world of work and its demands either in specific subjects, such as technology, or more broadly across the curriculum. It is often taught in the last two years of compulsory school, although it can start much earlier. In addition, vocational orientation is now streamlined across subjects in the responsibility of the class teacher in cooperation with external counsellors involving several internships, CV production and interview training.

Table 7.3 Degree of integration into curricula in eight European countries

Country	Degree	Way of integration into curricula
The Netherlands	High	Orientation towards 'learning and working' is included in the upper forms of all general subjects, and 'orientation towards the sector' in all vocational subjects, within *vocational* education. Within general education 'orientation on continued education' is an optional component within the so-called 'free space' periods
Finland	High	Career education is compulsory in grades 7–9, and new curriculum guidelines require it to be included in the full basic education. Two hours per week of lessons are provided in grades 7–9, and one hour per week in the optional tenth grade and in upper secondary education. Vocational school students receive one-and-a-half weeks of career guidance and counselling
Germany	Middle	Schools incorporate (learning about the world of work) into the curriculum, either in specific subjects such as technology or more broadly across the curriculum. It often takes place in the last two years of compulsory school, but may start much earlier
Slovenia	Middle	The social structure of society is regarded as an important issue in the curriculum, but does not have a strong relation to the teaching practice
The UK	Middle	Since 1997 career education has been a mandatory part of the national curriculum in England for the 14–16 age group, although its extent and content have not been specified and schools have adopted widely differing approaches
Italy	Weak	Integration of guidance into curricula remains very dependent on individual initiative from teachers
France	Weak	The new 'referential of personal competencies' introduced into curriculum is a first step of integration. The content is defined at the national level but the way of using it still varies. Integration of guidance into curricula remains very dependent on individual initiative from teachers
Poland	Weak	Integration of guidance into curricula remains very dependent on individual initiative from teachers. Activities are prepared ad hoc

The Netherlands has also developed this kind of programme within the curriculum. Schools have the freedom to develop their own curriculum within the framework of the core objectives. As a result, some career guidance programmes, for instance, 'Orientation towards learning and working', are included in the upper forms of all general subjects and 'orientation towards the sector' in all vocational subjects within pre-vocational education. Within general education 'Orientation towards continuing education' is an optional component within the so-called 'free space' periods.

The second model, based on helping students to develop skills for making decisions and managing transitions, is clearly more difficult to identify as it is an holistic approach where career guidance skills (autonomy, self-esteem, effective research of information) are infused within all subjects in the curriculum. No national directive can be found, and this kind of pedagogical approach often depends on school or teacher initiatives. Nevertheless, some clues exist in the local case studies. In France teachers are free to develop their own pedagogy – within the framework of the national core objectives – and some teachers (often the youngest) use a skills approach in their classes.

Hence, career programmes vary in their structure, depending on how much they can integrate into the curriculum. Furthermore, in some countries (the UK, France, Italy) several patterns can be seen due to the autonomy that schools (and teachers) are given to decide which model to use. In England, since 1997, career education has been a mandatory part of the national curriculum for 14–16-year-olds, although its extent and content has not been specified, and schools have adopted widely differing approaches. In Italy, besides the compulsory part called *Consiglio orientativo* (guidance suggestion), the Ministry concerned with education also suggests other actions, such as starting guidance in primary schools or focusing on pupils' emerging talents. However, authority and control over implementation largely is given to schools.

Another difference across education systems concerns the grade in which career guidance should be or is located. Countries have different degrees of tracking (see Tikkanen et al., in this volume) and key transitions are not located at the same grades. Nevertheless, the most common choice is to concentrate career education in lower secondary education in order to prepare for transitions towards upper secondary education and tertiary education. Only one country involved in the GOETE study extends career education into upper secondary education, and that is Finland.

Altogether, the comparative report on the local case studies involved in the GOETE study concludes that there is a conspicuous commonality in the governance of career guidance (Bledowski and Felczak, 2013; Mellottée and Julkunen, 2013). In none of these countries, however, does career guidance accompany the *whole* school career of a child, beginning with entrance to primary school and ending at the completion of compulsory schooling or even later (Tikkanen et al., 2015). It seems that the transition from primary to secondary school is perceived by institutions, as well as by personal actors (teachers, parents, pupils/students), as not requiring particular support. Instead, teacher advice and test results will do. Yet, there is growing insight in some school systems that it is precisely the first transition which is crucial for the further school career of a student. This is certainly the case in countries with selective systems, although it also pertains to comprehensive systems. Few pedagogical actors – including those involved in teacher training – pay attention to both transitions and regard them as belonging to *one* school career (cf. Baumert et al., 2009).

The issue of curriculum integration is closely connected to the question of who provides career guidance in schools. This question is, however, also related to the structure of school systems. A high level of differentiation may require a high level of career guidance or counselling, as students have to make educational choices at an early age (Germany and the Netherlands). Still, even though the issue is not covered in teacher training, guidance can be accessed through other providers or sources as Table 7.4 illustrates (cf. Mellottée and Julkunen, 2013).

From the analysis, three different models emerge: the 'class teacher' or the integrated model, the more specialized form of 'school specialized practitioners' and the 'out-of-school specialized practitioners' model. The more specialized forms of organization partly explain why career guidance is weakly covered in teacher training in countries such as Finland, Slovenia, Italy and the UK. In the Netherlands a 'class teacher' model is used, and career guidance is covered in teacher training. France and Germany have a more mixed system and training of future teachers in these issues is rather sparse, whereas they also have a

Table 7.4 Organizational forms in eight European countries

Model	Countries	Organization
Class teacher	The Netherlands, Germany (mixed), France (mixed), Italy	A teacher is responsible for guidance in addition to subject teaching
School specialized professionals	Slovenia, Finland, France (mixed)	Within the school a professional with dedicated training is in charge of guidance and counselling
Out-of-school specialized professionals	The UK, Poland, Germany (mixed)	Outside the school a professional with dedicated training is in charge of guidance and counselling

'class teacher' model and in Germany some schools also have out-of-school specialized professionals.

Concepts and Models of Guidance

Career guidance in the GOETE countries has been described on the basis of the national reports and a concluding comparative report (Parreira do Amaral et al., 2011). Looking more closely at the actors and roles in career guidance shows that there is a rather mixed variation with regard to its professional basis, and the types of actors involved (see also Amos et al., in this volume). In Table 7.5 we have further analysed the kinds of training the different professionals have. We also elaborate the conception of guidance, drawing on the different country contexts and how career guidance is understood and profiled (cf. Mellottée and Julkunen, 2013).

Table 7.5 gives an overall picture of the different actors, and the kinds of competencies involved. However, since it is very difficult to give general national pictures, because the actors vary *within* the countries, we will describe the different conditions in each country.

In the *Netherlands* there is a common trend according to which students prefer practical courses to working in class, and the teachers regard these courses as essential in enabling students to get a clearer view of their intended work field. Practical training is conducted in cooperation with local entrepreneurs, thus maintaining permanent contact between school and students. For teachers, individual career counselling in the work place has great importance. Other programmes have been designed to give students a broader view on what the labour market looks like and will expect from them. These programmes also make parents aware of the importance and necessity of decision making.

Germany has a very mixed system. Generally teachers are responsible for guidance, since it is part of the curriculum. However, in lower secondary there may also be specialized professionals who operate in school, distinct from the external pedagogical counsellors. Education oriented toward the labour market takes the form of informal education and occurs in students' spare time. In general, informal learning takes the form of voluntary or youth work. Competencies obtained in this way are very relevant, and facilitate understanding of the importance of education and interpersonal relations. As a result of the cooperation between schools and networks of external consultants, schools receive advice on how to build closer relationships with local companies

Table 7.5 Actors, contents and profiles in career guidance

Countries	Actors	Roles and training
The Netherlands	Class teachers	Theoretical knowledge is lacking and teachers mainly learn about career guidance in their practical in-service periods at school
Germany	Class teachers, counselling teachers	Teachers with extra training in educational science and psychology provide guidance and advice for learning or behavioural difficulties
France	Guidance counsellors	Specific training mainly in psychology
	Class teacher	Responsible for guidance in a class; receives no specific theoretical training
Italy	Counselling teacher	An appointed teacher who is not a specialist on career guidance and has to follow guidance projects and activities
Slovenia	Counselling service	Individuals or a team of counselling and guidance specialists (psychologists, pedagogues, social workers) provide guidance and support for pupils, students, parents and teachers
Finland	Guidance counsellors	A separate trained group of teachers give advice related to educational transitions and occupational orientation
The UK	Personal advisers	Not located within schools; provided by the local education authority, local council or the health service by full-time personal advisers who work with a range of young people's problems, not only career guidance. This holistic approach takes place in England and Northern Ireland. They have a postgraduate qualification in career guidance or its equivalent. In Scotland, there is a mix between guidance teachers and external counsellors
Poland	Psycho-educational counselling centres	Career counselling is mainly conducted in separate institutions

and improve matching processes and vocational guidance. This enables more encounters with practice, broader ranges of internships, support in finding training places and combines experience with occupational apprenticeship.

In *France* one in-service period is mandatory for all students during the last year of lower secondary. Some teachers are involved, but the main support for students in this case is family. Most of the students interviewed found an internship thanks to relatives. Networks of local enterprises have been built which host students for their in-service week. The purpose of this is to find a proper place for their first connection with the labour market. The weaknesses of the French education system are loose connections between the labour market and schooling, and the local character of the proposed solutions.

In *Italy* the school is understood as a social place where students, especially from disadvantaged families, may undertake activities and spend their time. This may enable the development of interests and help adjust students to the extra-curricular activities and future decisions on job selection. Nevertheless, there are problems in the lack of special resources and a more holistic approach. In addition, the lack of networking outside school may create unequal opportunities for students from different social background.

All primary schools in *Slovenia* start the transition procedure in the 8th and 9th grades and provide students with expert counselling, involving governmental and non-governmental organizations, formal and informal meetings with teachers, and school experts visiting secondary schools. Particular attention is paid to students in need of more support.

In *Finland*, the guidance counsellor has an important role in informing students about educational opportunities and work life. Students are in general oriented to continue to upper secondary education. Students visit upper secondary schools for one whole day, the significance of which seems to be gaining more concrete and practical knowledge of what the studies may be about. Cooperation between counsellors from lower to upper secondary schools is important and *both individual and group visits are arranged*. This improves the possibilities for tackling transitional challenges. Local and regional programmes are important elements in schools and have an added value. These may be important to tackle issues for disadvantaged young people and their transitions. The difficulties lie in the nature of these programmes as these are not often followed-up and the mechanisms of support remain unintegrated.

There are networks (albeit limited) between schools and the business community in the *UK* to give young people work experience, and they offer practical guidance such as filling applications and mock interviews to develop social competencies. There are a number of outside networks that help students manage the transition to the labour market, including Further Education Colleges, as well as youth charities and the government department that deals with apprenticeships and Further and Higher Education.

In *Poland*, there is no kind of extensive programme of supporting students in making decisions on their further education or the selection of a profession. The programmes that have been implemented are limited to a region, or even to a single school. Students with difficulties and in danger of falling behind in school who follow these programmes can participate in extra-curricular compensating classes and make use of educational and career counselling. Large groups of students are covered by the programmes and the emphasis is on the disadvantaged.

Constellations of Support

In this chapter, we have been interested in gaining a more in-depth understanding of how career guidance works in different settings. What are the demands and challenges that encompass the strategies of career guidance in different settings? What are the degrees of integration, the degrees of coherence and the conception of career guidance in eight European countries? And what are the challenges ahead?

In all countries career guidance is seen as a public good linked to policy goals related to learning, labour market and social equity. Career guidance brings learning and work together and stresses the interaction between them. This is operationalized in different ways in the different countries and the question remains whether the services and support provided are adequate to meet the challenges ahead.

The concepts and models of career guidance vary across the countries, and issues of access and coherence are evident. In the *low-level standardized and differentiated systems* (the UK, Italy, Poland) countries provide only little institutionalized support, which is more residual and directed towards disadvantaged students. This gives rise to a lack of transparency facing many students. Support is poorly integrated and oriented towards the resources and capabilities of the students, while career guidance is not accessible to all students or school leavers. Thus, it is difficult for individuals to find services adapted to their social background, capacities and specific needs. In *high-level standardized and comprehensive systems* (Finland, Slovenia) organizational differentiation and the degree of selectivity are low and there are no key transitions in compulsory education. This type of system seems to have the most potential for providing effective access to education and mitigating inequalities through functioning support systems. A functioning system encompasses a comprehensive and cooperative surrounding, including informal, indirect and external support.

A high level of differentiation seems to require a high level of career guidance or counselling as students have to make educational choices at an early age. The *high-level standardized and differentiated systems* (France, Germany, the

Netherlands) have inherent highly selective 'bottlenecks' and early decision-making points that have the potential to reinforce social and educational inequalities and disadvantage, thus offering less potential for providing effective access and mitigating inequalities.

In none of the GOETE countries does career guidance accompany the whole school career trajectory of a child, beginning at entrance to the first year of primary school and ending at the end of compulsory education. Finland is the only country which extends career guidance into further education. There is a need for closer coaching, certainly in countries with selective systems, although this also relates to comprehensive systems. Few educational actors – aside from teacher training institutions – pay attention to both of the transitions facing students. Paradoxically, guidance counsellors, as one means of formal support, face particular coping challenges within their own profession, in turn limiting their capacity to support students. Strengthening the professional expertise of career guidance within school and as the broker between education and work seems to be essential.

Reviewing the detailed data on the different career guidance concepts and models in the GOETE study, critical strategies to strengthen the expertise of career guidance as a broker between education and work seem to be related to: (1) regular national and regional round-table discussions with teachers, employers, parents and students about working life and the needs and changes in career guidance at schools; (2) regular meetings, discussions and visits with labour market representatives; (3) research on future employment strategies and students' satisfaction and effects of guidance; (4) acknowledgement of career guidance as an integrated concept requiring training and critical examination of good strategies; and (5) compiling students' occupational portfolios in order to make them aware about the interrelations between their individual interests and competencies, the school and the labour market. These all point at the importance of continual evaluation of the link between work and education, and the importance of their integration in the school system. It also points to the importance of broadening the discussions about school and work outside the school context and developing new spaces for career guidance.

Conclusion

> Sometimes it feels like the world is changing so fast so that the choices the students possibly make now are not valid any more at a later point. Nowadays

> you cannot trust the permanency of factory jobs or blue-collar jobs, not even universities. It is really hard to predict what really in the end will work. (Guidance counsellor, Finland)

School is seen to be a key to making young people aware of career pathways and of the importance of education through life (lifelong learning), but the issue of careers and career guidance is complex, as this quote from a Finnish guidance counsellor conceives. To prepare students for choosing their future paths, giving them as much information and encouragement as possible so that they can make informed choices, as well as offering practical guidance, is a key element in career guidance. However, this has to be set in the perspective of the general societal, economic and cultural contexts that provide the frame for understanding the challenges education systems and students are facing. The context of increasing globalization, internationalization and competitive knowledge societies is currently shaping many of the demands towards the education system and individuals (Parreira do Amaral et al., 2013). The institutional contexts also frame the issue, in terms of the degree of differentiation and comprehensiveness of education and training, the degree of support for students and the existing form of cooperation and integration between the two.

Traditionally, career guidance in schools has been viewed largely as an individualized service provided at key transitional phases, and a support to the curriculum rather than part of it. It has mainly been delivered through personal interviews and sometimes supported by psychometric testing. This type of guidance is not feasible when large numbers of pupils are involved, and this limits its availability. GOETE evidence also shows that in recent years there has been a trend for this more individualized career guidance to be supplemented with a curriculum-based approach. An emphasis upon lifelong learning and sustained employability greatly enhances the case for such an approach.

The challenge is to enrich the support offered at school to all students with additional opportunities for those who are in greatest need. Counselling and guidance do not necessarily have to take place at school. They can be organized outside, in dedicated centres and NGO institutions dealing with the labour market. These centres could also be places where teachers could improve their level of qualifications. It is crucial to offer appropriate opportunities for students from disadvantaged families, as schools are not organized to provide them with special classes.

The main challenge is to create a career guidance system that will provide students with enough skills and self-reliance to be able to take on challenges related to the changing labour market, changing professional qualifications and the need for lifelong learning.

8

Cooperation and Problems of Recognition between Schools and Parents in Supporting Young People's Educational Trajectories

Hülya Koşar Altinyelken
University of Amsterdam

Silvia Demozzi
University of Bologna

Felicitas Boron
Kreisjugendring Esslingen e.V.

Federica Taddia
University of Bologna

Introduction

Parental involvement in education has been a topic of intense debate for many decades. It is seen as key to students' academic achievement, school engagement and social and emotional development (Williams and Sanchez, 2011). Moreover, parental participation is increasingly linked to an inclusion agenda, to decentralization and to accountability policies at schools (OECD, 2006). It is perceived as crucial to the democratization of school governance and to achieve 'democratization of everyday life', through engaging parents in the processes of deliberation and dialogue at school (Vincent and Martin, 2000). Furthermore, within late modern knowledge societies, parent–school cooperation has been increasingly regarded as important, since it helps to bridge community knowledge and school validation of that knowledge: connecting practical, out-of-school, experiential knowledge with academic and abstract knowledge (Gonzalez and Moll, 2002). Hence, cooperation and communication between home and school are critical to integrating informal and non-formal learning with formal education provided in school settings.

Concerns with the relatively poor school achievement and high drop-out rates among children of low socio-economic status (SES) and migrant children have led to an increased scholarly interest in studying educational challenges in relation to family backgrounds and how students and parents cope with such challenges. A range of studies have been conducted in North America and around Europe highlighting the significance of parental engagement and home–school cooperation on educational success, particularly for low SES children (Desforges, 2003; Huntsinger and Jose, 2009). Nevertheless, actively involving parents from low socio-economic backgrounds has been a persistent challenge in many country contexts (Smalley and Reyes-Blanes, 2001). Several studies have demonstrated that individual and institutional, social, cultural and material factors influence the degree and quality of home–school cooperation (Crozier, 2001; Vincent and Martin, 2002), and these factors operate differently and discriminatingly across social classes and among individual parents (Desforges, 2003). Indeed, lower-class families appear to encounter more challenges in being involved in the education of their children and in cooperating with schools (Minke and Anderson, 2005).

This chapter seeks to analyse how parents and schools cooperate in schools in Europe, which are primarily located in disadvantaged urban areas or enrol students from disadvantaged backgrounds. Although parent–school cooperation in such contexts has been studied before, very few studies have adopted a comparative perspective (OECD, 2012b). The main questions addressed in our chapter include the following: (1) How is the importance of parent–school cooperation viewed by teachers and parents? (2) To what extent and in what ways do parents with low SES cooperate with teachers? (3) How do teachers and parents reflect on their cooperation experiences? And (4) what challenges do teachers and parents encounter in their cooperation? Our analysis draws from case studies conducted in eight European countries (Finland, France, Germany, Italy, the Netherlands, Poland, Slovenia and the UK) within the framework of the *Governance of Educational Trajectories in Europe* (GOETE) project. The project analysed how educational trajectories of young people are governed and how transition-related decisions are taken at individual, school and policy levels, by using a life course and governance perspective (see Parreira do Amaral et al., 2013).

We will first overview some relevant theoretical approaches and concepts on the topic and explain our methodological choices. Then, we will present the empirical findings and conclusions drawn from these findings by an analysis of the significance of parental involvement, its various forms, the mutual reflections of teachers and parents on their cooperation experiences, and the challenges and complexities that such cooperation entails.

Parental Involvement, Class and Exclusion

Organization of parental involvement

Parental involvement includes a wide range of activities, from participation in school governing bodies to joining cultural activities, from meetings with teachers to helping out with homework. Within the literature, such activities are categorized in various ways. Ozaki and Koshino (2008), for instance, differentiate among four types: *home based*, *school based*, *decision making* and *advocacy*. The first two types refer to the place where parental engagement in education occurs, while decision making and advocacy relate to power relations and parents 'having a voice' in their child's schooling. Moreover, Epstein (2001) describes six different forms of parental involvement: parenting, communicating, volunteering (helping in classroom or cultural events), teaching at home (help with homework and educational choices), decision making (participation in school governance bodies) and collaborating with the community.

Furthermore, Nordahl (2007, cited in Bæck, 2010) discusses three types of cooperation: *representative cooperation*, *direct cooperation* and *cooperation without contact*. Representative cooperation refers to participation of individual parents in schools' decision-making bodies. These parents are often elected and represent the voice of parents within such bodies. Direct cooperation is understood as the form of cooperation formalized through direct meetings and interactions between parents and teachers, by way of parent–teacher conferences, or individual meetings, for instance. Last, cooperation without contact points to home-based parental involvement in education, e.g. the support they provide through conversations, encouragement, affection and help with homework.

Benefits of parent–school cooperation

Parental involvement is considered very important by various actors involved in education as it offers unique opportunities for parents to be involved in their children's education and has important implications for children's academic, behavioural and development outcomes (Domina, 2005; Turney and Kao, 2009). Some studies on the topic have shown that students achieve better, obtain higher grades and are less likely to drop out of school when their parents are engaged in their education, by offering stimulation, meeting with teachers or participating in school activities (Epstein, 2001; Christenson, 2004). These patterns differ according to the age of the children, their school level and social and academic skills. Research indicates that parental engagement can contribute to the academic success even more strongly among at-risk groups of students (Hill, 2001).

Furthermore, various studies refer to parental involvement as a form of *social capital*, comprising networks and social structures that generate benefits for their members (Turney and Kao, 2009). Parental involvement significantly affects behavioural outcomes as it plays an important role in socializing children. Similarly, a social network generated by school–parent cooperation can serve as a source of information for parents to learn about the educational system, whether their children have problems at school and how these can be solved (Domina, 2005). Moreover, parental involvement can have a positive impact on children's self-esteem, psychological problems, drop-out rates and delinquent behaviour, as children get better adapted to the school system and tend to value education more (Geel and Vedder, 2009).

A class perspective to barriers in parental involvement

Various studies indicate that parents wish to participate in the schooling of their children and cooperate with schools; however, there are several barriers that constrain such involvement, particularly for low SES parents (Cooper and Crosnoe, 2007). In analysing class differences in patterns of parental involvement, Coleman (1988) points to three key forms of capital – economic, human and social, which are distributed unevenly between different social classes and have wide ranging ramifications on the level of parental participation in schooling processes. Low economic status often means fewer material resources, opportunities and time for parents to be involved in their children's education (Geel and Vedder, 2009; Turney and Kao, 2009). Human capital refers to the way parents can make use of their own knowledge resources to create a stimulating learning environment for their children. Social capital is intended as a resource deriving from specific social structures that can be used to pursue specific interests. It enables members of a social network to have access to information and resources to support their children in school. Both human and social capital tend to be limited among low SES parents.

Furthermore, parents with disadvantaged backgrounds appear to encounter difficulties in communicating with teachers on an equal level (Bourdieu, 1998). Parents' education level is important in this regard, since their consideration of teachers and their degree of communication with them are influenced by their previous educational experiences. Limited educational experiences tend to lead to lower parental confidence or relevant competences in supporting their children or communicating with the school staff. Consequently, some parents believe that they should not interfere with the school's authority (Kohl et al., 2000). A study conducted by Crozier (1999) on working class parents revealed that they viewed teachers as the 'experts' in education, and perceived them as superior and distant. Their perceptions of teachers were also reinforced by the way in which teachers approach them. Thus, working class parents were not inclined to be proactive in their partnership. Vincent and Martin (2002) also confirmed that parents with low SES perceive contacts with school as empty, contrived, insubstantial and awkward.

Within the European context, such debates often focus on parents with a migration background. These parents report having more barriers to participation at school, and are subsequently less likely and willing to get involved in activities at school. Teachers might also interpret the low levels of parental involvement at school as an indicator of their lack of interest or caring about their children's educational outcomes (Turney and Kao, 2009). However, most studies on this topic identify lack of language proficiency as one of the main barriers to migrant parents' participation in schools (Ozaki and Koshino, 2008; Turney and Kao, 2009). In some cases, the language barrier stems from social-class-associated differentiation in verbal styles. Teachers often speak a language that is associated with middle-class norms, which parents from lower economic/educational backgrounds do not feel comfortable with, or do not always fully understand (Dahlstedt, 2009). Moreover, parents' non-involvement in school may also stem from a different cultural approach to school–family relationships and their respective roles in education. When teachers do not recognize such cultural differences and express frustration at parents' assumed 'detachment', schools might miss an important opportunity to create meaningful relationships with parents (Protheroe, 2006).

Methodology

The GOETE project adopted a mixed-methods design integrating a number of quantitative and qualitative research methods. Our analysis is based on qualitative case studies on local school spaces in socially deprived areas. In each of the eight GOETE countries, three cities and one school in each city were selected as case studies, hence a total of twenty-four schools were involved in qualitative local studies. In most of our schools, there was a strong intersection of low SES, ethnicity and migrant status, except for the Polish schools. Since the case studies aimed at generating in-depth information about how educational transitions are governed from a multi-scalar level and multi-actor perspective, it included a range of qualitative research tools (interviews, focus group discussions and student essays) with a wide variety of actors, including students during (N=195) and after lower secondary school (N=109), parents (N=109), as well as professionals and experts (teachers, headmasters, internal and external experts, N=208) (du Bois-Reymond et al., 2012). Our analysis here is limited to interviews and focus group discussions conducted with parents and teachers.

A semi-structured interview guideline was developed during a joint meeting involving members from national research teams, and was translated into national languages by the respective teams. After data collection, a coding scheme was developed jointly through various consultations, and national teams have undertaken data analysis using a combination of content analysis (Krippendorff, 2004) and grounded theory approach (Glaser and Strauss, 1967). The analysis presented here is based on analyses conducted by national teams. The authors also had access to the English summary of the interview transcriptions with parents and teachers. During analysis and writing phases, there were ongoing communications with the national teams to cross-check interpretations and conclusions.

Having outlined some of the approaches to parental cooperation and its challenges, we will in the next sections present the GOETE findings. We will first explain how parents and teachers view the importance of cooperation, and how such cooperation is organized in our case study schools. Then, we will analyse how parents and teachers reflect on their cooperation experiences, and what challenges, shortcomings and tensions they identify. These discussions will highlight the problems of *recognition* which appear to be central to our discussion.

Perspectives from Case Studies on the Importance of Cooperation

Our findings reveal that both parents and teachers regard school cooperation as highly important for improving children's educational achievement, school belonging and the quality of their schooling experiences. In our research, cooperation was analysed in relation to the most important school transition stage: from lower secondary to upper secondary education. Cooperation at this stage was deemed critical for making the 'right' decisions. Good communication and cooperation between school and home were directly associated with improved knowledge and understanding about students' performance, capabilities and future aspirations. Furthermore, such interactions were seen as central to developing improved understanding of the education system, transition possibilities within the system and the realistic possibilities students might opt for. Teachers believed they cannot educate children alone, and this cannot be done only at school. Hence, the importance of dialogue, ongoing communication and cooperation was highlighted.

Most case studies within the GOETE project were conducted in schools located in disadvantaged neighbourhoods or schools that enrolled disadvantaged students. According to various teachers, parental cooperation is even more important in such disadvantaged contexts. They enumerate several reasons to justify this account. For instance, teachers argued that students from disadvantaged backgrounds need more support at school, and that schools need more information and interactions with parents in order to offer this support effectively. In other words, they believed that remedying the educational and developmental problems of disadvantaged students requires improved cooperation between schools and families. Moreover, parents from lower socio-economic or educational backgrounds may not be adequately informed about the education system and the transition possibilities, hence cooperation is central to enabling them to make informed choices. These accounts confirm some earlier studies indicating that parental involvement is critical particularly for children with low SES in order to overcome discontinuities between home and school (Mendez and Fogle, 2002).

Forms of parent–school cooperation

Cooperation between parents and schools involves a broad range of activities. In our analysis, we will use three categories suggested by Nordahl (2007, cited in Bæck, 2010): *representative cooperation*, *direct cooperation* and *cooperation without contact*.

Representative cooperation

In various countries, school governance structures allowed bodies in which parents could participate (e.g. Finland, the Netherlands and Slovenia). However, parent associations are often not known by parents or not utilized. In Finland, the schools had parent associations but they were not active due to parental disinterest. Lack of time and confidence in schools were also mentioned as explanatory reasons. Moreover, some parents did not believe that these associations had any real power to influence school policies, echoing similar concerns in Slovenia. In the Netherlands too, parents did not believe they could influence school decisions, hence, they hardly used formal bodies of participation:

> And if you want to discuss something, then … all kinds of excuses … No, I do not think that is alright. But it is as it is. (Parent 28, the Netherlands)

Consequently, in several schools, we observed that parents chose to express their voice individually rather than collectively, and there was little trust in the real decision-making power of governance bodies that involved parents. These concerns resonate with an OECD study on parent and community voice in schools (OECD, 2006).

Direct cooperation

Direct cooperation included visits to schools: to establish good relationships with teachers; to gather information about children's performance, curriculum or transition routes to upper secondary; to discuss emerging problems; or to assist with the organization of school activities. Moreover, parents joined parental meetings organized by schools, and made use of teachers' consultation hours. In Germany, exchanging phone calls and receiving letters were important forms of teacher–parent contact, and this was true for many other schools as well. In the Netherlands, contact between home and school is established mainly via cell phone, emails and letters from school or information posted on school websites. The issue of home visits was also raised. Teachers did not visit homes to initiate or intensify contact; most would not want to do so, even if there was time for it. They felt that home visits were the responsibility of social workers and other experts.

In general, direct cooperation appears to be a rather common form of parental involvement in our case-study schools. It was often organized on an individual and needs basis, and parents tended to prefer this form of cooperation for discussing problems and seeking solutions. Moreover, various accounts confirmed that this form of cooperation diminishes as children get older. For instance, in Finland, parental participation tended to decrease at lower secondary since schools do not contact parents as often as in primary school and, on their side, parents want to give more responsibility to students. Furthermore, parental participation tends to be *gendered*, since more mothers than fathers were actively seeking direct cooperation. Such gendered imbalance of parental participation is identified in other studies as well (Vincent and Martin, 2000), suggesting that it is labelled as 'soft' and accorded secondary status by men.

Cooperation without contact

This category refers to parents' at-home educational involvement, including modelling, expectations, support, discussions, encouragement and skills training. In our study, the following forms of support were highlighted the most during interviews with parents: discussing school progress and other educational issues, help with homework, arranging private lessons, providing educational materials, boosting children's motivation, advising on important decisions (e.g. on subject choice, internship places and transition to upper secondary school), offering emotional support and contributing to children's personality development and the development of certain competencies that are highly relevant for schooling and the labour market. These are highly important forms of home school cooperation; however, they are often invisible to teachers.

Help with homework emerged as one of the most common means of parental support. Some offered direct support and others supervised their children's work. Parents of children with learning difficulties offered more help with homework. Also, parents who placed high importance on academic performance were highly involved. Supervision of homework at lower grades was more common, while at higher grades, children were seen as more autonomous and parents had less confidence in their ability to help with homework. In addition, some parents arranged private lessons to supplement their children's learning, such as in Germany and the Netherlands, where the education system is highly selective and differentiated. Moreover, in countries where academic competition was high, private tutoring was common. For instance, in Slovenia, private tutoring was pervasive even among families who struggled to pay for such services. However, in countries where students receive additional support (as in Finland) via remedial teaching or special education classes, such strategies were not utilized.

Furthermore, parents sought to improve their children's motivation to study harder and achieve good results. For this purpose, some parents conversed about the importance of education, and some others offered immediate rewards. In Slovenia, where parental involvement was recorded as very high, parents controlled their children and exerted pressure to motivate them. Furthermore, parents tried to reinforce the development of competencies that are highly esteemed at school and more importantly in the labour market. For instance, in Germany, some parents encouraged the development of key competencies, such as being committed and ambitious, ability to set priorities, time management and assertiveness.

Views on cooperation experiences

Teachers' perspectives

As indicated earlier, cooperation was considered highly important, acknowledging that parents' full support is needed to maximize schooling outcomes. Nevertheless, there was a strong sense of dissatisfaction among teachers with regard to the *frequency* and *quality* of their cooperation with parents. In all schools, there were parents demonstrating high, intermediate and low levels of engagement. In some cases, teachers complained that parents were interfering too much in what should be their professional domain. For instance, in Slovenia, some teachers complained about their lack of authority and autonomy, and about increasing interference of parents in teaching and evaluation. Similar remarks were made by some Finnish teachers as well. Nevertheless, according to teachers, most parents demonstrated low levels of engagement; this implied attendance at parents' evenings organized once or twice per year and having minimal contact otherwise, and assuming a reactive rather than proactive attitude to cooperation with school. Teachers' conceptions of parent–school cooperation mainly referred to representative and direct cooperation, discounting parental involvement at home to a large extent.

Teachers believed that these 'passive parents' failed in cooperating with school. They did not show up at meetings, or teachers encountered difficulties in contacting them or arranging individual meetings. In some schools, teachers explicitly noted that parents were absent from school. For instance, in Poland, teachers complained about lack of cooperation with families and they argued that parents do not demonstrate any interest in their children's education. In many contexts, it was mainly the passive attitude of parents that was criticized by teachers. The reason for the inadequacies of parental cooperation was perceived as parental unwillingness to actively seek contact with school, which was often interpreted as not supporting their children's education. In France, for example, teachers recognized that parents come to institutionalized events such as parent–teacher meetings, but do not commit on their own initiative. Hence, their passivity was criticized and seen as proof of their lack of interest in their children's school career.

Teachers suggested that inadequacies in cooperation with parents are a general problem that becomes more severe in cases where students come from disadvantaged backgrounds. In many countries the lack of parental participation is considered as the main cause, or at least an explanatory factor, for disadvantage. For instance, in Germany, disadvantage is associated with family background, and working class families and families with migrant backgrounds came often into the discussion as being associated with a general lack of resources, with low parental aspirations and devaluation of the importance of education. Several teacher accounts of migrant parents often pointed to perceptions of migrant families being a 'big problem', very difficult to contact and ignorant.

Hence, we observed in such settings a strong discourse of 'othering' and failure to recognize migrant life courses with the specific challenges they might have, as well as competencies and potentials they generate. 'Othering' is defined as the generalizing and hierarchical speaking about others (West and Fenstermaker, 1995), and appears to be a severe problem parents have to cope with. For example a mother interviewed in a German case study complained about unjust and discriminatory treatment on the basis of a migration background that not only her son but also herself experience in their dealings with school:

> I have to have this appointment with her (principal). Permanently she (principal) debases my children, calling them sexually deviant, ascribing something negative to them all the time. Some others – I don't tell the names – they really disrespect others, are sanctioned the very same way. But this is not the education he gets (at home). So I ask myself: why are all these children put into the same waste bag and beaten? This is unfair … My son is accused to be not educated. And this I don't allow school to tell me. On the contrary, my education is failing at school, and not the other way around. (Parent 5, Germany)

Parental perspectives

When we explored how parents viewed cooperation experiences, we noted diverse parental accounts. Some were pleased with the cooperation (e.g. in Slovenia and Finland), but in some other schools there were criticisms and concerns about the frequency of parent–teacher contact and the quality of the interactions (e.g. Germany, the Netherlands and France). Parents who criticized cooperation experiences pointed to three issues: (1) how they were perceived by teachers; (2) information flows from school on their children's academic and behavioural development; and (3) how school advises children in their transition choices. In Germany, some parents complained that they were not seen by the school staff as competent partners, and regretted the waning efforts of the school to stay in contact with them. Some argued that teachers had little knowledge about parental efforts, and that there were hardly any real exchanges and cooperation between parents and teachers. Some migrant parents also felt that they were treated in discriminatory ways. These accounts pointed to problems of recognition, and a sense of not being acknowledged for their participation in the education of their children.

Moreover, there were also concerns that parents were not informed early enough about important issues concerning their children. For instance, one German mother complained that she was only informed when the problems of her child became severe. There were far more concerns in relation to cooperation on transition choices. Several parents noted that they were not pleased with the information they received and the talks they had on transition possibilities. Some Polish parents wished that teachers would show more interest in students' vocational future and would bring up that issue in discussions with parents. Not only Polish parents but also parents from several other schools expressed a desire for more information and knowledge on transition pathways. The role of teachers and parents in supporting students' educational transitions is discussed further in Chapter 12.

Challenges in parent–school cooperation

Parents' access to social, cultural and material resources differs widely due to a range of reasons. Their differential possession and deployment of such resources have consequences on their willingness and capacity to get involved in their children's schooling (Vincent and Martin, 2002). Understanding these resources and the challenges implicated by them helps us to identify which parents are more involved, and why some parents cooperate more compared to others. Our analysis has highlighted seven factors that enhance or constrain cooperation, including language, family background, parental interest in education, parental education level and knowledge about education system, distrust in schools, institutional factors and divergent teacher and parental expectations.

Language

Lack of language proficiency is cited as one of the most significant challenges in parent–school cooperation, confirming several other earlier studies on the subject (Matuszny et al., 2007). In Slovenia, Italy and Finland, teachers and experts referred to language problems as an impediment to cooperation with migrant families. For instance, in Finland, there were problems in providing support to immigrant families due to language barriers, hence the presence of an interpreter was often needed. In France, Germany and the Netherlands, the language problem was even more pervasive, as these countries host larger immigrant communities. In France, teachers discussed how parents and children suffered from lack of exposure to French. Teachers often felt misunderstood, as parents could not understand their messages adequately. The problem was most acute for Turkish families, even though they have been living in France for a long time. This phenomenon was also observed in Germany and the Netherlands.

Family background

Our findings suggest that challenges related to the home environment tend to undermine parental support at home, and make parent–school cooperation more difficult, if not impossible. According to teachers, families who are in the most precarious situation are single parent households (mostly single mothers), confirming some other studies on the subject (Kohl et al., 2000). This was particularly raised as a big concern in France, Finland and Germany. Other significant issues were poverty, alcoholism, drug abuse, domestic violence, precarious working situations of parents and unemployment. In Finland, teachers discussed instances of generational unemployment (up to three generations) and poverty inheritance. Also, teachers in Poland, Germany, the Netherlands and the UK expressed their concern about inter-generational poverty and living on benefits, and the type of modelling of values and expectations these parents offered to their children.

In Poland as well, these issues were often raised by teachers. A teacher noted in a group discussion that:

> The families are really poor, confused. They have a lot of domestic problems; they are often broken families what is often associated with permanent lack of money. I think these children are really needy … there is a neglected environment. (Teacher 1, Poland)

Several families experienced the challenges of poverty, high levels of unemployment, domestic strife, divorce (or separation), financial difficulties and domestic violence. Moreover, alcohol abuse appears to be a huge problem among Polish families. Parental involvement in the upbringing of children and supporting their education is viewed as limited. Such disengagement is particularly acute for parents who move abroad to find temporary employment, leaving their children with other relatives. These children, often referred to as 'Euro orphans', were seen as at-risk since they had diminished motivation, disengagement from school and demonstrated learning difficulties. Absence of parents also negatively influenced parent–school cooperation.

Parental interest in education

School–parent cooperation was positively associated with parental interest in education. Teachers tended to believe that parents with a low SES placed less value on education and had lower educational aspirations, hence they were less disposed to cooperate with school. In many schools (e.g. in Slovenia), we met parents who had high aspirations for their children. Conversely, in Poland teachers were alarmed by low parental interest in education. Moreover, in one of the French case studies situated in a rather disadvantaged area, parents appeared to have little interest in education. Teachers raised concerns about high absenteeism rates among students, which was attributed to parents' failure to convince their children to attend schooling regularly. In another French case study, where a gipsy community constitutes an important part of student population, parents noted that they did not wish to deal with public institutions as they did not share their values. Similar concerns were raised in Italy as well, about Roma families who do not perceive education as a possible tool for promoting social and professional integration of their children, and 'force' their daughters to get married at young ages. The relevance of education was perceived as very limited in disadvantaged areas and hence interest in education was low.

Some teachers particularly pointed to migrant families as lacking such interest and having low aspirations for their children. However, several other accounts from teachers, as well as parents, revealed that many migrant parents view education as an important tool of social mobility, one of the very few available to this group. They were often anxious to secure their children's future and hence had rather high aspirations for them. We noted such aspirations among various parents in the Netherlands, Germany, Italy and Slovenia. These seemingly contradictory accounts and perceptions warn us against viewing migrants as one homogenous group, and attributing specific characteristics to them. The comments of one teacher in the Bristol case study illustrate this point very clearly:

> With some of the ethnicities, with some of Somali lads for example, their aspirations are quite low. So, that has a knock-on effect – many of their family members are either struggling to get jobs, or have jobs that they do not particularly enjoy, but that brings money in for them. They lack aspiration, but they have very high aspirations at the same time. For example, the parents of students with D and E grades come in and are desperate for their child to be a doctor or a lawyer or something. (Teacher 1, the UK)

Parental education level and knowledge about education system

Teachers associated low parental education level and inadequate knowledge about education systems negatively with parental involvement. In several countries, particularly among non-native populations, teachers believed that such knowledge was inadequate. In various country contexts (e.g. in France, Poland, the UK, Italy and the Netherlands), there were concerns that parents from disadvantaged (migrant) backgrounds did not know how the education system is organized, and what support is available at school. The explanatory reasons for this included low parental education level, being educated abroad and language problems. Indeed, some migrant families may lack confidence in becoming more involved due to their limited experience with formal education, and may not be able to understand how the education system works and what role they can play within education or what is expected from them.

Parental distrust in school

Another concern undermining family–school cooperation was parents' lack of trust in school. This was raised as an issue by teachers in France and Italy. In one of the French schools, parents felt excluded from public institutions and did not believe that the school provided equal opportunities to their children. Hence there was a sense of discrimination and feelings of resentment. Some parents were unable to understand expectations of the school from their children, and this has led to a total delegation to school. In Italy, lack of parental participation was viewed by some as a cultural issue. Some believed that the differences might be due to parenting styles. For instance, parents might care very much about the education of their children, but do not demonstrate it in a way that schools expect. This was perceived as common among migrant families who tend not to 'interfere' with school affairs. Their attitude is informed by trust in public institutions, lack of confidence in their role in interacting with school staff due to lack of language proficiency, lack of knowledge of the system or differences in educational levels. Furthermore, in various other settings, teachers also believed that parents appear to distrust teachers particularly when it comes to their advice for future transitions, a phenomenon that negatively influences cooperation between the parties. According to teachers, parents with low SES or a migrant background tend to overestimate their children's capacities and have ambitious plans themselves for their children. Therefore, they do not agree with teachers' advice on transition.

Institutional factors

How schools position themselves and their degree of openness and responsiveness to parents are also critical factors in home–school cooperation. For instance, parental perceptions of schools as impermeable institutions would undermine their willingness to intervene (Vincent and Martin, 2002). Although teachers often made critical remarks about parents during discussions on parent–school cooperation, some of them also reflected on their own role. In France, for instance, teachers maintained that they were equally concerned with lack of communication between schools, and among teachers and experts working at the same school. Lack of cooperation between school staff constrained cooperation with parents. In Italy and the Netherlands, some parents complained about high teacher turnover and absences (due to sick leave or burnout) as having negative effects on education quality as well as on home–school cooperation efforts. For instance, prolonged absences made teachers less available for meetings with parents and created discontinuities in communication.

Divergent teacher and parental expectations

Definitions of roles and responsibilities for teachers and parents are informed by family and cultural experiences and might be subject to conflict and tension between the parties (Hoover-Dempsey and Sandler, 1997). Indeed, in our schools we encountered different teacher and parent narratives on this topic.

For instance, parents expected teachers to impart key competencies that are necessary for educational success, while teachers in many schools complained that parents left much socialization to schools. Teachers tended to feel that parents delegated a lot of responsibility to schools inadvertently, or due to adopting a customer attitude.

Hence, teachers often pointed out their 'original qualification' as teachers and not social workers. In the Netherlands, for instance, teachers complained that parents were inclined to leave much socializing education to school, while they as teachers could not exercise their profession properly. Moreover, in Germany a teacher noted the following:

> What we are doing here partially at the moment, is more social work than normal lessons, that's the way it is. But actually I am a conveyor of knowledge and of course I have an upbringing effect in that, but … at the moment it's sometimes the other way round … but we are not qualified for that. (Teacher 2, Germany)

Similar tensions on the roles and responsibilities of teachers and parents were found in other schools as well, causing in some instances conflicts between the parties and leading to a blaming of each other. This was particularly acute when teachers and parents communicated on transition-related issues. In some cases, parents who were very engaged in their children's education were criticized by teachers for trusting too little in teacher advice related to transition. Parents were blamed for overestimating their children's capacities and for being overly ambitious, especially if they had a lower socio-economic or a migration background. A principal of an Italian school illustrates this tension between parents and teachers very well:

> If parents were more present in some cases, but more absent in some others, they would help us to solve the main problems we have with their children. (Principal 15, Italy)

Conclusion

Our study confirms the significance of parent–school cooperation, particularly for students from disadvantaged backgrounds. Yet, school staff identified this group as 'problematic', suggesting that parents with low SES are often absent from school, and their interaction with school is often reactive rather than proactive. Parental absences generated negative teacher perceptions, as teachers often concluded that parents from disadvantaged backgrounds lack interest in education, have low educational aspirations, are not involved in education of their children and are not motivated to cooperate with school. Migrant families often came up in these discussions, since in many contexts there were concerns that migrant families are almost absent at school. Although teacher narratives often hold parents responsible for their apathy and non-participation, there might be other reasons that explain their detachment. Our interviews with migrant families point to how parents deeply care about their children's learning and view education as an important tool for socio-economic mobility (see also Crozier, 2001). These accounts also reveal that migrant families support their children's education at home in ways that are not so visible and apparent to educators. Hence, we encountered several parents who felt that their efforts and contribution were not acknowledged at school. Some also felt that they were not treated respectfully and therefore they withdrew from school. In such situations, there was a high risk of both teachers and parents engaging in an unproductive 'blame game', as identified in some other studies as well (Dahlstedt, 2009).

Our findings also confirm that parental involvement is strongly class-related. Access to, and deployment of, a set of social, cultural and material resources shapes parental voice in schools. Hence, different reactions and reasons might be underlying what is perceived as 'parental silence' (Vincent and Martin, 2002). We identified factors such as language proficiency, parental education level, knowledge of education system, trust in school, institutional factors, and divergent teacher and parental expectations as mediating parental involvement. Lack of active relationships with schools might be more related to these complex issues rather than to parental inertia. Furthermore, the recurrent tension between schools and families can also be explained by looking at the differences between the socio-economic backgrounds of teachers and families. Analysis of teacher training shows that in most countries, teacher–students come from middle-class families and only very few of them have a migrant background (Cramer et al., 2012). Hence they often have limited understanding of how families from disadvantaged backgrounds live, what challenges they encounter in their daily lives and how these contextual factors impede their involvement in education. Moreover, schools tend to be middle-class institutions, and teachers expect parents to socialize their children in a 'normal' way, which is mainly informed by middle-class norms. Such perceptions and expectations can generate conflicts when school staff cooperate with families from low SES families, especially when the values and norms of these groups are ignored or refused (Ferguson, 2005; Waanders et al., 2007).

The current approach to parental involvement is characterized by a 'one size fits all' approach, assuming that all parents are the same and have the same needs, so that their children can be treated in the same way. Such an approach 'masks the complexity of needs, the roles that ethnic minority parents are playing, or the constraints that impede their involvement, and at the heart of this is structural racism' (Crozier, 2001: 330). Based on our findings, we suggest that educators need to move beyond such universalist approaches, and improve their understanding of the effects of contextual factors that mediate parental involvement. This can potentially foster more positive teacher attitudes towards parental involvement, and enable educators to target their efforts more effectively (Waanders et al., 2007). Moreover, educators may have to think outside of their own cultural lenses and acknowledge that what is considered 'good' parental involvement is largely culturally defined (Epstein, 2005). Hence, instead of having a deficit approach, educationalists may come to see that low SES may have different ways of supporting their children's learning (Protheroe, 2006; Huntsinger and Jose, 2009). Recognizing this means that home-based parental support is highly important because studies show that how parents interact with their children at home and provide educational support is a more important predictor of academic achievement than the extent to which parents cooperate with schools (Zellman and Waterman, 1998). Furthermore, intervention programmes need to have an integrated approach, involving activities that aim to enhance the connectivity between schools and parents, as well as training programmes that target parents. Stimulating high-quality parental involvement in schooling may help reduce performance differences across diverse socio-economic groups (OECD, 2012b), and contribute to the efforts to promote social justice through educational approaches.

Part 4

Relevance of Education

9

Comparing the Views of Students, Parents and Teachers on the Emerging Notions of Relevance of Education

Joanne McDowell
University of Hertfordshire

Andreja Živoder
University of Ljubljana

Alessandro Tolomelli
University of Bologna

Introduction and Methodology

Tackling educational disadvantage depends on the successful balancing of societal and individual demands, as well as the actual returns of education. Consequently, this is reflected in the different notions of 'relevance' that various groups attribute to education, and how this impacts on youths' aspirations and investment, be it emotional, financial or cultural, within their education and schooling experience. Against this paradigm, this chapter examines various actors' notions of the relevance of education today as they emerge in the individual learner context. It compares the views of students who are in transition from lower secondary to upper secondary education, as well as that of the parents and teachers who are also involved in these transition processes.

Understanding the relevance of education to the aforementioned actors is a complex undertaking due to the intertwined factors and circumstances, some of which are more *systemic* (such as the form, accessibility and permeability of the education system, welfare state, labour market or the economic position and related education background of the families), while others are more *subjective* (such as the motives and abilities of individual learners, or the social and cultural capital of the families). Furthermore, individuals' notions of the relevance of education are often embedded in a highly interactive process, where teachers frequently play a crucial role in the mediation of societal and subjective needs, thus shaping notions of relevance. In most cases, the individual notions of relevance derive from the interaction of *all* these factors, which is why they cannot be attributed exclusively to either subjective or systemic factors.

In order to grasp *why* and *how* subjective notions of the relevance of education emerge, they must be placed within wider societal settings to account for the specific contemporary conditions in which the lives of students and their families are embedded. The most notable and influential contemporary trends highlighted by recent research on education and youth are *individualization* and the related increasing *individual responsibility* for managing life choices and societal reproduction (Beck, 1992; Bauman, 2001; Beck and Beck-Gernsheim, 2002); the *de-standardization* and *pluralization* of life courses and transitions (Brückner and Mayer, 2005; du Bois-Reymond and Chisholm, 2006; Walther, 2006; Kohli, 2007); the *changing relationships* between parents and children (especially in terms of prolonged youth, education and economic dependence on parents) (Beck-Gernsheim, 2002; Biggart et al., 2002; Leccardi and Ruspini, 2006; Ule, 2013; Ule et al., 2015); and the insecure, precarious and rapidly *changing labour markets*.

Notions of relevance of education are also significantly shaped by the features of the respective education systems in which students' educational trajectories and transitions take place. For the purposes of this chapter we utilize Allmendinger's (1989) typology of education systems (see Tikkanen et al., in this volume), which proposes that schools can be classified according to the criteria of stratification and standardization of educational systems.[1] Social class and its related social, economic and cultural position is also a factor that might have considerable influence on the formation of perceptions regarding the relevance of education, as well as the reproduction of socio-economic and educational disadvantage. In the words of Pierre Bourdieu: 'it [education] is in fact one of the most effective means of perpetuating the existing social pattern, as it both provides an apparent justification for social inequalities and gives recognition to the cultural heritage, that is, to a social gift treated as a natural one' (Bourdieu, 1974: 32). Consequently, the analysis of empirical data will also address the socio-economic and cultural context.[2]

This chapter draws on the quantitative and qualitative data gathered in the GOETE project[3] that involves eight European countries: Finland, France, Germany, Italy, the Netherlands, Poland, Slovenia and the UK. Standardized individual surveys were carried out with students (N=6390) in their last year of compulsory education (aged 13–16 years), and their parents (N=3290).[4] In-depth interviews and focus group discussions were held with students (N=195), ex-students (N=109), parents (N=109) and teachers (N=109) as part of qualitative case studies taking place within twenty-four local schools in disadvantaged city areas (one school per city, three schools in each country). This generated in-depth information about the processes and outcomes of the governance of educational trajectories of students in local settings (du Bois-Reymond et al., 2012).

Relevance of Education: Empirical Evidence

The current empirical analysis is structured and analysed in three thematic sections. We begin by identifying and analysing the key notions of ir/relevance of education for students' lives in contemporary society as they emerged in the quantitative surveys, qualitative interviews and focus groups with students, their parents and teachers. By comparing students', parents' and teachers' notions of relevance, we will attempt to determine their mutual interdependence and establish the complex role and influence of both parents and families, as well as giving consideration to teachers as institutional representatives beyond constraining socio-economic and systemic factors. We continue by examining the links between ir/relevance of education and the future of students as perceived by respondents and, finally, identify and analyse the key barriers, concerns and worries related to education, as well as considering experts' suggestions for breaking through existing barriers. Throughout the chapter, empirical findings are contextualized in terms of the contemporary socio-economic and institutional setting, particularly in terms of the characteristics of educational systems and socio-economic and cultural capital of students and their families.

The following analysis will also be based on the concepts of 'cultural arbitrary' (Bourdieu and Passeron, 1990) and 'habitus' (Bourdieu, 1974). According to this perspective, the predominant ideas on education are the result of the ability of a particular mainstream group(s) who impose their own conception of 'culture' or 'relevance' as 'cultural arbitraries' that reflect their own interests (cf. Bourdieu and Passeron, 1990). Bourdieu and Passeron emphasize that it is mainly the educational system that institutionalizes these cultural arbitraries: for instance in the form of making them into qualifications, and by making the allocation of those qualifications appear as the result of individual ability (or the lack thereof). The specific content of the dominant cultural or linguistic form – or cultural capital – is less important for Bourdieu's theory than the mere existence of an arbitrary standard which is recognized as legitimate even by those unable to reach it. Lower-class students do not, in general, possess these traits, so the failure of the majority of these students is inevitable. However, this failure is often explained as 'natural' rather than socio-politically constructed. Therefore, for Bourdieu, educational credentials help to reproduce and legitimate social inequalities, as higher-class individuals are seen to deserve their privileged access to them. Bourdieu (1990) also forged the concept of 'habitus', which is a system of durable and transportable dispositions inculcated by objective structural conditions (such as family background, experiences and ways of seeing the world). Crucially, the habitus is seen as being embodied, and as generating practices for members of particular social groups (and it should be noted that all social groups have their own habitus, not just the socially disadvantaged; indeed it is precisely habitus that distinguishes the academically, socially and economically successful) (Bourdieu, 1990). Bourdieu regards school as a productive 'locus of habitus', which gives rise to patterns of thought that 'organize reality by directing and organizing thinking about reality by directing and makes what he thinks thinkable for him as such and in the particular form in which it is thought' (1971: 194–5), so that 'it may be assumed that every individual owes to the type of schooling he has received a set of basic deeply interiorized master patterns' (Bourdieu, 1971: 192–3). Consequently, together, the cultural arbitrary and the habitus powerfully, though not automatically or definitively, shape conceptions of educational relevance. In essence, the cultural arbitrary means that everyone is guided to want the same things and the habitus means that they all have different and durable capacities to achieve those ends.

Key notions of ir/relevance of education

'Education' and *Bildung* are two different concepts that refer to the same topic. While 'education' within contemporary social and policy discourses regards the provision and acquisition of a certain set of skills (which means more practical abilities and competencies are interpreted as being useful in terms of occupational qualification and hence better life chances), *Bildung* sees education as an end-in-itself for the individual, which refers to their human development and pedagogical interactions (Stojanov, 2012: 1).

The analysis of the relevance of education according to different actors mirrors the more recent trends of educational policy in the view of this restricted concept of 'education' as previously defined, much more than that of the *Bildung* perspective. Moreover, the role of education varies according to the actors. Relevance of education from the students' perspective depends on the level of importance that young people assign to getting an education, as well as on their 'objective' possibilities of being able to do so (Walther, 2009). Therefore, students have different ideas as to what they can do with their current level of education, and what it may do for them at this stage in their lives (move into work or further education).

It is evident from the data that both systems and theoretical concepts of education condition students' decisions through family and educational professional influence. However, we found interesting contradictions in our data. Students who appeared to be more sceptical about the links between education and access to the labour market (e.g. Germany, where access to elite secondary education is highly contested) stressed that education was more than just a means for accumulating economic capital, stressing the cultural and social aspects of education as well. On the other hand, students who strongly believed that education can open the door into a good career emphasized a more systematic interpretation of education in terms of access to the labour market, economic capital and material wealth.

The parents' viewpoint is generally in consensus with the 'education' paradigm due to the fact that their perspective is driven by the socio-economic security of their children. According to the concept of *Bildung*, teachers also frequently refer to the reflexive process of their students, who in their view should realize their human potential. The interesting aspect of many of the teachers' perspectives is that they mirror the contents and values of their own education pathways. One dimension of the relevance of education for teachers is the belief that they need to guide students to become active and contributing members of society. While students and parents both stress the future occupational aspect of education, teachers tend to place more emphasis on the *Bildung* idea of education. But this idealistic view of education conceals a discrepancy as even though teachers' representation seems to reflect a more *Bildung* concept of education, the school systems of the eight contributing countries are based on a social selective framework. Therefore, the 'relevance of education' has also to be considered in terms of social and cultural reproduction. Despite teachers' professional perspectives based on the *Bildung* concept, the nature and consequences of social class differences also play an extremely important role which is often opposed to this idea. Bourdieu's ideas of 'cultural arbitrary' and 'habitus' as well as 'forms of capital' (cultural, social and economic) represent a very interesting and useful framework for analysis. As Bourdieu writes:

> the structure of the distribution of the different types and subtypes of capital at a given moment in time represents the immanent structure of the social world, i.e. the set of constraints, inscribed in the very reality of that world, which govern its functionality in a durable way, determine the chances of success for practices. (Bourdieu, 1986: 46)

Drawing on the GOETE data (Litau et al., 2013) the cultural, social, economic and symbolic capital of students plays an important role in their educational process because these factors contribute to the perception of the relevance of their education. The majority of the students recognized that occupations are differentiated by a hierarchy of power and status, and that education is the key to getting a job that can offer higher social status providing the symbolic capital of possessing credentials. However, even with some variations across the eight countries, students generally acknowledged not only the symbolic capital of education but also its cultural, social and economic capital. Students who are quite sceptical about the links of education to work (economic capital) found it to be relevant for other reasons (social, cultural, symbolic) and embraced a more subjective interpretation of the relevance of education. Furthermore, students' motivation is influenced by their own interpretations. Examining students' perspectives of the relevance they assigned to education highlighted some differences between those with a mainly subjective interpretation (e.g. France) and those with a systematic interpretation of education (e.g. the UK), while certain students held both views (e.g. Slovenia, Finland, Germany).

From the perspective of the theory of social mobility, one's belonging to a social class is not fixed for the whole life course – she or he is able to move up or down in the social hierarchy (Schüren, 1989). Today, this type of vertical mobility is strongly connected to occupational change. This was especially true for females, who aimed for higher education levels than their male counterparts as they regarded education as a means of independence, self-provision and status (e.g. the Netherlands). Almost overriding habitus at one level in the form of educational aspirations – an indication of the power of the cultural arbitrary that places the highest emphasis on economic achievement – parents regard education as very important for their children's future. The great majority (almost 90 per cent) would like their child to remain in full-time education after finishing compulsory education, and over 60 per cent of that cohort wants their child to reach the tertiary educational level.

Nevertheless, socio-demographic analysis has revealed highly distinctive patterns as parents with more socio-economic and cultural capital express considerably higher educational aspirations. The differences between these groups of parents are extremely evident. For example, 81 per cent of parents who possess tertiary education qualifications, compared to 41 per cent of parents with a more basic education, want their children to achieve higher/further education. Such significant differences in educational aspirations are certainly not coincidental. On the one hand, they are the reflection of not only the perceived relevance of education in terms of different social or cultural capital of families, but also of the different educational possibilities, opportunities and systems that are available to the different families in contemporary society – largely as a consequence of high-level governance, especially in respect to the first transition. They therefore point towards the confirmation of Bourdieu's thesis on the social reproduction of capitals, e.g. the reproduction of educational inequalities, which then leads to the overall reproduction of socio-economic inequalities.

Teachers' perspectives of the relevance of education are dominated by an understanding of education as knowledge transfer rather than considering all the capital dimensions of education as relevant. This means that for teachers, the main task of education is seen to be providing knowledge that gives young people a better chance in the labour market so they can care for themselves and become valuable full-value members of society. This attitude and understanding of the relevance of education is evident across a vast range of their teaching methods (McDowell et al., 2012). Lessons and support are more organized in terms of knowledge transfer and less on self-reflection and reasonable thinking. This can be interpreted as an implicit aim to make students accumulate all three types of capital on their own. Of course, teachers cannot provide economic capital, but they have the potential to provide the social and cultural capital required for students to be able to develop during their life course in order to enhance their economic capital.

Regarding the issue of qualification and allocation, it was evident that all teacher trainers agreed that school and education were about delivering knowledge in order to prepare students for their future occupation and therefore the main duty of teachers (Cramer et al., 2012). However, we also need to appreciate that educational credentials do not convert directly into economic and cultural capital. Research results indicate that despite high hopes that education should enable social mobility, educational inequalities are most likely to be reproduced throughout society. But we cannot ignore the claim that the relevance of the social dimension of education also means the preparation of young people to act responsibly in a diverse world. The conjunction of the cultural arbitrary and the embeddedness of habitus produce quite different conceptions of relevance in education. However, we have to recognize that the conceptions and practices of educational relevance that operate within this framework are certainly not completely deterministic, though nevertheless quite predictable. There are even hints that a different conception of educational relevance could lead to schools becoming involved in forms of individual and social capacity building that are not reduced to, or dependent on, success in the terms framed by the cultural arbitrary and the habitus.

Education and the future

As illustrated in the previous section on Relevance of Education, this chapter's empirical findings demonstrate that quite different conceptions of relevance of education coexist, depending on the various systemic characteristics of educational systems, social, economic and cultural capital, and the subjective perspective of individual respondents. What all these conceptions about the importance of education have in common, however, is their inherent link to the *future lives of students*. As life course studies have shown, individual biographies, transitions and choices, including educational transitions and trajectories, are not only dependent on present opportunities and motivations, or even past achievements and experiences, but are crucially bound to future expectations, hopes and plans (du Bois-Reymond, 1998; Payne, 2003; Reiter, 2003; Leccardi, 2008; Grytnes, 2011).[5] As a Slovenian student explains:

> Education is actually also a part of your life. It decides how you will live, what kind of life you will have. It is not only the money, but your decision, how you will live.

Or, even more directly, a female student from the Netherlands:

> I think education is highly important and I'm not someone who would consider finding a rich husband, sit at home and watch daytime TV shows.

The most direct testimonies about the high relevance of education for future lives of students are the very high educational aspirations of students and their parents. McDowell et al. (2012) found that 47 per cent of students hoped to achieve at least a tertiary level of education, while the aspirations of their parents are higher, with 62 per cent of parents wanting their children to achieve this tertiary level of education. A mother from Slovenia expressed her high ambitions in the following way: 'I see it this way, for my children, I want them to attain a high education, right. And if there is even more, then even better' (McDowell et al., 2012).

Educational aspirations are closely related to the expectations and hopes for the future, but as McDowell et al. (2012) illustrate, aspirations are also significantly related to the systemically available opportunities, where socio-economical dis/advantage plays a crucial role – educational aspirations of disadvantaged students and their parents are considerably lower than those of their more affluent and educated counterparts. To illustrate this: 41 per cent of mothers who have tertiary education, and only 11 per cent of mothers who have basic education, expect their children to achieve tertiary education.

Furthermore, parents who are more disadvantaged are less satisfied with their child's school performance, have minimum access to private tutoring and are least confident that their child will achieve their desired level of education. They are also the most convinced that there are barriers standing in their child's way, especially concerning a lack of financial resources, which means they think they will not be able to support the child financially to achieve their educational goals. All this illustrates that the more disadvantaged families face the greatest difficulties when supporting their child despite the fact that the majority of parents believe education to be very important for the child's future. In terms of life course, this increases the feelings of subjective disadvantage, feelings of personal failure and a lack of control over one's life, especially if we consider that modern societies have successfully shifted the burden and responsibility for its reproduction to individuals (families). A hindered access to education leads to a lowering of aspirations and confidence, which transmutes into a 'cooling out', lowering hopes and goals for the future, i.e. students face decreased possibilities to plan their future life course.

The link between education and employment opportunities is one of the key concerns of all actors in students' future educational trajectories. Future employment opportunities can be singled out as the most important and most distinctly voiced reason for the relevance of education by students and parents, as well as teachers. Future employment opportunities, however, have a twofold significance. The first is their *systemic or instrumental significance*, which is related especially to external social, economic and employment circumstances in present society. Here, getting a job in the first place is of prime importance.

Students are aiming to get an education that will allow them to get a relatively secure job: one with little risk in the current uncertain and changing labour market. In addition, they want a job that allows a relatively prosperous socio-economic position.

Such an understanding of the relevance of education often aims at its instrumental value, that is, the value of educational or vocational certificates, where education is seen mostly as a tool in achieving other goals, while knowledge per se is less valued. McDowell et al. (2012) have shown that 56 per cent of students opted for an instrumental reason as most important in choosing a job: 37 per cent chose gaining a good income and 13 per cent chose wanting a safe job with no risk of unemployment as the number one reason for choosing a job. When parents were asked the main reason they wanted their child to get a certain level of education, their answers were considerably less instrumental: 13 per cent of parents chose a good income and 17 per cent secure employment.

On the other hand, there is *the subjective or personal significance* of future employment opportunities, which is related to subjective and even an emotional view of employment. Students and their parents would like children to have interesting, enjoyable jobs to deliver feelings of accomplishment and achieve self-realization. For example, as one parent from Poland highlighted: 'How can I hurt my kid making him learn? That is not the point. I would do more harm if I had made him go to work that is unsatisfactory.' According to McDowell et al. (2012), 20 per cent of students want an interesting job regardless of pay, 17 per cent want an important job that gives feelings of accomplishment, while for 5 per cent the most important aspect is working with people they like.

Parents, on the other hand, are more prone to the subjective significance of education, with more than 67 per cent of all parents pointing to one of the subjective reasons for importance of education. However, a more detailed analysis revealed that parental reasons for desired education are dependent on their socio-economic position; subjective reasons are more prominent in families that are more affluent. The more affluent the parents are or the more socio-economic-cultural capital they have, the more they can afford to plan or think about their child's future in line with their children's interests, desires and abilities. The more disadvantaged parents are, the more their wishes, plans and aspirations are subjected to external fluctuations of capital, demands in the labour market and current socio-economic prospects in the society. All these factors intertwine and reinforce both the subjective and objective shortcomings of the more disadvantaged students and families and thus have considerable and negative long-term influence over the life course trajectories of the students involved.

What is more, some common understandings of the relevance of education of socially disadvantaged families were found (McDowell et al., 2012). For example, in many countries, these families view education as a method to gain upward social mobility (for example Turkish families in Germany and the Netherlands, some parents in France, the UK, Poland and Slovenia). These families regard education as the most promising strategy for their children to reach a higher social and economic standing. In relation to this understanding, many see education as providing a better life than they themselves had. As a parent from Poland states: 'I wish he would get more than I'. Many more disadvantaged parents left education too early for various reasons (financial, family, migration, disliked it, education was not regarded as necessary, etc.) and/or were unemployed or working in poorly paid positions. What is most important here is that some socially disadvantaged families hope or believe that education is the only possible path out of the reproduction of social inequalities, while others are much more sceptical about the link between education and labour market opportunities or even the well-being of children in general.

Teachers too share the view about the high relevance of education, particularly when it comes to the future lives of their students. They emphasize a twofold character of education, according to which education is not only about knowledge transfer, but, also importantly about the acquisition of social and/or life skills. For example, as one Italian teacher vividly illustrated: 'School is a gym for life, a gym for training the citizens of tomorrow, learning to interact with all kinds of people, representing different cultures and ways of thinking.' A similar comment was made by a French teacher: 'For most of our students what we are teaching to them does not make sense and I think they won't use it. Yet, interpersonal skills, relations with others as future citizens, that's more than all the theoretical knowledge we can bring to them.'

However, compared to students and their parents, teachers often showed a more pessimistic view about students' future plans (McDowell et al., 2012). They highlighted that some students have very unrealistic plans for their future as they often overestimate their own capabilities. Such students enrol on demanding programmes where they cannot academically manage, and this can have adverse consequences in the short or long term, sometimes even resulting in education dropout.

Although educational aspirations are generally high, and education is considered crucial to educational trajectories, students, parents and teachers have also expressed considerable cynicism about the link between education and job possibilities. This indicates a rising awareness that in contemporary European society, education alone is no longer a guarantee for later career possibilities or secure, long-term employment. Each group of actors has raised concerns that education today does not guarantee getting a job (especially due to the poor employment prospects and economic recession), nor sufficiently well-paid or secure (long-term) employment. Parents are especially concerned about the unpredictability of present labour markets; a statement from a parent from Finland illustrates:

> Sometimes it feels like the world is changing so fast so that the choices the students possibly make now are not valid any more at a later point. Nowadays you cannot trust the permanency of factory jobs or blue-collar jobs, not even universities. That it is really hard to predict what really in the end will work.

Students and parents both expressed their doubts about the 'meaning' and 'power' of education when they discussed their dissatisfaction with contemporary employment possibilities, claiming that having the proper 'connections and acquaintances' is often much more important than having adequate qualifications (du Bois-Reymond et al., 2012). Another important issue is whether education is considered important to the students with regard to the knowledge it provides and transmits, and whether this knowledge is relevant to everyday life. Many teachers complained about a lack of motivation in students, which they interpreted as an incorrect understanding of the relevance of education.

Barriers, concerns and worries

As reported before, over 70 per cent of the student cohort in nearly every country wishes to stay on in education. However, this desire to remain in education varies from country to country. For example, in France, 56 per cent of students wish to remain in full-time education, in Germany 75 per cent and the Netherlands only 41 per cent, illustrating that despite being in similar education systems (highly stratified/high standardized), the students in these countries place different emphasis on staying in education beyond compulsory schooling. We can assume that besides personal problems, young people have to face multi-dimensional institutional barriers at points of transition from compulsory to secondary/vocational school, which could account for such differences. Alongside an examination of the level of importance students place on their education and their future transition pathways, it is important to address such foreseen barriers to their pathways and how they may be addressed, as such issues directly affect students' and parents' perceptions of the relevance of education (McDowell et al., 2012).

Socio-economic factors were a key barrier to educational aspirations, with students in disadvantaged schools much less likely to aspire to a university education (McDowell et al., 2012). While nearly two-thirds of students from disadvantaged backgrounds did not want to go to university, over half of those (61 per cent) from affluent schools did, with the average schools falling somewhere in between. At the European level there is a relative balance between students in vocational and general education; nevertheless high variations exist between individual countries (McDowell et al., 2012). In some countries (Germany, the UK, the Netherlands) vocational education still has low status and academic pathways are seen to be more prestigious especially among more affluent families. This may help explain the differences in attitudes toward attending university between the disadvantaged and affluent schools.

Education systems also played a role in the future transition expectations of the pupils, with gaining further academic education of less relevance in high stratified/high standardized education systems than in others. In terms of Allmendinger's typology, 81 per cent of students in the low stratified/low standardized cohort wanted to remain in full-time education compared to 77 per cent in the low stratified/high standardized group, and only 58 per cent in the high stratified/high standardized group. These differences may be explained by the expectations these students have of their capabilities in relation to their school, especially in highly stratified systems where it remains very difficult to proceed onto higher education if students start within vocational education. Therefore highly stratified systems may prevent students from even acknowledging university as a possibility (du Bois-Reymond et al., 2012). These results are certainly a reflection of barriers to education: in countries where the education system is more differentiated and stratified, some educational routes are not available to some students (those in lower tracks), which is why they are 'beyond' expectations and thus not necessarily an indication of lower aspirations in general. Nevertheless, the Netherlands is an exception in Allmendinger's (1989) group of high stratification/high standardization systems, since it shows the second highest educational aspirations among all of the countries.

For parents, the barriers facing their child were one of the important factors affecting their thoughts on the relevance of education, as highlighted in the section on Education and the Future. In the overall sample of parents, almost a quarter of respondents stated there was some form of barrier standing in their child's way. Analysis revealed the most common barriers to be: their child might not do well enough in school to continue with education (23 per cent); lack of financial resources (18 per cent); and an intensely high competition for places at the university (16 per cent). However, how parents feel that these barriers will affect their children substantially differs across the countries and respective educational systems. Parents with the most concerns were located in Poland and in Italy (countries where standardization and stratification of the educational system are low), and those with the least concerns in Finland and Slovenia (countries where the educational system is highly standardized, but with low stratification). Moreover, parents who have the lowest levels of education (ISCED) and socio-cultural capital feel they face the majority of existing barriers to their children attaining desired levels of education, which could also partially explain why their educational aspirations are lower. Results show that these parents worry considerably more about their child's inability to find employment and doing badly in school because they cannot provide enough help or support to improve their child's chances. These results confirm that students with higher socio-cultural capital have better opportunities, more available support from their educated parents and better access to resources, meaning a higher level of school performance and hence employment possibilities. Once again, data confirms the likely social reproduction of educational and social inequalities. The concerns that parents have in regard to their child finding employment, or performing badly in school, are not directly explained by the specifics of the educational systems in the individual countries. Instead, these worries are more related to the general conditions/prospects of the labour market and the economy of each country, as well as to the level of socio-economic deprivation and socio-cultural capital of the families themselves.

Interestingly, one of the most influential barriers to our students was their gender. Males appear to be significantly more sceptical about the relevance of education than females, illustrating that the young women in the GOETE study find education more essential for their future success than young men do (Hodgson, 2008). When asked what they think they will be doing after compulsory education, 75 per cent of females wanted to remain in full-time education in comparison to 67 per cent of the male cohort. Women want to achieve higher education levels than the men (McDowell et al., 2012). This was explored further in interviews, and for many of the female participants their preference for a prolonged education was a result of fewer opportunities for them as women in the labour market, especially in the world of business and commerce, and the assumption that more education may widen their access. This supports both school assessment and qualitative research that suggests that young women find education more relevant for future success than young men (Hodgson, 2008). This may be a result of the desire women have to climb the ladder to gain social status and have independence, to move away from just being housewives and mothers. Many desire to work, and therefore know they must do well in school in order to achieve this. This illustrates how relevance is constructed according to different social positions. From the perspective of the *theory of social mobility*, one's belonging to a social class is not fixed for the whole life course; she or he is able to move up or down in the social hierarchy (Schüren, 1989). Today, this kind of vertical mobility is strongly connected to occupational changes, and upward social mobility and status can be achieved through one's occupation.

Breaking the barriers: Experts' perspective on making education more relevant

In all eight GOETE countries, we can find barriers caused by inequalities in the education systems. Socially disadvantaged students self-report facing the most barriers, so are more likely to enter vocational rather than academic streams, and are statistically much more likely to end up as early school leavers, which often leads them to unemployment. Also, the likelihood of socially disadvantaged students being able to access the highest performing secondary schools (for example those with the highest proportions of their students progressing onto tertiary education) is much lower than for those from more prosperous backgrounds. These outcomes of poverty are 'unintended' but nevertheless persistent and almost universal across the eight countries (Dale et al., 2012). Experts in all GOETE countries are aware of these inequalities and therefore many see it as an important task of the school to reduce or compensate social inequalities, especially in cases where the student does not receive support from the family. However, as yet no education system, comprehensive or differentiated, has succeeded in erasing social inequalities.

To support a fairer education with the removal of some of these barriers, experts and teachers feel that it is important to provide multilevel tools. For students, it would be important to develop school and community-based counselling services to give young people an opportunity to face their problems and get support, but also to focus on their own educational desires and needs. For the schools as well as for social care systems, early recognition of students in disadvantaged situations is crucial to provide individual tutoring and support and thus help the student avoid early school dropout. Parents also need to be supported about their educational and care commitments and need assistance on how to support their children. In this regard, it would be useful to provide training for parents so they will be prepared to support their own offspring in the education process. A differentiated school system and early selection is one important feature, which is regarded as putting students in a disadvantageous position. A unified school system without any separation in different school tracks is seen as key to removing barriers by many experts as it avoids early selection and therefore early disadvantage which often follows. European and local institutions are recommended to elaborate policy responses inspired by an opportunity-focused approach and aimed to a strategic financial investment. This step must be addressed by reflexive forms of policymaking, inspired by evidence of best practices, which are available in the European environment and are oriented to reduce the impact of transitions within the educational process.

Of course, it is very difficult to draw a Europe-wide picture because of the large variations in: the policy systems in the different European countries; the problems of youth at risk of social exclusion; the socio-economic conditions and cultural environments; and the scale of migration, ethnic minority presence, youth unemployment and numbers of excluded young people in these countries. Nevertheless, it is hoped that the ideas shared in our research will increase awareness of the particular social, economic and political needs of young people within their educational European space to make their needs more visible in policy agendas. These needs include the opportunities for students to gain their desired educational credentials, and preventing potential social disadvantage developing into social exclusion.

Conclusion

This chapter was concerned with outlining multiple perspectives to address the following questions: how important education is for young people (how relevant) and why it is seen to be relevant in that particular sense (why and in what sense relevant). As students are surrounded by a plethora of different actors that may have similar or different views on their educational trajectories, this chapter examined the different interpretations and understandings of the relevance of education within and between each group of actors (students, parents, teachers and experts).

A number of similarities and differences in perceptions of the relevance of education have been found, and not only among the different actors within the participating countries and educational systems. Regardless of the various argumentations and reasons for the relevance of education, there is a commonly shared view across the majority of the respondents that educational choices have a significant influence on the future lives of students. Despite the fact that the majority of respondents are aware that education is not a guarantee for a successful and secure position in the labour market, the link is still seen to be crucial, with students evaluating the relevance of education in relation to their life course and to their future transition plans. For the majority of young people, education is relevant for achieving the skills and certificates required in terms of gaining opportunities for their future career as well as forging good relationships with their peers in their school environment. In terms of influence, students' opinion on relevance of education has largely been influenced both by their parents' opinion and by their educational system and the current economic climate in their country. Although some students also mention the importance of making a contribution to their society, the majority in every country stressed some form of economic influence as to why they needed an education.

For parents, the 'relevance of education' largely means providing their children with the knowledge, necessary skills and educational certificates that would offer them prosperous and secure future possibilities and opportunities, especially in terms of access to the (insecure and rapidly changing) labour market. As with students, education was seen primarily as key to ensure a good and secure socio-economic position in society. However, to assert that parents mainly view education from the instrumental perspective would be rather misleading, since parents also emphasized the subjective side of future employments, such as feelings of accomplishment, fulfilment, enjoyment in future professions, where the path towards such rewarding employments is precisely through attaining high and relevant education. Although some of these families believe that the education is the right and possible path out of the reproduction of social inequalities, the research results show that on the overall level, educational and social inequalities are likely to be reproduced (Bourdieu and Passeron, 1990).

Teachers in all GOETE countries emphasize the twofold character and tasks of education that shape their view of its relevance. In their view, it is undisputed and unquestioned that education is about knowledge transfer and about conveying social or life skills. The former is knowledge based, in the same way as language proficiency or numeracy. The latter covers the whole personality and includes behaviour, manners or general competence in dealing with aspirations in terms of what students can do in the future. For many teachers both dimensions are intertwined in their orientation to make their students able to find a job after finishing school. To achieve that, they believe that knowledge transfer on the one hand, and social skills one the other, are the keys to be more able to cope with the demands in transition, and with the demands of the labour market more generally, as well as being better able to become, and to stay, integrated in the society. The aim to enjoy learning or to have fun in school (like in the case of the UK) seems to be subordinate or irrelevant. Indeed this perspective has passed onto students.

For experts, the relevance of education is judged on a meta-level. Their discussions on the relevance of education are closely linked to a discourse of preventing marginalization, e.g. preventing unemployment. Experts underline that aims, methodology and each school's teaching approach are related not only to pupils' achievements in school subjects, but also to the transmission of tools and skills aimed at social integration.

Education and school not only have an important role in preparing young people for the labour market, but also contain a crucial socializing aspect of schools' work, as well as an important role in decreasing social inequalities. However, different education systems provide students with different opportunities. In some differentiated education systems that have early selection for example, a student cannot easily change his or her educational trajectory, while comprehensive systems provide students with more opportunities to change and an educational trajectory even if it has already commenced. In countries with well-developed apprenticeship or work placement training (e.g. Germany and the Netherlands), students may choose to enrol in full-time education or enter the labour market after compulsory education, while in others full-time education is considered to be the only real option (e.g. Finland and Slovenia). Because of the different education systems' emphases on the nature and aspects of relevance, conceptions of relevance of education differ across the GOETE countries. Polish students see that education is something they must earn, and so want to gain as many qualifications as possible. On the other hand, French students see apprenticeship training or a full-time job as an opportunity they all have once compulsory education finishes. In differentiated and stratified education systems, some routes to higher education are not available for students in lower tracks; they are 'beyond' their expectations and cannot therefore necessarily be seen as an indicator of low aspirations of students and parents.

The differences between education systems as well as country differences make it difficult to provide general recommendations on policy and practice. However, results show that family background is of great importance in influencing the opportunities students can have in their life course, and how they perceive the relevance of education. It not only shapes how students perceive the relevance of education for their future life, but is also significant in providing different learning opportunities. There seems to be a general trend in reducing schools' role in providing students with different learning opportunities outside the curriculum, which has been shown to be important in providing them with the learning experiences that they do not receive from home. Therefore, it is important for the schools to have sufficient knowledge on how to support students who are typified as disadvantaged. Socially disadvantaged students who do not receive support from home are in the most vulnerable position if they do not receive support from their school. Schools should therefore be encouraged to provide students with different non-formal learning opportunities and out-of-school activities in order to increase their levels of student support.

10

The Relevance of Informal Learning and Out-of-School Contexts for Formal Educational Transitions

Veronica Salovaara
University of Helsinki

John Litau
University of Frankfurt

Introduction

In the transition phase from lower secondary school to upper secondary education and training, formal education is often regarded as the main important factor in determining a successful transition. However, contemporary Western society is characterized by an unstable labour market, widespread youth unemployment and uncertainty about the exact type of skills and knowledge that are required on the labour market. Consequently, there has been a shift towards a discourse of lifelong learning, a continuous need of re-educating oneself in order to cope with the demands of, and managing oneself on, the labour market. In this discourse, informal learning and learning in out-of-school contexts have gained a more important role (e.g. Coffield, 2000; Scheerens, 2009; Werquin, 2010).

Learning occurs in all kinds of situations: 'learning, apart from being stimulated by formal and explicit teaching, is seen as also taking place during the daily experiences inside and outside classrooms' (Scheerens, 2009: 3). Hence, by informal learning we mean learning that takes place in everyday life, inside and outside school, and is not organized. Although it is indisputable that young people learn informally in everyday life and non-formally in out-of-school contexts, this fact has not been much acknowledged in schools in practice (Coffield, 2000; Bekerman et al., 2006; Young, 2007; Jarvis, 2009). This leads to reasonable doubts whether the discourse of lifelong learning with its emphasis on the relevance of informal and non-formal learning is rather a mere rhetorical reality in schools.

Therefore, in this chapter we want to focus on informal learning and out-of-school contexts and their relevance for the transition phase. We analyse views of young people, teachers and other educational experts on the role and relevance of informal learning in young people's educational trajectories in Finland and Germany. The chapter draws on an extensive qualitative interview data set with students, teachers and educational experts (Litau et al., 2013). The analytical focus of the chapter captures the question of how informal learning and out-of-school learning are dealt with in school. This also involves examining to what extent different actors, involved directly and indirectly in education in school and educational trajectories, are conscious and aware of young people's informal learning. What relevance do they ascribe to informal learning and out-of-school contexts, and how is this learning recognized and made visible, or even being supported in, through or in relation to school?

Due to the diversity of European education systems we will analyse data from two countries, Finland and Germany, that have been classified as representing different transition regimes (Walther and Pohl, 2005; see also Tikkanen et al., in this volume). Although we are not able to systematically compare the data due to its complex diversity, we will highlight the views of different actors who are enrolled in the different education systems and may therefore be expected to reflect differently upon the relevance of informal learning and learning in out-of-school contexts.

1. The *Finnish education system* is a comprehensive system, where the selection of students happens for the first time in the transition phase from lower secondary to upper secondary school. Students apply either to general upper secondary school (which is the traditional route to university) or to vocational upper secondary school. Both routes lead to the tertiary level which consists of universities and polytechnics. Although vocational education can alternatively be taken as apprenticeship training, this is not a common route for Finnish students.
2. The *German education system* is more complex, due to its federal organization, with some significant specificities. One is the differentiation of lower secondary education which selects students into different tracks leading to qualifications with different status, and the system comprises therefore a strong stand of special schools. Another is the 'dual' vocational

training system which combines apprenticeship training in companies with vocational education in professional schools, according to centrally standardized profiles and curricula. Germany has a complex but developed system of apprenticeship and/or work placement training, and students may choose to enrol in full-time education or enter the labour market after compulsory education.

We will first discuss the theoretical concepts of formal education, informal learning and out-of-school contexts and address informal learning as a social practice. After a description of the methods and sample, the results of the analysis will be presented. Here we will explain how teachers, students and experts discuss informal learning and non-formal learning in out-of-school contexts. Subsequently we analyse how these actors reflect upon the relevance of learning in out-of-school contexts for educational transitions.

Theoretical Framework: Informal Learning and Learning in Out-of-School Contexts as Discourse and Social Practice

School is not only a place where students learn what is taught formally according to the formal curricula. Students also learn informally in school – with regard to hidden curricula, discrepancies between rhetoric and reality of participation, or the career destinations of peers in their communities (Jackson, 1968; Colley et al., 2002; Walther et al., 2006; Machacek and Walther, 2008). At the same time school is a meeting point and arena of youth cultures (e.g. Willis, 1977; Helve and Bynner, 2007) and for young people these areas might be experienced as even more important than formal education (Walther, 2009). In particular, the discourse on *lifelong* and *life-wide* learning and its recognition in the European educational space has led to a precise distinction of different forms of learning that are based on the institutional settings and social life worlds where, and in what ways, particular knowledge can be acquired (Delors et al., 1996). In line with the development and increasing relevance of knowledge societies, formal education alone is no longer a guarantee for a safe or secure employment in the contemporary European society. In the discourse of lifelong learning all learning, i.e. also learning that happens informally and non-formally in out-of-school contexts, is acknowledged as relevant (e.g. Coffield, 2000; Werquin, 2010). Or as Frank Coffield writes: 'Informal learning should no longer be regarded as an inferior form of learning whose main purpose is to act as the precursor of formal learning; it needs to be seen as fundamental, necessary and valuable in its own right, at times directly relevant to employment and at other times not relevant at all' (Coffield, 2000: 8). That means that informal learning and out-of-school contexts play a significant role for young people in contemporary society. For some, this can even result in an understanding of leisure time activities as a way of improving the curriculum vitae in order to increase their chances on the labour market (Määttä and Tolonen, 2011). This type of functionalization of informal learning processes raises questions regarding the meaning and relevance of informal learning contexts in school.

Before we can answer the question of relevance of informal learning and learning in out-of-school contexts empirically by analysing the perspectives of educational actors on that issue, we have to draw a theoretical distinction between what is understood as formal, non-formal and informal learning (based on the explanations of Schugurensky, 2000; Cedefop, 2008; Werquin, 2010) as well as explaining how learning is embedded in social relationships and interactions, and why informal learning is crucial for that understanding:

1. Formal learning refers to learning that occurs in an organized and structured environment, such as the institutionalized education system, and is explicitly designated as learning. Formal learning is intentional from the learner's point of view and often leads to certification. For young people, formal learning usually means learning in school by the formal school curricula.
2. Non-formal learning refers to all organized educational programmes that take place outside the formal school system. Non-formal learning is also intentional from the learner's point of view and is embedded in planned activities not explicitly designated as learning. For young people, non-formal learning usually means learning in extra-curricular activities in out-of-school contexts.
3. Informal learning refers to learning that takes place in everyday life and is unintentional from the learner's point of view. The idea with informal learning is that people are constantly exposed to learning situations, and that they learn unintentionally by experience. For young people, informal learning can take place inside formal and non-formal educational institutions, but the learning occurs independently of (and sometimes against) the intended goals of the explicit curriculum.

As there is no precise setting to which informal educational processes are bound, learning that is informal may take place everywhere and anytime. Self-referred learning in the sense of self-reflection may be one aspect of that process but even this type of learning is related to a social context. Self-reflection in this sense can be understood as coping with everyday life and as making sense of the daily routines. Informal learning therefore can be understood primarily as a social practice. At the same time it points to the individual as an active learner situated within social contexts (Lave and Wenger, 1991; Wenger, 1998; Coffield, 1999; Field, 2005; Mørch and du Bois-Reymond, 2006; Chisholm, 2008).

To understand how informal learning becomes visible and is relevant for formal educational contexts, it is crucial to examine how individual learning is embedded in relationships and practices with peers, role models and/or intentional educators. The perspective of informal learning as social practice is even key to understanding a general concept of learning as it is used in sociology and educational science. One of the most influential studies dealing with that issue is the idea of 'communities of practice' elaborated by Jean Lave and Etienne Wenger (Lave and Wenger, 1991; Wenger, 1998). In communities of practice, learning and education are referred to as social practices within social life worlds in which education is negotiated and experienced. In particular, Wenger (2009: 211) refers to learning as a process of: (1) *belonging* to a community; (2) *becoming* in the sense of identity development; (3) *experience* through which meaning is elaborated; and (4) *doing* in the sense of learning as a shared practice. The idea of the communities of practice is important as it helps to understand that social reproduction through social capital requires relationships, where learning habits are internalized and subjective identities are reworked in relationships (Bourdieu, 1990; Wenger, 1998; Field, 2005; Helve and Bynner, 2007). Children experience norms, values and practices in their early social relationships, e.g. in their families, and are encouraged to explore (or prevented from exploring) their wider social environment. Later the main social networks consist of friendships, peer networks and youth cultures. Also informal work or other extra-curricular activities can have different meanings, functions and consequences across different contexts (Ball et al., 2000; Raffo and Reeves, 2000; Walther et al., 2005; Foljanty-Jost et al., 2008; Hungerland et al., 2008; Invernizzi, 2008).

Taking this idea as an approach for analysing how informal learning is reflected in formal educational settings involves emphasizing the enjoyment of learning. When individuals enjoy what they are learning, it may nurture their identity and show greater success in learning. This is how learning obtains an individual instead of a socially mediated sense, such as learning to get a job. From the other side, it is necessary to recognize, as stressed by Wenger (1998), that today school is structured in a way that gives students a taster of many subjects, so that realistically they have no chance to learn anything in any real depth. One consequence of this is that they cannot apply what they are learning to their future lives, or get the chance to enjoy what they are learning, when school is all about exams and how they influence their occupational future. Therefore they are likely to become bored, discouraged and dispassionate.

Methods and Sample

In this chapter we analyse interviews and focus groups conducted in three different schools each in Finland and Germany. The focus group discussions aimed at learning about informal views of groups on the researched issue through the initiation of self-steered discussion processes in which participants confirm each other's speech, complete and correct it, and in doing so actualize a specific group opinion (Mangold, 1960; 1973). In individual interviews we aimed at different perspectives through the eyes of the different actors. Both perspectives give room to the issues and relevance systems of the interviewees, both by open narrations and by research questions from structured interview guidelines.

Our Finnish data set consists of interviews and focus groups with seventeen teachers, thirty-one students and thirty-three experts working in the closer field of the researched schools (see also Salovaara et al., 2012). The German data set consists of interviews and focus groups with seventeen teachers, forty-nine students and thirty-two experts respectively (see also Boron et al., 2012). The respective educational experts are guidance counsellors, school nurses and psychologists, school social workers, social workers, transition phase workers, etc. The student data was mainly collected before the transition from lower secondary school to the upper secondary level. However, some of the students were also interviewed after their transition phase.

Data analysis has been carried out on the basis of fully transcribed interviews, their postscripts, and summaries of all group discussions and interviews, which highlighted the salient topics coming out of the discussion or interview. We applied a mix of content analysis (Mayring and Gahleitner, 2010) and grounded theory (Corbin and Strauss, 2008; Strübing, 2011). This decision resulted from the need to compromise between an inductive and a deductive procedure – the first one to get insights into new, unexpected issues, problems and constellations of informal learning and education in formal educational settings, the second to fulfil the tasks given by the research question focusing on students' educational and life course trajectories (see also Parreira et al., in this volume).

Empirical Insights of Informal Learning and Out-of-School Contexts

Informal learning in school

The school is a formal educational institution, so it is not surprising that for a great part learning in school means learning in formal structures organized in lessons. However, what students learn in school and even in lessons does not have to be confined to what is intended by the curriculum. There are different informal learning settings and processes to be found within a school day or even a single lesson. Social interaction is probably the most significant one in this context. This means meeting friends, interacting with teachers or using the spaces of school as places where learning that is informal in nature can take place. This type of learning is at the same time much more related to the out-of-school life of students, as a much wider range of issues may be discussed and negotiated there. Schools, on the other hand, in some cases have their own normative system, which can conflict with what students are used to in their out-of-school life. These different sets of norms and values can cause frictions. The question we are interested in is: how are different types of learning processes recognized by educational actors in the formal context of school, and what relevance do they ascribe to them?

How learning is embedded in social relationships and interactions

As elaborated above, school is an important place of socializing and interaction with and in different elements of youth culture. In both Finland and Germany, a sense of belonging to a group or to single friends at school may be seen as a motivational tool for young peoples' education. Friends seem to be even more important in the decision-making process regarding the transition phase from primary school to lower secondary school when students are younger (Salovaara et al., 2012), but are, however, still important when attending upper secondary education. Asking students about their memories and experiences from school, the first reply is often 'friends'. Friends are a reason for attending school and a reason for enjoying or disliking it. A Finnish girl who had changed schools several times due to her family moving was asked how she felt about changing schools so often and replied: 'My friends changed when we moved to a new place and I didn't know anyone, so it was nice to go to school and get to know new people.'

This means that school can be seen as a place where one can meet new peers, who can become new friends and that can help in coping with new situations and integration into new environments. Friends at school are an asset for young people, as is also emphasized in previous research (Määttä and Tolonen, 2011).

Although many students appreciate the social context of schools, especially interacting with peers, one demotivating factor is to be seen in experiences of bullying and when finding friends in school becomes difficult. On the other hand, students who do not receive support from peers or who do not feel integrated tend to be less motivated to attend school and might even quit or change schools:

> I changed schools, because the school was so far away … and there (in school) was not anyone of my friends, not anyone I knew … and to this place (the school) many people had come from the same school and they had their own groups and they didn't really take anyone in … and in the cafeteria I was always sitting alone. (Student 4, Finland)

Other students also mention the lack of leisure time, time for extra-curricular activities or time for meeting friends. The reasons they give for this are the demanding curricula in upper secondary school, which can be interpreted as a frustration gap that school can create for students' sociality demands.

Another crucial prerequisite for students' learning formally is their motivation, which they develop – and this is the interesting part – mainly through informal experiences. Students who work together are more motivated to learn, and do tend to learn even better. They seem to enjoy learning more than those who work in a class with bad atmosphere. We found out that both students and teachers agree that a good atmosphere in the class is not only closely connected to higher learning motivation, but is also a prerequisite of efficient learning (formally). Teachers who have experience working with young people also recognize the importance of developing a good relationship with students, not only because of empowering them, but also because their experience tells them that is important for students' school achievements:

> Because it is so much about personal talks … students … with whom you have to have extra talks, or initiate class conferences … or project work … This is something which I have learned now, these social-pedagogical aspects.

> And this is in my opinion much, much more important in a school like this, to get good relationship with students, to empower them, so they become strong, not only with regard to their marks but also as a person. (Teacher 1, Germany)

Our analysis of social aspects of learning in school shows that interacting with peers and teachers is important as a motivational tool for young people in the formal context of school. Good informal social experiences in school can have a positive outcome on students' learning formally, whereas bad informal experiences may have the opposite effect.

Learning (and teaching) norms and values in school

Values and norms regarding education or educational aspirations are usually internalized primarily in students' family contexts but also in interaction with their peers and of course in school, although more for some and less for others. Students learn and internalize these values and norms unintentionally and mostly informally in their everyday life. Sometime they may be contradictory to the norms and values of their teachers or the school. In analysing how teachers and educational experts reflect upon these issues and how they deal with the challenges of different norms and values, we found out that many are aware of the differences between values that students learn in and out of school.

In discussions with teachers, informal learning is not explicitly discussed – neither as a concept nor as a significant or relevant process that they find important. However, one distinction that teachers drew seems to be interesting, as some of them strongly argue that particularly socially disadvantaged students lack important basic skills they need in order to learn in school. They reinterpret this observation as their task to provide (especially disadvantaged) students with values they do not learn at home, with their family or friends. This can be interpreted in the sense that teachers who think this way ascribe lacking particular values to individual deficits of students. Values and norms learned in school seem to have another quality and to be more relevant than everything that is gained and lived informally by students.

It comes as no surprise that teachers agree upon the necessity of good manners and behaviour, and that these skills are part of the most important tasks in their teaching. This shift in relevance from transmitting knowledge to explaining and imparting the importance of manners is again an indication that teachers find it hard to appreciate the norms and values gained informally, as can be seen in the group discussion below:

Interviewer: What are the most important tasks in education?
Teacher 1: To calm the class down in a condition that they can get a grasp of something
Teacher 3: To motivate students
Teacher 1: I would also say that, but that has of course to do with taking control of the situation
Teacher 4: Of course going through basic matters, so that they are able to follow the news, in order to understand e.g. the situation in Japan, what's happening there and why it happens ... And of course to raise an interest so that they also want to follow the news
Teacher 2: I think it is important to teach them to speak, so that they have the courage to speak without paper
Teacher 1: Plus to learn some human behaviour. 'I'm sorry', 'Thank you'. And also how to treat other people

(Focus group with teachers, Finland)

Some teachers have accepted these tasks as a part of their teaching and even talk about how they 'raise' their students, a word that is usually connected with parenting. Interestingly, teachers in Germany often even use comparisons between teaching and being a social worker to underline the contradiction between the job for which they 'originally' qualified and the mismatch with current daily occupational requirements. By being a 'social worker' they understand all tasks other than teaching, i.e. talking to parents, management of classroom discipline and cooperating with non-school agencies. Many teachers reflect on these aspects of their job in an especially critical way when considering that this task consumes most of their working time and there is less time left for the 'classical' knowledge transfer.

> What we are doing here partially at the moment, is more social work than normal lessons, that's the way it is. But actually I am a conveyor of knowledge and of course I have an upbringing effect in that, but ahm, at the moment it's sometimes the other way round. And that is ... but we are not qualified for that. (Teacher 2, Germany)

By doing that, they are leaning towards their interpretation of their job description as a 'conveyor of knowledge' who is not able to take aspects of informal learning into account at the same time. By realizing that they are not trained or qualified to be social workers, this can be interpreted as a realization of what kind of resources and skills they think not only students, but also schools, are lacking.

Taken together, school can be seen as a place where different cultures, norms and values meet and can collide. In the decision-making process regarding the transition phase from lower secondary school to further education and training the students' different norms and values regarding education can become evident. Teachers struggle in particular with students who come from families with different values regarding education and upbringing.

Informal learning and labour market demands

Non-teaching educational experts, e.g. particular guidance counsellors, school psychologists and school social workers, who work closely with students in school but who also are aware of the changing labour market, have a somewhat different view from teachers on what kind of skills are important for young people to learn. These educational experts seem to have a much stronger focus on informal and non-formal learning than teachers. This is characterized by a stronger emphasis on socialization aspects of education and achievement of disciplinary skills. Teachers and experts agree that skills required on the labour market are not very closely related to formal education and qualifications. They think that students need to be aware that lifelong learning is an essential part of the contemporary society and that young people will have to undergo several different forms of training throughout their working career. However, while teachers need to focus on teaching subjects according to the formal school curriculum, experts may focus also on guiding students in their own individual educational trajectory.

That is why non-teaching educational experts tend to focus less on the achievements in school, and more on the harmonious development of students. According to experts it is less important what students study compared to showing motivation and flexibility. In young peoples' careers, motivation and flexibility are important skills young people need to learn:

> As I have made clear to the young people … work or do something, in some way, if it feels too hard to struggle with books, then go to vocational education and try to learn at work or finish your studies with apprenticeship training … or something, so you won't be left out without an education … Because I say, even though you have a profession of making hats, that you have completed one vocational education, it tells something to the work life. That you are trainable, you have that something. (Guidance counsellor 2, Finland)

Experts' views on these informal skills young people need to learn have also to do with the changing nature of the labour market. Experts think that a particular education does not necessarily provide the student with adequate tools for the whole of their working career. The labour market has changed and school needs to change as well. The labour market demands flexible workers who are able to re-educate themselves according to new demands and requirements during the whole life course. However, it is unclear what the school's role is in supporting and preparing students for the new demands of the labour market.

The relevance of out-of-school contexts for formal educational transitions

For young people, a significant part of learning takes place outside school: e.g. at extra-curricular activities, during experiences of their hobbies, at youth clubs or by just hanging around with peers and family. In this section we will discuss the role of these types of activities as well as the role of family and peers for students' educational transitions, especially transitions from lower secondary school to upper secondary education and training.

Non-formal education activities in and out of school

According to our data, out-of-school learning is not visibly recognized in school. It is remarkable how little teachers – both in Finland and Germany – actually know about their students' out-of-school lives. Missing that type of insight, it is hard for them to really value what students learn besides what is taught in school. However, teachers from both countries agree that a broad knowledge is needed to meet the demands of contemporary society. Nowadays it is not only about studying to a profession. Students also need a broad knowledge base and experience, which is important for a successful educational trajectory. Interestingly, teachers also admit to knowing very little about their students' perspective in this regard. This might be because they are aware that in the transition to upper secondary education, it is less the experience or the broad knowledge base than the certificate that counts.

Although teachers in theory recognize the current and future need of lifelong and life-wide learning, in the interviews they distinguish between the more important studying and learning in school according to the formal curricula, and learning that takes place in out-of-school contexts which they do not consider as important as the formal learning:

> Well, it´s cooler not to study. The striver is never the cool one. That´s often a big obstacle. And laziness is a big factor. It´s clear, adolescents in the middle of the

> puberty … they have a lot of other interests and then school is not so important. (Teacher 4, Germany)

This quotation shows how teachers complain about students who are 'lazy' and have 'other interests' and for whom 'school is not so important'. At the same time, many students complain about missing practical experiences in school. However, a student who has other interests may be very active and a good learner/student in his/her after-school life. Yet, this kind of out-of-school learning seems not to be valued by the teachers. Nevertheless, the knowledge students develop in their after-school life may be very relevant for their educational trajectories and may have an impact on the students' further education after lower secondary school. However, there are teachers who also want to promote other talents that students have, talents that are not learned formally at school but are part of their youth culture. Some teachers actually seem to realize the potential in promoting the interests students have developed in out-of-school contexts, and realize that these skills can be very important in the student's educational trajectory:

> Some of them are really bad in the lessons, but they nevertheless have other talents, and … we try … to promote these. We have some, who are completely bad in German, but they are writing amazing raps and do Hip Hop in a band, or we have a highly talented drawer, who did Graffiti for a theatre exposition. Like that we try to promote their strengths a bit and to get them prepared for vocational training, hopefully. (Teacher 5, Germany)

Extra-curricular activities seem to have an impact on students' decisions as to which school to apply to after compulsory education, especially in Finland. Almost all students in our Finnish data who had applied to a vocational school which specialized in sports or art, for example, had pursued this activity in their leisure time or in the lower secondary school within the so called weighted curriculum.[1] In Germany, on the other hand, extra-curricular activities are not as important for choosing schools. However, sports or arts could be a reason to attend a specific school, although usually there are very few of them in one city or even a region.

This comparison is of special interest for our analysis. In their extra-curricular activities students learn not only the activity, e.g. to play football or dance ballet, but they also learn what their strengths and interests are. Students might be motivated to learn more in extra-curricular activities or other out-of-school contexts, or they may learn what they are not interested in (e.g. Walther et al., 2006). However, students do not have equal opportunities to participate in extra-curricular activities. Some of the students are put in a disadvantaged position if parents do not have the financial means or desire to support extra-curricular activities, for instance. Out-of-school contexts can also be significant for young people when they decide what they want to study or work with after compulsory education.

Both Finnish and German experts agree that out-of-school contexts may be very important for the well-being of students and that students benefit from learning that takes place outside the formal curricula. However, often in school there are very little or no financial means to support any learning other than what is expressed in the formal curriculum, which is so tightly organized that there is little or no room for any additional learning. In Finland there has been a tradition of arranging voluntary afternoon clubs in schools, after the school day. However, due to cuts in school budgets, the number of afternoon clubs has decreased. According to some teachers in Finland, the afternoon school had a positive impact on the well-being of students, and they regarded this as an unfortunate development.

In Germany learning motivation is stimulated through non-formal courses and extra-curricular activities offered in the youth work or community work sector. Although sometimes rooms of the school buildings are used in this regard, this learning takes place mainly outside school. Also the school doesn't contribute to its funding. The relevance of this type of out-of-school context and learning is seen as being extremely important, especially as a contrast to the formal context of school or a non-formal place such as a youth club, as expressed by an expert:

> We have the chance to visit kids at their informal meeting points on the street, where they have a completely different kind of self-assuredness, and where most of them more easily talk about their problems than in the context of a youth club. This is something very important, besides the transfer to other institutions. (Youth worker 1, Germany)

Although an increase in non-formal courses or extra-curricular activities arranged in school outside the formal curricula could benefit disadvantaged students in particular, it seems that the development in both Finland and Germany is going in the opposite direction. In neither the Finnish nor German schools in our data does there seem to be sufficient financial resource to support non-formal learning.

The role of family and peers for students' educational transitions

In the context of the transition phase, out-of-school contexts become extremely important. This is based on our observation that school and school actors seem to be not the only, or maybe not the most important, source for support. In both Finland and Germany, peers and family members are much more important for students' decisions about which school to apply to after lower secondary school, for example. Students mainly discuss their alternatives after compulsory education with their parents, but also make their own assessments by observing their parents, other relatives or significant persons that are close to them (see Cuconato et al. and Ule et al., in this volume).

In our interviews we asked young people how they decide what they wanted to do after compulsory education. All students explained that it has been their own decision to which school they were going to apply, or what to do after compulsory education. Of course this is evaluated by them within the limits and restrictions such as previous school achievements, grades, entrance tests or even health issues. However, in some cases it became evident that students not only listen to their parents and value their opinion, but follow in their footsteps by choosing the same career. The following focus group discussion is an example of how four boys in Finland explain how they made the decision on where to apply to after compulsory education.

> Interviewer: How did you come up with this plan?
> Boy 1: With my parents, and family
> Boy 2: Well, I figured it out with my father
> Boy 4: Dad has always built his own cars, that's probably why. And then he has always been working with cars
> Interviewer: What about you?
> Boy 3: Well, for me it has been, like, my mum owns her own firm, so that's like business, so that's why … my mum was like, if you choose business, you can come and work for me

On the other hand, there are students who have very little experience and knowledge about work and the labour market. Some teachers and experts are very concerned about students who come from families with long-term unemployed parents, because in their view these students have never seen their parents do any work and so are experiencing a way of life that is based on unemployment which they interpret as normal.

Students learn a considerable amount of the understanding about work life and the labour market from their family. For some students this knowledge may be very limited and in these cases schools have a significant supporting role. However, both in Finnish and German schools there seems to be a lack of reflection about what the role of the school can be in these types of situation.

Conclusion

In this chapter, we have analysed what relevance students, teachers and experts ascribe to informal and non-formal learning as well as to out-of-school contexts in the transition phase from lower secondary school to further education and training.

Young people are constantly exposed to learning situations. At school they learn according to the formal curriculum, but also outside the curriculum they learn through interacting with peers, or unintentionally by experience (Werquin, 2010). According to our findings, informal and non-formal learning in and out of school find very little recognition in school in practice, although this is valued in the discourse of lifelong and life-wide learning.

In our analysis we have found different aspects of informal learning in school which have an impact on decision making at transitions: social interactions, e.g. friendship and a sense of belonging, as well as aspects of norms and values learned in school. Students internalize values and norms from their homes, peers and school. In the transition phase from lower secondary school to further education students stress that the decision is their own and not dependent on their peers. However, for motivation as well as school satisfaction and contentment, it is important to find friends, or at least not to feel left out.

Teachers are aware of different sets of values and norms students have learned informally and internalized from home, in particular regarding education and behaviour. They aspire to influence these values by teaching students good manners and behaviour, and they agree that these skills are part of the most important tasks in their teaching. Educational experts, on the other hand, stress that socialization aspects of education and achievement of disciplinary skills have to be considered together, and even more so in the future.

The perceived problem of motivational challenges among youth needs to be reviewed and opened up for discussion within the school context and educational research. In both countries, Finland and Germany, teachers complain that students are not motivated and that they need a lot of time and energy to motivate them. Because they are aware of the challenges young people have with motivation to studying formal curricula, they try to find new ways of learning within the formal curricula. Drawing on the interviews with students, the problem seems not to be that students are not eager to learn; on the contrary, students learn all the time, but this takes place in particular informally, and in out-of-school contexts. In students' active out-of-school lives the knowledge is perceived through experience and (different) social practice. But if teachers don't know what students learn in out-of-school contexts and what they learn informally, how can they know what motivates them or what their interests are? Students may have a very active out-of-school life, which needs to be considered more, as this is exactly what may be relevant in the decision-making process when transferring to further education after lower secondary school.

Despite the structural differences between the comprehensive Finnish education system and the German one with a strong emphasis on early selection and with a more developed apprenticeship training, our results show no distinct differences regarding attitudes towards informal and non-formal learning in and outside school. In fact, it is interesting that we found quite similar attitudes and views in both countries despite the structural differences. In both systems, informal and non-formal learning are not explicitly appreciated. In both countries, teachers seem to know very little about the students' after-school lives, even though their leisure time hobbies and activities might play a very important role in the transition phase from lower secondary school to upper secondary school. In Finland, both the weighted curricula and the variety of upper secondary schools with the possibility of individual choice could be seen as providing students a slightly broader range of possibilities in connecting informal and formal learning. However, it is up to the individual rather than being facilitated in a systematic way.

Education in school – formal education – is indeed important in the fight against youth unemployment and social marginalization; without proper education young people do not have a fair chance on the labour market. However, formal education is not the only factor that plays an important role in students' future opportunities. The unstable labour market puts different demands on today's young people. Experts stress that students will most certainly undergo several training experiences throughout their working career, and that flexibility and motivation are therefore important skills on the contemporary labour market.

Social origin is often regarded as one of the most important predictors of selection in school (OECD, 2001). Social origin is of course not per se the significant factor, but other features, such as, for example, the financial opportunities parents have to support extra-curricular activities and more importantly the parents' attitudes towards education, also have an impact. These attitudes, values and financial opportunities can put students in disadvantaged positions and influence their own reflections on education. In our data we find teachers and experts who are concerned about students who internalize different values regarding work and the labour market from those taught in school: for instance, according to these teachers and experts, some students learn informally from their unemployed parents that it is acceptable not to work. We also find teachers and experts who are concerned about students who don't have the same opportunities to learn non-formally in extra-curricular activities as students who apply to specialized upper secondary schools after having the opportunity to learn more activities according to their interests in school (e.g. students who have studied according to a weighted curriculum). However, for further research, both formal and informal learning need to be considered even more in terms of social advantage and disadvantage, as this might be of high relevance for students' school success and integration into society.

Part 5

Educational Transitions in the Life Course

11

Students' Decision-making Strategies at Transitions in Education

Morena Cuconato
University of Bologna

Karolina Majdzińska
Warsaw School of Economics

Andreas Walther
Goethe University, Frankfurt

Annegret Warth
University of Frankfurt

Introduction

As lifelong learning represents the ground on which knowledge societies should be based, it is not surprising that both political discourse and educational research increasingly underline the importance of longer schooling as the prior condition for socializing students as future independent lifelong learners, and in this respect the importance of decision making. However, while in political discourses educational decision making is mostly considered as an individual choice for which students and their families are made accountable, scientific debate is controversial with regard to how educational trajectories evolve differently and the factors that are involved. Different authors conceptualize choice according to different epistemological perspectives as 'rational', 'constrained' or 'structured' (cf. Folbre, 1994; Breen and Goldthorpe, 1997; Furlong and Cartmel, 2007).

While there is a range of theoretical concepts on educational decision making, little empirical knowledge exists on how students experience and reconstruct decision making themselves. In this chapter, we try to reduce this research gap, presenting and discussing findings of an analysis of quantitative and qualitative data collected in the framework of the GOETE project on how young people (re)construct their educational trajectories and especially their transitions from lower to upper secondary education. The aim is to understand how decisions are being made at this critical point in young people's educational and life course trajectories, who is involved and how structural factors and individual agency are related. In order to do this, we analysed two sets of data. The first comes from a survey with students in the final year of lower secondary education across different socio-economic contexts and types of schooling in Finland, France, Germany, Italy, the Netherlands, Poland, Slovenia and the UK, in three cities per country. The second comes from qualitative interviews with 106 young people from schools located in socio-economically disadvantaged urban areas after their transition from lower to upper secondary education.

The chapter starts with a discussion of existing theoretical concepts and empirical findings regarding decision making in young people's educational trajectories. The dimensions of operationalization we identified as relevant were: ruptures versus smooth progression through school careers; expected and actualized upper secondary destinations; and experiences of choice and/or constraint in educational transitions. Following this, we analysed survey data with regard to how previous ruptures, expectations concerning destinations, and experiences of choice are distributed among students at the end of lower secondary school. This is contrasted with a qualitative reconstruction of the trajectories of young people who had attended schools in disadvantaged areas, still along ruptures, (realized) destinations and choice. In order to understand how young people refer to decision making in their biography, the criteria they consider relevant, the ways in which they experience choice and constraint, and with whom they interact, a smaller sub-sample of 18 interviews with young people from Finland, Germany, Italy, the Netherlands and Slovenia is analysed in depth. From this, four constellations of decision making at transitions in educational trajectories are elaborated. The chapter concludes with a discussion relating these key individual factors to structural dimensions involved in decision making – including the influence of different national education and welfare systems – presenting the analytical and heuristic value of modelling patterns and constellations in this respect.

Decision Making: Theoretical Concepts and Empirical Evidence

Both structuralist and individualistic theories have been generated to explain how students make decisions, and what types of factors influence their decision making at institutionally foreseen transition points. However, applying an interactionist perspective to discourses of individualization in individual decision making appears to be embedded in, enhanced or hindered by social structure which in turn does not exist independently from how it is being interpreted by individuals (cf. Giddens, 1984; Emirbayr and Mische, 1998). Consequently, the relationship between individual choice and structures of inequality articulated in decision-making processes during transitions in individual life course trajectories is conceptualized as interrelated and dialectical (cf. Beck, 1992; Alheit and Dausien, 2002; Walther, 2009; Woodman, 2009). It takes shape through individuals' assignment of meaning to the norms, resources and opportunities structuring their social environments. In other words, educational, training and occupational opportunities result from structural and subjective elements.

Educational trajectories – understood as individual movements through the education system and education processes (see Walther et al., in this volume) – are structured by socio-economic factors and educational systems and appropriated by individuals in the process of biographical construction. Trajectories involve transitions scheduled institutionally at the same moment for all students of the same cohort. However, decision making – this is the assumption underlying this analysis – evolves as a particular configuration between life course and biography in each individual case, otherwise it would be impossible to explain how some students from disadvantaged backgrounds succeed in school despite the structural constraints they are faced with (cf. OECD, 2010b; Cuconato et al., 2014; Miethe et al., 2014). Bloomer and Hodkinson (2000) refer to *learning careers* as dispositions for learning in a comprehensive perspective towards the developing self. Of course, these are influenced by structures of education and welfare systems providing different levels of accessibility and support (see also Tikkanen et al. and Stauber et al., in this volume).

In order to gain an overview of the state of art, Paton (2007) has identified three models of educational decision making: models of *economic/instrumental rationality, structural models* and *hybrid models*. The first model applies classic 'economic' rationality to the field of educational and vocational decision making. It assumes that individuals take instrumental decisions on the basis of their evaluation of investments and returns and that students would prioritize educational pathways promising utmost economic prosperity, particularly when it comes to higher education (cf. Le Claire, 1988; Breen and Goldthorpe, 1997; Choy et al., 2000). This model neglects the possibility that educational returns come only after a long time, while sociological research on youth has revealed the shorter time perspectives of young people (cf. Leccardi, 2005). Furthermore, it reduces the complexity of biographical construction involving the reconciliation of contradictory demands, and downplays consequences of social inequality to available resources of investment (cf. Archer, 2000; Bynner, 2005; Coté and Bynner, 2008; Walther, 2009). Despite these shortcomings, the persisting 'appeal' of rational choice theory may be due to its concurrence with neoliberal ideologies of 'activation' aiming at making individuals responsible for their own life course trajectories (cf. Walther et al., 2009).

The second model recognizes that educational decision making is determined by institutional, economic and cultural constraints transmitted by family, friends, teachers and school experts, educational policies and institutions, and labour market opportunities, over which young people generally have no control. This model derives from the classic studies of educational sociology like those of Bourdieu and Passeron (1977) or Willis (1977), focusing on the power of economic, cultural and social capital or of class culture in reproducing inequality through education. Also, contemporary authors like Furlong and Cartmel (2007) consider that individual agency is overestimated by individualization theory. However, they do not take into account the exceptions and (statistical) minorities of young people who actually take decisions and realize particular trajectories despite structural barriers (cf. Walther et al., 2009).

We agree with Paton that educational decision making is explained most adequately by *hybrid models* relating structural, individual and interactive factors with sociological and social-psychological knowledge. According to Hodkinson and Sparkes (1997) educational and career decisions are bound to 'horizons for action', determined by both external opportunities for a job and personal perceptions of what is possible, desirable and appropriate, depending on the wider context and the individual's life history. They suggest that students' decision-making processes are part of a lifestyle structured by social and cultural contexts as well as of an ongoing biographical process in life course trajectories evolving from interactions with others. This approach connects three interacting dimensions: pragmatic identification of preferences (according to different rationalities), interactions with other persons, and 'the location of decisions within the partly unpredictable pattern of turning points and routines that make up the life course' (cf. Hodkinson and Sparkes, 1997: 33; du Bois-Reymond and Stauber, 2005).

An interactionist perspective implies that decision making is the expression of individual attitudes and dispositions, which in turn are embedded in and negotiated with social structures, institutions and networks. As a matter of fact, children and young people from less advantageous social backgrounds have difficulties in reconciling school norms with the structural possibilities of their life worlds, and in responding adequately to school requirements. In contrast, those coming from families with higher social and cultural capital appear from the beginning to be more motivated (at least extrinsically) for schooling (cf. Willis, 1977; Ball et al., 2000; Walther et al., 2006). However, structuration does not occur automatically without contingency. While on the one hand social reproduction is regulated by institutions and/or by increasingly complex constellations of governance, on the other hand it depends on how individuals perceive, interpret and thereby (re)produce them. This means that individual (educational) trajectories consist of a life course and a biographical dimension. The life course dimension refers to the expectation of a linear course following an institutional script of subsequent levels of education, while the biographical dimension refers to the subjective meaning individuals ascribe to their life course trajectory and the ways in which they construct their identities across past, present and future (cf. Kohli, 1985; Alheit and Dausien, 2002; Heinz et al., 2009).

With regard to education, the relation between life course and biography can be analysed in terms of social learning. Social learning theories understand learning as situated and collective processes of individuals' meaningful participation in communities of practice embedded in particular social contexts (cf. Lave and Wenger, 1991; Wenger, 1998). Correspondingly, social psychologists conceive of decision making as a 'goal-directed behaviour in the presence of options' (cf. Lipshitz and Strauss, 1997; Hansson, 2005: 6). Thus, they acknowledge both the given alternatives structured by social relationships and the cognitive process which eventually leads to a choice (cf. Gigerenzer, 2002; Elster, 2007). Social contexts act as *decision frames* (Kahneman and Tversky, 1981), while knowledge is filtered through subjective interpretations which never coincide completely with 'objective' facts or data (cf. Ule, 2009). In educational decision making 'habitus, personal identity, life history, social and cultural contexts, actions and learning are interrelated' (Bloomer and Hodkinson, 1997: 46; cf. Miethe et al., 2014). They are structured by ascriptions according to gender and ethnicity which are inherent to the 'doing difference' inherent to institutional settings (Crul et al., 2012).

Like the relationship between structure and agency (cf. Emirbayr and Mische, 1998) or between life course and biography, decision making in educational trajectories has a *temporal* dimension. Education aims at preparing students for future (occupational) roles while biographical construction links personal past, present and future. Super (1990) conceptualizes educational decision making as an integral part of the processual development of young people's self-concepts which is characterized by complex interactions between physical and mental growth, individual experience and environmental factors. He suggests a developmental framework including five ideal typical life stages: growth, exploration, establishment, maintenance and disengagement. In each stage individuals have to cope with the educational and vocational developmental tasks institutionally foreseen in that chronological age range. In the stage of exploration, young people are expected to understand their own interests, skills and values, and to pursue professional goals consistent with that understanding, re-shaping the vocational stereotypes constructed previously in the growth stage. However, self-concepts evolve dynamically as individuals make new experiences.

Other research on the timing of decision making has found that the decision making of students who leave education early is often rooted in the first stages of their school careers (Payne, 2003: 16). While their job preferences are still inconsistent, they develop a highly instrumental approach to education. They do not expect that staying on will increase their options. Those with no specific career goals tend to stay in full-time education mostly because of their good academic performance or because they do not yet feel ready or confident enough to face the responsibilities of a job. For both groups employment is a central aspect of their considerations (cf. Furlong and Cartmel, 2007).

The discussion of existing research reveals that empirical analysis of educational decision making needs to be open to both structural and subjective as well as to temporal dimensions. The institutionalized life course relies on the normative expectation of linearity, while subjective biographies are concerned with continuity between individual past, present and future. Ruptures, destinations and choice are therefore suggested as relevant dimensions of analysis: ruptures represent risk factors as well as indicators of discrepancy between individual aspirations and societal demands in transitions; choice is a key value in individualized societies – expected and claimed by individuals who are at the same time made accountable for their trajectories as if they were resulting from 'free' choices (cf. Walther, 2009); the destinations young people envisage represent the degree to which they have accepted and internalized the normative implications of lifelong learning for their own biographical planning, and the destinations they achieve reflect the degree to which this is accessible for them depending on their cultural and social capital (cf. Bourdieu and

Passeron, 1977; Parreira do Amaral et al., 2015). Against this backdrop, analysis of quantitative and qualitative empirical data aims at identifying the influence of structural factors on the one hand and reconstructing students' subjective experiences with decision making at the end of lower secondary school on the other.

Ruptures, Destinations and Choice at the End of Lower Secondary School: Survey Findings

The survey conducted in the framework of the GOETE project with students in the final year of lower secondary school aimed at collecting their views of their previous school careers as well as their outlooks to their future pathways. Data was collected through questionnaires distributed and completed in the classroom. The weighted sample[1] from the eight countries included 6,390 students, with one third each from schools in disadvantaged, average and affluent contexts. The sample is balanced for gender, with an average age of 15.5 years. In the following, the focus lies on how the ruptures they experienced, and the destinations and the degrees of choice they expected, are distributed across the sample and how they correlate with socio-economic status, gender and migration background, as well as with structures of national education and training systems.

Ruptures and choices in the past

In order to understand whether students experienced their trajectories as ruptured or smooth, they were asked whether they had ever changed school or repeated a school year, and to what extent they were satisfied with previous transitions, especially from primary to lower secondary school.

There were 31.6 per cent of students that stated that they had *changed school* at least once, for different reasons such as having to repeat a school year, being relocated to another school for low achievement or disciplinary reasons, family reasons such as moving home, separation of parents, or own or a parent's health problems. In terms of statistical significance,[2] fewer students than average changed school in Slovenia, Italy, Poland and the UK, and more than average in France, the Netherlands and Germany (in countries with the more differentiated education systems), but surprisingly also in Finland (implying that changing school is a rather broad and heterogeneous category). Socio-economic contexts of schools in terms of affluent, average or disadvantaged areas have statistically significant impacts, but differences are small:[3] the highest proportion of students who have changed school at least once are those from average schools (34.2 per cent), followed by students from disadvantaged schools (31.4 per cent) and affluent schools (29.3 per cent). While there are no significant differences on the basis of gender (male: 31.5 per cent; female: 31.7 per cent), students with a migration (56.6 per cent) or minority background (46.8 per cent) experienced school change more often.[4] Here, factors such as mobility due to migration as such, as well as having to change school due to under-achievement and/or language problems, may play a role (cf. Crul et al., 2012).

A change of school is also more common among students whose mothers have a low level of education (basic: 36.9 per cent; secondary: 30.2 per cent; tertiary: 27.1 per cent).[5] The analysis suggests that families with higher levels of education are less likely, or less obliged, to subject their children to school change. This means that educational ruptures associated with individual reasons such as limited abilities and effort or special needs may also be a consequence of external circumstances such as a low level of support or difficulties resulting from a migrant status (e.g. language problems, discrimination).

Differences between proportions of students who had to *repeat a school year* (a total of 12 per cent across countries) are statistically significant, with students from disadvantaged schools being more likely to repeat a school year (14.9 per cent) than from average (12.7 per cent) or affluent schools (8.3 per cent). Differences between countries are most likely to be explained by the differences between educational systems. Data from Finland, Slovenia and the UK shows that the structure of the education system has a stronger influence than the socio-economic context. In general, repeating school years is considerably more frequent in education systems with high stratification and high standardization like in France, Germany and the Netherlands.[6]

Other factors connected with class repetition are mothers with the lowest level of education, migration background and gender,[7] although differences are minor: 13.6 per cent of boys compared to 10.4 per cent of girls had to repeat a school year which confirms other research findings (cf. Ule and Šribar, 2008; Eurydice, 2010).

For a vast majority (89.8 per cent) of students the transition from primary to lower secondary school occurred according to their choice. However, country analysis shows that perceived accessibility is lower in countries with a highly standardized and stratified education system, including barriers according to performance and early selection into educational tracks with unequal status such as Germany (82.4 per cent), France (84.9 per cent) and the Netherlands (90.0 per cent).[8] Enrolment to the desired school is also statistically related to the country of birth, to the ethnic group, to the socio-economic status of the families and slightly to context of school, while gender is not a significant variable in this respect.[9]

Reflecting back on their first school transition, 74.3 per cent of students declare their satisfaction with the chosen school, whereas 17.6 per cent think they might have got on better at another school, and 8.1 per cent would have definitely preferred to attend another school. Mostly students from France, the Netherlands and Germany would have preferred another school.[10] Moreover, the sons or daughters of migrants, and/or students with a migration background, were more likely to be less satisfied with their schools. With regard to gender, girls were less satisfied than boys, although it is not clear if this is due to gender discrimination or to the higher aspirations and expectations of girls.[11]

Expected destination and experiences of choice

As students were surveyed at the end of lower secondary school, they still were in the decision-making process regarding upper secondary education or training. They were asked about their educational and career expectations, aspirations, confidence and worries.

Educational aspirations are almost equally distributed between secondary (46.6 per cent) and tertiary (46.8 per cent) education. The correlations with gender, place of birth and nationality are all statistically significant, but the relationships among variables are weak.[12] The strongest one regards nationality: educational aspirations of students from migrant and/or ethnic minorities are higher, which may result from a strong desire to improve their disadvantaged social position in relation to the native majority population and/or in relation to the education of their parents (a similar trend was noticed in the qualitative interviews; cf. du Bois-Reymond et al., 2012).

There are also significant differences in educational aspirations according to social contexts of schools and country which are statistically significant. Aspirations of students from average schools are almost equally distributed between secondary and tertiary education (48.7 per cent and 44.7 per cent), 36.3 per cent of students from disadvantaged schools compared to 59.1 per cent from affluent schools aim at tertiary education, which may reflect both socio-economic family background as well as different aspirations raised in different social contexts.[13]

Seventy-one per cent of all students surveyed planned to remain in full-time education after lower secondary school, 21.9 per cent thought they would get a full-time job, enter a work placement or an apprenticeship scheme, while 7.1 per cent expected to have a caring role in the family or at home, become a full-time parent or be unemployed. Specificities of national education systems play a role inasmuch as countries with higher standardization and stratification (France and the Netherlands, surprisingly not so in Germany) have lower rates of students expecting to be in full-time education and instead expecting to be in an apprenticeship or work.[14]

Both the socio-economic contexts of school and the education level of parents influence students' future expectations. The highest proportion of students who expect to remain in full-time education are those attending schools in affluent areas and those whose parents have a higher education level. One factor affecting the educational plans of students from families with lower socio-economic status may be the urgency of finding a job and contributing to the family budget.[15]

The expected destination is also strongly related to previous educational ruptures which make students less inclined to continue with education. Girls (75.2 per cent) are more inclined to remain in full-time education, which may reflect their consciousness of the gendered nature of employment opportunities requiring from them higher educational levels than from boys for comparable job opportunities. Girls worried about their chances of finding a job in the future considerably more often than boys.[16]

Not surprisingly, worries are also related to the socio-economic position of the families: students with less educated parents are more dependent on the external circumstances of society and the labour market; they have less decision-making power, weaker support networks and fewer strategies regarding job opportunities. In contrast to native students, who seem to have more opportunities to choose their jobs in line with their subjective interests, students with a migration background have fewer opportunities and more frequently have to limit themselves to survival strategies. The criteria for future jobs were also cross-analysed with the expected future activity and educational status of students. Both correlations are statistically significant and confirm expected patterns; subjective or expressive reasons are more important for those students who expect to remain in full-time education and increase in line with the expected level of education and decrease according to previously experienced school rupture.

The question whether these expectations represent individual choice or anticipate structural constraint can be answered only indicatively. On the one hand, their self-efficacy in achieving aims can be interpreted as reflecting identification with and choice of goals (cf. Walther et al., 2006). On the other hand, when students were also asked to what extent they could raise issues and were listened to in school, their perception of possibilities to express views and of being listened to in school was that they were rather low. While 10.6 per cent of students report having no possibilities to raise issues in school, 26.2 per cent say that their views are not listened to. Significant differences were found with regard to the social context of school and between countries.[17] More students in affluent contexts reported experiences of participation (could express their views), though surprisingly this was more common in school systems with high differentiation and high standardization like Germany or the Netherlands.

The quantitative analysis of ruptures, destinations and choice in students' educational trajectories largely confirms existing research showing that structural factors like national education and social support systems as well as family background have a clear influence on the patterns of trajectories through lower secondary school. Future educational aspirations are concerned to a lesser extent, while migration background and gender affect educational aspirations, confidence and worries about future employment. In contrast to quantitative data, qualitative data provided insight into how these influences occur in individual trajectories and how they are experienced differently.

Patterns of Educational Trajectories

While the analysis of survey data has revealed that young people have different experiences during their school careers with regard to ruptures, expected destinations and degrees of choice, the qualitative analysis aimed at reconstructing educational trajectories according to the dimensions ruptures, choice and destinations (cf. Evans, 2002; Walther et al., 2006). The sample of this qualitative analysis differed from the survey in terms of its limitation to students from schools located in socially disadvantaged areas and of the timing of data collection. The interviews were carried out after transitions from lower secondary school to upper secondary school or vocational training. Therefore they provide information on actual rather than on expected or preferred destinations. They were fully transcribed and coded first by an open coding process from which a joint code system was generated, allowing for comparability across cases while leaving openness for contextual and individual aspects. A first step of analysis consisted in reconstructing the steps young people had made since primary school up to their actual stage of upper secondary education or training; this resulted in five patterns of educational trajectories:

1 *Smooth academic*: This pattern clusters educational trajectories of young people who change from lower secondary education to general upper secondary without ruptures in their school career, and make this transition on the basis of their own choice. These trajectories are consistent with the (standard) institutional scripts of the respective education systems. Not surprisingly, this pattern is more common in comprehensive school systems that postpone tracking to post-compulsory stage and where educational choices are not totally conditioned by prior achievement. Regarding the individual level, the sample is heterogeneous in terms of family background, experience of support and motivation.
2 *Discontinuous academic*: In this pattern, educational trajectories lead into general upper secondary education but consist of ruptures and/or require compromise with regard to subjects or type of school. In comparison to the first pattern, they indicate a more heterogeneous and eventful development at the individual level due to low achievement, health problems, conflicts with teachers or a dynamic and/or problematic family life, etc. Here, parents are inclined to push their children towards general upper secondary school, thus exposing them to competition without adequate support. This pattern is also associated with comprehensive schools, although they are predominant in contexts in which vocational education has a low status and does not represent a relevant alternative.
3 *Smooth vocational*: These educational trajectories lead to vocational education and training without any ruptures according to the choices of the young people. This can be either for intrinsic reasons or follow processes of adjusting aspirations to under-achievement in lower secondary school (e.g. entrance requirements are lower in vocational routes). Although vocational routes are more explicitly gendered than academic ones (with higher rates of male students in representative statistics), the qualitative sample included both male and female students. The meaning of this pattern differs across institutional contexts: in differentiated education systems (Germany, France, the Netherlands) vocational routes do not provide access to higher education (which partly applies also for Poland and Slovenia).
4 *Discontinuous vocational*: This pattern refers to young people's educational trajectories as they enter vocational education and training not on the basis of their own choice and/or after ruptures in their school career. Key factors

are low socio-economic status, migration or ethnic minority background, and/or problematic school careers. Either young people intentionally reduce their aspirations in favour of more accessible and manageable routes in advance, or they are forced to do so because of their low achievement. Both institutional guidance and informal influence from parents or friends are involved in this process of 'cooling out' (Goffman, 1959; cf. Walther, 2003). In our sample, such trajectories are over-represented in Germany and the Netherlands, where vocational routes are differentiated and segmented and early selection limits the choices of students.

5 *Remedial or intermediate*: This final pattern refers to the educational trajectories of young people who enter interim courses or compensatory pre-vocational schemes. Normally, these routes do not represent individual choices but result from under-achievement in lower secondary school and/or a lack of sufficient and adequate education or training opportunities. Most of these young people have experienced earlier ruptures in their trajectories. Low socio-economic status, migration or ethnic minority background as well as traumatic experiences (e.g. addiction, health problems or parents' separation) are key factors. This pattern is associated with differentiated education and training systems like Germany and France where schemes tend to be stigmatizing 'parking lots' for those who fail to enter regular education and training. In contrast, in a comprehensive system like Finland similar routes provide qualifications allowing for return to regular education and training.

This first finding provides in itself relevant insights into students' educational trajectories. First, in contrast to dominant discourses in which so-called 'disadvantaged youth' are homogenized, their educational trajectories through lower secondary school and their transitions to upper secondary school or vocational training are highly heterogeneous, covering a range from smooth to remedial trajectories. Second, socio-economic factors prove to be relevant, but are not sufficient to explain individual trajectories. Third, the context of educational systems – their differentiation versus comprehensiveness but also their integration with and backing up by social support and welfare – has some potential to reinforce or to mitigate the impact of socio-economic factors. A closer look reveals, fourth, that structural factors are interrelated with individual agency, inasmuch as young people interpret situations and possibilities differently on the basis of biographical experiences and orientations, motivational careers (cf. Walther et al., 2006) and relationships with gatekeepers and significant others in and out of institutional frameworks (see Ule et al., in this volume). In the following section, we will therefore analyse young people's narratives with regard to their decision making in the transition from lower to upper secondary education or training.

Constellations of Decision Making

It should be noted that in order to understand how young people experienced and reflected their decision-making processes at the end of lower secondary school, the interview transcripts of a sub-sample of eighteen young people (limited to Finland, Germany, Italy, the Netherlands and Slovenia) was analysed in depth. The analysis revealed key factors on the basis of which constellations of decision making have been elaborated. In the following section, four out of five constellations are presented and discussed. Each one is introduced by an exemplary case and then contrasted by a counter case displaying similarities of decision making but differing with regard to other factors of the respective educational trajectories. This reveals how the complex interrelationship between cases relates to decision making in a concrete situation rather than to persons or their entire biographies.

Step-by-step

Matteo lives in a major city in a poor region of Southern Italy. His trajectory can be classified as *smooth academic* as the transition to commercial school – a middle road between grammar school and professional school in the Italian

Table 11.1 The case of Matteo (Italy)

Background and social context	Pattern of educational trajectory	Original idea → actual destination	Central actors	Criteria of decision making	Choice/ constraint
Low SES, father died early, weak region, comprehensive school	Smooth academic	Confusion, then chooses commercial school	Himself Teachers in primary/ lower secondary school	Occupational choice, goals he can reach by himself	Presents decision as own choice

upper secondary school system – occurred without problems. His aim is to study law and to become director of a company. He presents his decision making as self-determined and self-responsible:

> First, I want to get the high-school certificate, as nowadays with middle school [lower secondary] you don't get anything … The teachers said, we don't force you … but you have possibilities to get everywhere … I followed nobody … I have taken all my choices by myself.

His narrative reveals an individualized approach, including distancing himself from his peers, for instance when advising teachers to be stricter. The 'choice' of commercial school – instead of grammar school which, according to his teachers, would have been possible with his previous achievements – reflects his awareness of the limited support he can expect from his family. He has to opt for a middle road which he feels confident he can manage alone – while keeping options open for continuing towards his desired academic destination.

This constellation of decision making has been categorized as *step-by-step*. It refers to cases in which young people have high ambitions but are conscious of poor family background and/or institutional barriers and therefore are not fully confident in their ability to reach them. They break down their trajectory into smaller steps which lead to intermediate goals from which they may continue further.

Poja's decision making can also be categorized in this way. She has a migrant background but was born in the Netherlands. Her trajectory was *discontinuous (vocational)* as she had to change school early, experienced bullying and had to repeat a grade. Her decision for secondary education was mainly motivated by making 'sure to never see' her classmates again. Although she has to accept the lowest level of lower secondary school, the transition into a new environment opened new chances: 'My marks were simply so good … As a matter of fact, I started a new grade each year and it was so nice in the group.' Poja is supported and encouraged by her mother and sister, by teachers in lower secondary school and by a personal advisor. Although her trajectory remains affected by health problems, she has developed a subjective interest in care and manages entering upper vocational education in this sector.

Comparison shows that *step-by-step* decision making develops more easily in comprehensive than in differentiated systems where it depends on comprehensive support and intrinsic motivation.

Too weak to follow own plans

The trajectory into scientific upper secondary of *Nina*, a 15-year-old Slovenian girl, initially looks smooth. A closer look at the decision-making process at the end of lower secondary school, however, reveals a rupture classifying it as an example of a *discontinuous academic* pattern.

Originally intrinsically motivated to enrol in a vocational school for floriculture, she eventually attends a biotechnical gymnasium, as she puts it: 'First of all I wanted to go to three-year vocational floriculture school but everybody recommended me to choose a gymnasium instead'. Her parents wanted to prevent her from possibly regretting her decision later, worrying that in the future she would be dissatisfied that she was 'just a florist', and ignored her strong desire to work in this field. Also the school staff perceived her choice as a degradation of her chances. She accepts their advice but after only two months she regrets not having listened to herself:

> If I compare it, in a way I regret it, because now I know I could make some concrete physical things – like different bouquets of flowers, things that make me happy … I am sorry that I did not listen to myself, but I somehow listened to the opinions of others.

Nina experiences the decision for general upper secondary education as a misleading trajectory, alienating her from her dream profession and self-fulfilment. Her explanation why she did not resist parental and teacher pressure expresses an even bigger lack of self-confidence than in the constellation step-by-step which results in prioritizing safety (as much cultural capital as possible) over all other criteria of decision making.

Table 11.2 The case of Nina (Slovenia)

Background and social context	**Pattern of educational trajectory**	**Original idea → actual destination**	**Central actors**	**Criteria of decision making**	**Choice/ constraint**
Working class, comprehensive system	Discontinuous academic	From floriculture vocational school to biotechnical gymnasium	Parents, school advisor	Security: Avoiding low qualifications (vocational school) – keeping future options open	Giving up intrinsic interest under pressure from parents and school

This constellation of decision making *too weak to follow own plans* regards students whose educational and vocational wishes are more or less pronounced, but they are not able to realize them due to external constraints and a lack of individual resources. *Lemi* from Germany, who only achieved the leaving certificate from *Hauptschule* with some difficulties, is diverted from his original plan (remedial trajectory). In his attempts to upgrade his qualification in a full-time professional school in order to get into computing training, he is advised against this by his teachers as well as by the career guidance: 'She told me right in the face, "you will not make it" … Just like this. How can she? I do not like that.' Coming from a Turkish background his family gives emotional support without being able to sustain him in terms of schooling or decision making, while imposing the burden of expectations to the first-born son regarding career and income. Thus, Lemi is fully dependent on institutional advice and support.

Nina's case is untypical for this constellation inasmuch as it coincides with an academic trajectory, i.e. cooling out does not imply lowering aspirations regarding level of education. In her case, cooling out refers to alienation from intrinsic interest, and it might be seen as typical of how the relevance of education is negotiated in the knowledge society in terms of 'the more education, the better', and of how individualized responsibility leads to the fear of missing chances and to neglecting subjective interests. In contrast, Lemi's decision-making processes are typical of how stratified and standardized education and training systems translate into poor school performance, lower familial social and cultural capital or failing applications for apprenticeship, more or less directly into destinations of reduced status and/or choice.

Fighting for dreams

Sirin, a 16-year-old young woman from the Netherlands with a migration background, has experienced a *discontinuous vocational* trajectory: she had already started at a so-called second chance secondary school (HAVO/VWO), combining vocational with general elements, but after two years she was further downgraded to pre-vocational school (VMBO) because of low grades.

In her narrative, Sirin portrays herself as a very determined student. Most important for her is continuing after VMBO with higher vocational education (HBO) and from there entering university. Looking back to the previous transition, Sirin expresses anger about teachers' unjust treatment: 'other children [who had even worse marks], they got a chance, not me'. In spite of the disappointing experience of being downgraded, Sirin constructs herself

Table 11.3 The case of Sirin (the Netherlands)

Background and social context	Pattern of educational trajectory	Original idea → actual destination	Central actors	Criteria of decision making	Choice/ constraint
Migration background, differentiated system	Discontinuous vocational	Orientation towards economy developed after change to higher level of vocational education	Supportive family, close friend, later also teachers	Career and social mobility rather than intrinsic interest	Downgraded but later climbed up due to support and effort

as a straightforward student who takes her decisions rationally. Being asked why she chose a specialization in economy, she explains: 'I asked my mentor: what is the best thing I can do if I want to go on with HBO.' She did not choose it because of her interest in this subject but because she wanted to reach an academic trajectory. In the new school she experienced more support. However – apart from her family, her most important source of support was a close female friend whose trajectory took a similar course. In fact, they encourage each other mutually. Sirin says the most important factor was 'that we came across each other … Together we are strong.'

We refer to the decision-making constellation of students who resist unfavourable external conditions and cooling out mechanisms as *fighting for dreams*, although in Sirin's case 'dream' rather refers to a strong ambition of success and social mobility than to a particular activity. They share the ability to adapt to adverse circumstances and maintain their educational and professional plans. They also share a strong self-determination and mobilize and accept support from different persons, partly by re-interpreting support relationships in terms of friendship and recognition. In these cases young people are driven by a strong wish for achievement and social mobility, or a concrete professional dream.

Also *Rojda*, a Kurdish refugee from Turkey, with a highly *discontinuous vocational* trajectory, with several stays in Germany, Sweden and Norway, presents her trajectory primarily as her life story, active in mobilizing supportive relationships wherever she is. After lower secondary school, she has concrete wishes like becoming a journalist to document the situation of the Kurdish people, or a family care worker since in her biography such a professional figure played a supportive role: 'I would like to do with children what she did with us.' However, in the context of the differentiated German education and training system, these destinations are out of reach. She follows a short-term vocational course in social assistance instead, but insists at least on changing the school: 'They wanted to send me to the other school … but I didn't want to go there, it was a school of bitches … And then, they accepted me [in the actual school].' A key supporting figure in this process was a personal advisor appointed to lead students from lower secondary school into vocational training to whom she assigns qualities of a significant other: 'she's my darling'.

Family convoy

Julia from Germany originally attended a comprehensive school but decided to change school in grade 7, because she felt uncomfortable with classmates and teachers, and accepted a downgrading to *Hauptschule*. Her case is an example of a *discontinuous vocational* trajectory.

Her decision-making process was also marked by ruptures. Her original wish was to train in geriatric nursing. However, a complex mix of factors – feeling uneasy with colleagues, experiences of death and the fact that it was unclear whether her school certificate would actually suffice – led her to abandon a (compulsory) internship which she pursued in a home for the elderly. She loses orientation and motivation and school performance declines. She explains how she ended up in an apprenticeship as a bakery saleswoman:

Table 11.4 The case of Julia (Germany)

Background and social context	Pattern of educational trajectory	Original idea → actual destination	Central actors	Criteria of decision making	Choice/ constraint
Parents working class, SES low to middle	Discontinuous vocational	From geriatric nurse to saleswoman in a bakery	Mother, aunt	Availability of training place, trust in mother and aunt, urgency in getting some training	Turning adaption towards available options into own choice

> I always wanted to become a saleswoman … and then I had the idea with the bakery, through my mum and my aunt. They do the same … they advised me a lot.

In fact, the female family members simply took her to the bakery in which they work. Social capital as well as control and support during the internship made sure that Julia completed the compulsory internship. Her motivation developed and she performed so well that she was offered the apprenticeship place. It is striking that family influence was much more effective than various institutional support inside and outside of school – including in enabling Julia to internalize adaptation to available options as own choice.

Cases like Julia's have been interpreted as a constellation of *family convoy*, where the role of the family is the outstanding factor in decision making, yet in an ambivalent way. The family provides protective support while also strongly channelling young people's choices in a way that extrinsic factors such as security are prioritized over intrinsic goals. Compared to other constellations, the influence of school guidance is low.

This is also the case with *Giovanna* from Italy (*discontinuous academic trajectory*), whose self-confidence is very low due to experiences of dyslexia and bullying. Her professional aspirations lack intrinsic motivation; they appear random and reflect attainable gendered careers: 'simple jobs, hairdresser … baby-sitter, or kindergarten teacher, things like this'. Asked if the school she actually attends, with arts-based general upper-secondary education, was her own choice, she answers: 'No, I wanted to go to another school,[18] but … then it became different.' Her narrative reveals that this decision was more or less taken by her mother who has tried to protect Giovanna from the challenges of life since the diagnosis of dyslexia in primary school. While the fact that the family acts as a compensator for social disadvantage is not surprising in Italy with its structural deficit of support structures for young people, this does not apply for Germany. Here, young people often do not perceive institutional support measures as subjectively useful, but need to complement them by support from trusted significant others.

Resuming and reflecting the exemplary cases presented in the previous section, the following dimensions emerge as distinctive features of constellations of decision making.

1 *Actors*: In the narratives different actors, especially significant others and/or institutional gatekeepers, are presented as central, which highlights the role of relationships with other persons in decision making – either a positive

or an ambivalent and restrictive one concerning young people's intrinsic aspirations (cf. Hodkinson and Sparkes, 1997; see also Ule et al., in this volume).

2 *Timing*: In some cases young people refer to a lengthy process involving different stages and turning points and changes – voluntarily or not; in others, they presented decision making as an integral element of their life history, while others again referred to a single moment. This points to the processuality and interwovenness of decision making with a biographical past, present and future (cf. Super, 1990; Emirbayr and Mische, 1998).
3 *Reflexivity*: Some stories are more elaborated and differentiated than others, with some talking in explicit ways about the process of decision making that remained more implicit in others. Both could, but not necessarily, be a sign of different consciousness and the tolerance of ambiguity in contexts of individualized and uncertain transitions (cf. Miethe et al., 2014).
4 *Criteria*: Young people present different criteria of decision making, including security, accessibility, compatibility with other life themes, or intrinsic interest.
5 *Strategies*: Depending on their reflexivity and criteria of decision making, young people consciously develop strategies of decision making – involving specific actors, seeking for information, trying out alternatives – or rather appear drifting (cf. Sennett, 1997).
6 *Choice and constraint*: Some young people refer explicitly to their experience of choice and constraint, but in other cases this can be interpreted from how they present their decision making and their own role in relation to possibilities, barriers or cooling out mechanisms; *too-weak-to-resist* was the only constellation in which young people explicitly did not present them as the centre of decision making in their trajectories.

Apart from these factors related to the decision-making processes as such, the analysis has also revealed the relevance of *contextual factors*. These are first socio-economic factors in terms of cultural and social capital. Second, there are institutional factors related to differentiated or comprehensive education systems with more or less support available (see also Tikkanen et al., in this volume). This is especially visible in the constellation *step-by-step*, requiring a system which is open for a flexible approach between individual ambition and keeping options open, or *too-weak-to-resist* which has rather different effects in comprehensive or differentiated systems. Interestingly, the constellation *family convoy* is typical not only for systems with low levels of support, but also those where a lot of support mechanisms are provided – though these may not be experienced as relevant, effective or trustworthy.

The constellations of decision making emerging from this analysis must not be understood as ideal-type biographies, or even individual biographies, but as decision-making processes, which may occur differently in other moments of the same biographies. Additionally, some of the decision-making processes had not been completed at the time of the interview and therefore may have taken different directions or been reconstructed differently at a later moment.

Conclusion

This chapter aimed at analysing how young people's educational trajectories evolve differently, and how decision making occurs at transitions between lower and upper secondary education.

Theoretically, it started from the assumption that decision making is neither a purely individual choice nor determined by structural forces; rather, it results from a complex interplay at macro, meso and micro levels requiring 'hybrid' models of explanation and reconstruction. The structural factors at play have been revealed by the quantitative analysis. These include the educational level of parents, the social contexts of schools, migration background and gender, as well as the comprehensiveness/differentiation aspect and the level of support available in national education systems. They all play a role in the ruptures young people experience up to the end of lower secondary education, in the destinations they envisage and in the degree of choice they feel they have. While correlations were significant, though in most cases rather weak, the qualitative reconstruction of the trajectories of students attending lower secondary schools in disadvantaged areas showed a high heterogeneity with regard to ruptures, destinations and degrees of choice which points to complex and contingent relationships of structure and agency. The in-depth analysis of constellations of decision making finally revealed that even within similar trajectories decisions are being taken in different ways through interactions between different actors, on the basis of different criteria, in different processes and time horizons and on different levels of reflexivity. Thus, in contrast to what might have been expected, it was impossible to recombine the patterns of educational trajectories and constellations of decision making into a single typology. Except for *smooth trajectories*, which evolve in a linear way according to their own intrinsic motives, thus excluding decision making in terms of *too-weak-to-resist*, there is no constellation of decision making typical for a single pattern of trajectory. This expresses the complexity of educational trajectories in which not only do institutional factors reinforce or mitigate socio-economic factors of reproduction, but young people's subjective agency also filters socio-economic, institutional and discursive factors; only analysis of individual cases can reveal *how* reproduction occurs in different ways and with different outcomes. For example, the discourse of lifelong learning is being interpreted in different ways: some, like for example Matteo, accept the need to achieve higher qualifications to secure career options; others, like Rojda, interpret it as possibilities to revise their own trajectory in the future. One very striking finding is the relevance of support which – in all cases discussed in this chapter – only becomes relevant in particular relationships with concrete persons who are ascribed qualities of significant others. These can be teachers or personal advisors, but also parents, relatives, siblings or friends. However, biographical significance of support does not necessarily mean overcoming processes of selection and cooling out. In some cases, like the constellation of *family convoy*, it is only through family mediation that young people accept reducing vocational and occupational aspirations.

This complexity of interrelations, of structures requiring interpretations, of choices being structured, of options and possibilities being negotiated both indirectly and face to face, justifies characterizing decision making in educational trajectories in terms of *doing transitions*. Referring to Fenstermaker and West's (1987) analysis and reflection, 'doing' must not be misunderstood as individual action but as interplay of practices at micro, meso and macro level which are in constant interaction and thereby contribute to the construction and structuring of reality – including the governance of young people's educational trajectories.

12

Teachers and Parents as Actors in the Students' Educational Transitions

Mirjana Ule
University of Ljubljana

Andreja Živoder
University of Ljubljana

Harry Lunabba
University of Helsinki

Manuela du Bois-Reymond
Leiden University

Introduction

A life course perspective on the educational careers of students reveals that educational trajectories and transitions have become more complex and prone to risks and failures than was the case for former generations. Therefore, in educational governance, young people are increasingly dependent on their two main reference groups, their parents and their teachers. This chapter aims at analysing how parents and teachers view their roles in young people's transitions. Their perspectives and attitudes are compared, and implications of discrepancies concerning the trajectories and transitions of young people are discussed. Taking their different positions in and for the lives of young people into account, we start from the assumption that teachers represent the institutional perspective as to how transitions should be realized, following the logic of the educational system, while the parents will define their task more in terms of protection and emotional support. In that sense, teachers will act more as gatekeepers as opposed to parents, who will first of all look to the well-being of their child and act as way-keepers. But teachers and parents are bound together in their undertaking of influencing the decisions of students. In our contribution, we ask how much parents and teachers differ or agree about students' transitions under conditions of individualization and growing pressure of achievement.

Education is a central element of the interplay between structure and agency, or between individual life course trajectories and biographies (Walther et al., 2006). Institutionalized pathways are intended to prepare children and young people for adulthood and thus have created the youth phase as 'educational moratorium' (Zinnecker, 1995), while 'new learning life courses' extend over the whole life span (Chisholm, 2008). Inasmuch as individuals interpret and appropriate their life course in constructing their life history, educational trajectories are interrelated with subjective learning biographies.

The professional role of teachers in this is to fulfil the societal expectations of socializing and qualifying students to become competent and self-sufficient adults. These expectations are translated into formal education curricula (Ezer et al., 2010). Consequently, they have to prepare students for internalizing these expectations and acquire the respective skills and knowledge in order to reach their educational goals (Beck, 2008). But they also have a role as gatekeepers, as they assess students' achievements and influence their educational opportunities (Cuconato et al., 2015; see also Walther et al., in this volume). Teachers today must be aware of the fact that they prepare students for a life that demands continuous learning beyond formal education. But when we informed teachers about that side of their profession, we found hardly any consciousness among the professionals about the broader ramifications of their work with students. They are inclined to restrict their attention to the micro level, which is the classroom. Learning deficiencies of the students are more likely to be blamed on the parents than analysed in the framework of lifelong learning and informal learning (Lima and Guimaraes, 2011).

In contrast to teachers, parents are concerned with the individual or biographical aspect in their child's educational transitions and their future life chances; they care for the general well-being and the life chances of their children and accordingly support them in their educational trajectories. And as uncertainty about individual life courses grows, family support can be expected to be increasingly relevant and will affect parenting. Parents have by definition a broader view on their child's well-being compared to teachers, whose formal interests are more limited to cognitive and knowledge aspects. At the same time, though, representatives of both groups act as significant others (Mead, 1934) in the sense that they are persons who might complement each other's roles by providing students recognition in their decision-making processes.

In answering our question about divergences or concurrence of teacher–parent perspectives on student transitions, we draw on qualitative data gathered in the GOETE project: interviews and focus groups with parents and teachers of lower secondary school students in eight European countries: Finland, France, Germany, Italy, the Netherlands, Poland, Slovenia and the UK. Interviews and focus groups were carried out as part of case studies in twenty-four local schools in disadvantaged city areas (one school per city, three schools in each country), which aimed at generating in-depth information about the processes and outcomes of the governance of educational trajectories of students in local settings.[1] In order to secure a comparable analysis across the different national, cultural, social and institutional contexts, interviews were semi-structured by identifying key orientation questions. All interviews were fully transcribed and coded. Coding comprised a combination of deductive qualitative content analysis (Mayring and Gahleitner, 2010) and an inductive grounded theory approach (Strauss and Corbin, 1990). The coding was followed by extensive analysis of the interview contents by applying a categorization developed via cross-communication between the research members involved. The meaning of long statements was transformed and rephrased into synthesized categories. With these condensations of meaning, relevant themes were identified to facilitate the interpretation of the findings. A potential bias may exist in the parental sample, in that only those parents who were more interested and involved in their children's education and/or those who felt comfortable and competent enough participated in an interview. However, quantitative data obtained from the survey on a much more representative sample of parents (Cuconato and Walther, 2013; see also Walther et al., in this volume) have confirmed the general trends in parental involvement, support and educational aspirations for their children.

Theoretical Background: Parents and Teachers in the Educational Trajectories of Students

In recent years, we have witnessed substantial changes in family and upbringing patterns, in the importance of family support structures and in parental involvement in their children's educational trajectories. The notion of *parental involvement* has become an important and apparently self-evident concept in understanding the role of parents in the educational trajectories of their children (Arendell, 1997). 'The relationships of control and obedience are supplemented by the relationships of help, encouragement and confidentiality' (Holmer Nadesan, 2002). These characteristics are part of a general shift towards familialization, which has been traced in a series of research on youth in Europe (Biggart and Walther, 2006; du Bois-Reymond and Chisholm, 2006). Familialization means that children are understood as their parents' responsibility, supervising their sons and daughters in the home and keeping them in familial dependency (Qvortrup, 1995; Edwards and Alldred, 2000). In this way, parents have become their children's confidants and advisers for psychological as well as educational problems. A parallel contemporary social process is institutionalization, which refers to the process by which children's lives are organized in 'separate and protected organized settings, supervised by professionals and often structured according to their age', where the focus is 'on their educational attainment and development' (Edwards and Alldred, 2000: 436). Cooperation between the home and the school has thus become a forming part of the social construct of 'good parenting'. In this social construct, parents, especially mothers, take over the care of and responsibility for their child's school attainment (Ule, 2013).

Research on family patterns and parent–child relationships confirms significant changes in upbringing patterns and parent–child relationships, which are evident throughout modern societies and can be characterized as a shift from a model of the upbringing family to a model of the emotional and supportive family with a more equal power balance between the generations (du Bois-Reymond, 2001; Beck-Gernsheim, 2002). Social-cultural changes in childhood resulting in intensification of protective parenting reflect the intensive care for children and their welfare (Clayton, 2004; Hodgkinson, 2010). Protective parenthood means the creation of a new discursive space within which children are perceived as individuals whose autonomy should be protected and maintained, but at the same time involves the opposite process of distinguishing children from adults through increased control and protection (James et al., 1998). Despite the great popularity of the concept of parental involvement, critics point to systemic deficits and related educational practices. They call attention to the incoherencies in the very definition of the concept, to shortcomings of applied tests and measurement methods, as well as to socially and racially conditioned models of positive parental involvement, for example, a preoccupation with the conceptions of white middle-class parents and teachers about what influences the child's school performance and welfare (Turney and Kao, 2009).

Hegemonic discourses of good parenting and corresponding practices are often adapted to the middle class. They overlook the social, economic and political obstacles as well as inequities that make the norm of good, responsible parenting unattainable for families from de-privileged social backgrounds. They also blame marginalized parents for their children's low school achievements (Crozier, 2000; Edwards and Alldred, 2000; Holmer Nadesan, 2002; Lareau, 2003; Griffith and Smith, 2005). Not all families are able to deliver adequate support for various reasons: unemployment or precarious jobs, migrant status, health problems or divorce, among others. Thus, parental support is one of the sources for the reproduction of social differences and is also a mechanism of social exclusion (Golombok, 2008).

In this changed framework, teachers remain crucial for the learning biographies of students. From a life course perspective, their role has at least two dimensions: as representatives of the school system they act as gatekeepers, thus making sure that their students' educational trajectories comply with the existing social, economic and cultural order. But they also play a role in the biographies of young people, either as significant others if they succeed in creating a trusting relationship with students, or in a negative way if they alienate them from meaningful learning.

Social and economic changes affect the developing rhetoric of knowledge society, which influences the role and meaning of education and consequently the teaching profession. Today it is much less evident than a few decades ago what kind of knowledge is relevant besides basic skills and faculties. What is clear, though, is that knowledge creation and application has to be continuously updated and re-evaluated in the light of new developments in society and the economy. Lifelong learning has become imperative not only for students, but for teachers as well (Coolahan, 2002; European Commission, 2010b; Lima and Guimares, 2011). It is no longer sufficient for teachers to base their profession exclusively on subject matter knowledge and traditional didactics. On the contrary, they are increasingly confronted with social and emotional demands and dilemmas of students and their parents (as well as themselves) when educating students and preparing them for individualized life courses.

Empirical Findings: Parents' and Teachers' Involvement in the Educational Transitions of Students

Parents as supporters and 'way-keepers'

Parents have a significant and often decisive role in their children's lives. Their views, attitudes and involvement influence their child's educational trajectories and consequently their further life course trajectories. For a majority of parents included in the GOETE research, education is seen as a key to professional and personal success in a competitive world. Most straightforwardly, this is evident in high parental educational aspirations: that is to say, parents would most like their children to attain tertiary levels of education[2] (Litau et al., 2013; Ule et al., 2015). But even if their aspirations are lower, aiming at vocational certificates, parents want their children to attain the proper qualifications and skills required for later employment and careers. In both cases, education matters and is in the eyes of parents crucial for the future lives of their children. Higher education is understood as a safeguard – the more education the better and often associated with a wider range of employment opportunities which means that the parents have an awareness about the link between education and the employment system.

For parents the personal development and the educational trajectories of their children are part of their own biographical life project. Many of them tend to view school as an opportunity for their child to climb up the social ladder: they hope for upward social mobility. Parents as well as students consider degrees and certificates to be the primary objective of education, not knowledge per se. They are willing to do a lot to achieve this aim of social and economic status by any means: they stimulate their children, help them with their schoolwork and projects, acquire information on further educational courses, search in-service places, act as their children's advocates in case of conflict with official intuitions, pay for additional instruction, etc., even if their social and economic situation is stretched. Such attitudes reflect the systemic structures of disadvantage as well: the more disadvantaged the parents, the more crucial their children's educational chances become.

Examples of parental ambition were some Turkish families at a Dutch school, where parents (usually mothers) had very high aspirations for their daughters. In these families, educational achievement is treated as a family project where the mother, the daughter, relatives and older siblings will come together to combine all resources available to promote the success of the student in question. As a 16-year-old daughter put it, 'If I do not study further, my parents would simply kill me.' A similar example was given by a very ambitious mother from Germany who disregarded her son's desire to get a blue-collar job but urged him instead to continue his education so he could be qualified for white-collar work. In another case, a Slovenian student, Nina, wanted to become a florist by all means. Her parents disregarded her dream, however, and claimed that a vocational school was not good enough and advised her to enrol in a gymnasium, which would provide more access to better educational options in the future. Nina listened to her parents while completing her first year of the gymnasium but complained: 'I am sorry that I did not listen to myself' (see also Cuconato et al., in this volume).

On the other hand, there are many parents who value education for more subjective reasons. Such parents would like their children to be educated according to their interests and find jobs that allow them self-realization and enjoyment. For example, one parent from France stated, 'What I urge them (children) to do is to find work to make something you choose and something you like, have pleasure in it and find professional fulfilment.' The desire that children will secure interesting and important jobs that would give them a feeling of accomplishment and satisfaction was found in parents from all countries and also confirmed by the quantitative data (Cuconato and Walther, 2013; Litau et al., 2013). Nevertheless, this desire is more often found among affluent and educated families, which is not surprising as such families dispose of more social, cultural and economic resources to support their children to follow the desired higher education, even when links with the labour market might not be as evident or direct.

Therefore, if parents from various social milieus agree on the high relevance of education, a new and somewhat subtle division is emerging between the different goals and attitudes attached to education. Whereas middle- and upper-class parents try to equip their children with the skills and capital needed to ensure meaningful and interesting jobs (self-developmental approach), disadvantaged families who traditionally believe in the functional role of education would try to equip their children with formal educational certificates, and in this way hope that they will achieve upward mobility and have a secure future. Some parents from lower classes might develop a sort of contempt for education, viewing it as a mere necessity in order to gain employment. Although educational aspirations are generally high, parents express considerable scepticism about the link between education and job opportunities. That shows their awareness that in contemporary European society education alone is no guarantee for later career options or safe employment. Not surprisingly, the most educated parents, who are usually also those with the most decision-making power in governing the life courses of their children, are least sceptical.

Parents have considerable influence on their children's educational transitions not only as caregivers, but also because children often choose them as their first advisors and trustworthy persons who always ensure their best interests (Ule, 2013). From the interviews in all the countries involved, two contrasting parental attitudes could be distinguished, and these then influenced how much and in what way parents are involved in their children's educational decision making. The first attitude leads to no direct interference at all. These parents support their children's choices but do not want to interfere with their decisions. The second attitude leads to varying degrees of interference, from blunt coercive to persuading educational strategies (Ule et al., 2015).

Parents with a non-direct interference attitude believe that their children have to find their own path and see their child as a decision maker on his or her own. A parent from Finland: 'I cannot tell him: your place is there and that is your profession.' There is general consensus among these parents to allow children to choose their school career and vocation according to their own liking. In their view it is an imperative condition for the child's well-being and involvement in his studies, as a parent from France explained: 'I don't influence my children, I let them choose because it's not a good thing to … all the parents who influenced their children, they didn't succeed, even in their family life.' A similar attitude was expressed by a parent from Poland: 'Eh, I have already said that I won't influence her choice. We advised our son before and it turned out to be a bad deal.' Yet, such a lenient parental attitude is possible only if there are no social, economic or institutional barriers such as a selective and stratified educational system with early selection which limits the range of possible vocations and professions, such as for example in Germany or in the Netherlands (see also Tikkanen et al., in this volume).

Our qualitative findings suggest that most parents in their statements 'leave' educational decision making to the children. However, this is mostly only true in the framework of their own expectations, of what they consider 'good' or 'appropriate' choices. The range of choices that a child has in term of parental expectations is often implicitly (or even explicitly) normative and obliging for the children, precisely due to the high level of familialization. In most cases, though, parents act as 'way-keepers': they offer soft guidance or support when their children are making a school decision, and the child generally gladly accepts it.

Some other parents were more clearly inclined to give advice. They might even have very definite plans and aspirations, a 'set agenda' for their children. The following statement from a parent from Poland is a vivid example of that attitude: 'Well, I would like him to become a lawyer. That is my dream.' The following statement made by a mother from Slovenia illustrates a less direct influence: 'My mother said to me: enrol in whatever school you want, but I would advise you not to choose a three-year school. Because this is vocational school and the education you will obtain is not so good, she said.'

While many parents show a great deal of understanding for their children's personality, abilities, wishes and needs, at the same time they try to push them towards what they themselves perceive to be 'key competencies': being agreeable, committed, motivated, ambitious, taking responsibility for one's own life, showing discipline, preciseness and punctuality, the ability to prioritize educational and life goals, know about time- and self-management and the value of assertiveness. As a parent from Germany emphasized:

> This is what I want to give him on his way: that he becomes more self-confident in a lot of things, and that he doesn't care so much about what others think … So you cannot always act in accordance with them, otherwise you will be the downfall of this society. Yes, you have to go your way, and this I give him and I think, with the years, this attitude will come, I hope, yes. Because these are the things I find important.

There exist external barriers to parental engagement and involvement, as another parent from Germany highlighted: 'but there are limits for being highly active as a parent, especially when being a single parent: employed parents have less time'. A relatively new problem concerns parents and children who have to cope with temporary economic migration of one or both parents, which emerged in the case study schools in Poland. Children of temporary emigrants (referred to as Euro orphans) live under the care of their grandparents or their extended family's care during the extended absence of their parents. A lack of communication between school and parent not only affects the child's education and level of motivation, but may carry high risk for the whole education trajectory.

The findings about the role of parents as educational and vocational 'way-keepers' point to a latent contradiction between the social processes of familialization and individualization that becomes visible in the way children's educational trajectories develop: familialization binds children and parents closely together, while individualization emphasizes the child's autonomy as does institutionalization, which reduces the child to 'individual performance' and calls for self-responsibility. This contradiction is smaller than it seems, however: there is a tacit consent between parents and children about educational and vocational decisions, at the same time as choices are made within the framework of the more or less explicit expectations of parents that define how children should achieve their well-being and independence. Parental support has become even more crucial in conditions where the state and institutions are shifting the responsibility for educational success on the shoulders of individuals. A lack not only of economic but also social and cultural resources might close the doors to further education and thereby contribute to the reproduction of educational and socio-economic inequality.

Teachers as gatekeepers?

When teachers were asked how they prepare students for their future lives in late modern society, they referred to the growing importance of education, independent of country, school type or teacher training. Generally, we found two main teaching styles: one more subject-oriented, that is to say less focused on the individual learner; the other more social-pedagogical oriented, those teachers giving more attention to problems students may have with the subject taught. This does not mean, though, that all teachers adapt or understand the notion of knowledge society and its implications for the further lives of the coming generations, or their role as promoters of a lifelong learning attitude to their students (Coolahan, 2002). Instead, studies suggest that knowledge about sociological concepts of society and youth as well as cultural and economic developments in contemporary society exist only to a limited extent in the minds of teachers. Such knowledge is not regarded as an essential part of the profession (Cuconato and Walther, 2013). There are teachers who mainly focus on their role as formal educators and on guiding their students towards a certification that will hopefully help students to integrate into the labour market (Cuconato et al., 2015). These teachers concentrate primarily on teaching and do not value extensive knowledge about the family conditions in which their students live outside school. Our experience is that those teachers who see their professional identity only as formal educators regard families who do not live up to current expectations of parental involvement as 'problem families'. But our case studies supported results from previous studies (Beijaard et al., 2000) which point to teachers' efforts to understand and value the challenges their students might confront outside school. For example, an Italian teacher explained how she tried to motivate students to learn and offered them the possibility of broadening their horizons: 'These are socially excluded students who desire to get around, to know … When we go downtown, they are so grateful.' In similar vein, a teacher in a school in Amsterdam in a group discussion about how teachers and schools should have a broader and emancipatory function in society said: 'I think you are not ready when the school day is over. You should have a kind of function … the school as a kind of social centre for the neighbourhood.'

Although teachers in our reference countries may not refer explicitly to broader societal developments implied by 'knowledge society' and its underlying educational paradigm of lifelong learning, they do refer to the labour market and the chances it provides or withholds for school leavers. Many teachers we interviewed pointed out that general education in the long run pays better off than (lower) vocational education. In all our countries, they either encourage students to enrol in upper secondary education, or 'cool out' their aspiration according to labour market demands and education and training requirements needed to enter it (see Walther et al. and Cuconato et al., in this volume). 'Cooling out' takes on two forms: teachers either discourage students, despite their explicitly shown ambitions and learning motivation, arguing that for 'this type of student' vocational education is good enough, or they urge students to stay within vocational education in the student's best interest and not take the risk of failing in higher school forms.

Across comprehensive versus differentiated educational systems with different models of vocational and educational orientation, teachers stress the importance of learning motivation and the necessity of anticipating the implications of vocational decisions for the future of a student. From the perspective of a comprehensive system, Italian teachers were concerned that their students often disregard the harsh reality of unresponsive labour markets, for example: 'When they say "I'd like to become", they have a model in mind which is empty of contents … They have no idea of the engagement they have to spend to achieve that goal, no idea if they have a real attitude towards their activity or not.' By contrast, teachers in selective systems would rather advise their students to follow the safe path of a (good) vocational education, although our interviews also suggest that Dutch teachers more than their German colleagues are inclined to encourage promising students to pursue higher general school levels.

Our interviews showed that Italian, German and Dutch teachers were particularly worried about the structural factors in their respective educational systems, which impede smooth transitions. In the Netherlands and Germany, the transitions from primary to lower secondary vocational school take place between 10 and 12 years of age, which is deemed much too young for pupils to make deliberate choices, with many parents feeling the same. This is also true in Italy (decisions are taken at 13 years) and Finland (15–16 years), where teachers also regard students as too young and immature to be ready for transition and making life-important decisions. Actually, transition to upper secondary school or vocational training is a real breaking point in a student's life, as this decision-making step will have a deep impact on their future educational trajectories and labour market positioning. Especially in the selective German and Dutch systems with standardized labour market entry, students are tracked not only on an educational path but also on a differentiated work path, when they still have limited life experiences and few possibilities to make informed decisions. This greatly contributes to the reproduction of social inequality, as the primary school path is too short to compensate for the learning gap created by disadvantaged socio-economic and cultural backgrounds.

Beside the different educational philosophy and tradition of the involved countries, teachers' pedagogical style and work orientation are somewhat influenced by the interplay between the nature of the education systems (comprehensive vs selective) and the structure of labour markets (standardized vs flexible access) and their capacity (low/high youth unemployment rate). It could be argued that in comprehensive education systems teachers are under less pressure to comply with labour market claims than in a selective system. Germany and the Netherlands, with their selective systems, are indeed much more focused on the labour market, with more standardized entry demands. One might regard this option as ambivalent: on the one hand it implies the 'cooling out' of students' ambitions; on the other, teachers want to save students from the experience of failure and secure a safe option for them. Both attitudes are recorded as professional dilemmas. A teacher from a school in Amsterdam shared this dilemma during a focus group discussion: 'Many parents expect that their children will continue with higher professional education … children must become a lawyer or something with medicine. But that is certainly not for everybody.'

Within comprehensive educational systems such as Finland and Italy we found that teachers of lower secondary schools oscillate in their professional self-perception between preparing their students in an instrumental way for the labour market and yet giving way to the students' present wishes and inclinations, supporting their self-confidence and learning motivation. As an example, a Finnish teacher explained how she tried to encourage students to follow their dreams and desires. 'I always tell the students to go and get a profession or a vocation that makes them happy … If they go to places where they don't want to be in and don't feel comfortable they will get frustrated with their lives.' An Italian teacher shows in her reflection, similarly, how teachers need to support students' self-esteem and encourage students' open mindedness.

> If they [students] feel frustrated in their working ambitions from the very beginning, they will disengage as soon as they meet the first learning difficulties. Pupils should have more self-esteem; actually they seem to be very severe on themselves. We should try to teach them to be more open minded and to stay curious.

Teachers did not see the two professional orientations – the economic-bound and the subjective-bound – as opposites. They would rather adhere to the dominant (European) discourse and ideology that both orientations are each other's equivalents and would lead to social integration. We quote a Finnish teacher who stressed, more than his colleague from the quote above, the systemic side of education:

> I somehow think that an important objective of school is to show the students that we are part of a functioning society and in that functioning society people cannot just do whatever they please and feel like doing.

Home–school relations: Contradicting tendencies

A longstanding topic in understanding educational transitions is the relationship between parents and teachers/schools. It is remarkable how this relationship continues to be perceived as problematic, not only by scholars in the field but also by parents and teachers (Ule et al., 2015). This points to the tension that exists between the two social processes we identified as familialization and institutionalization.

Some teachers complained about parents who would not show up to school meetings and regretted that some parents tended to leave much socializing education to the school. Schools (teachers and principals) most often complained about the lack of parental involvement in their children's education and their limited participation in school affairs, while sometimes, for example in Slovenian case study schools, teachers also criticized parents for doing the opposite: they interfered too intensely with their children's education, which undermines the work of teachers and contests their judgement about students' (missing) potential. For example one teacher told us:

> Counselling takes part [in school], but our role here is not so important any more, the parents' role has become more important. Parents have become so

> strong and ambitious for their children that they do not allow the school to suggest something. So, here we have loosened up, but it was the only way for us.

In general, the empirical findings suggest that schools have definite ideas and expectations about how parents should support their children and how this should be manifested in their participation in the school (attending school meetings is the best example), which is adapted to middle-class parents regardless of other factors such as times of change, different socio-economic conditions, working terms, migrant backgrounds, language deficiencies, among other factors. Nevertheless, teacher accounts indicate that disadvantaged students tend to receive less support from parents, even though they need it the most; in the eyes of the teachers, many parents simply did not know what kind of support they could receive at school. In general, weak parental participation is seen as a problem. Teachers may realize that the reasons lie outside school (Barberis et al., 2012). In other cases, lack of participation is considered a cultural issue influenced by parenting style. Parents do care for their children, but in such a way that it does not match the behavioural norms of the institution and society at large. An Italian expert provided an insightful view by referring to differences in perspective between the two parties:

> The school perceives the parents as the origin of the problem, while parents perceive the school as overemphasizing the problem … true, it could be a family with problems, but in our opinion if you can consider the other as a resource, you can do something.

Parents might often feel misunderstood by teachers who suggest that they fail to motivate their children to do their best in school. For parents, such an attitude strengthens formal and asymmetric relationships rather than open and sympathetic collaboration. As an Italian parent recounted during the interview: 'They are much too "ologist" … they keep parents at a distance, underlining their power of deciding about health and fairness.' Forms of participation and support are not only individually diverse, but are also bound to wider social and cultural milieus as well as financial resources. One example is parents' working schedules that might make it difficult for them to attend afternoon school meetings. Another is language barriers, as was vividly expressed by a social worker in a Dutch school:

> I deeply regret that only few parents are engaged in their child's education here at school. You must move heaven and earth to get them come to school. But then, I can understand why. If we have an information evening and you don't

> understand 70 per cent of what is being said there – why come? We have asked ourselves to translate what we have to say in a couple of languages. But where should you start and end? At our school we have some 30 different nationalities. How do you do that? Take the biggest group, the smallest?

This quote is not so much an example of cultural ascription as an expression of powerlessness of out-of-school professionals whose task it is to mediate between the involved parties of teachers and parents (and by implication students).

For immigrant parents, it is sometimes difficult to understand how the educational system and support offers work; parents simply do not know what kind of support they can ask for and receive at school. They feel they are being discriminated against as their children receive systematically lower advice for further education. A German mother with a migration background, for instance, had a very frustrating communication with the principal of her child's school in which she felt highly disrespected:

> Relentlessly, she [principal] debases my children, calling them sexually deviant, ascribing something negative to them all the time ... But this is not the education he [her son] gets [at home] ... My son is accused of not being educated. And this I don't allow the school to tell me. On the contrary, education is failing at school, not the other way around.

It needs to be said at this point that the teachers themselves in all discussions vehemently denied discriminatory attitudes and behaviours against migrant parents – again a question of perspectives.

Some parents suggest that teachers should adopt a more individualized (teaching) approach, taking the individual personality of students into account; for example one Italian parent proposed that:

> Teachers should change their methods: sometimes it is too schematic and too much based on the assumption that pupils are part of general categories. They should try to see pupils according to their way of expressing themselves.

Parents stress that it is up to them to get information about offers of support from teachers, not the other way round. Parents must therefore cope with institutional demands of individual responsibility. Yet, despite complaints, the majority of parents evaluate the support system in predominantly positive terms, as this description from a German mother illustrates: 'This school is on all accounts the best lower secondary school in the whole region, this is for sure.' In fact, this means the best school within the lowest track in the German educational system. This quote illustrates how parents whose children have no other options but to attend lower track schools (with no possibilities of later attaining higher level of education) have to accept the selection applied by the school system and try to make the best of it.

Conclusion

Our main aim in this chapter has been to analyse and discuss how teachers and parents deal with the reality and problems of students who must be prepared for educational trajectories and transitions in advanced knowledge societies. Presently, parents and teachers face a situation which is rich in transitions and decision-making moments, due to a prolongation of the youth phase and an extensive stay in educational institutions. Students are urged to keep on learning beyond obligatory education, and lifelong and life-wide learning are at the heart of national and European educational discourses. In this new social situation, biographically meaningful learning has become an influential force in the lives of the young generation shaping their educational trajectories in a life course perspective. At the same time, students face a precarious labour market and are by no means confident any more to enter it without much uncertainty and delay. They are all the more dependent on informed advice and support of their parents and their teachers.

Parents are the main supporters and advisors of their children in the decision-making processes of their educational trajectories. They function as gatekeepers and as way-keepers, but the modern trend towards familialization gives more space for the way-keeping function, that is to say, a non-authoritarian and emotionally rich socialization with mutual understanding and respect. Parents display their influence and authority through conversation and negotiation with their children when giving advice and support for the child's education. Parents of all social classes follow this trend, but with different outcomes. While middle-class parents with ample social and cultural capital and many resources within and outside their family, and sufficient knowledge of the educational order and organization to be able to make use of it in advising and supporting their children's educational trajectories, this is the case to a much lesser degree for lower class parents, among them migrant parents. The latter feel individually guilty for real or supposed socialization failures manifested in educational disadvantages. They do not understand and accept why their efforts of support do not pay off according to their ambitions for their child's school career. The school is for them much more terra incognita than for parents of higher socio-economic status.

Most teachers working in vocational schools and with disadvantaged students interpret their professional role also in terms of social work, and try to integrate elements of such practice in their professional identity and daily teaching practice, albeit to different degrees. We found that these professional styles are independent from country and education system, that is to say, there exists, to our knowledge, no 'German' or 'Italian' teaching style and none which is more pronounced in comprehensive versus selective school systems. Yet we did find that teachers in selective systems – in our countries of Germany and the Netherlands – have a closer relationship with the labour market and are more inclined to advise their students to enter it without delay, avoiding taking the risk of failing in further education than their colleagues in comprehensive systems – Finland or Slovenia for example – who would rather encourage their students to continue their educational trajectories. But a word of caution here: our empirical material is not extensive enough to generalize these spurious trends and we would hope that further research throws more light on the matter.

What we can confirm more confidently is the finding that teachers in all our countries, and again independent of school form, are poorly prepared during their study for working with disadvantaged students and parents. Despite the European discourses about lifelong and especially life-wide learning – learning also outside school in non-formal settings – many teachers are focused on the 'inside' of school and are barely cognizant of the living conditions of the families of their students. This impacts negatively on their relationship with the parents of such families. Teachers, of course, see problems of language insufficiencies, poor learning motivation and other unfavourable influences for successful educational trajectories. But they are inclined to blame the parents for insufficient home socialization instead of analysing the situation in a broader societal context, taking into account the interplay between subjective factors and objective conditions (see also Cramer et al., 2012).

Parents of disadvantaged migrant and non-migrant students are most dependent on the advice of the teacher concerning the further educational course of their children. We found two parental (mothers') approaches in this respect: one is characterized by anger and distrust, suspecting 'cooling out' the learning ambitions of their child; the other, and more frequent, attitude is characterized by trust and respect and the belief that the teacher 'knows best' what is best for their child. Teachers on their side interpret 'best for the child' in two opposite ways. In the first way, they encourage the student to aim as high as possible in their ambitions and professional wishes, even if they may not be convinced that the student will succeed, but they do want to give them a good chance and not frustrate them. The other way is that the teacher calculates the risk of failure if the student (and his or her parents) aims too high, and rather advises a more moderate trajectory. These ways or approaches are not directly, but possibly indirectly, connected with the two above-mentioned professional identity and teaching styles: it would be rather the social-pedagogically oriented teacher who would encourage student and parents in realizing educational and professional ambitions and dreams, and it may be the subject-matter oriented colleague who would be hesitant to do so.

All teachers, in all countries and education systems, concur in their opinion about the great importance of parental engagement for the learning biographies of their students. But they are inclined to put the burden of active engagement on the shoulders of the parents: it is they who must come to school; the teacher will not be able to meet them outside school, and most teachers would not want to either. This issue, and its implications for furthering or inhibiting more social equality as well, is neglected in current teacher training.

In all this one has to take into account mounting pressures on the school – not only vocational but up to university – to increase 'output' in terms of educational achievement and economic efficiency under neoliberal regimes. That contradicts an individualized biographical transition approach, which is not based on 'product' but on 'process'. It is not only teachers who suffer under these new demands, which make teaching less satisfactory, but parents as well. When they encourage their children to meet upgraded achievement standards and obtain favourable professional qualifications and prosperous jobs, they can do that only by simultaneously increasing pressure to perform according to school norms. In that way, teachers as well as parents are caught in an opposite but complementary dilemma: adhering to biographically motivating learning according to the discourses of individualism and lifelong learning on the one hand; complying with efficiency standards with less respect for student wishes and family circumstances on the other. Neither of these contradictions can be solved in the present context of family life and school life. A counterproductive division of labour derives from this situation: individualized and self-directed learning (Long, 1989) tends to move out of school and take place in the family and other places of non-formal learning, while institutionalized teaching and learning remains in the school to the detriment of disadvantaged students and their families who do not have enough resources to bridge the gap, which becomes wider rather than narrower. This is perhaps the most relevant problem to be tackled in teacher education of the near future.

13

Conclusion: Comparative Multilevel Analysis of Educational Trajectories

Marcelo Parreira do Amaral
University of Münster

Andreas Walther
Goethe University, Frankfurt

Who takes decisions in education? This provokingly short question lies at the heart of the project 'Governance of Educational Trajectories in Europe. Access, coping and relevance of education for young people in European knowledge societies'; it may as well be used to summarize the key findings documented and discussed in this volume. The subtitle of the project further specifies the question with regard to how access to education is regulated, how young people cope with educational demands and what support they can mobilize, and what makes education relevant for them as well as for other societal actors.

The underlying conceptual perspective on educational trajectories results from a combination of a life course and governance perspective with regard to education. The need for such an approach has been identified and justified against the background of a changing role of education in what has been termed knowledge societies: the concept of lifelong learning signals that education has become ever more important in organizing social integration while the organization of education is less and less regulated top down in a bureaucratic way, but by complex processes of negotiation between different actors across different societal levels from local to transnational, from individual to institution, holding more or less power. Consequently, research and analysis have been designed as a mixed-method and comparative multilevel approach in order to take into account as many different perspectives as possible as well as their dynamic and interactive nature (see Walther et al., in this volume). These new modes of governance need to be contextualized with regard to social contexts that have developed differently throughout the modernization process. Education systems on the one hand and welfare states on the other have developed interdependently and created specific transition and life course regimes (see Tikkanen et al., in this volume). Referring to these contexts simply as nation states would do little justice to the complexity of the opportunity structures for individual life course trajectories *in* and *through* education but also miss the specificities of current social change. Dale et al. (in this volume) argue that educational governance needs to be analysed with regard to discourses as modes of structuring practice as well as with regard to processes of re-scaling between individual, organizational, local, regional, national and transnational levels. These new mechanisms of governance imply that general transversal discourses gain influence and power while at the same time being constantly translated and adapted by concrete actors with regard to specific social contexts. These processes of translation have been analysed in particular with regard to the scope of influence of students and parents in the education process. In contrast to public discourses, the scope for parents' involvement, however, remains limited (see Amos et al., in this volume). A specific aspect of policy translation relates to how students and their parents perceive and interpret institutional access regulations to and within education. Especially, the current debate on Early School Leaving (ESL) suffers from a simplistic assumption that access equates to attendance and participation. It has been suggested that understanding the use individuals make of education requires extending the perspective from access to include the *accessibility* individuals ascribe subjectively to education (see Stauber et al., in this volume). The interaction between individuals and education systems reflected by the relation between access and accessibility, however, is not a dualistic one but needs rather to be seen as embedded in social practice in which other actors are involved, especially peers, counsellors and teachers. For example, the way in which professionals interpret their role and the opportunity structures for action within existing institutional arrangements contributes to different modes of producing and reproducing educational trajectories (see Barberis et al., in this volume). The same applies to the fact that schools interpret education as more than teaching, including different mechanisms and ways of support. Vocational and educational guidance is central in this respect, at least as far as transitions from lower to upper secondary education are concerned. These measures differ as to the extent that they are integrated with general teaching, to the extent they aim at allocating students to specific routes or assisting them in developing their own career plans, and whether they are provided by school or external actors (see Felczak and Julkunen, in this volume). Guidance schemes as well as measures aimed at preventing ESL increasingly try to involve parents in order to interrupt milieu-specific effects of social reproduction. However, relationships between school and parents often rather resemble a 'blaming game', characterized by reciprocal expectations and responsibilizations. Especially, parents from disadvantaged social backgrounds tend to feel controlled and disrespected by teachers in their educational competence and aspiration (see Koşar Altinyelken et al., in this volume). Such conflicts reflect different, and often contradicting, expectations towards education and the meanings attached to it. Most actors agree that education is relevant for acquiring the skills and the knowledge needed for positioning oneself in society and the labour market. However, while students and parents expect to maximize their life chances through it, teachers have to mediate this expectation with the allocative function of education (see McDowell et al., in this volume). This points to the complex relationship between formal learning represented by the school curriculum and teaching, and non-formal and informal learning, which occur both inside and outside school. Our analyses reveal that for young people the relevance of education splits between formal and informal aspects. The latter, however, tend not to be fully recognized by the other school actors (see Salovaara and Litau, in this volume). While access, coping and relevance are obviously involved in the decisions taken in young people's educational trajectories, understanding their specific influence requires analysing decision making not in terms of young people making individual choices, but rather in terms of constellations of decision making involving negotiation between a range of actors (see Cuconato et al., in this volume). While parents and teachers agree on the relevance of education, they play different roles, having specific interests in and thus different perspectives on young people's education. The degree to which parents understand school mechanisms, on the one hand, and the extent to which their aspirations are recognized by teachers, on the other, tends to reflect structures of social inequality (see Ule et al., in this volume).

The remaining part of this concluding chapter deals with drawing insights from and expanding on the possibilities of the research presented in the preceding chapters that can further multilevel comparative analysis as a methodological approach to education research in Comparative and International Education. First, we discuss how multilevel comparative analysis has been conceptualized and conducted as reflecting the complexities of the research object and its needs for contextualization. Second, we illustrate the added-value of this approach by discussing in detail three exemplary educational trajectories. The chapter ends with a discussion of its contribution to educational research and emerging research perspectives.

Comparative Multilevel Analysis

The analyses conducted in the chapters of this volume resorted to different but related comparative strategies with the aim of adequately addressing the research questions and techniques as well as types of data available specific to a particular level. As the preceding chapters in this volume have discussed them in detail, they will be only briefly referred to in this chapter.

In terms of accounting for the macro-level or socio-economic dimension, our research has referred to typological and cross-national comparison of education and welfare (Allmendinger, 1989; Esping-Andersen, 1990) for systematic case selection and in order to reach a balanced coverage and sampling criteria, including as many contextual variables as possible (cf. Tikkanen et al., in this volume). For instance, GOETE countries differ substantially in their rates of participation in education and training as well as in the ways in which education and training are organized (cf. Eurydice and Eurostat, 2012: 72). In order to give just a brief idea of variation in this respect, one may look at two indicators which are at the centre of current educational discourses: the rate of ESL and the public expenditure on education in EU member states; the levels of ESL are medium or low in GOETE countries, with the highest share in Italy (15 per cent) and the lowest in Slovenia (4.4 per cent) (see Figure 13.1).

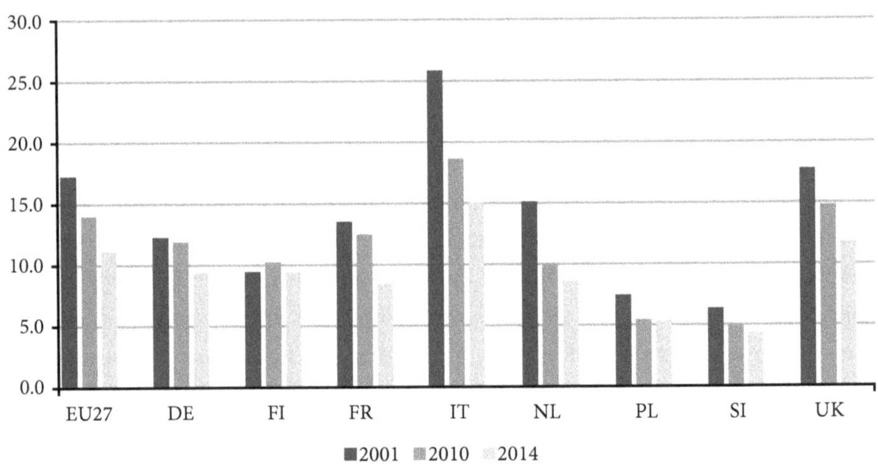

Figure 13.1 ESL rates in GOETE, per cent in 2001–2014

Source: Eurostat, 2015a

On the policy level, there is variation in the level of expenditure on education across the countries, as seen in the percentage of the gross domestic product. Expenditure for education in GOETE countries reflects different degrees of investment into their younger generations and consequently allowing for different provisions of teaching and support (see Figure 13.2).

Our analyses allowed us to further differentiate the typology proposed by Allmendinger (1989) – according to which three main clusters were distinguished among the eight GOETE countries (cf. Tikkanen et al., in this volume) – to include the different organizational frameworks and regulations of access as well as the different provisions of support available for young people throughout their educational trajectories. These systemic frameworks do not completely determine individual trajectories, but rather provide varying levels of everyday life experience of accessibility at the individual-subjective dimension. This is reflected, for instance, in parents' expectations of the educational destinations of their children (see also Biggart et al., 2015).

1 In *high-level standardized and comprehensive* systems (Finland, Slovenia) organizational differentiation and degree of selectivity is low and no transitions in compulsory education exist. Thus the degree to which students are selected and grouped according to individual or group characteristics (e.g. level of achievement, language proficiency, etc.) is by definition (and also in practice) substantially lower. This type of system

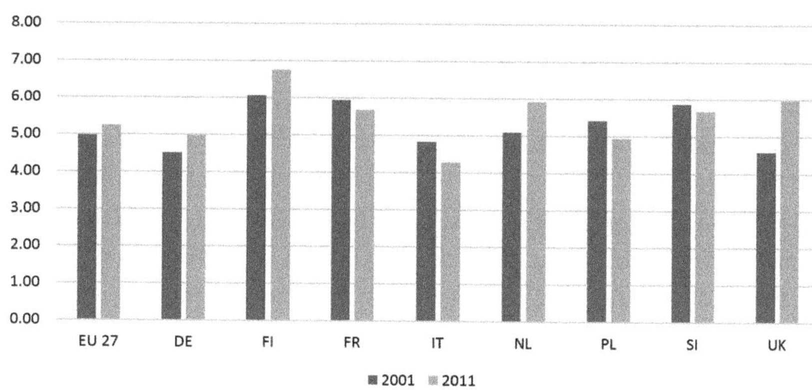

Figure 13.2 Total public expenditure on education in GOETE countries, as per cent of GDP

Source: Eurostat, 2015b

has the most potential for effectively providing access to education and mitigating inequalities.

2 In *low-level standardized and differentiated systems* (the UK, Italy, Poland) there is a medium degree of organizational differentiation, a low degree of selectivity and the existing transitions are 'smoother'. This, however, has to be seen in the context of the level of support pupils receive to cope with transitions: all three countries provide only little institutionalized (state) support. While pupils consequently have to count predominantly on their families' support (often reproducing social inequalities), they also experience fewer 'cooling out' processes.

3 In *high-level standardized and differentiated systems* (France, Germany, the Netherlands) there is a substantial organizational differentiation; a medium to high degree of selectivity and transitions exists which represents a medium to high threshold from one education level to the next. The systems have inherent highly selective 'bottlenecks' and early decision-making points that have the potential to reinforce social and educational inequalities and disadvantage, thus offering less potential for providing effective access and mitigating inequalities.

Focusing on institutional and discursive elements of the governance of educational trajectories, analysis at the macro and national/regional level compared how educational trajectories are framed, as was argued in Dale et al. (in this volume), by two distinct but related opportunity structures in the wider field of education: *Institutional Opportunity Structures* and *Discursive Opportunity Structures*. Opportunity structures basically indicate what is possible and desirable in particular policy fields. Thus, instead of comparing the 'content' of the educational trajectories – which would remain at the surface, showing both similarities and differences – this approach compares 'opportunity structures' that have a shaping effect on them, for instance by shaping policy on a particular issue, by impacting on whether and how a particular issue is problematized and for whom, by suggesting or indeed urging particular types of intervention and mechanisms of achieving them (see also Dale et al., in this volume; cf. Dale and Parreira do Amaral, 2015). A general insight from these analyses is that the 'governance of educational trajectories' is experienced almost wholly indirectly and insensibly through the ways it shapes opportunity structures available to those involved. While opportunity structures do not determine policies, they do set broad limitations on their stated purposes and objectives, providing powerful institutional and discursive framings that operate *proscriptively* and on a basis of *exclusion* rather than inclusion, i.e. ruling out policies that do not conform. For instance, Parreira do Amaral and Rinne (2015) have illustrated how the discourse on the 'knowledge-based economy' impacts deliberations of the governance of education trajectories.

Besides distinguishing between various types of regulation and organizational frameworks and between different opportunity structures provided to policy, multilevel comparative analysis also required an interpretative framework accounting for the interplay of individual agency and socio-economic, institutional and cultural elements. Walther's model of 'transition regimes' (2006) offers a broad set of categories useful in understanding the distinct realities and 'normalities' across the cases involved in the project by linking these differences and similarities to life course structures – which includes not only the education system but also welfare, labour market, cultural or discursive dominant understandings of young people as well as their individual experiences, orientations and strategies (see Figure 13.3).

GOETE countries can be clustered into five different regime types that result from the interplay of cultural, institutional and socio-economic factors: liberal regime (the UK), employment-centred regime (Germany, France, the Netherlands), universalistic regime (Finland), post-socialist countries (Poland, Slovenia) and sub-protective regime (Italy) (cf. Tikkanen et al., in this volume).

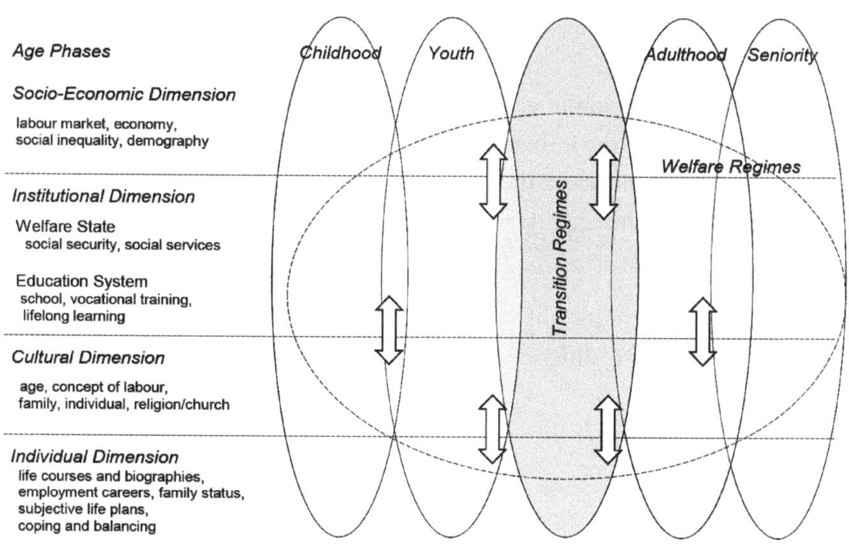

Figure 13.3 Dimensions of transition regimes

Source: Walther, 2015b: 201 (translated)

At the local level, the comparative analyses conducted focused on the *individual level* of subjective experiences. By doing this, they did not conceive of individuals simply as rational choosers, but rather as embedded in local school spaces comprising various webs of relationships with multiple actors at various levels. Comparative analyses focused thus on these interactive and dynamic processes from which actual educational trajectories evolve. Emphasis was placed on the *inter-subjective level* regarding all kinds of interactions and relevant practices within schools and in the local contexts of schools by means of individual interviews, focus groups or participatory observation. These different techniques allowed for insights into the issues from different angles: individual interviews (with students, teachers, professionals) gave access to subjective interpretations of inter-subjective topics, but at the same time allowed reconstruction of subjective meaning; group discussions allowed reconstruction of collective meaning and aspects of social practice.

Adapting the model of qualitative multilevel analysis developed by Helsper et al. (2010), we elaborated a model of *comparative multilevel analysis* (see Walther et al., in this volume). In correspondence with the model of transition regimes (see Figure 13.3) the most relevant levels of analysis related to educational trajectories are:

1 The socio-economic dimension: different structures of labour market and economy, social inequality and demography.
2 The institutional dimension: with a focus on both the welfare state and the education system.
3 The cultural dimension of varying context-dependent understandings of age, labour, family, the individual, etc.
4 The individual dimension: the subjective perspectives of young people, their aspirations and experiences as well as the transitions and trajectories in their life courses.

These analyses provide insight into different patterns of young people's educational trajectories with different constellations of decision making, as will be discussed below.

Educational Trajectories as Cases of 'Doing Transitions' between Actors across Levels

In the following, we illustrate what comparative multilevel analysis means with regard to what we have conceptualized as 'doing transitions' in young people's educational trajectories. We refer to three different cases already presented and analysed in Chapter 11 by Cuconato et al. These trajectories follow different patterns and include different constellations of decision making at the end of lower secondary school. Moreover, they represent different clusters of relationships between education and welfare. The aim is to explore how different actors and levels of governance are interrelated in these cases.

The case of Matteo

> Nowadays with [lower secondary] you don't get anything … I followed nobody … I have taken all my choices by myself.

Matteo lives in the outskirts of a major city in a poor region of Southern Italy characterized by high levels of unemployment, poverty and criminality. In keeping with the neighbourhood, his family can also be characterized as low to middle SES (his father died when he was very young). As regards the institutional context of his educational trajectory, the Italian constellation of education and welfare has been characterized as low-level-differentiated: school is regulated centrally as comprehensive and permeable; however, the links to employment are weak. Central regulation does not foresee support services for students, which therefore differ depending on political will and resources available at the level of a single school or municipality. Especially, the region in which Matteo lives is known for a scarcity of social and educational out-of-school infrastructure. At the same time, school autonomy is emphasized in public discourses and individuals are held more self-responsible for their education and social mobility. In the neighbourhood, his former school is the only relevant public actor, and school actors appear to have accepted this role and responsibility for supporting students as much as possible. In fact, school offers out-of-school activities as well as counselling and support related to the transition to upper secondary school. This is facilitated by a teacher–student ratio of 1:3.5 (half of the teachers being special needs teachers) and by the school management's engagement in attracting additional project funds and staff (cf. du Bois-Reymond et al., 2012: 306). Matteo remembers being warmly accompanied, recognized and supported. He adapted to the rules and norms of school life and is proud that he gets along well even with strict teachers. Actually, he thinks they should be even stricter. His adaptation to school illustrates the internalization of the current discourse of individual self-responsibility for learning and life course and distancing himself from his peers who – according to him – do not understand the relevance of education but aim at entering the labour market early. It needs to be noted that in Italy unemployment figures among young people under the age of 30 do not differ as much according to education as in Northern European countries.

Although teachers in lower secondary encouraged him to go to general upper secondary school (*liceo*), he opted for a technical institute for commerce which is not as demanding (and middle-class oriented) while still giving access to higher education (he wants to study law and become a company director):

> First, I want to get the high-school certificate as nowadays with [lower secondary] you don't get anything … The teachers said, we don't force you … but you have possibilities to get everywhere … I followed nobody … I have taken all my choices by myself.

This individualized career plan reflects his awareness of having to rely on himself as his family cannot support him. On the one hand, the figure of company director represents a gendered stereotype of the male, self-responsible and independent leader. A hypothesis could be that growing up without a father (his mother does not appear as a competent support in his narrative) is a reason for seeking close relationships with teachers which in turn helps him in accepting and internalizing the individualized norms of modern schooling. On the other hand, preferring a middle track of upper secondary education can be interpreted in terms of 'safety first' as he is aware that he must succeed without family backup and without the support of his old school. This constellation of decision making has been characterized as *step-by-step* (Cuconato et al., in this volume). It is facilitated by a permeable school system with postsecondary pathways being open for everyone, by a good student–teacher ratio in quantitative and a good teacher–student relation in qualitative terms. However, this support does not only reflect a pedagogical approach but also confirms the dominant policy agenda of preventing early school leaving at any cost. This happens especially in Southern Italy where schools and universities are the only 'safe' acknowledged and accessible places for young people, even if return rates of education are uncertain. Moreover the official discourse is being undermined by a local and subcultural discourse according to which staying on in education is a waste of time. This places a heavy burden on school and staff as they have to compensate for this 'passive subsidiarization' by which the task of reducing ESL is passed over to lower levels without additional resources (see Dale et al., in this volume).

The case of Matteo is both typical and untypical for the governance of educational trajectories in (Southern) Italy. It is untypical inasmuch as unlike many of his peers he has adapted to school and accepted being self-responsible for his education. Also, the way school engages in supporting young people in their educational trajectories is special. At the same time, both individual and school attitudes reproduce the national and European discourse of lifelong learning, school autonomy and of reducing social inequality to the problem of early school leaving.

The case of Nina

> I am sorry that I did not listen to myself but ... to the opinions of others.

The trajectory of *Nina*, fifteen years old, living in a suburb of a major city in Slovenia, also appears smooth as she passes from primary school – which in Slovenia includes both primary and lower secondary education without a transition in between – to general upper secondary education (*gymnasium*). Her family is from the lower middle class and her parents have high educational aspirations for her. This corresponds to a widespread discourse and policy in the country according to which investment in education is both an individual and public duty, especially in general education (84 per cent of all students in the school year 2011/12), while vocational routes undergo a decline in status and recognition (du Bois-Reymond et al., 2012: 380). The power of this discourse, on the one hand, results from policy reforms which have strongly referred to the idea of lifelong learning interpreted largely in terms of keeping young people as long as possible in education. On the other hand, for young people and their parents this discourse allows postponing vocational and occupational choices and maintaining hopes for social mobility and successful labour market entry.

At least until the recent economic crisis, Slovenian lifelong learning policies have been made possible by public expenditure for education being higher than in many other European countries (see Figure 13.2). In Nina's school, the ratio between multi-professional pedagogical staff (including social worker, psychologist, social pedagogue and special needs educator) is 1:9 which in Nina's narrative is summarized as '*all the people around me*', including both her parents and school staff (du Bois-Reymond et al., 2012: 380).

A closer look at the decision-making process in Nina's educational trajectory at the end of lower secondary school reveals that the trajectory is less smooth than at first sight. There is a rupture classifying it as a *discontinuous academic* pattern. Originally intrinsically motivated to enrol in a vocational school for floriculture, she eventually attends a biotechnical gymnasium as 'everybody recommended me to rather choose a gymnasium'. Her parents wanted to prevent her from possibly regretting her decision later, worrying that in the future she would be dissatisfied with being 'just a florist', and ignored her strong desire to work in this field. Also, school staff perceived her choice as spoiling her chances. As the floriculture school is also at greater distance from home, she accepted their advice. However, after only two months she regretted not to have listened to herself:

> In a way I regret it, because now I know I could make some concrete physical things – like different bouquets of flowers, things that make me happy … I am sorry that I did not listen to myself, but … to the opinions of others.

Nina experiences the decision for general upper secondary education as a misleading trajectory alienating her from her professional dream and self-fulfilment, a pattern which has been termed as *too-weak-to-resist* to mechanisms of cooling out. In her case, however, cooling out does not mean lowering aspirations of disadvantaged youth with the consequence of reproducing social inequalities, but subjecting students to a quantitative human capital logic: The more education, the better. Her explanation why she did not resist parental and teacher pressure expresses an even bigger lack of self-confidence than in the constellation *step-by-step* illustrated by Matteo's trajectory. This needs to be contextualized with regard to a discourse climate in which prioritizing subjective interest over getting as far and high as possible – at least in the case of good achievement – is addressed in moral terms of individuals being consciously wasting one's human capital and therefore being self-responsible for narrowing future life course options. This individualizing discourse may be interpreted as a shift from work ethics in labour societies to education ethics in knowledge societies.

The case of Julia

> They held me an apprenticeship place right under my nose, but without a school leaving certificate I wouldn´t have got it. Yes, and then I didn´t want to stand there as a fool, so I made some efforts to get the apprenticeship place.

Julia has grown up in a deprived area in a de-industrialized city and region in Germany characterized by high rates of immigrant population, unemployment and poverty. She lives with both her parents; the family is of low to middle SES. Originally she had attended a comprehensive school but then in grade 7 decided to change school as she did not get along with classmates and teachers. This implied accepting downgrading to *Hauptschule*, which represents the lowest track of lower secondary school in the highly differentiated German education system. Leavers from *Hauptschule* (after grade 9 or 10) do not have access to higher education. Entering vocational training in the dual system of apprenticeship training or in the few school-based vocational courses is the only option for them. However, due to a decline in the offer of apprenticeship places by enterprises since the 1990s, many of them remain without upper secondary general or vocational qualifications. Employers justify this with regard to the low degree of 'trainability' of this group. Consequently, most leavers from *Hauptschule* do not enter vocational education or training directly but are obliged to attend pre-vocational measures, in many cases more than once as transition into regular training succeeds only in one out of two cases. This so-called 'transition system' has increased since the 1990s and extended towards lower secondary education where vocational orientation towards 'realistic' perspectives tends to start as early as in grade 7, with 'trainability' as the accepted orientation for all actors in this area (cf. Walther, 2015b).

Julia describes her lower secondary school as a caring and supportive place. Teachers seem to feel responsible for supporting young people in coping with social disadvantage and accept not only being teachers but also acting as social workers. Yet, the teacher–student ratio of 1:13 sets clear limits (du Bois-Reymond et al., 2012: 250). Therefore, the school cooperates with a broad range of external actors – in most cases funded by local youth welfare authorities – who provide school with social work, counselling, leisure activities and vocational orientation. Cooperation with companies provides access – while also introducing and reinforcing the discourse and the criteria of 'trainability' into school. Originally, Julia wanted to enter a school-based vocational training for care of the elderly. However, during an internship in a home for elderly persons she did not feel very comfortable. Additionally, the coincidence of experiences of death in the home and of a girl from her school causes her a depression and undermines her motivation for working in the care field. She abandons the internship, her school achievement declines and her transition into vocational training seems at high risk.

At this point her family intervenes, especially her mother and aunt who both work as saleswomen in a bakery. They convince their boss to offer Julia an internship. Backed up by this female support network, Julia recovers and manages to perform well during the internship. She is promised an apprenticeship place on the condition of achieving the school leaving certificate. As discussed in detail in Chapter 11, her case is an example of a *discontinuous vocational* trajectory as she had to compromise with – and actually lower – her original professional aspiration as a nurse for the elderly. Nevertheless she says: 'I always wanted to become a saleswoman … and then I had the idea with the bakery, through my mum and my aunt. They do the same … they advised me a lot.' Obviously the social embedding facilitated by the female family allowed accepting and internalizing this compromise as her individual choice. It is striking that in her case, family influence seems to be more effective than the various institutional support inside and outside of school.

Cases like Julia's have been interpreted as a constellation of *family convoy* due to the central, yet ambivalent roles of the family: it provides protective support while also channelling young people's choices according to available (social) capital. A potential explanation for the relevance of this constellation in Germany could be that in the differentiated and selective school system, vocational orientation and transition support imply obvious and powerful mechanisms of stigmatization.

Taking a comparative perspective, we see that the contexts of these trajectories differ:

1. Discourses of lifelong learning and prevention of early school leaving are interpreted differently: in Slovenia lifelong learning has been taken up explicitly by the government as the main reference of policy reforms that aim at keeping as many students in education as long as possible; in Italy lifelong learning is primarily interpreted in terms of school autonomy and self-responsibility of students to stay in education as long as possible, yet without backing this up with resources (however, there is a local, subcultural counter-discourse according to which staying in school does not pay off); in Germany, the lifelong learning discourse is interpreted primarily in terms of 'trainability' reflecting the role of employers in providing vocational opportunities and trajectories.
2. Institutionally, access to post-compulsory routes is open in Italy and Slovenia, but selective in Germany. Welfare services for young people are integrated with education in Slovenia, largely lacking in Italy and separated with a subordinate, compensatory role in Germany.
3. As regards staff, the highest teacher–student ratio is found in the Italian case study school; in qualitative terms Italian school staff mainly comprise

teaching staff, compared to multi-professional teams in Slovenia and cooperative networks between schools and youth welfare agencies in the German case.

4 Consequently, students in Slovenia tend to be directed towards general upper secondary school, in Italy students get differentiated recommendations which however are not binding, while in Germany school leavers from *Hauptschule* are clearly directed towards the apprenticeship system and/or the so-called transition system of pre-vocational schemes for those classified as 'not trainable'.

However, neither the trajectories nor the constellations of decision making reflect these conditions directly. As summarized in Table 13.1, they rather represent conditions and influences that are perceived, interpreted and negotiated at local level, at institutional and milieu level, at the level of direct interaction between students and parents, peers or professionals, and at individual level as a part of the biographical construction and identity work of the young people concerned:

1 The case of Matteo seems to differ from how trajectories are seen as typical nationally and locally; due to his specific biographical situation he has close contact with teachers who in turn – not untypically – aim at compensating the infrastructural deficits affecting young people's trajectories; thus he internalizes a general discourse of lifelong learning (and of tackling early school leaving) although this is not facilitated by concrete policy programmes.
2 The case of Nina is particular and paradoxical as she 'suffers' from success and support within the inclusive and permeable lifelong learning-driven Slovenian context. In her case teachers, counsellors and parents – for different reasons – cooperate in convincing her to take up general upper secondary education instead of a vocational route for which she shows intrinsic interest. In this case, it is unclear whether and how long she will be motivated to follow this destination.
3 The case of Julia reflects the structures of the German education and transition system quite explicitly. Nevertheless, it is less teachers and professionals than informal support through family members that accomplishes the cooling out process to accepting a lower status training for saleswoman as an individual choice.

In sum, these cases reveal that opportunity structures work their way 'down' from macro to micro, or from transnational discourses to local practices.

Table 13.1 'Doing transitions' in the educational trajectories of Matteo, Nina and Julia

Levels of meaning	Society/macro	Milieus/institutions	Interaction and practices	Individuals
Society/macro: Education and welfare Structures of inequality Discourses	**Education:** between permeability (Slovenia) and selectivity (Germany) **Welfare**: structural deficit (Italy), integrated (Slovenia), external-compensatory (Germany) **Lifelong learning:** individualized responsibility (Slovenia), passive subsidiarity (Italy), trainability (Germany)		**Orientation:** towards general upper secondary (Italy, Slovenia), 'realistic' training (Germany)	**Education:** as way out/up (Matteo), as feasible but meaningless (Nina), as difficult and inevitable (Julia)
Milieus/institutions: Local politics Authorities and institutions Experts and teachers Policy programmes	**School policies:** between centralization and autonomy (Italy, Slovenia), social disadvantage (Italy, Germany), segmented training and labour markets (Italy, Germany)	**Schools acting:** between social responsibility (Germany, Italy), social mobility (Slovenia), prevention of ESL (Italy), occupational allocation (Germany)	**Career/educational guidance:** visiting schools (Nina), internships (Julia), reflection (Matteo) – based on achievement (Matteo, Nina), school type, labour market (Julia)	**Experience of school support:** socio-emotional support (Julia, Matteo), pressure and alienation (Nina), less effective and meaningful than family support (Julia)
Interaction and practices: Teaching Counselling Family and peers	**Families:** aiming at higher cultural capital (Slovenia), investing social capital (Germany), lack of social and cultural capital (Italy)	**Parents/school:** confirm pressure for upward mobility (Slovenia), accept individual preference (Italy), mitigate/complement vocational orientation/cooling out (Germany)	**Use of school support:** acceptance due to lack of family support (Matteo), acceptance without meaning (Nina), 'replaced' by family support (Julia)	**Constellations of decision making:** Matteo: step-by-step; Nina: too-weak-to-resist; Julia: family convoy
Individuals: Subjective meaning, experience, interest, motivation, coping strategies, decisions trajectories	**Gendered career plans:** between accessibility and intrinsic interest; resisting (Slovenia), using (Italy), replacing **lifelong learning** by trainability ('cooling out', Germany)	**Experience of parents:** as pressure (Slovenia), unconditional love but ineffective (Italy), caring and channelling role models (Germany)	**Individual 'choice':** own in accordance with school (Matteo), induced, overruled by school/parents (Nina), suggested by family role models and internalized (Julia)	**Patterns of trajectories:** Matteo: smooth; Nina: discontinuous academic; Julia: discontinuous vocational

Between-levels policies and programmes from 'above' need to be 'translated' into strategies and aims of concrete actors 'below'. At each change of level, structures, meanings and practices are produced and reproduced. At the same time, 'doing transitions' works itself up inasmuch as the individual is considered as the main decision-making unit while her/his actions are always embedded in and structured, negotiated and framed by interactions with others.

Closing Remarks

The analyses in this volume called attention to the need for a more differentiated conceptualization of educational trajectories, which are not simply seen as the outcome of individual rational choices, but rather as embedded in various layers of structural, institutional and discursive frameworks as well as in social practice and subjective positioning. However, the more important issue educational research needs to address is to ask what kinds of changes, rather than just how many changes, are going on, and with what consequences, for whom. In essence, the challenging complexity related to studying the governance of educational trajectories derives from the fact that how educational trajectories and transitions are governed is the product of activities and actors at a range of different scales, from the global to the local school. The nature of this increasing complexity is certainly experienced quantitatively – there is just more 'governance' going on, at more levels, and involving more actors, many times, at the cost of the loss of influence of other actors (cf. Parreira do Amaral et al., 2015).

In this concluding chapter, we have tried to outline rather than fully elaborate in a systematic way a comparative perspective on how decisions in education are being made. We have summarized the life course and governance as the overarching theoretical perspectives and access, coping and relevance as cross-cutting dimensions of operationalization. We have introduced *doing transitions* and *opportunity structures* as two fundamental conceptual approaches to the interactive nature of the governance of educational trajectories. Due to the multilevel, multi-actor and multi-perspective approach of the GOETE project, comparative analysis of this general question does not mean simply drawing findings together across different contexts but requires integration at another level of analysis. For comparative analysis of educational trajectories this implies, first, more than juxtaposing different types of institutions or variables; second, as nature, forms and consequences of patterns of governance are extremely, and increasingly, complex, they cannot simply be homogenized in terms of national models or patterns.

Using the model of multilevel qualitative analysis in our research can be seen as experimenting with a heuristic model that has been developed for the analysis of social interrelations without reducing their complexity. One of the major contributions of GOETE to research, policy and practice pertains to applying multilevel analysis methodology to empirical research. While educational and social research has long discussed multilevel analysis (Bray and Thomas, 1995), its empirical use has been mostly restricted to quantitative research (Hox, 2010). GOETE drew from the model of qualitative multilevel analysis developed by Helsper et al. (2010) in designing research and analysis, while at the same time integrating both quantitative and qualitative data and paying adequate attention to the highly interactive nature of the research questions at hand. In face of the increasing complexity of the governance of education, this represents one promising avenue for further research.

In reviewing some of the main thematic dimensions of our research, GOETE contributed to a more differentiated view of issues of access to education in educational trajectories. It discussed crucial issues related to *access to education and inequality* pointing to the interactive and iterative nature of providing and effectively 'getting' access to education. Access reflects socio-economic factors such as class, gender and ethnicity as well as the social context of schools and depends on the stratification inherent to the institutional structure of education and training. Differences occur especially between high-level standardized and comprehensive systems (Finland, Slovenia) and high-level standardized differentiated systems (France, Germany, the Netherlands). Yet, findings revealed also that access needs to be expanded by *accessibility*, thus referring to individuals' subjective interpretation and realization of access. Apart from this, also the discretionary practice of teachers and other professionals contributed to different degrees of accessibility of education and training. Here, in particular the concept of accessibility may be viewed as a contribution both to research and to policy and practice inasmuch as it points to the complexity of a research object and to the need to account for it when studying issues of access to education and inequality. Additionally, GOETE findings provide insights for policy and practice inasmuch as they reveal how institutional and organizational arrangements of access play out on individual trajectories, but also by pointing to the need to reflect on the interaction among those involved in these processes, both those providing education and those directly concerned – namely young people and their parents.

Against the background of differing conceptions, traditions and perspectives of education, one crucial issue related to the role of education in social integration in knowledge societies pertains to its ability to integrate and reconcile subjective meanings and relevancies at individual level with more instrumental needs and requirements at societal level in order to facilitate educational trajectories which are individually meaningful and societally sustainable. With regard to the meaning and *relevance of education*, GOETE demonstrated that an instrumental view of education as a means of securing employability and life chances based on employment prevailed among all actors: from teachers and teacher trainers, school principals and policymakers, counsellors and social workers, employers and civil society representatives, to parents and students themselves. Other meanings of education such as personal development and emancipation as well as the relevancies more directly related to young people's everyday lives seem to remain hidden amid this discourse. This predominant view of education is also reflected by the recent EU policy agenda on education and training.

The latter is related to the increasing role of transnational discourses such as knowledge society, knowledge-based economy, lifelong learning, employability or disadvantage in the governance of education. The ways in which educational trajectories are currently being shaped occur more and more indirectly and insensibly through a complex interaction of multiple actors and increasingly less through top-down state policies. A new vertical and horizontal division of labour in educational governance has emerged contributing to different *opportunity structures* being produced at different scales by different actors, institutions and processes of governance. In this framework, parents and students are expected to take responsibility for their own education. Yet, possibilities of participation in decision making at school are limited. The adopted conceptualization of governance as our research object may be in itself considered as one major contribution to research in the governance of education. The framework adds to the conceptual and analytical repertoire of researchers, allowing for a more differentiated view of governance that distinguishes scales, activities and actors/institutions of governance, thus opening up issues to theoretical and empirical analyses. Policy and practice also profit from these insights inasmuch as they need critical reflection upon the different messages they receive from different actors, but also from the distinction of scales, activities and actors/institutions which allows for a clearer understanding of the complexity they all are part of, thus pointing to the need for careful coordination.

Unequal access and accessibility is also related to different abilities and resources for *coping* with educational demands. GOETE investigated how students, especially those from deprived social backgrounds, cope with educational demands and the *support* they receive for it. Evidence of a powerful discourse of individualism was found, putting students under pressure. Young people believe themselves to be solely responsible for success or failure in their educational trajectories. GOETE findings showed that academic demands seem to be the most pressing challenge for students to cope with and this may be related to the predominant instrumental view of education mentioned above. Students feel especially burdened with decision making at transition points which implies that more and better guidance and counselling are needed. However, formal support measures suffer from little trust by students. Four times more students refer to informal sources of support in the case of school or transition problems than to teachers or other professionals. Informal support in turn suffers from a lack of recognition from institutional actors. In fact, findings reveal a 'blaming game' between school and family.

The complexity of dimensions, actors and levels involved in the emergence and governance of individual educational trajectories reveals that the relationship between education and the *life course* results from complex interaction and negotiation processes. It reveals that neither discourses as mechanisms of transnational governance, nor access regulations as institutional structures of national education systems or local policies compensating for structural deficits, nor teachers' intentions or parents' expectations, nor students' orientations and achievements alone can explain how educational trajectories evolve differently; nor is there a linear top-down or bottom-up model of explanation. For educational research – comparative or not – this implies recognizing the specificity of individual cases (whether individual refers to young people, particular schools or local school spaces). From here, recognizing and understanding the processes – or better, constellations – of 'doing transitions' that are at the core of educational pathways remains a crucial task for future educational research, policy and practice.

Notes

Chapter One

1 'Governance' has been criticized for being 'notoriously slippery' (Pierre and Peters, 2000: 7). It is used in substantially different ways (as a practical, normative, melioristic, etc. concept) and amid diverging discussions in fields such as economics and foreign policy, among others, which makes it even more important to be clear about our usage (Pierre and Peters, 2000). In this volume, we favour a descriptive-analytical usage of the term 'governance' while acknowledging a more normative usage such as in 'good governance' or 'New Governance'. The latter usage points to preferred ways of governing respectively to a model against which ineffective governing may be contrasted. Illustrations of this normative usage may be found in the documents of the International Monetary Fund, the World Bank and the United Nations (cf. Agere, 2000).

2 The usage of the term in so many different disciplines and in the analysis of so many different issues also makes clear that 'governance' fulfils different functions in academic debates (see Schuppert, 2011).

3 This stands in contrast to quantitative research, where multilevel analysis refers to multiple regression techniques for the analysis of hierarchical or clustered data aiming at correct inference of coefficients, at the estimation of group effects, etc. (see, for example, Browne and Rasbash, 2004).

Chapter Two

1 Due to recent changes in early childhood education legislation, pre-primary education became part of compulsory education in Finland in August 2015.

2 This is true with the exception of Northern Ireland and some parts of England, which retain a selective system for entry into grammar school based on a test sat by pupils at the end of primary schooling.

Chapter Three

1 A good example is given by Italy where compulsory education does not finish when the lower secondary cycle finishes, but in the middle of upper secondary schooling. This is not even synchronized with regionally regulated vocational systems which are highly differentiated (Barberis et al., 2012).
2 See European Commission (2003, 2005 and 2006).

Chapter Four

1 For example, new curricular standards introduced in countries like England and the Netherlands both restricted autonomy and increased teachers' responsibility to find out proper mixes of strategy to cope with school-specific issues (Eurydice, 2008).
2 PISA data indicates that the path towards an effective autonomy is far from linear. Autonomy is often associated with better results: autonomy in teaching, assessment and resource allocation has a positive effect on pupils' performance – but only where and when some sort of coordination takes place, e.g. with accountability rules, cooperative more than competitive learning environments, standardized testing, national investments, equitable distribution of resources among schools (OECD, 2010a).

Chapter Five

1 See GOETE Comparative Analysis Individual Survey, Litau, J., McDowell, J., Salovaara, V., Živoder, A., Dale, R., Tolomelli, A. and Cramer, C. (2013): *Education! (What Is It Good For?) – The Relevance of Education in Contemporary Knowledge Society. Governance of Educational Trajectories in Europe. Thematic Report on Relevance*. GOETE Working Paper. Frankfurt: University of Frankfurt.
2 See GOETE Comparative Analysis Institutional Survey 2012, online at: http://goete.eu/download/working-papers (accessed 15 June 2015).
3 It is in this sense that Fairclough writes 'Discourse is a difficult concept, largely because there are so many conflicting and overlapping definitions formulated from various theoretical and disciplinary standpoints' (1992: 3).
4 It is important to note the influence of Michel Foucault (for instance the issue of knowledge and power as well as social theories of discourse; see Fairclough, 1992: Chapters 2 and 3; see also: Foucault, 1972) as well as of Antonio Gramsci (e.g. the

concept of hegemony) in the work of Norman Fairclough (see Fairclough, 1992: 91).

5 These differences have to be understood against the background of different national, regional or local socio-economic, institutional/organizational and cultural arrangements and discourses. Here the concepts of life course and of youth transition regimes prove useful in helping us account for and interpret these variations (Lessenich, 1995; Walther, 2006).

Chapter Six

1 Help-seeking orientation is defined as a person's proclivity to resolve personal and academic problems through the seeking of social support.

2 In development and health research, this has been considered the lack of a specific social capital called 'linking', i.e. the competences and relationships to access and use institutional resources, which is related to the resources available to interact with services: knowledge and understanding of their operations, language and structures; access to formal and informal 'gatekeepers' able to ease access; and trust in interactions among people with different power (Szreter and Woolcock, 2004) – a concept that can also be useful to consider in our context.

3 Regarding personal problems, about one student out of two believes that social support is available from informal resources only, and a similar number considers both informal and formal. About only 3 per cent of student interviewees do not fit into either of these two categories. Therefore, students' perceptions of helping resources appear different in relation to problems concerning school life.

4 Legitimacy can be blurred and can undergo unclear ranking processes since, in complex bureaucratic systems, coexisting norms and practices may be contradictory. Any decision looks legitimate, but specific paths can differently affect students with similar needs.

5 The 'normal' age for lower secondary students in Italy is between twelve and fourteen.

6 An external student who applies for a school final exam without being enrolled and without attending official courses.

7 Transition from lower to upper secondary education, usually at fourteen years old.

8 This item is rated 3.2 on a scale of 1 to 5 by French principals, against an average of 2.3 in the whole sample.

9 Finnish principals rate this item 3.2 on average in a 1 to 5 range, against 2.6 for the whole sample.

Chapter Nine

1 Educational systems of participant countries are distributed into three Allmendinger types: low standardization and low stratification (the UK, Italy and Poland); high standardization and high stratification (France, Germany and the Netherlands); and high standardization and low stratification (Finland and Slovenia).

2 For the purpose of this chapter, this is classified as the level of school disadvantage (disadvantaged, average and affluent schools) and socio-economic-cultural status of the families (parental education).

3 For more detailed description of the methodological design of the research within the GOETE project see Cuconato et al., in the Introduction of this volume.

4 To ensure equivalence in the national samples' data structure for the purpose of the statistical analysis the data was weighted (both students and parents); post-stratification weights were made by two criteria: the country sample size and the national school sample distribution (disadvantaged, average and affluent schools). The parental sample has a gender bias as a great majority of respondents are female (82); however, because of the dominance of females, the data could not be weighted in terms of gender. UK parental data was excluded following consideration of the small and biased sample (McDowell et al., 2012).

5 Choice and decision-making processes in educational transitions are addressed in Cuconato et al. and Ule et al., in this volume. For a more comprehensive analysis of the patterns of parental involvement in educational trajectories of their children see also Ule et al., 2015.

Chapter Ten

1 Weighted curriculum means a special emphasis on a particular subject in the formal curriculum. There are many lower secondary schools which have a special emphasis in particular languages, sports or arts, for example.

Chapter Eleven

1 Data was weighted according to country sample size and the distribution of schools in disadvantaged, average and affluent areas per country (see McDowell et al., 2012).

2 Sig.=<0.000, Cramer's V 0.241.

3 Sig.=<0.003, Cramer's V 0.043.

4 Sig.=<0.000, Cramer's V 0.172 for migration; Sig.=<0.000, Cramer's V 0.125 for ethnic minorities.

5 Sig.=<0.000, Cramer's V 0.079.

6 Sig.=<0.000, Cramer's V 0.305.

7 Mother's education: Sig.=<0.000, Cramer's V 0.163; migration background: Sig.=<0.000, Cramer's V 0.062; gender: Sig.=<0.000, Cramer's V 0.048.

8 Sig.=<0.000, Cramer's V 0.140.

9 Country of birth: Sig.=<0.000, Cramer's V 0.047; migration/minority: Sig.=<0.000, Cramer's V 0.084; socio-economic status of family: Sig.=<0.000, Cramer's V 0.081; context of school: Sig.=<0.000, Cramer's V 0.026; gender: Sig.=<0.000, Cramer's V 0.001.

10 Sig.=<0.000, Cramer's V 0.172.

11 Born abroad: Sig.=<0.000, Cramer's V 0.064; other nationalities: Sig.=<0.000, Cramer's V 0.121; gender: Sig.=<0.000, Cramer's V 0.049.

12 Gender: Sig.=<0.000, Cramer's V 0.056; place of birth: Sig.=<0.000, Cramer's V 0.060; nationality: Sig.=<0.000, Cramer's V 0.093.

13 Disadvantaged: Sig.=<0.000, Cramer's V 0.238; average: Sig.=<0.000, Cramer's V 0.284; affluent: Sig.= <0.000, Cramer's V 0.239; total: Sig.=<0.000, Cramer's V 0.234.

14 Sig.=<0.000, Cramer's V 0.286.

15 Context of schools: Sig.=<0.000, Cramer's V 0.085; education of parents: Sig.=<0.000, Cramer's V 0.106.

16 Sig.=<0.000, Cramer's V 0.149.

17 Raising issues – context of schools: Sig.=<0.000, Cramer's V 0.047; country: Sig.=<0.000, Cramer's V 0.129; expressing views – context of schools: Sig.=<0.007, Cramer's V 0.033; country: Sig.=<0.000, Cramer's V 0.128; and being listened – context of schools: Sig.=<0.000, Cramer's V 0.049; country: Sig.=<0.000, Cramer's V 0.117.

18 A fifth constellation found in the material 'choosing the simple path' has not been presented due to space restrictions (cf. Walther et al., 2015).

Chapter Twelve

1 For more about the methodological design of the research within the GOETE project see Cuconato et al. and Walther et al., in this volume.

2 For a more detailed discussion of educational aspirations and quantitative data of the GOETE survey on students and parents see McDowell et al., in this volume.

References

Agere, S. (2000), *Promoting Good Governance. Principles, Practices and Perspectives*, London: Commonwealth Secretariat.

Alheit, P. and Dausien, B. (2000), 'Biographicity as Basic Resource of Lifelong Learning', in P. Alheit et al. (eds), *Lifelong Learning Inside and Outside Schools*. Conference Proceedings, vol. 2, 400–23, Roskilde: RUC, 2.

Alheit, P. and Dausien, B. (2002a), 'The Double Face of Lifelong Learning: Two Analytical Perspectives on a Silent Revolution', *Studies in the Education of Adults* 34: 3–22.

Alheit, P. and Dausien, B. (2002b), 'Lifelong Learning and "Biographicity": Two Theoretical Views on Current Educational Changes', in A. Bron and M. Schemmann (eds), *Social Science Theories in Adult Education Research*, 211–41, Hamburg, London: LIT Verlag.

Allmendinger, J. (1989), 'Educational Systems and Labour Market Outcomes', *European Sociological Review* 5 (3): 231–50.

Allmendinger, J. and Leibfried, S. (2003), 'Education and the Welfare State: Four Worlds of Competence Production', *Journal of European Social Policy* 13 (1): 63–81.

Altrichter, H. and Helm, C. (2011), 'Schulentwicklung und Systemreform', in H. Altrichter and C. Helm (eds), *Akteure and Instrumente der Schulentwicklung*, 9–10, Baltmannsweiler: Schneider Verlag Hohengehren.

Altrichter, H., Brüsemeister, T. and Wissinger, J. (eds) (2007), *Educational Governance. Handlungskoordination und Steuerung im Bildungssystem*. Wiesbaden: VS Verlag.

Amos, S. K. (ed.) (2010), *International Educational Governance. International Perspectives on Education and Society*, 12, Bingley: Emerald.

Amos, S. K. and Radtke, F.-O. (eds) (2007), 'Die Formation neuer Bildungsregime: Zur Durchsetzung von Regierungstechniken in der post-nationalen Konstellation', *Tertium Comparationis* 13 (2).

Anthias, F. (2005), 'Social Stratification and Social Inequality: Models of Intersectionality and Identity', in F. Devine, M. Savage, J. Scott and R. Compton (eds), *Rethinking Class. Culture, Identity, and Style*, Basingstoke: Palgrave Macmillan.

Apple, M. W. (2006), 'Producing Inequalities: Neo-Liberalism. Neo-Conservatism, and the Politics of Educational Reform', in H. Lauder, P. Brown, J. Dillabough and A. H. Halsey (eds), *Education, Globalization and Social Change*, 468–89, Oxford: Oxford University Press.

Archer, M. (2000), *Being Human: The Problem of Agency*, Cambridge: Cambridge University Press.

Arendell, T. (ed.) (1997), *Contemporary Parenting: Challenges and Issues*, London: Sage.

Arnett, J. J. (1999), 'Adolescent Storm and Stress, Reconsidered', *American Psychologist* 54: 317–26.

Aro, M. (2014), 'Pitääkö koulutus lupauksensa?' ['Does Education Keep its Promise?'], *Sosiologia* 40: 313–28.

Aro, M., Julkunen, I. and Treptow, R. (2013), 'Formal Support for Students', in H. Koşar Altinyelken and I. Julkunen (eds), *Coping and Support in Educational Transitions, Thematic Working Paper*, 72–90, University of Helsinki/University of Amsterdam.

Aro, M., Järvinen, T., Rinne, R., Tikkanen, J., Buchowicz, I., Fedorczuk, M., Bledowski, P., Parreira do Amaral, M. and Walther, A. (2012), *Governance of Educational Trajectories in Europe: Comparative Analysis Institutional Survey*, GOETE Working Paper, Turku: University of Turku, available online: http://goete.eu/download/cat_view/69-working-papers (accessed 2 July 2015).

Bæck, U. K. (2010), 'Parental Involvement Practices in Formalized Home–School Cooperation', *Scandinavian Journal of Educational Research* 54 (6): 549–63.

Baer, S. (2009), 'Wozu und was macht Gender? Notwendige Erweiterungen der Governance-Perspective', in S. Botzem, J. Hofmann, S. Quack, G. F. Schuppert and H. Straßheim, (eds), *Governance Als Prozess. Koordinationsformen Im Wandel*, 99–124, Baden-Baden: Nomos.

Ball, S. J. (1990), *Politics and Policymaking in Education*. London: Routledge.

Ball, S. J. (1998), 'Big Policies/Small World: An Introduction to International Perspectives on Education Policy', *Comparative Education* 34 (2): 119–30.

Ball, S. J. and Junemann, C. (2012), *Networks, New Governance and Education*, Bristol: Policy Press.

Ball, S. J., Macrae, S. and Maguire, M. (2000), *Choice, Pathways and Transitions Post-16: New Youth, New Economics in the Global City*, London: Routledge.

Bandura, A. (1997), *Self-efficacy: The Exercise of Control*. New York: Freeman.

Barberis, E. and Loncle, P. (2015), 'Governance and Disadvantage: Institutional Opportunity Structures at Local Level', in M. Parreira do Amaral, R. Dale and P. Loncle (eds), *Shaping the Futures of Young Europeans: Education Governance in Eight European Countries*, 151–69, Bristol: Symposium Books.

Barberis, E., Cuconato, M., De Luigi, N., Demozzi, S., Martelli, A., Taddia, F. and Tolomelli, A. (2012), *Governance of Educational Trajectories in Europe: National Case Study Report Italy*, GOETE Working Paper, Bologna: University of Bologna; Urbino: University of Urbino Carlo Bo.

Barbier, J. C. (2008), *La Longue Marché vers l'Europe sociale*, Paris: PUF.

Bauman, Z. (2001), *Individualized Society*, London: Sage.

Baumert, J. and Schümer, G. (2001), 'Familiäre Lebensverhältnisse, Bildungsbeteiligung und Kompetenzerwerb', in J. Baumert, E. Klieme, M. Neubrand, M. Prenzel, U. Schiefele, W. Schneider, P. Stanat, K.-J. Tillmann and M. Weiß (eds), *PISA 2000. Basiskompetenzen von Schülerinnen und Schülern im internationalen Vergleich*, 323–407, Opladen: Leske and Budrich.

Baumert, J., Maaz, K. and Trautwein, U. (eds) (2009), 'Bildungsentscheidungen' ('Educational Decisions'), *Zeitschrift für Erziehungswissenschaft*, special issue 12.

Beck, S. (2008), 'The Teacher's Role and Approaches in a Knowledge Society', *Cambridge Journal of Education* 38 (4): 465–81.

Beck, U. (1992), *Risk Society: Towards a New Modernity*, New Delhi: Sage.

Beck, U. and Beck-Gernsheim, E. (2002), *Individualization: Institutionalized Individualism and its Social and Political Consequences*, London: Sage.

Beck-Gernsheim, E. (2002), *Reinventing the Family. In Search of New Lifestyles*, Cambridge: Polity Press.

Becker, G. (1975), *Human Capital: A Theoretical and Empirical Analysis, with Special Reference to Education* (second edition), New York: Columbia University Press.

Becker, R. (2000), 'Klassenlage und Bildungsentscheidung. Eine empirische Anwendung der Wert-Erwartungstheorie', *KZfSS Kölner Zeitschrift für Soziologie und Sozialpsychologie* 52 (3): 450–75.

Becker, R. and Hecken, A. E. (2008), 'Warum werden Arbeiterkinder vom Studium an Universitäten abgelenkt? Eine empirische Überprüfung der "Ablenkungsthese" von Müller und Pollak (2007) und ihrer Erweiterung durch Hillmert und Jacob (2003)', *KZfSS Kölner Zeitschrift für Soziologie und Sozialpsychologie* 60 (1): 7–33.

Beijaard, D., Verloop, N. and Vermunt, J. D. (2000), 'Teachers' Perceptions of Professional Identity: An Exploratory Study from a Personal Knowledge Perspective', *Teaching and Teacher Education* 16: 749–64.

Bekerman, Z., Burbules, N. and Silberman-Keller, D. (eds) (2006), *Learning in Places. The Informal Education Reader*, New York: Peter Lang.

Benz, A. (ed.) (2004), *Governance – Regieren in komplexen Regelsystemen. Eine Einführung*, Wiesbaden: VS Verlag.

Benz, A., Lutz, S., Schimank, U. and Simonis, G. (eds) (2007), *Handbuch Governance. Theoretische Grundlagen und empirische Anwendungsfelder*, Wiesbaden: VS Verlag.

Bernstein, B. (1971/72), *Class, Codes and Control*, 2 vols, London: Routledge and Kegan Paul.

Biggart, A. and Walther, A. (2006), 'Coping with Yo-yo Transitions: Young Adults' Struggle for Support between Family and State in Comparative Perspective', in C. Leccardi and E. Ruspini (eds), *A New Youth? Young People, Generations and Family Life*, 41–63, Aldershot: Ashgate.

Biggart A., Bendit, R., Cairns, D. and Hein, K. M. (2002), *Families and Transitions in Europe: State of the Art Report*, Brussels: European Commission, HPSE-CT2001-00079.

Biggart, A., Järvinen, T. and Parreira do Amaral, M. (2015), 'Institutional Frameworks and Structural Factors Relating to Educational Access Across Europe', *European Education* 47: 26–45.

Bledowski, P. and Felczak, J. (2013), 'Concepts of Lifelong Learning in Vocational Orientation', in M. Cuconato and A. Walter (eds), *Education and Life Course Thematic Working Paper*, 55–93.

Block, F. (1990) *Post Industrial Possibilities: A Critique of Economic Discourse*, Cambridge: Cambridge University Press.

Bloomer, M. and Hodkinson, P. (1997), *Moving into FE: The Voice of the Learner*, London: Further Education Development Agency.

Bloomer, M. and Hodkinson, P. (2000), Learning Careers: Continuity and Change, Young People's Dispositions to Learning, *British Educational Research Journal* 26 (5): 583–98.

Böhnisch, L. and Schefold, W. (1985), *Lebensbewältigung. Soziale und Pädagogische Verständigungen an den Grenzen der Wohlfahrtsgesellschaft*, Weinheim/München: Juventa.

Bokhorst, C. L., Sumter, S. R. and Westenberg, P. M. (2010), 'Social Support from Parents, Friends, Classmates, and Teachers in Children and Adolescents Aged 9 to 18 Years: Who is Perceived as Most Supportive?', *Social Development* 19: 417–26.

Boldero, J. and Fallon, B. (1995), 'Adolescent Help-seeking: What do They Get Help for and from Whom?', *Journal of Adolescence* 18: 193–209.

Boote, D. N. (2006), 'Teachers' Professional Discretion and the Curricula', *Teachers and Teaching: Theory and Practice* 12 (4): 461–78.

Boron, F., Bosch, A., Litau, J., Pohl, A., Stauber, B. and Walther, A. (2012), *Governance of Educational Trajectories in Europe: National Case Study Report Germany*, GOETE Working Paper, Frankfurt: University of Frankfurt; Tübingen: University of Tübingen and IRIS e.V.

Boudon, R. (1974), *Education, Opportunity and Social Inequality. Changing Prospects in Western Society*, New York: Wiley.

Bourdieu, P. (1971), 'Systems of Education and Systems of Thought' in M. F. D. Young (ed.), *Knowledge and Control*, 189–207, London: Macmillan.

Bourdieu, P. (1974), 'The School as a Conservative Force: Scholastic and Cultural Inequalities', in J. Eggleston (ed.), *Contemporary Research in the Sociology of* Education, 32–46, London: Methuen.

Bourdieu, P. (1986), 'The Forms of Capital', in J. Richardson (ed.), *Handbook of Theory and Research for Sociology of Education*, 241–58, New York: Greenwood.

Bourdieu, P. (1990), *The Logic of Practice*, Stanford, CA: Stanford University Press.

Bourdieu, P. (1998), *Practical Reason: On the Theory of Action*, Cambridge: Polity Press.

Bourdieu, P. and Passeron, J. C. (1970), *La reproduction. Eléments d'une théorie du système d'enseignement*, Paris: Minuit.

Bourdieu, P. and Passeron, J. C. (1977/1990), *Reproduction in Education, Society and Culture*, London: Sage.

Bradley, H. and Devadason, R. (2008), 'Fractured Transitions: Young Adults' Pathways into Contemporary Labour Markets', *Sociology* 42 (1): 119–36.

Bray, M. and Thomas, R. M. (1995), 'Levels of Comparison in Educational Studies. Different Insights from Different Literatures and the Value of Multilevel Analyses', *Harvard Educational Review* 65 (3): 472–90.

Breen, R. and Goldthorpe, J. (1997), 'Explaining Educational Differentials: Towards a Formal Rational Action Theory', *Rationality and Society* 9: 275–305.

Breen, R., Luijkx, R., Müller, W. and Pollak, R. (2009), 'Non-Persistent Inequality in Education Attainment: Evidence from Eight European Countries', *American Journal of Sociology* 114 (5): 1475–521.

Breen, R., Luijkx, R., Müller, W. and Pollak, R. (2010), 'Long-term Trends in Educational Inequality in Europe: Class Inequalities and Gender Differences', *European Sociological Review* 26 (1): 31–48.

Brenner, N., Peck, J. and Theodore, N. (2010), 'Variegated Neoliberalization: Geographies, Modalities, Pathways', *Global Networks* 10 (2): 182–222.

Brint, S. (1998), *Schools and Societies*, Thousand Oaks, CA: Pine Forge Press.

Browne, W. and Rasbash, J. (2004), 'Multilevel Modelling', in M. Hardy and A. Bryman (eds), *Handbook of Data Analysis*, 459–78, London: Sage.

Brückner, H. and Mayer, K. U. (2005), 'De-standardization of the Life Course: What it Might Mean? And If it Means Anything, Whether it Actually Took Place?', in R. Macmillan (ed.), *The Structure of the Life Course: Standardized? Individualized? Differentiated?*, 22–53, Amsterdam: Elsevier.

Budde, J., Scholand, B. and Faulstich-Wieland, H. (2008), *Geschlechtergerechtigkeit in der Schule: Eine Studie zu Chancen, Blockaden und Perspektiveneiner gender-sensiblen Schulkultur*, Weinheim: Juventa.

Bynner, J. (2005), 'Reconstructing the Youth Phase of the Life Course: The Case of Emerging Adulthood', *Journal of Youth Studies* 8: 367–84.

Caplan, G. (1974), *Support Systems and Community Mental Health*, New York: Basic Books.

Castel, R. (2000), *Transformation of the Social Question: From Manual Workers to Wage Labourers*, New Jersey: Transaction.

Castel, R. (2003), *L'insécurité sociale, qu'est-ce qu'être protégé?*, Paris: Seuil.

Castel, R. and Haroche, C. (2001), *Propriété privée, propriété sociale, propriété de soi. Entretien sur la construction de l'individu moderne*, Paris: Fayard.

Catalano, R. F., Berglund, M. L., Ryab, J. A. M., Lonczak, H. and Hawkins, J. D. (2004), 'Positive Youth Development in the United States: Research Findings on Evaluations of Positive Youth Development Programs', *The ANNALS of the American Academy of Political and Social Science* 591 (1): 98–124.

Cauce, A. M. and Srebnik, D. S. (1991), 'Returning to Social Support Systems: A Morphological Analysis of Social Networks', *American Journal of Community Psychology* 18: 609–16.

Cauce, A. M., Reid, M., Landesman, S. and Gonzales, N. (1990), 'Social Support Networks in Young Children: Measurement, Structure, and Behavioral Impact', in I. G. Sarason, B. R. Sarason and G. Pierce (eds), *Social Support: An Interactional View*, New York: Wiley.

Cauce, A. M., Mason, C., Gonzales, N., Hiraga, Y. and Liu, G. (1994), 'Social Support During Adolescence: Methodological and Theoretical Considerations', in F. Nestmann and K. Hurrelmann (eds), *Social Networks and Social Support in Childhood and Adolescence*, Berlin: de Gruyter.

Cedefop (European Centre for the Development of Vocational Training) and European Commission (2008), *European Guidelines for the Validation of Non-formal and Informal Learning.*

Chaiklin, S. and Lave, J. (eds) (1996), *Understanding Practice: Perspectives on Activity and Context*, Cambridge: Cambridge University Press.

Chase-Lansdale, P. L. and Brooks-Gunn, J. (2014), 'University Two-generation Programmes in the Twenty-first Century', *The Future of Children, Helping Parents, Helping Children: Two-Generation Mechanisms* 24 (1): 13–39.

Chisholm, L. (2008), 'Re-contextualizing Learning in Second Modernity', in R. Bendit and M. Hanh-Bleibtreu (eds), *Youth Transitions. Process of Social Inclusion and Patterns of Vulnerability in a Globalised World*, 135–50, Opladen: Barbara Budrich.

Choy, S., Horn, L., Nunez, A.-M. and Chen, X. (2000), 'Transition to College: What Helps At Risk Students and Students whose Parents did not Attend College', in A. Cabrera and S. M. La Nasa (eds), *Understanding the College Choice of Disadvantaged Students*, 45–63, San Francisco: Jossey-Bass.

Christenson, S. L. (2004), 'The Family–School Partnership: An Opportunity to Promote the Learning Competence of all Students', *School Psychology Review* 33 (1): 83–104.

Clark, B. R. (1960), 'The "Cooling-Out" Function in Higher Education', *The American Journal of Sociology* 65 (6): 569–76.

Clayton, V. (2004), *Overparenting: When Good Intentions Go Too Far, Kids can Suffer*, available online: http://www.msnbc.msn.com/id/6620793/# (accessed 9 September 2012).

Coffield, F. (1999), 'Lifelong Learning as a New Form of Social Control', in F. Coffield (ed.), *Why's the Beer always Stronger up North? Studies of Lifelong Learning in Europe*, 1–12, Bristol: Policy Press.

Coffield, F. (2000), 'The Structure Below the Surface: Reassessing the Significance of Informal Learning', in F. Coffield (ed.), *The Necessity of Informal Learning. The Learning Society*, Bristol: Policy Press.

Coleman, J. S. (1988), 'Social Capital in the Creation of Human Capital,' *The American Journal of Sociology* 94: 95–120.

Colley, H., Hodkinson, P. and Malcolm, J. (2002), 'Non-formal Learning: Mapping the Conceptual Terrain. A Consultation Report', Leeds: University of Leeds Lifelong Learning Institute.

Colombo, M. (2001), *Scuola e comunità locali: un'introduzione sociologica*, Roma: Carocci.

Compas, B. E., Hinden, B. R. and Gerhardt, C. A. (1995), 'Adolescent Development: Pathways and Processes of Risk and Resilience', *Annual Review of Psychology* 46: 265–93.

Coolahan, J. (2002), *Teacher Education and the Teaching Career in an Era of Lifelong Learning*, OECD Education Working Paper No. 2.

Cooper, C. E. and Crosnoe, R. (2007), 'The Engagement in Schooling of Economically Disadvantaged Parents and Children'. *Youth and Society* 38: 372–91.

Corbin, J. and Strauss, A. L. (2008), *Basics of Qualitative Research. Techniques and Procedures of Developing Grounded Theory*, Thousand Oaks, CA: Sage.

Coté, J. and Bynner, J. (2008), 'Exclusion from Emerging Adulthood: UK and Canadian Perspectives on Structure and Agency in the Transition to Adulthood', *Journal of Youth Studies* 11: 251–68.

Cramer, C., Bohl, T. and du Bois-Reymond, M. (2012), *Governance of Educational Trajectories in Europe: Comparative Report Teacher Training*, GOETE Working Paper, Tübingen: University of Tübingen, available online: http://goete.eu/download/cat_view/69 -working-papers (accessed 2 July 2015).

Crenshaw, K. (1989), 'Demarginalizing the Intersection of Race and Sex: A Black Feminist Critique of Antidiscrimination Doctrine, Feminist Theory and Antiracist Politics', *The University of Chicago Legal Forum* 140: 139–67.

Crozier, G. (1999), 'Is it a Case of "We know when we're not wanted"? The Parents' Perspective on Parent–Teacher Roles and Relationships', *Educational Research* 41 (3): 315–28.

Crozier, G. (2000), *Parents and Schools: Partners or Protagonists?*, Trentham Books: Stoke-on-Trent.

Crozier, G. (2001), 'Excluded Parents: The Deracialisation of Parental Involvement', *Race, Ethnicity and Education* 4 (4): 329–41.

Crul, M., Schneider, J. and Lelie, F. (eds) (2012), *The European Second Generation Compared. Does Integration Context Matter?*, Amsterdam: Amsterdam University Press.

Cuconato, M. (ed.) (2014), *Il tempo delle medie. Esperienze scolastiche e transizioni generazionali [The Time of Middle School. School Experiences and Generational Transitions]*, Roma: Carocci.

Cuconato, M. and Walther, A. (eds) (2013), *Education and the Life Course*, GOETE Working Paper, Frankfurt: University of Frankfurt. Available online: http://www.goete.eu/download/working-papers/doc_download/56-thematic-report-on--education-and-the-life-course (accessed 21 May 2013).

Cuconato, M. and Walther, A. (2015), '"Doing transitions", in Education', *International Journal of Qualitative Studies in Education* 28 (3): 283–96.

Cuconato, M., du Bois-Reymond, M., Lunabba, H., Ule, M., Walther, A., Warth, A. and Živoder, A. (2013), '"Do I stay or do I go?" Constellations of Decision-making in Young People's Educational Trajectories', in M. Cuconato and A. Walther (eds), *Education and the Life Course. Governance of Educational Trajectories in Europe: Thematic Report on Life Course*, GOETE Working Paper, 129–56, Bologna: University of Bologna.

Cuconato, M., Martelli, A. and Pitti, I. (2014), 'Transizioni e processi decisionali tra passato, presente e futuro' ['Transitions and Decision Processes between Past, Present and Future'], in M. Cuconato (ed.), *Il tempo delle medie. Esperienze scolastiche e transizioni generazionali [The Time of Middle School. School Experiences and Generational Transitions]*, 159–79, Roma: Carocci.

Cuconato, M., du Bois-Reymond, M. and Lunabba, H. (2015), 'Between Gate-keeping and Support: Teachers' Perception of their Role in Transition', *International Journal of Qualitative Studies in Education* 28 (3): 311–28.

Dahlstedt, M. (2009), 'Parental Governmentality: Involving "Immigrant Parents" in Swedish Schools', *British Journal of Sociology of Education* 30 (2): 193–205.

Dale, R. (1997), 'The State and the Governance of Education: An Analysis of the Restructuring of the State–Education Relationship', in A. H. Halsey, H. Lauder, P. Brown and A. S. Wells (eds), *Education: Culture, Economy and Society*, 273–82, Oxford: Oxford University Press.

Dale, R. (2007/2008), 'Changing Meanings of "the Europe of Knowledge" and "Modernizing the University", from Bologna to the "New Lisbon"', *European Education* 39 (4): 27–42.

Dale, R. and Robertson, S. (eds) (2009), *Globalisation and Europeanisation in Education*, Oxford: Symposium Books.

Dale, R. and Parreira do Amaral, M. (2015), 'Discursive and Institutional Opportunity Structures in the Governance of Educational Trajectories', in M. Parreira do Amaral, R. Dale and P. Loncle (eds), *Shaping the Futures of Young Europeans: Education Governance in Eight European Countries*, 23–41, Bristol: Symposium Books.

Dale, R., Amos, K., Barberis, E., Kazepov, Y., Parreira do Amaral, M. and Treptow, R. (2012), *Governance of Educational Trajectories in Europe. Comparative Report High Level Governance*, GOETE Working Paper, Bristol: University of Bristol; Tübingen: University of Tübingen; Urbino: University of Urbino; Frankfurt: University of Frankfurt, available online: http://goete.eu/download/cat_view/69-working-papers (accessed 27 June 2015).

Daly, M. (2012), 'Paradigms in EU Social Policy: A Critical Account of Europe 2020', *Transfer* 18 (3): 273–84.

Deane, F. P. and Todd, D. M. (1996), 'Attitudes and Intentions to Seek Professional Psychological Help for Problems or Suicidal Thinking', *Journal of College Student Psychotherapy* 4: 45–60.

Deci, E. L. and Ryan, R. M. (1985), *Intrinsic Motivation and Self-determination in Human Behaviour*, New York: Plenum Press.

Degryse, C. and Pochet, P. (2012), 'Worrying Trends in the New European Governance', in D. Natali and B. Vanhercke (eds), *Social Developments in the European Union 2011*, 81–108, Brussels: ETUI.

Delors, J. et al. (eds) (1996), 'Learning: The Treasure Within', Report to UNESCO of the International Commission on Education for the Twenty-first Century, Paris: UNESCO Publishing.

Demaray, M. K. and Malecki, C. K. *(2002)*, 'The Relationship Between Perceived Social Support and Maladjustment for Students at Risk', *Psychology in the Schools* 39*:* 305–16.

Denzin, N. K. (1970), *The Research Act: A Theoretical Introduction to Sociological Methods*, Chicago, IL: Aldine.

Desforges, C. (2003), 'The Impact of Parental Involvement, Parental Support, and Family Education on Pupil Achievement and Adjustment: A Literature Review', *Research Report, RR433*, London: Department for Education and Skills.

Diefenbach, H. (2007), *Kinder und Jugendliche aus Migrantenfamilien im deutschen Bildungssystem. Erklärungen und empirische Befunde*, Wiesbaden: VS Verlag.

Diepstraten, I., du Bois-Reymond, M. and Vinken, H. (2006), 'Trendsetting Learning Biographies: Concepts of Navigating through Late-Modern Life and Learning', *Journal of Youth Studies* 9 (2): 175–93.

Ditton, H. (1989), 'Determinanten für elterliche Bildungsaspiration und für Bildungsempfehlungen des Lehrers', *Empirische Pädagogik* 3 (3): 215–31.

Dogan, M. and Pelassy, D. (1990), *How to Compare Nations,* Chatham, NJ: Chatham House Publishers Inc.

Domina, T. (2005), 'Leveling the Home Advantage: Assessing the Effectiveness of Parental Involvement in Elementary School', *Sociology of Education* 78 (3): 233–49.

Domina, T., Conley, A. M. and Farkas, G. (2011a), 'The Link between Educational Expectations and Effort in the College-for-all Era', *Sociology of Education* 84 (2): 93–112.

Domina, T., Conley, A. M. and Farkas, G. (2011b), 'The Case for Dreaming Big', *Sociology of Education* 84 (2): 118–21.

du Bois-Reymond, M. (1998), 'I Don't Want to Commit Myself Yet: Young People's Life Concepts', *Journal of Youth Studies* 1 (1): 63–79.

du Bois-Reymond, M. (2001), 'Negotiation Families', in J. L. Kincheloe and J. Jipson (Series eds) and M. du Bois-Reymond, H. Sünker and H. H. Krüger (Vol. eds), *Rethinking Childhood: Vol. 15 Childhood in Europe, Approaches, Trends, Findings*, 63–90, New York: Peter Lang.

du Bois-Reymond, M. and Stauber, B. (2005), 'Biographical Turning Points in Young People's Transitions to Work across Europe', in H. Helve and G. Holm (eds), *Contemporary Youth Research: Local Expressions and Global Connections*, 63–75, Aldershot: Ashgate.

du Bois-Reymond, M. and Chisholm, L. (eds) (2006), *The Modernization of Youth Transition in Europe*, San Francisco: Jossey-Bass.

du Bois-Reymond, M., Koşar Altinyelken, H., Stauber, B., Svab, A., Ule, M., Živoder, A. and Parreira do Amaral, M. (2012), *Governance of Educational Trajectories in Europe: Comparative Analysis Case Studies*, GOETE Working Paper, Tübingen: University of Tübingen; Amsterdam: University of Amsterdam; Ljubljana: University of Ljubljana; Frankfurt: University of Frankfurt.

Dubow, E. F., Lovko, K. R. and Kausch, D. F. (1990), 'Demographic Differences in Adolescents' Health Concerns and Perceptions of Helping Agents', *Journal of Clinical Child Psychology* 19: 44–54.

Duru-Bellat, M. (2006), *L'inflation Scolaire. Les Désillusions de la Méritocratie*, Paris: Seuil.

Duru-Bellat, M. and Meuret, D. (2001), 'Nouvelles formes de régulation dans les systèmes éducatifs étrangers: autonomie et choix des établissements scolaires', *Revue française de pédagogie*, 135 (1) 173–221.

EDUCATIONAL GUIDANCE (1921), in *The Journal of Education* 94 (20): 544.

Edwards, R. and Alldred, P. (2000), 'A Typology of Parental Involvement in Education Centring on Children and Young People: Negotiating Familialisation, Institutionalisation and Individualisation', *British Journal of Sociology of Education* 21 (3): 435–55.

Elster, J. (2007), *Explaining Social Behavior. More Nuts and Bolts for the Social Science*, Cambridge: Cambridge University Press.

Emirbayr, M. and Mische, A. (1998), What is Agency?, *American Journal of Sociology* 4: 962–1023.

Epstein, J. L. (2001), *School, Family and the Community Partnerships: Preparing Educators and Improving Schools*, Colorado: Westview Press, Perseus Book Group.

Epstein, J. L. (2005), 'Attainable Goals? The Spirit and Letter of the No Child Left Behind Act on Parental Involvement', *Sociology of Education* 78 (2): 179–82.

Esping-Andersen, G. (1990), *The Three Worlds of Welfare Capitalism*. Princeton, NJ: Princeton University Press.

Eurofound (2012), 'NEETs. Young People not in Employment, Education or Training: Characteristics, Costs and Policy Responses in Europe', Luxemburg: Publications Office of the European Union.

Eurofound (2014), *Mapping Youth Transitions in Europe*, Luxembourg: Publications Office of the European Union.

Euroguidance (2014), 'Guidance in Europe. National guidance systems', available online: http://euroguidance.eu/guidance-in-europe/national-guidance-systems/ (accessed 12 November 2015).

European Commission (2003), *Communication from the Commission: The Role of the Universities in the Europe of Knowledge*, Brussels.

European Commission (2005), *Communication from the Commission: Mobilising the Brainpower of Europe: Enabling Universities to Make their Full Contribution to the Lisbon Strategy*, Brussels.

European Commission (2006), *Communication from the Commission to the Council and the European Parliament: Delivering on the Modernization Agenda for Universities: Education, Research, Innovation*, Brussels.

European Commission (2010a), *Youth on the Move. An initiative to unleash the potential of young people to achieve smart, sustainable and inclusive growth in the European Union*, COM(2010) 477, SEC(2010) 1047 Communication from the Commission to the European Parliament, the Council, the European Economic and Social Committee and the Committee of the Regions, Brussels.

European Commission (2010b), *Common European Principles for Teacher Competences and Qualifications*, Brussels: European Commission, Directorate-General for Education and Culture.

European Parliament (2000), 'Lisbon European Council 23 and 24 March 2000. Presidency Conclusions', available online: http://goo.gl/lLhw4 (accessed 18 March 2013).

Eurostat (2015a), 'Early Leavers from Education and Training', available online: http://ec.europa.eu/eurostat/tgm/table.do?tab=table&init=1&language=en&pcode=tsdsc410&plugin=1 (accessed 7 August 2015).

Eurostat (2015b), 'Expenditure on Education as % of GDP or Public Expenditure', last update: 24-07-2014, available online: http://appsso.eurostat.ec.europa.eu/nui/show.do? dataset=educ_figdp&lang=en (accessed 7 August 2015).

Eurydice (2007), *School Autonomy in Europe. Policies and Measures*, Brussels: Eurydice.

Eurydice (2008), *Levels of Autonomy and Responsibilities of Teachers in Europe*, Brussels: Eurydice.

Eurydice (2010), *Gender Differences in Educational Outcomes: Study on the Measures Taken and the Current Situation in Europe*, Brussels: Eurydice.

Eurydice (2012a), *Citizenship Education in Europe*, Brussels: Eurydice.

Eurydice (2012b), *Key Data on Education 2012*, Brussels: Eurydice.

Eurydice (2013), *Funding of Education in Europe. The Impact of the Economic Crisis, Education, Audiovisual and Culture Executive Agency*, Brussels: Eurydice.

Eurydice (2014). 'Countries. Description of National Education Systems', available online: https://webgate.ec.europa.eu/fpfis/mwikis/eurydice/index.php/Countries (accessed 24 November 2015).

Eurydice and Eurostat (2012), 'Key Data on Education in Europe 2012', available online: http://eacea.ec.europa.eu/education/eurydice/documents/key_data_series/134EN.pdf (accessed 7 August 2015).

Evans, K. (2002), 'Taking Control of their Lives? Agency in Young Adult Transitions in England and the New Germany', *Journal of Youth Studies* 3: 245–70.

Evans, T. and Harris, J. (2004), 'Street-level Bureaucracy, Social Work and the (Exaggerated) Death of Discretion', *British Journal of Social Work* 34 (6): 871–95.

Ezer, H., Gilat, I. and Sagee, R. (2010), 'Perception of Teacher Education and Professional Identity among Novice Teachers', *European Journal of Teacher Education* 33 (4): 391–404.

Fairclough, N. (1992), *Discourse and Social Change*, Cambridge: Polity Press.

Fazekas, M. and Burns, T. (2012), *Exploring the Complex Interaction Between Governance and Knowledge in Education* (Working paper), Paris: OECD.

Feagin, J. and Feagin, C. B. (1986), *Discrimination American Style – Institutional Racism and Sexism*, Malabar: R. E. Krieger Publishing Company.

Feldman, S. and Elliott, G. (1990), *At the Threshold: The Developing Adolescent*. Cambridge, MA: Harvard University Press.

Fend, H. (2006), *Neue Theorie der Schule. Einführung in das Verstehen von Bildungssystemen*. Wiesbaden: VS Verlag.

Fenstermaker, S. and West, C. (1987), 'Doing Gender', *Gender and Society* 1 (2), 125–51.

Fenstermaker, S. and West, C. (1995), 'Doing Difference', *Gender and Society* 1 (9): 8–37.

Ferguson, C. (2005), *Reaching out to Diverse Populations: What can Schools do to Foster Family–School Connections?*, Texas: Southwest Educational Development Laboratory.

Field, J. (2000), *Lifelong Learning and the New Educational Order*, Stoke-on-Trent and Stirling: Trentham Books.

Field, J. (2005), *Social Capital and Lifelong Learning*, Bristol: Policy Press.

Field, S., Kuczera, M. and Pont, B. (2007), 'No More Failures: Ten Steps to Equity in Education', FP7-SSH-2009-A-1.1.1: Governing Educational Trajectories in Europe (GOETE) – Part B, 10 January 81, Paris: OECD.

Folbre, N. R. (1994), *Who Pays for the Kids? Gender and the Structures of Constraint*, London: Routledge.

Foljanty-Jost, G., Helsper, W., Krüger, H.-H., Hummrich, M. and Kramer, R.-T. (eds) (2008), *Family, Youth, and School Culture*, Frankfurt am Main: Peter Lang.

Foucault, M. (1972), *The Archaeology of Knowledge and the Discourse on Language*, trans. A. M. Sheridan Smith, London and New York: Pantheon Books.

Frydenberg, E. and Lewis, R. (1993), *Adolescent Coping Scale*. Melbourne: Australian Council for Educational Research.

Furlong, A. and Cartmel, A. (2007), *Young People and Social Change: New Perspectives*, Buckingham: Open University Press.

Furman, W. and Buhrmester, D. (1992), 'Age and Sex Differences in Perceptions of Networks of Personal Relationships', *Child Development* 63: 103–15.

Gallie, D. and Paugam, S. (eds) (2000), *Welfare Regimes and the Experience of Unemployment in Europe*. Oxford: Oxford University Press.

Galligan, D. J. (1990), *Discretionary Power*, Oxford: Clarendon.

Gangl, M. (2003), 'Returns to Education in Context: Individual Educational and Transition Outcomes in European Labour Markets', in W. Müller and M. Gangl (eds), *Transitions from Education to Work in Europe: The Integration of Youth into EU Labour Markets*, 156–85, Oxford: Oxford University Press.

Geddes, M. (2000), 'The Limits to the New Orthodoxy of Local Partnership', *International Journal of Urban and Regional Research* 24: 782–800.

Geel, van M. and Vedder, P. (2009), 'The Role of Family Obligations and School Adjustment in Explaining the Immigrant Paradox', *Youth Adolescence* 40 (2): 187–96.

Gennep, A. van (1960), *The Rites of Passage*. London: Routledge Library Edition.

Giddens, A. (1984), *The Constitution of Society: Outline of the Theory of Structuration*, Cambridge: Polity Press.

Gigerenzer, G. (2002), *Calculated Risks: How to Know When Numbers Deceive You*, New York: Simon and Schuster.

Gildemeister, R. (2004), 'Geschlechterdifferenz – Geschlechterdifferenzierung. Beispiele und Folgen eines Blickwechsels in der empirischen Geschlechterforschung', in S. Buchen, C. Helferich and M. S. Maier (eds), *Gender methodologisch. Empirische*

Forschung in der Informationsgesellschaft vor neuen Herausforderungen, 27–45, Wiesbaden: VS Verlag.
Glaser, B. G. and Strauss, A. L. (1967), *The Discovery of Grounded Theory*, Chicago, IL: Aldane.
Glaser, B. G. and Strauss, A. L. (1971), *Status Passage*, London: Routledge.
Goffman, E. (1952), 'On Cooling the Mark Out: Some Aspects of Adaptation to Failure', *Psychiatry*, XV: 451–63.
Goffman, E. (1959), *The Presentation of Self in Everyday Life*, New York: Doubleday Anchor.
Golombok, S. (2008), *Parenting. What Really Counts?*, London: Routledge.
Gomolla, M. (2006), 'Tackling Underachievement of Learners from Ethnic Minorities: A Comparison of Recent Policies of School Improvement in Germany, England and Switzerland', *Current issues in Comparative Education* 9 (1): 46–59.
Gomolla, M. and Radtke, F.-O. (2009), *Institutionelle Diskriminierung. Die Herstellung ethnischer Differenz in der Schule* (third edition), Wiesbaden: VS Verlag.
Gomolla, M. and Rotter, C. (2012), 'Zugewanderte und einheimische Eltern: über Gemeinsamkeiten und Unterschiede in der Beurteilung von Schulpolitik und Schulpraxis', in D. Killus and K.-J. Tillmann (eds), *Eltern ziehen Bilanz. Ein Trendbericht zu Schule und Bildungspolitik in Deutschland*, 2, JAKO-O Bildungsstudie, 113–42, Münster/New York: Waxmann.
Gonzalez, N. and Moll, L. C. (2002), 'Cruzando el Puente: Building Bridges to Funds of Knowledge', *Educational Policy* 16 (4): 623–41.
Goodin, R. E. (1986), 'Welfare, Rights and Discretion', *Oxford Journal of Legal Studies* 6 (2): 43–70.
Grek, S. and Lawn, M. (2009), 'A Short History of Europeanizing Education: The New Political Work of Calculating the Future', *European Education* 41: 32–54.
Gresch, C., Baumert, J. and Maaz, K. (2010), 'Empfehlungsstatus, Übergangsempfehlung und der Wechsel in die Sekundarstufe I: Bildungsentscheidungen und soziale Ungleichheit', in K. Maaz et al. (eds), *Der Übergang von der Grundschule in die weiterführende Schule. Leistungsgerechtigkeit und regional, soziale und ethnisch-kulturelle Disparitäten*, 201–27, Bonn: BMBF.
Griffith, A. and Smith, D. (2005), *Mothering for Schooling*, New York: Routledge.
Grundmann, M., Bittlingmayer, U. H., Dravenau, D. and Groh-Samberg, O. (2008), 'Bildung als Privileg und Fluch – zum Zusammenhang zwischen lebensweltlichen und institutionalisierten Bildungsprozessen', in R. Becker and W. Lauterbach (eds), *Bildung als Privileg. Erklärungen und Befunde zu den Ursachen der Bildungsungleichheit*, 47–74, Wiesbaden: VS Verlag.
Grytnes, R. (2011), 'Making the Right Choice! Inquiries into the Reasoning Behind Young People's Decisions about Education', *Young* 19 (3): 333–51.
Han, B. C. (2014), *Psychopolitik: Neoliberalismus und die neuen Machttechniken*, Frankfurt am Main: Fischer Verlag.

Hansson, S. O. (2005), *Decision Theory. A Brief Introduction*, Stockholm: Royal Institute of Technology (KTH).

Hantrais, L. (2009), *International Comparative Research: Theory, Methods and Practice*, Basingstoke and New York: Palgrave Macmillan and St Martin's Press.

Hay, C. (2002a), *Political Analysis: A Critical Introduction*, Basingstoke: Palgrave Macmillan.

Hay, C. (2002b), 'Globalisation as a Problem of Political Analysis: Restoring Agents to a "Process Without a Subject" and Politics to a Logic of Economic Compulsion', *Cambridge Review of International Affairs* 15 (3M): 379–92.

Heckhausen, H. (1991), *Motivation and Action*. New York: Springer.

Heinrich, C. J. (2014), 'Parents' Employment and Children's Wellbeing', *The Future of Children, Helping Parents, Helping Children: Two-Generation Mechanisms* 24 (1): 121–46.

Heinz, W. R. (1992), *Institution and Gate-keeping in the Life Course*. Weinheim: Deutscher Studien Verlag.

Heinz, W. R., Weymann, A. and Huinink, J. (eds) (2009), *The Life Course Reader: Individuals and Societies across Time*, Frankfurt am Main: Campus.

Helsper, W. (2004), 'Schülerbiographie und Schulkarriere', in W. Helsper and J. Böhme (eds), *Handbuch der Schulforschung*, 903–21, Wiesbaden: VS Verlag.

Helsper, W., Kramer, R.-T., Brademann, S. and Ziems, C. (2008), 'Children's Biographical Orientations toward Selection Procedures at School', in G. Foljanty-Jost, W. Helsper, H. H. Krüger, M. Hummrich and R.-T. Kramer (eds), *Family, Youth, and School Culture*, 179–98, Frankfurt am Main: Peter Lang.

Helsper, W., Hummrich, M. and Kramer, R.-T. (2010), 'Qualitative Mehrebenenanalyse', in B. Friebertshäuser, A. Langer and A. Prengel (eds), *Handbuch qualitative Forschungsmethoden in der Erziehungswissenschaft* (third edition), 119–35, Weinheim/München: Juventa.

Helve, H. and Bynner, J. (eds) (2007), *Youth and Social Capital*, London: The Tufnell Press.

Hill, M. J. and Ham, C. (1993), *The Policy Process in the Modern Capitalist State*, New York: Harvester Wheatsheaf.

Hill, N. E. (2001), 'Parenting and Academic Socialization as they Relate to School Readiness: The Role of Ethnicity and Family Income', *Journal of Educational Psychology*, 93 (4): 686–97.

Hillmert, S. (2008), 'Soziale Ungleichheit im Bildungsverlauf: zum Verhältnis von Bildungs-institutionen und Entscheidungen', in R. Becker and W. Lauterbach (eds), *Bildung als Privileg. Erklärungen und Befunde zu den Ursachen der Bildungsungleichheit*, 75–102, Wiesbaden: VS Verlag.

Hodgkinson, T. (2010), *The Idle Parent: Why Less Means More When Raising Kids*, London: Penguin Books.

Hodgson, D. (2008), *Understanding Early School Leaving. A Narrative Research Approach*, Saarbrücken: VDM.

Hodkinson, P. (2010), 'Informal Learning: A Contested Concept', in P. Peterson, E. Baker and B. McGaw (eds), *International Encyclopedia of Education* (third edition), 42–6, Oxford: Elsevier.

Hodkinson, P. and Sparkes, A. (1997), 'Careership: A Sociological Theory of Career Decision-making', *British Journal of Sociology of Education* 10, 23–35.

Holmer Nadesan, M. (2002), 'Engineering the Entrepreneurial Infant: Brain Science, Infant Development Toys, and Governmentality', *Cultural Studies*, 16, 401–32.

Honneth, A. (2007), *Reification – A New Look at an Old Idea*, Oxford: Oxford University Press.

Hoover-Dempsey, K. V. and Sandler, H. M. (1997), 'Why do Parents become Involved in their Children's Education?', *Review of Educational Research* 67 (1): 3–42.

Horn, D. (2009), 'Age of Selection Counts: A Cross-country Analysis of Educational Institutions', *Educational Research and Evaluation* 15: 343–66.

Hox, J. J. (2010), *Multilevel Analysis: Techniques and Applications* (2nd edn), New York: Routledge.

Hungerland, B., Liebel, M., Liesecke, A. and Wihstutz, A. (2008), 'Paths to Participatory Autonomy. The Meanings of Work for Children in Germany', *Childhood* 14 (2): 257–77.

Huntsinger, C. S. and Jose, P. E. (2009), 'Parental Involvement in Children's Schooling: Different Meanings in Different Cultures', *Early Childhood Research Quarterly* 24 (4): 398–410.

Hupe, P. and Hill, M. (2007), 'Street-level Bureaucracy and Public Accountability', *Public Administration* 85 (2): 279–99.

Invernizzi, A. (2008), 'Perspectives on Children's Work in the Algarve (Portugal) and their Implications for Social Policy', *Critical Social Policy* 25 (2): 198–222.

Isaksson, J. (2011), 'Re-evaluating the Meaning of School Difficulties', in A. E. Sjölander and J. G. Payne (eds), *Tracking Discourses. Politics, Identity and Social Change*, 113–41, Lund: Nordic Academic Press.

Jackson, P. W. (1968), *Life in Classrooms*, New York: Holt, Rinehart and Winston.

James, A., Jenks, C. and Prout, A. (1998), *Theorizing Childhood*, Cambridge: Polity Press.

Jarvis, P. (ed.) (2009), *The Routledge International Handbook of Lifelong Learning*, London/New York: Routledge.

Jessop, B. (1990), *State Theory: Putting the Capitalist State in its Place*, Cambridge: Polity Press.

Jessop, B. (1999), 'The Changing Governance of Welfare: Recent Trends in its Primary Functions, Scale, and Modes of Coordination', *Social Policy and Administration* 33 (4): 348–59.

Jessop, B. (2001), 'Institutional Re(turns) and the Strategic–Relational Approach', *Environment and Planning A* 33 (7): 1213–35.

Jessop, B. (2008), *State Power*, Cambridge: Polity Press.

Jessop, B., Fairclough, N. and Wodak, R. (2008), *Education and the Knowledge-based Economy in Europe*, Rotterdam: Sense Publishers.

Jessop, B., Brenner, N. and Jones, M. (2008), 'Theorizing Socio-spatial Relations', *Environment and Planning D: Society and Space* 26: 389–401.

Johnson, M. E. (2001), 'Influences of Gender and Sex Role Orientation on Help-seeking Attitudes', *The Journal of Psychology*, 122: 237–41.

Jones, K., Cunchillos, C., Hatcher, R., Hirtt, N., Innes, R., Joshua, S. and Klausenitzer, J. (2008), *Schooling in Western Europe: The New Order and its Adversaries*, Basingstoke: Palgrave Macmillan.

Kahneman, D. and Tversky, A. (1981), 'The Framing of Decision and the Psychology of Choice', *Science* 21: 453–8.

Kazepov, Y. (ed.) (2010), *Rescaling Social Policies: Towards Multilevel Governance in Europe*, Farnham: Ashgate.

Kazepov, Y. and Barberis, E. (2012), 'Social Assistance Governance in Europe. Towards a Multilevel Perspective', in I. Marx and K. Nelson (eds), *Minimum Income Protection in Flux*, 239–70, Basingstoke: Palgrave Macmillan.

Keep, E. (2006), 'State Control of the English Education and Training System – Playing with the Biggest Train Set in the World', *Journal of Vocational Education and Training* 58: 47–64.

Keiser, L. R., Mueser, P. R. and Choi, S.-W. (2004), 'Race, Bureaucratic Discretion, and the Implementation of Welfare Reform', *American Journal of Political Science* 48 (2): 314–27.

Kelly, M. (1994), 'Theories of Justice and Street-level Discretion', *Journal of Public Administration Research and Theory* 4 (2): 119–40.

Kelly, M. (2000), 'Youth as an Artefact of Expertise: Problematising the Practise of Youth Studies', *Journal of Youth Studies* 3 (3): 301–15.

Kersbergen, K. van and van Waarden, F. (2004), 'Governance as a Bridge Between Disciplines: Cross-disciplinary Inspiration Regarding Shift in Governance and Problems of Governability, Accountability and Legitimacy', *European Journal of Political Research* 43: 143–71.

Killus, D. and Tillmann, K. J. (2012), '2. Elternbefragung als kontinuierliche Forschung Zur Einführung in die 2. JAKO-O Bildungsstudie', in D. Killus and K.-J. Tillmann (eds), *Eltern ziehen Bilanz. Ein Trendbericht zu Schule und Bildungspolitik in Deutschland, 2,* JAKO-O Bildungsstudie, 9–19, Münster/New York: Waxmann.

Kohl, G. O., Lengua, L. J. and McMahon, R. J. (2000), 'Parent Involvement in School: Conceptualizing Multiple Dimensions and their Relations with Family and Demographic Risk Factors', *Journal of School Psychology* 38 (6): 501–23.

Kohli, M. (1985), 'Die Institutionalisierung des Lebenslaufs. Historische Befunde und theoretische Argumente', *Kölner Zeitschrift für Soziologie und Sozialpsychologie* 37 (1): 1–29.

Kohli, M. (2007), 'The Institutionalisation of the Life Course: Looking Back to Look Ahead', *Research in Human Development* 4 (3–4): 253–71.

Koller, H.-C. (2011), 'The Research of Transformational Education Processes: Exemplary Considerations on the Relation of the Philosophy of

Education and Educational Research', *European Educational Research Journal* 10 (3): 375–82.

Kooiman, J. (1993), *Modern Governance, New Government–Society Interactions*, London: Sage Publications.

Koşar Altinyelken, H. and Julkunen, I. (eds) (2013), *Coping and Support. Governance of Educational Trajectories in Europe. Thematic Report on Coping and Support*, GOETE Working Paper, Amsterdam: University of Amsterdam.

Kränzl-Nagl, R. and Zartler, U. (2010), 'Children's Participation in School and Community: European Perspectives', in B. Percy-Smith and N. Thomas (eds), *A Handbook of Children and Young People's Participation, Perspectives from Theory and Practice*, 164–73, Abingdon: Routledge.

Krippendorff, K. (2004), *Content Analysis: An Introduction to its Methodology*, Thousand Oaks, CA: Sage Publications.

Lange, B. and Alexiadou, N. (2010), 'Governing through Learning about Policy: Just all Words? An Introduction to Policy Learning in the Context of Open Methods of Coordinating Education in the European Union (EU)', *Journal of Education Policy* 25 (4): 443–63.

Langer, R. (2011), 'Schüler/innen, Eltern und weitere Anspruchsgruppen', in H. Altrichter and C. Helm (eds), *Akteure Und Instrumente Der Schulentwicklung*, 103–14, Baltmannsweiler: Schneider Verlag.

Lareau, A. (2000), *Home Advantage: Social Class and Parental Intervention in Elementary Education* (2nd edn), Lanham, MD: Rowan and Littlefield.

Lareau, A. (2003), *Unequal Childhoods: Class, Race, and Family Life*, Berkeley: University of California Press.

Lasonen, J. and Young, M. (1998), *Strategies for Achieving Parity of Esteem in European Upper Secondary Education*, Jyväskylä: Institute for Educational Research.

Lauder, H., Young, M., Daniels, H., Balarin, M. and Lowe, J. (eds) (2012), *Educating for the Knowledge Economy?*, London and New York: Routledge.

Laval, C. and Weber, H. (eds) (2002), *Le nouvel ordre éducatif mondial: OMC, Banque Mondiale, OCDE, Commission Européene* [*The New Worldwide Educational Order: WTO, World Bank, OCSE, European Commission*], Paris: Syllepse.

Lave, J. and Wenger, E. (1991), *Situated Learning. Legitimate Peripheral Participation*, Cambridge: Cambridge University Press.

Lawn, M. (2013), 'The Understories of Education: The Contemporary Life of Experts and Professionals', *Sisyphus – Journal of Education* 1 (1): 18–35.

Lawn, M. and Grek, S. (2012), *Europeanizing Education: Governing a New Policy Space*, Oxford: Symposium.

Lawn, M. and Lingard, B. (2002), 'Constructing a European Policy Space in Educational Governance: The Role of Transnational Policy Actors', *European Educational Research Journal* 1 (2): 290–307.

Lazarus, R. and Folkman, S. (1984), *Stress Appraisal and Coping*, New York: Springer.

Leccardi, C. (2005), 'Facing Uncertainty. Temporality and Biographies in the New Century', *Young* 2: 123–46.

Leccardi, C. (2008), 'New Biographies in the 'Risk Society'? About Future and Planning', *21st Century Society* 3 (2): 119–29.

Leccardi, C. and Ruspini, E. (2006), *A New Youth. Young People, Generations and Family Life*, Aldershot: Ashgate.

Le Claire, K. A. (1988), 'University Choice Behaviour. A Preliminary Analysis', *Education and Research Perspectives* 15: 83–96.

Le Galès, P. (2004), 'Gouvernance', in L. Bousssaguet, S. Jacquot and P. Ravinet (eds), *Dictionnaire des politiques publiques*, 242–50, Paris: Presses de Sciences Po.

Lessenich, S. (1995), 'Wohlfahrtstaatliche Regulierung und die Strukturierung von Lebensläufen', *Soziale Welt*, 46: 51–69.

Lima, L. C. and Guimarães, P. (2011), *European Strategies in Lifelong Learning: A Critical Introduction*, Opladen and Farmington Hills, MI: Barbara Budrich Publishers.

Lipshitz, R. and Strauss, O. (1997), 'Coping with Uncertainty: A Naturalistic Decision-making Analysis', *Organizational Behavior and Human Decision Processing*, 69: 149–63.

Lipsky, M. (1980), *Street-level Bureaucracy. Dilemmas of the Individual in Public Services*, New York: Russell Sage Foundation.

Lipsky, M. (2010), *Street-level Bureaucracy*, New York: Russell Sage Foundation.

Litau, J., McDowell, J., Salovaara, V., Zivoder, A., Dale, R., Tolomelli, A. and Cramer, C. (2013), *Education! (What Is It Good For?) – The Relevance of Education in Contemporary Knowledge Society. Governance of Educational Trajectories in Europe: Thematic Report on Relevance*, GOETE Working Paper, Frankfurt: University of Frankfurt.

Loncle, P. (2011), 'La jeunesse au local, comment analyser les spécificités locales dans les interventions publiques?', *Sociologie* 2 (2): 129–47.

Loncle, P., Cuconato, M., Muniglia, V. and Walther, A. (eds) (2012), *Youth Participation in Europe, Beyond Discourses, Practices and Realities*, Bristol: Policy Press.

Long, H. B. (1989), 'Self-directed Learning: Emerging Theory and Practice', in H. B. Long et al. (eds), *Self-directed Learning: Emerging Theory and Practice*, Norman: University of Oklahoma.

Määttä, M. and Tolonen, T. (eds) (2011), 'Otettu, annettu, itsetehty. Nuorten vapaa-aika tänään' (Taken, Given and Selfmade. The Leisuretime of Young People in Contemporary Finland), *Nuorisotutkimusverkoston ja seuran julkaisuja*, 112, Helsinki.

Machacek, L. and Walther, A. (2008), 'Participation and Learning', in P. Loncle and V. Muniglia (eds) (2008), *Youth Participation, Agency and Social Change*, Thematic Report of the UP2YOUTH Project, 62–80.

Mangold, W. (1960), *Gegenstand und Methode der Gruppendiskussion: aus der Arbeit des Instituts für Sozialforschung*, Frankfurt am Main: Univ. Diss.

Marks, G. (1992), 'Structural Policy and 1992', in A. Sbragia (ed.), *The Political Consequences of 1992 for the European Community*, 191–224, Washington, DC: The Brookings Institution.

Maroy, C. (2004), 'Regulation and Inequalities in European Education Systems. Final Report', available online: http://goo.gl/LPa5FF (accessed 18 March 2013).

Maroy, C. (2006), *Ecole, régulation et marché: Une analyse de six espaces scolaires locaux en Europe*, Paris: PUF.

Martelli, A. (2007), 'Verso una nuova governance locale delle politiche sociali?, Autonomie locali e servizi sociali', *ALSS Il Mulino* 1: 97–108.

Martelli, A. (2013), 'The Debate on Young People and Participatory Citizenship. Questions and Research Prospects', *International Review of Sociology* 2: 421–37.

Marx, K. (1852/1954), *The Eighteenth Brumaire of Louis Bonaparte*, Moscow: Foreign Languages Publishing House.

Mattioli, E. and Volturo, S. (2014), 'Famiglie, insegnanti e vita scolastica: le relazioni all'interno dei local school spaces', in M. Cuconato (ed.), *Il tempo delle medie*, 124–44, Bologna: Carocci.

Matuszny, R. M., Banda, D. R. and Coleman, T. J. (2007), 'A Progressive Plan For Building Collaborative Relationships with Parents from Diverse Backgrounds', *Teaching Exceptional Children* 39 (4): 24–31, Council for Exceptional Children.

Mayer, K.-U. (1997), 'Notes on a Comparative Political Economy of Life Courses', *Comparative Social Research* 16: 203–26.

Maynard-Moody, S., Musheno, M. and Palumbo, D. (1990), 'Street-wise Social Policy: Resolving the Dilemma of Street-level Influence and Successful Implementation', *The Western Political Quarterly* 43 (4), 833–48.

Mayntz, R. (2004), 'Governance im modernen Staat', in A. Benz (ed.), *Governance – Regieren in komplexen Regelsystemen. Eine Einführung*, 65–76, Wiesbaden: VS Verlag.

Mayntz, R. (2006), 'From Government to Governance: Political Steering in Modern Societies', in Scheer, D. and Rubik, F. (eds), *Governance of Integrated Product Policy*, 18–24, Aizlewood Mill: Greenleaf Publishing.

Mayring, P. and Gahleitner, S. B. (2010), 'Qualitative Inhaltsanalyse', in K. Bock and I. Miethe (eds), *Handbuch qualitative Methoden in der Sozialen Arbeit*, 295–304, Opladen: Budrich.

McDowell, J., Biggart, A., Živoder, A., Ule, M., Martelli, A., De Luigi, N. and Litau, J. (2012), *Governance of Educational Trajectories in Europe: Comparative Analysis Individual Ssurvey*, GOETE Working Paper, Belfast: Queens University of Belfast.

McNeish, W. and Loncle, P. (2003), 'State Policy and Youth Unemployment in the EU: Rights, Responsibilities and Lifelong Learning', in A. López Blasco, W. McNeish and A. Walther (eds), *Young People and Contradictions of Inclusion: Towards Integrated Transition Policies in Europe*, 105–26, Bristol: Policy Press.

Mead, G. H. (1934), *Mind, Self and Society from the Standpoint of a Social Behaviourist*, Chicago: University of Chicago Press.

Meier, K. and Bothe, J. (2001), 'Structure and Discretion: Missing Links in Representative Bureaucracy', *Journal of Public Administration Research and Theory* 11 (4): 455–70.

Mellotée, L. and Julkunen, I. (2013), 'Career Guidance in Transitions – Policies and Practices', in H. Koşar Altinyelken and I. Julkunen (eds), *Coping and Support. Governance of Educational Trajectories in Europe: Thematic Report on Coping and Support*, GOETE Working Paper, 87–109, Amsterdam: University of Amsterdam.

Mendez, J. L. and Fogle, L. M. (2002), 'Parental Reports of Preschool Children's Social Behavior: Relations among Peer Play, Language Competence and Problem Behavior', *Journal of Psychoeducational Assessment* 20: 374–89.

Miethe, I., Ecarius, J. and Tervooren, A. (eds) (2014), *Bildungsentscheidungen im Lebenslauf. Perspektiven qualitativer Forschung*, Opladen, Berlin/Toronto: Verlag Barbara Budrich.

Minke, K. M. and Anderson, K. J. (2005), 'Family–School Cooperation and Positive Behaviour Support', *Journal of Positive Behaviour Interventions* 7: 181–5.

Mons, N. (2009), *Les nouvelles politiques éducatives, La France fait-elle les bons choix?*, Paris: Presses Universitaires de France.

Mørch, S. and du Bois-Reymond, P. (2006), 'Learning in Times of Modernisation. The Writers Take a Close Look at Changing Relationships between Education and Learners in Light of Demands and Consequences of Modernization', in P. du Bois-Reymond and L. Chisholm (eds), *The Modernisation of Youth Transitions in Europe*, 23–35, San Francisco: Jossey-Bass.

Müller, W. and Wolbers, M. (2003), 'Educational Attainment in European Union: Recent Trends in Qualification Patterns', in W. Müller and M. Gangl (eds), *Transitions from Education to Work in Europe. The Integration of Youth into EU Labour Markets*, 23–62, Oxford: Oxford University Press.

Musheno, M. C. (1986), 'The Justice Motive in the Social Policy Process', *Policy Studies Review* 5 (4): 697–704.

Myles, J. (1993), 'Is there a Post-Fordist Life Course?', in W. R. Heinz (ed.), *Institutions and Gatekeeping in the Life Course*, 171–85, Weinheim: Deutscher Studienverlag.

Nadler, A. (1997), 'Personality and Help-seeking: Autonomous versus Dependent Seeking of Help', in G. Pierce, B. Lakey, I. G. Sarason and B. Sarason (eds), *Sourcebook of Theory and Research on Social Support and Personality*, New York: Plenum.

Naumanen, P., Leppänen, R. and Rinne, R. (2008), 'Euroopan unionin muuttuva koulutuspolitiikka' ['The Changing Education Policies of the European Union'], in R. Rinne, L. Jõgi, R. Leppänen, M. Korppas and K. Klemelä (eds), *Suomalainen ja virolainen koulutus ja EU:n uusi koulutuspolitiikka* [*Finnish and Estonian Education and the New Education Policy of the EU*], 227–326, Turku: The Faculty of Education of the University of Turku.

Nespor, J. (1997), *Tangled Up in School: Politics, Space, Bodies, and Signs in the Educational*, New York and Abingdon: Routledge.

Nordin, A. and Sundberg, D. (eds) (2014), *Transnational Policy Flows in European Education. The Making and Governing of Knowledge in the Education Policy Field*, Oxford: Symposium Books.

Nóvoa, A. and Lawn, M. (2002), *Fabricating Europe: The Formation of an Educational Space*, Dordrecht: Kluwer.

Oberti, M. (2007), 'Social and School Differentiation in Urban Space: Inequalities and Local Configurations', *Environment and Planning A* 39 (1): 208–27.

Oerter, R. and Montada, L. (eds) (2008), *Entwicklungspsychologie*, München: Urban and Schwarzenberg.

Organisation for Economic Cooperation and Development (OECD) (2001), *Knowledge and Skills for Life. First Results from the OECD Programme for International Student Assessment (PISA)*, Paris: OECD.

Organisation for Economic Cooperation and Development (OECD) (2003), 'Career Guidance: New Ways Forward', in *Education Policy Analysis*, Paris: OECD.

Organisation for Economic Cooperation and Development (OECD) (2004a), *Career Guidance. A Handbook for Policy Makers*, Paris: OECD.

Organisation for Economic Cooperation and Development (OECD) (2004b), *Career Guidance and Public Policy. Bridging the Gap*, Paris: OECD.

Organisation for Economic Cooperation and Development (OECD) (2005), *School Factors Related to Quality and Equity*, Paris: OECD.

Organisation for Economic Cooperation and Development (OECD) (2006), 'Parent and Community Voice in Schools', in *Demand-sensitive Schooling? Evidence and Issues*, Paris: OECD.

Organisation for Economic Cooperation and Development (OECD) (2009), *Equally Prepared for Life? How 15-Year-old Boys and Girls Perform in School*, Paris: OECD.

Organisation for Economic Cooperation and Development (OECD) (2010a), *PISA 2009 Results: What Students Know and Can Do*, Paris: OECD.

Organisation for Economic Cooperation and Development (OECD) (2010b), *Learning for Jobs. Synthesis Report of the OECD Reviews of Vocational Education and Training*, Paris: OECD.

Organisation for Economic Cooperation and Development (OECD) (2012a), *Education at a Glance 2012*, OECD Indicators, Paris: OECD.

Organisation for Economic Cooperation and Development (OECD) (2012b), *Parental Involvement in Selected PISA Countries and Economies*, Education Working Paper No. 73, Paris: OECD.

Ozaki, N. and Koshino, K. K. (2008), 'Parental Involvement and Immigrants: Suggestions for Future Teacher Education', *International Journal of the Humanities* 6 (1): 99–104.

Parding, K. (2007), *Upper Secondary Teachers' Creation of Discretionary Power*, Lulea: Department of Human Work Sciences, Lulea University of Technology.

Parreira do Amaral, M. and Rinne, R. (2015), 'Reading Discourses in the Governance of Educational Trajectories of Youth in Europe', in M. Parreira do

Amaral, R. Dale and P. Loncle (eds), *Shaping the Futures of Young Europeans: Education Governance in Eight European Countries*, 69–89, Bristol: Symposium Books.

Parreira do Amaral, M., Litau, J., Cramer, C., Kobolt, A., Loncle, P., Mellottée, L., Ule, M., Walther, A. and Živoder, A. (2011), *Governance of Educational Trajectories in Europe. State of the Art Report*, GOETE Working Paper, Frankfurt: University of Frankfurt, available online: http://goete.eu/download/cat_view/69-working-papers (accessed 2 June 2015).

Parreira do Amaral, M., Walther, A. and Litau, J. (2013), *Governance of Educational Trajectories in Europe: Access, Coping, Relevance of Education for Young People in European Knowledge Societies in Comparative Perspective*, Final Report, Frankfurt: University of Frankfurt.

Parreira do Amaral, M., Dale, R. and Loncle, P. (eds) (2015), *Shaping the Futures of Young Europeans: Education Governance in Eight European Countries*, Bristol: Symposium Books.

Parreira do Amaral, M., Stauber, B. and Barberis, E. (eds) (2015), 'Access to and Accessibility of Education Throughout the Educational Trajectories of Youth in Europe', *European Education* 47 (1).

Paton, K. (2007), *Conceptualising 'Choice': A Review of the Theoretical Literature.* [Working Paper 5. NPinHE Project].

Payne, J. (2003), *Choice at the End of Compulsory Schooling: A Research Review*, Research Report RR414, London: Department for Education and Skills.

Pereyra, M. A. (1993), 'The Social Participation in the Construction of the European Dimension in Education', *CESE Newsletter* 36, 7–12.

Périer, P. (2012), 'De quelques principes de justice dans les rapports entre les parents et l'école', *Education et didactique* 6: 85–96.

Pierre, J. and Peters, G. B. (2000), *Governance, Politics and the State*, Basingstoke: Macmillan.

Pierson, P. (2000) 'Increasing Returns, Path Dependency, and the Study of Politics', *American Political Science Review*, 94: 251–67.

Ploesser, M. and Mecheril, P. (2012), 'Neglect – Recognition – Deconstruction. Approaches to Otherness in Social Work', *International Journal of Social Work* 55 (6): 794–808.

Pohl, A. and Walther, A. (2007), 'Activating the Disadvantaged: Variations in Addressing Youth Transitions Across Europe', *International Journal of Lifelong Education* 26: 533–53.

Power, S. (2007), *Education. Policy Synthesis of EU Research Results Series No. 4*, Brussels: European Commission DG Research.

Protheroe, N. (2006), 'Cultural Diversity and the School–Family Connection', *Principal*, available on-line: http://www.naesp.org/ (accessed 30 June 2015).

Przyborski, A. and Slunecko, T. (2009), 'Against Reification. Praxeological Methodology and its Benefits', in J. Valsiner, P. Molenaar, M. Lyra and N. Chaudhary (eds),

Dynamic Process Methodology in the Social and Developmental Sciences, 141–70, New York: Springer.

Qvortrup, J. (1995), 'Childhood and Modern Society: A Paradoxical Relationship?', in J. Brannen and M. O'Brien (eds), *Childhood and Parenthood*, London: Institute of Education.

Raffo, C. and Reeves, M. (2000), 'Youth Transitions and Social Exclusion – Developments in Social Capital Theory', *Journal of Youth Studies* 3 (2): 127–46.

Raviv, A., Sills, R., Raviv, A. and Wilansky, P. (2000), 'Adolescents' Help-seeking Behaviour: The Difference between Self and Other-referral', *Journal of Adolescence* 23: 721–40.

Reisel, L. (2011), 'Two Paths to Inequality in Educational Outcomes: Family Background and Educational Selection in the United States and Norway', *Sociology of Education* 84 (4): 261–80.

Reiter, H. (2003), 'Past, Present, Future: Biographical Time Structuring of Disadvantaged Young People', *Young* 11 (3): 253–79.

Rhodes, R. A. W. (1997), *Understanding Governance. Policy Networks, Governance, Reflexivity and Accountability*, Buckingham: Open University Press.

Riegel, C. (2012), 'Dealing with Diversity and Social Heterogeneity. Ambivalences, Challenges and Pitfalls for Pedagogical Activity', in Z. Bekerman and T. Geisen (eds), *International Handbook of Migration, Minorities and Education. Understanding Cultural and Social Differences in Processes of Learning*, 331–47, Dordrecht: Springer.

Rinne, R., Kivirauma, J. and Simola, H. (2002), 'Shoots of Revisionist Education Policy or just Slow Readjustment? The Finnish Case of Educational Reconstruction', *Journal of Education Policy* 17 (6): 643–58.

Robertson, S. and Dale, R. (2006), 'Changing Geographies of Power in Education: The Politics of Rescaling and its Contradictions', available online: https://susanleerobertson.files.wordpress.com/2009/10/2006-kassem-geographies.pdf (accessed 30 June 2015).

Rode, N. (2009), 'Comparative Research between Description and Speculation: Some Pitfalls of Comparative Research and How to Deal with them', in S. Ramon and D. Zavirŝek (eds), *Critical Edge Issues in Social Work and Social Policy. Comparative Research Perspectives*, 29–46, Ljubljana: Faculty of Social Work, University of Ljubljana.

Rusche, S. N. and Jason, K. (2011), '"You Have to Absorb Yourself in It": Using Inquiry and Reflection to Promote Student Learning and Self-knowledge', *Teaching Sociology* 39 (4): 338–53.

Salamon, L. M. (2002), *The New Tools of Governance, A Guide to the New Governance.* Oxford: Oxford University Press.

Salovaara, V., Lunabba, H. and Julkunen, I. (2012), *Governance of Educational Trajectories in Europe: National Case Study Report Finland*, GOETE Working Paper, Helsinki: University of Helsinki.

Scharpf, F. W. (1997), *Games Real Actors Play: Actor-Centered Institutionalism in Policy Research*, Boulder: Westview.

Scheerens, J. (2009), *Informal Learning of Active Citizenship at School – An International Comparative Study in Seven European Countries*, Dordrecht: Springer.

Scherger, S. (2009), *Destandardisierung, Differenzierung, Individualisierung. Westdeutsche Lebensläufe im Wandel*, Wiesbaden: VS Verlag.

Schröer, W., Stauber, B., Walther, A., Böhnisch, L. and Lenz, K. (2013), *Handbuch Übergänge*, Weinheim/Basel: Beltz Juventa.

Schugurensky, D. (2000), 'The Forms of Informal Learning: Towards a Conceptualization of the Field', Wall Working Paper No. 19, Toronto: Centre for the Study of Education and Work Department of Sociology and Equity Studies in Education.

Schultz, T. W. (1961), 'Investment in Human Capital', *American Economic Review* 51 (1): 1–17.

Schuppert, G. F. (2005), 'Governance im Spiegel der Wissenschaftsdisziplinen', in G. F. Schuppert (ed.), *Governance-Forschung. Vergewisserung über Stand und Entwicklungslinien*, 371–469, Baden Baden: Nomos.

Schuppert, G. F. (2011), *Alles Governance oder Was?*, Baden Baden: Nomos.

Schüren, R. (1989), *Soziale Mobilität*, St. Katharinen: Scripta Mercaturae.

Sen, A. (2001), *Development as freedom*. Oxford, New York: Oxford University Press.

Sennett, R. (1997), *The Corrosion of Character: The Personal Consequences of Work in the New Capitalism*, New York: W. W. Norton.

Severance, T. A. and Starr, P. J. (2011), 'Beyond the Classroom: Internships and Students with Special Needs', *Teaching Sociology* 39 (2): 200–7.

Shavit, Y. and Müller, W. (2000), 'Vocational Secondary Education, Tracking, and Social Stratification', in M. T. Hallinan (ed.), *Handbook of the Sociology of Education*, 437–52, New York: Kluwer Academic/Plenum.

Sheard, M. K. and Avis, J. (2011), 'Schools, Governance and Community: A Next Practice Intervention', *Educational Management Administration* 39 (1): 84–104.

Sheffield, J. K., Fiorenza, E. and Sofronoff, K. (2004), 'Adolescents' Willingness to Seek Psychological Help: Promoting and Preventing Factors', *Journal of Youth and Adolescence* 33: 495–507.

Simola, H., Rinne, R. and Kivirauma, J. (2002), 'Abdication of the Education State or just Shifting Responsibilities? The Appearance of a New System of Reason in Constructing Educational Governance and Social Exclusion/Inclusion in Finland', *Scandinavian Journal of Educational Research* 46 (3): 237–46.

Smalley, S. Y. and Reyes-Blanes, M. E. (2001), 'Reaching out to African American Parents in an Urban Community: A Community–University Partnership', *Urban Education* 36: 518–33.

Snyder, B. R. (1971), *The Hidden Curriculum*, New York: Knopf.

Sosin, M. H. (2010), 'Discretion in Human Service Organizations', in Y. Hasenfeld (ed.), *Human Services as Complex Organizations*, London: Sage.

Spillane, J. P., Gomez, L. M. and Mesler, L. (2009), 'Notes on Reframing the Role of Organizations in Policy Implementation', in G. Sykes, B. Schneider and D. N. Plank (eds), *Handbook of Educational Policy Research*, New York and London: Routledge.

Spivak, G. C. (1985), 'The Rani of Sirmur: An Essay in Reading the Archives', *History and Theory* 24 (3): 247–72.

Stauber, B. (2010), 'Transdisziplinäre Jugendforschung: Ein neuer Anlauf zu einer integrativen Forschungsperspektive', in C. Riegel, A. Scherr and B. Stauber (eds), *Transdisziplinäre Jugendforschung. Grundlagen und Forschungskonzepte*, 25–45, Wiesbaden: VS Verlag.

Stauber, B. and Parreira do Amaral, M. (eds) (2013), *Access and Education: Inequality and Diversity*, available online: http://www.goete.eu/download/category/4-executive-summaries?download=1:goete-access-thematic-working-paper-executive-summary (accessed 15 June 2015).

Stauber, B., Pohl, A. and Walther, A. (eds) (2007), *Subjektorientierte Übergangsforschung*, Weinheim and München: Juventa.

Stocké, V. (2007), 'Explaining Educational Decision and Effects of Families' Social Class Position: An Empirical Test of the Breen-Goldthorpe Model of Educational Attainment', *European Sociological Review* 23 (4): 505–19.

Stojanov, K. (2012), 'The Concept of Bildung and its Moral Implications', in K. Schneider (ed.), *Becoming Oneself. Dimensions of 'Bildung' and the Facilitation of Personality Development*, 75–88, Wiesbaden: VS Verlag.

Strauss, A. and Corbin, J. (1990), *Basics of Qualitative Research: Grounded Theory Procedures and Techniques*, Newbury Park, CA: Sage Publications.

Stromquist, N. (2000), 'Editorial', *Compare* 30 (3): 261–4.

Strübing, J. (2011), 'Grounded Theory', in B. Bertrand, D. Berg-Schlosser and L. Morlino (eds), *IPSA Encyclopedia of Political Sciences*, Thousand Oaks, CA: Sage.

Sultana, R. G. (1995), 'A Uniting Europe, a Dividing Education? Supranationalism, Euro-centrism and the curriculum', *International Studies in Sociology of Education* 5 (2): 115–44.

Sultana, R. G. (2002), 'Quality Education for Tomorrow's Europe. A Contrapuntal Reading of European Commission Documents', in A. Nóvoa and M. Lawn (eds), *Fabricating Europe: The Formation of an Educational Space*, 109–30, Dordrecht/Boston/London: Kluwer Academic Publishers.

Sultana, R. G. and Watts, A. G. (2004), *Career Guidance in Public Employment Services across Europe*, Paris: OECD.

Super, D. E. (1990), 'A Life-span, Life-space Approach to Career Development', in D. Brown and L. Brooks (eds), *Career Choice and Development: Applying Contemporary Theories to Practice*, 197–261, San Francisco: Jossey-Bass.

Szalai, J. (2011), 'Ethnic Differences in Education and Diverging Prospects for Urban Youth in an Enlarged Europe', EDUMIGROM Summary Findings, Budapest: Central European University, Center for Policy Studies, available online: http://

www.edumigrom.eu/sites /default/files/field_attachment/page/node-23788/ edumigromsummary-findings.pdf (accessed 2 July 2015).

Szreter, S. and Woolcock, M. (2004), 'Health by Association? Social Capital, Social Theory, and the Political Economy of Public Health', *International Journal of Epidemiology* 33 (4): 650–67.

Taylor, I. and Kelly, J. (2006), 'Professionals, Discretion and Public Sector Reform in the UK: Revisiting Lipsky', *International Journal of Public Sector Management* 19 (7): 629–42.

Tikkanen, J., Bledowski, P. and Felczak, J. (2015), 'Education Systems as Transition Spaces', *International Journal of Qualitative Studies in Education, Special Issue: 'Doing Transitions' in Education* 28 (3): 297–310.

Tolonen, T. (2013), 'Youth Cultures, Lifestyles and Social Class in Finnish Context', *Young 2013* 21 (1): 55–75.

Trautwein, U. and Baeriswyl, F. (2007), 'Wenn leistungsstarke Klassenkameraden ein Nachteil sind: Referenzgruppeneffekte bei Übertrittsentscheidungen', *Zeitschrift für Pädagogische Psychologie* 21 (2): 119–33.

Troyna, B. and Williams, J. (1986), 'Racism, Education and the State: The Racialisation of Educational Policy', *Capital and Class* 10 (2): 222–4.

Turney, K. and Kao, G. (2009), 'Barriers to School Involvement: Are Immigrant Parents Disadvantaged?', *The Journal of Educational Research* 102 (4): 257–71.

Tyack, D. and Tobin, W. (1994), 'The "Grammar" of Schooling: Why Has It Been So Hard to Change?', *American Educational Research Journal* (31) 3: 453–79.

Ule, A. (2009), 'Konteksti odlo-čanja' ['Contexts of Decision-making'], in A. Ule, O. Markič and U. Kordeš (eds), *Konteksti odločanja* [*Contexts of Decision-making*], 6–16, Maribor: Aristej.

Ule, M. (2013), '"I trust my mom the most": Trust Patterns of Contemporary Youth', in H. Warming (ed.), *Participation, Citizenship and Trust in Children's Lives*, *Studies in Childhood and Youth*, 174–94, Basingstoke: Palgrave Macmillan.

Ule, M. and Šribar, R. (2008), 'Status and Social Opportunities of the Girl-child in EU, Education Accentuated', *Teor. praksa* 45: 301–23.

Ule, M. and Živoder, A. (2013), 'Parents as Decision-making Actors in the Educational Trajectories of Students', in M. Cuconato and A. Walther (eds), *Education and the Life Course. Governance of Educational Trajectories in Europe: Thematic Report on Life Course*, GOETE Working Paper, 157–91, Bologna: University of Bologna.

Ule, M., Svab, A., Walther, A. and Litau, J. (2014), *Far from Frozen. Creative Strategies of Young People in Disadvantaged Circumstances*, Brussels: European Commission.

Ule, M., Živoder, A. and du Bois-Reymond, M. (2015), 'Simply the Best for my Children: Patterns of Parental Involvement in Education', *International Journal of Qualitative Studies in Education* 28 (3): 329–48.

United Nations Educational, Scientific and Cultural Organization (UNESCO) (1994), *The Salamanca Statement and Framework for Action on Special Needs Education*, Paris: UNESCO.

Vanttaja, M. and Järvinen, T. (2006), 'The Young Outsiders: The Later Life Courses of "Drop Out Youths"', *International Journal of Lifelong Education* 25 (2): 173–84.

Verger, A., Novelli, M. and Koşar Altinyelken, H. (eds) (2012), *Global Education Policy and International Development. New Agendas, Issues and Policies*, London: Bloomsbury.

Vincent, C. and Martin, J. (2000), 'School Based Parents' Groups – a Politics of Voice and Representation', *Journal of Educational Policy* 15 (5): 459–80.

Vincent, C. and Martin, J. (2002), 'Class, Culture and Agency: Researching Parental Voice', *Discourse: Studies in the Cultural Politics of Education* 23 (1): 109–28.

Waanders, C., Mendez, J. L. and Downer, J. T. (2007), 'Parent Characteristics, Economic Stress and Neighborhood Context as Predictors of Parent Involvement in Preschool Children's Education', *Journal of School Psychology* 45: 619–36.

Walther, A. (2003), 'Empowerment or Cooling-out? Dilemmas and Contradictions of Integrated Transition Policies', in A. López Blasco, W. McNeish and A. Walther (eds), *Young People and the Contradictions of Inclusion: Integrated Transition Policies in Europe*, 183–205, Bristol: Policy Press.

Walther, A. (2005), 'Risks or Responsibilities? The Individualisation of Youth Transitions and the Ambivalence between Participation and Activation in Europe', *Social Work and Society* 2 (1): 116–27.

Walther, A. (2006), 'Regimes of Youth Transitions. Choice, Flexibility and Security in Young People's Experiences across Different European Contexts', *Young* 14 (1): 119–41.

Walther, A. (2009), 'It was Not my Choice, you Know? Young People's Subjective Views and Decision Making Processes in Biographical Transitions', in I. Schoon and R. Silbereisen (eds), *Transitions from School to Work: Globalisation, Individualisation and Patterns of Diversity*, 121–45, Cambridge: Cambridge University Press.

Walther, A. (2012a), 'Youth – Actor of Social Change? Differences and Convergences across Europe', *Studi di Sociologia* 13 (1): 17–41.

Walther, A. (2012b), 'Learning to Participate or Participating to Learn', in P. Loncle, M. Cuconato, V. Muniglia and A. Walther (eds), *Youth Participation in Europe. Beyond Discourses, Practices and Realities*, 189–207, Bristol: Policy Press.

Walther, A. (2015a), 'The Struggle for "Realistic" Career Perspectives: *Cooling-out* versus Maintenance of Aspirations in Transitions to Work', *Italian Journal of Sociology of Education* 7 (2): 18–42.

Walther, A. (2015b), 'Bildung und Bewältigung in unterschiedlichen Lebenslaufregimen. Ein Beitrag zu einer international vergleichenden sozialpädagogischen Forschung', in M. Parreira do Amaral and K. Amos (eds), *Internationale und Vergleichende Erziehungswissenschaft. Geschichte, Theorie, Methode und Forschungsfelder*,189–208, Münster: Waxmann.

Walther, A. and Pohl, A. (2005), *Thematic Study on Policy Measures for Disadvantaged Youth*, Tübingen: IRIS, available online: http://nbn-resolving.de/urn:nbn:de:101:1-2013011217002 (accessed 15 June 2015).

Walther, A., du Bois-Reymond, M. and Biggart, A. (eds) (2006), *Participation in*

Transition. Motivation of Young Adults in Europe for Learning and Working, Frankfurt am Main: Peter Lang.

Walther, A., Stauber, B. and Pohl, A. (2009), *Youth – Actor of Social Change. Up2Youth Final Report*, available online: http://www.up2youth.org/ downloads/ task,doc_ download /gid,113/ (accessed 30 June 2015).

Walther, A., Warth, A., Ule, M. and du Bois-Reymond, M. (2015), '"Me, My Education and I": Constellation of Decision Making in Young People's Educational Trajectories', *International Journal of Qualitative Studies in Education* 28 (3–4): 349–71.

Wang, M. T. and Eccles, J. S. (2012), 'Social Support Matters: Longitudinal Effects of Social Support on Three Dimensions of School Engagement from Middle to High School', *Child Development* 83 (3): 877–95.

Watts, A. G. and Kidd, J. M. (2000), 'Guidance in the United Kingdom: Past, Present and Future', *British Journal of Guidance and Counselling* 28: 485–502.

Watts, A. G. and Sultana, R. (2004), 'Career Guidance Policies in 37 Countries: Contrasts and Common Themes', *International Journal for Educational and Vocational Guidance* 4: 105–22.

Wenger, E. (1998), *Communities of Practice. Learning, Meaning and Identity*, Cambridge: Cambridge University Press.

Wenger, E. (2009), 'A Social Theory of Learning', in K. Illeris (ed.), *Contemporary Theories of Learning. Learning Theorists in their Own Words*, 209–18, London: Routledge.

Werquin, P. (2010), *Recognising Non-formal and Informal Learning: Outcomes, Policies and Practices*, Paris: OECD Publishing.

West, C. and Fenstermaker, S. (1995), 'Doing Difference', *Gender and Society* 9 (1): 8–30.

Williams, T. T. and Sanchez, B. (2011), 'Identifying and Decreasing Barriers to Parent Involvement for Inner-city Parents', *Youth and Society* 45 (1): 54–74.

Willis, P. (1977), *Learning to Labour. How Working Class Kids Get Working Class Jobs*, New York: Columbia University Press.

Wills, T. A. and Shinar, O. *(2000)*, 'Measuring Perceived and Received Social Support', in S. Cohen, L. G. Underwood and B. H. Gottlieb (eds), *Social Support Measurement and Intervention: A Guide for Health and Social Scientists*, Oxford: Oxford University Press.

Winker, G. and Degele, N. (2011), 'Intersectionality as Multi-level Analysis. Dealing with Social Inequality', *International Journal of Women's Studies* 18 (1): 51–66.

Wolf, A. (2011), *Review of Vocational Education: The Wolf Report*, London: The Department for Education.

Woodman, D. (2009), 'The Mysterious Case of the Pervasive Choice Biography: Ulrich Beck, Structure/Agency and the Middling State of Theory in the Sociology of Youth', *Journal of Youth Studies* 12: 243–56.

Wrana, D. (2011), 'Den Diskurs lernen – Lesarten bilden. Die Differenz von

Produktion und Konsumption in diskursiven Praktiken', in R. Keller, W. Schneider and W. Viehöver (eds), *Diskurs Macht Subjekt*, 229–45, Wiesbaden: VS Verlag.

Young, M. F. D. (2007), 'Bringing Knowledge Back', in *From Social Constructivism to Social Realism in the Sociology of Education*, London: Routledge.

Zanten, A. van (2001), *L'école de la périphérie. Scolarité et ségrégation en banlieue*, Paris: PUF.

Zellman, G. L. and Waterman, J. M. (1998), 'Understanding the Impact of Parent School Involvement on Children's Educational Outcome', *The Journal of Educational Research* 91 (6): 370-80.

Zinnecker, J. (1995), 'The Cultural Modernization of Childhood', in L. Chisholm, P. Büchner, H. H. Krüger and M. du Bois-Reymond (eds), *Growing Up in Europe*, 85–94, Berlin: Walter de Gruyter.

Index

The letter *f* following an entry denotes a figure.
The letter *t* following an entry denotes a table.

Lightning Source UK Ltd.
Milton Keynes UK
UKHW02f2352041217
313887UK00004B/576/P

9 781350 053380